Black Market

STUDIES IN UNITED STATES CULTURE

Grace Elizabeth Hale, *series editor*

Series Editorial Board
Sara Blair, University of Michigan
Janet Davis, University of Texas at Austin
Matthew Guterl, Brown University
Franny Nudelman, Carleton University
Leigh Raiford, University of California, Berkeley
Bryant Simon, Temple University

Studies in United States Culture publishes provocative books that explore U.S. culture in its many forms and spheres of influence. Bringing together big ideas, brisk prose, bold storytelling, and sophisticated analysis, books published in the series serve as an intellectual meeting ground where scholars from different disciplinary and methodological perspectives can build common lines of inquiry around matters such as race, ethnicity, gender, sexuality, power, and empire in an American context.

AARON CARICO

Black Market
The Slave's Value in National Culture after 1865

The University of North Carolina Press *Chapel Hill*

*This book was published with the assistance of the
Authors Fund of the University of North Carolina Press.*

© 2020 The University of North Carolina Press
All rights reserved
Set in Arno Pro by Westchester Publishing Services
Manufactured in the United States of America

The University of North Carolina Press has been a member of the
Green Press Initiative since 2003.

Library of Congress Cataloging-in-Publication Data
Names: Carico, Aaron, author.
Title: Black market : the slave's value in national culture after 1865 /
 Aaron Carico.
Other titles: Studies in United States culture.
Description: Chapel Hill : University of North Carolina Press, [2020] |
 Series: Studies in United States culture | Includes bibliographical references
 and index.
Identifiers: LCCN 2019052241 | ISBN 9781469655574 (cloth) |
 ISBN 9781469655581 (paperback) | ISBN 9781469655598 (ebook)
Subjects: LCSH: Freedmen—United States—Social conditions. | Freedmen—
 United States—Economic conditions. | Slavery—Economic Aspects—
 United States. | Black market—United States.
Classification: LCC E185.61 .C265 2020 | DDC 306.3/620973—dc23
LC record available at https://lccn.loc.gov/2019052241

Cover illustration: Kerry James Marshall, *Great America* (1994, acrylic and collage on
canvas, 103 × 114 in.). © Kerry James Marshall. Courtesy of the artist and Jack Shainman
Gallery, New York.

Contents

Introduction: The Unabolished 1

CHAPTER ONE
Freedom as Accumulation 17

CHAPTER TWO
The Spectacle of Free Black Personhood 51

CHAPTER THREE
Cowboys and Slaves 105

CHAPTER FOUR
Southern Enclosure as American Literature 138

Conclusion: In the Trap 184

Acknowledgments 201

Notes 205

Bibliography 257

Index 279

Illustrations

Letter from Henry L. Thomas to President Warren G. Harding,
    27 March 1921 46
Response to Henry L. Thomas from the Office of the Comptroller
    of the Currency, 1 April 1921 49
William Harnett, *Attention, Company!* (1878) 50
Raw Recruits (1862) 57
The Contraband, from Thomas Waterman Wood, *A Bit of War
    History* (1865) 59
The Recruit, from Thomas Waterman Wood, *A Bit of War
    History* (1866) 60
The Veteran, from Thomas Waterman Wood, *A Bit of War
    History* (1866) 61
Thomas Nast, *Pardon* and *Franchise* from *Harper's Weekly*
    (5 August 1865) 63
A Typical Negro, from *Harper's Weekly* (4 July 1863) 65
Black America broadside 77
Photographs of *Black America*, from *The Illustrated American*
    (29 June 1895) 81
Emancipated Slaves, White and Colored, from *Harper's Weekly*
    (30 January 1864) 98
These Children, carte-de-visite (verso and recto) 99
Isaac and Rosa, Emancipated Slave Children, carte-de-visite 102
Detail of *Isaac and Rosa* with detail of *Attention, Company!* 103
Dorothea Lange, *Cotton Sharecropper Family Near Cleveland, Mississippi*
    (June 1937) 143
Arkansas sharecropping family evicted 144
Ben Shahn, *Poverty on the March, a Destitute Ozark Family, Arkansas*
    (October 1935) 144

Pages from George Washington Harris, *Sut Lovingood* (1867) 158
Walker Evans, photograph of Floyd Burroughs' fireplace (1936) 171
Speaking of Pictures, from *Life* (31 October 1938) 185
Two paintings from *American Art Comes of Age*, from *Life* (31 October 1938) 186

Black Market

Introduction
The Unabolished

Verily, the work does not end with the abolition of slavery, but only begins.
—Frederick Douglass

What is, so to speak, the object of abolition? Not so much the abolition of prisons but the abolition of a society that could have prisons, that could have slavery, that could have the wage, and therefore not abolition as the elimination of anything but abolition as the founding of a new society.
—Stefano Harney and Fred Moten, *The Undercommons*

So much had been achieved. Slaves had fled the plantations en masse, seizing their own freedom, and through that act, changed the course and the meaning of the Civil War.[1] Their multitude made the war about abolition, and when the war ended, they had made themselves free.[2] In Charleston, thousands celebrated in March 1865—signs called for free homes and free schools; children marched with a banner that read, "We Know No Master but Ourselves"; festive mourners paraded a coffin with the inscription "Slavery Is Dead."[3] "I felt like a bird out of a cage. Amen. Amen. Amen," Houston H. Holloway recalled. "The week passed off in a blaze of glory."[4] So much achieved, and so much left to accomplish. Abolition would be the democratic work of uprooting slavery, of ripping that institution from the ground of the nation's public life—from its economy, its laws, its culture, its mores—where slavery had grown and thrived for more than two hundred years. All the thieving, the killing quick and slow, the debasement, the exclusion would be gone for good; the fictions of blood, the badges of servitude, the architectures of production, of reproduction, all would be ended and destroyed. Slavery—root, branch, and vine—would be thrown into the war's bonfire. Slavery made America, and abolition would make it over.

Would.

But didn't.

That didn't happen, and hasn't happened. Having bravely crossed Union lines, freeing themselves, many ex-slaves straightaway found themselves stranded in refugee camps. They already knew of and were terrified by these camps, which were overcrowded with people plagued by sores, wracked with diarrhea, and "eaten up with vermin."[5] According to eyewitnesses, these were "vast charnel house[s]," for "thousands of people dying without well ones enough to inter the dead."[6] The corpses of the freed were loaded into carts with horses and mules and then dumped into the same ditch.[7] In some, half who entered would never leave. Meanwhile, convinced that former slaves might become too "dependent" on government assistance, future president Andrew Johnson refused to issue winter tents to the contrabands. Unprepared, neglectful, and cruelly indifferent, the North and its armies fought for an ideal of free labor and not for the sake of black life. By now, abolition's limits and failings are well known, even to many white Americans, and most former slaves did not have to wait long to learn them. The Union emancipated many thousands into open graves.[8] It was a bellwether.

By war's end, both houses of Congress had passed versions of a bill that would have permanently confiscated Confederate lands, with an eye toward redistributing them among the freed. The full name of the Freedmen's Bureau bore the trace of that prospect—the Bureau of Refugees, Freedmen, and Abandoned Lands.[9] In Georgia, with the authorization of U.S. officers, the foreman at a national cemetery, a former slave named Floyd Snelson, along with the federal employees in his charge and their families—around two hundred people—had built houses on land previously occupied by the Confederate government. "Many of them had built these houses at their own expense, and cleared, fenced, and cultivated gardens of from one to four acres, which were covered with corn, potatoes, and other vegetables," according to Snelson.[10] With its promises of land, as well as power and material equality, the period of "radical Reconstruction," as it came to be known, was short, lasting just a few years. In the end, the promises were empty, and reconstruction was ineffectual beyond the realm of formal rights and recognition, which were soon enough negated.[11] All the while, Freedmen's Bureau officials strong-armed the freed into signing labor contracts, often with the very families who had enslaved them.[12]

After the departure of the bureau's teachers and the U.S. lieutenant in command in July 1868, a claimant to that Georgia property where Snelson and others had made homes, Mr. B. B. Dikes, appeared and ordered every black resident to quit the premises within four days. When residents appealed to stay as renters or sharecroppers, Dikes refused, "and said they could not stay on any terms."[13] On the fourth day, Dikes arrived, "along with most of the white people in from six to ten miles around... with their arms," the sheriff and the magistrate in tow, and "went to the houses of all these people ... and threw all their furniture, and provisions of every kind, out of doors. They then nailed up the doors of all their cabins, on the inside.... By about two P.M., all these people, with their furniture, bedding, provisions, and everything that they possessed, were turned out of doors." A rainstorm soaked their belongings that night. "Many women and children lay out of doors guarding their things, and exposed to the weather nearly a week," Snelson stated, "before they could get any shelter at all—their husbands and fathers roaming over the country to find some kind of a home." That Saturday, whites "set fire to nine (9) of the buildings, that had been built by the colored people, and burnt them up, and tore down their fences and destroyed their crops."[14] No federal army or agency came to defend the evicted.

This would be repeated across the South.[15] By 1870, Georgia was being wrested back by white Democrats, as federal power, in the form of troops and bureau agents, retreated. Snelson's experience was atypical only in that no blacks were murdered. Five years later, in 1873, when whites overtook the town of Colfax, Louisiana, which black residents had barricaded for fear of political retribution, whites breached the perimeter and slaughtered 280 people, including 50 who had already surrendered.[16] In a late chapter of *Black Reconstruction*, titled "Back Toward Slavery," W. E. B. Du Bois's references to firsthand accounts of this violent white "Redemption" can seem endless: "There was not much law in the land"; "The life of a Negro is not worth much there"; "much disorder, and a condition of lawlessness toward the blacks"; "Murders, or attempts to murder, are numerous. Whippings are without number."[17] The Ku Klux Klan and its ilk arose and ran rampant. Across the region, with the end of the war came the enactment of Black Codes, which legally required of free blacks proof of employment and included laws against vagrancy, renting land, and insulting language or gestures, as well as statutes that bound black "orphans" over to court-ordered "apprenticeship" under whites, with preference being given to their former owners. The "whole criminal system came to be used as a method of keeping Negroes at work and intimidating them," with blacks "arrested on the slightest provocation and given long sentences or fines which they were compelled to work out."[18]

"Prison" across the South meant labor camp. Many Southern states dismantled their penitentiaries after the war and developed a convict-lease system, compelling black men and women to labor for public works and private profit, about which much has already been written.[19] "The South's 'penitentiaries' were great rolling cages that followed construction camps and railroad building, hastily built stockades deep in forest or swamp or mining fields, or windowless log forts in turpentine flats," writes C. Vann Woodward. Eight feet wide, fifteen feet long, and eight feet high, each cage housed more than twenty men.[20] In Du Bois's words, "Probably in no country in the civilized world did human life become so cheap."[21] Those who survived imprisonment were generally stripped of whatever rights they nominally enjoyed, as their sentences entailed "the customary loss of citizenship for life."[22]

Meanwhile, across the Southern countryside, landowners and lawmakers renovated and re-entrenched the plantation system. Instead of redistributing Southern lands, federal legislation cleaned the slate of prior debts for the region's planters and merchants, while state legislation filled their empty pockets by allowing small farmers to pledge in advance the profit of next year's crop.[23] So began the generations of blacks consigned to sharecropping's pillage and sentenced to its life of destitution.

SLAVERY'S ABOLITION IN THE United States amounted to three public laws, the Reconstruction Amendments: the Thirteenth, which declared that slavery "shall not exist" except as punishment for crime; the Fourteenth, which conferred birthright citizenship and affirmed due process of law; and the Fifteenth, which extended suffrage regardless of "race, color, or previous condition of servitude." Soon after ratification, the courts rapidly began to turn back Congress's efforts to extend the amendments' purpose through new legislation. When the Supreme Court overturned (before it could even be enforced) the Civil Rights Act of 1875, which was meant to curb racial discrimination and Southern political violence against blacks, the majority opinion stated: "This amendment [the Thirteenth], as well as the Fourteenth, is undoubtedly self-executing, without any ancillary legislation, so far as its terms are applicable to any existing state of circumstances. By its own unaided force and effect, it abolished slavery and established universal freedom."[24] For the courts, citizenship became the tautological evidence of freedom's accomplishment after Reconstruction. To be a citizen was to be free.[25] Slavery was conceived to be a status, a legal condition, and one that could be expunged instantly by proclamation. So understood, the law had no truck with the residue of history or the contemporary experience of former slaves like Floyd Snelson.

The deficiencies of abolition are a historical truism now beyond dispute. The histories we've been handed, though, mitigate the scale and scope of abolition's failure and its ongoing disaster. Slavery's basic architecture, infrastructure, political economy, the wealth it generated, its hierarchies, its culture, its whole habitus were left largely untouched in and after 1865, and in some instances remain untouched. The category of *slave* didn't just name a captive person or a status but also designated a form of value, a commodity, even a kind of money. Indeed, considering that the value of the slave population in 1860 surpassed by multiples the amounts invested in any other sector (manufacturing, railroads, banks—even the assessed value of land in slaveholding states), slaves were arguably more than *a kind* of money. They were money itself—the general equivalent, the standard of all value in the United States.[26] Slavery wasn't just a system of labor. It was also a system of capital accumulation.[27] That system ramified across the United States, and beyond, and was integral to the nation's existence. The dead and destroyed bodies generated by slavery's holocaust were, obscenely, only ever the collateral damage of that system.[28]

Strangely, the apparatuses of slavery have been considered incidental to abolition. Chattel slavery comprised the nation-state as a market in slaves, as abolitionists argued in the decades before the war.[29] The internal slave trade and the operation of fugitive slave laws made this truth about the United States apparent, a truth also revealed in the North's development, in its financial and industrial innovations, in its affluence, in its political culture, and in its vision of continental imperialism as the march of white liberty. "The black workers of America bent at the bottom of a growing pyramid of commerce and industry ... [and] became the cause ... of new dreams of power and visions of empire," Du Bois wrote at the beginning of *Black Reconstruction*.[30] Abolition in 1865 did not fundamentally alter this world. Neither did it dismantle the plantation as a means of production, nor place the black body or blackness itself beyond the reach of commerce.

Abolition prohibited the trade in black flesh. But such a prohibition doesn't necessarily extinguish the motivating desire, or its symptoms or rationalizations—and could as well be said to incite them. The greed that stood sentinel over the properties of whiteness, the prerogatives to use and destroy nonwhite bodies systematically, the vast stores of hoarded and augmenting white wealth and profit, blackness itself as a cipher for such relations of exchange and accumulation and domination—abolition did not address these. Instead, as aspects of what historian Walter Johnson calls "slave racial capitalism," these persisted.[31] Formal and incomplete, "abolition" created an impossible contradiction, as what had supposedly been erased and undone actually continued to determine the nation's social relations. Abolition merely shaved away the tip of slavery's iceberg. The larger frozen mass of the institution remained, submerged, mostly invisible beneath the surface of everyday life.

Slavery used to be called the "peculiar institution," which we take to mean an oddity, a transgression confined to a defeated South. But there's been an etymological slip along the way, and so we misunderstand. *Peculiar* didn't meant "odd"; it meant "ours." *Peculiar* here didn't signify the strange, the out of place, or what didn't belong; quite the contrary, it denoted proprietorship, precisely what *did* belong (from the Latin, *pecūliāris*, "of or relating to a person's peculium, belonging to a person, one's own, personal, private, that characterizes or belongs to a person, thing, or place"). And although it has come down to us as a defensive parry used by Southern elites, the peculiar institution didn't belong only to the South but to the whole nation. "If you black, you were born in jail, in the North as well as the South," Malcolm X said. "Stop talking about the South. As long as you south of the Canadian border, you South."[32] Slavery was and remains central to the American project. Slavery is ours. It is our American institution. And whatever happened in 1865 was no act of absolution or of restitution, and certainly not of divestment.

BEGINNING WITH THE sleight of hand that hid the slave's value after abolition, namely the metamorphosis of the plantation, *Black Market* diagrams the absent presence of this "peculiar institution" in the United States after 1865. The struggle to conjure a disavowed history animates the following pages. The commodity logic of slavery was not reversed by formal abolition and the slave as a value form survived. American law, political economy, and national culture express this history. Long after the supposed fact, slavery has continued to shape the United States. Our freedom, our equality, our national values, our national character, our national culture (and for *our*, read *white*)—all remain deeply rooted in a living history of slavery. "How could one speak of profit, economy, labor, progress, suffragism, Christianity, the frontier, the formation of new states, the acquisition of new lands, education, transportation (freight and passengers), neighborhoods, the military—of almost anything a country concerns itself with—without having as a referent, at the heart of the discourse, at the heart of definition, the presence of Africans and their descendants?" Toni Morrison asks. "It was not possible. And it did not happen."[33]

But how does one compel such a phantom to materialize? Most often, in histories of Reconstruction and its aftermath, any continuation of slavery has been located almost exclusively in the South, in whites' ongoing physical violation of black bodies and in the legal precincts of crime and punishment. A traduced abolition has been recognized in the vigilante death squads of lynchers and Klansmen—antiblack terrorism toward which the federal government turned a blind eye. For our own historical moment of mass incarceration, the convict labor camp has been the primary site of "slavery by another name," as one popular history's title has it, such camps now seen as authorized by the Thirteenth Amendment itself.[34] Convicts chopping cotton, distilling turpentine, mining coal, laying rails, or building roads: these scenes of reinstated captivity have most clearly rendered the lethal travesties of freedom, revealing the Möbius strip that joined prison and plantation after 1865.[35] But to focus on physical bondage or racist violence misrecognizes the systemic nature of slavery as an institution—its sheer breadth and depth. Through that telling, its institutional effects become intensely localized: a problem of bodies, of prison farms, of counties and states, a problem of the South. This also renders those effects vestigial.

Making slavery a Southern problem has long served an ideological purpose. From the moment of the nation's founding, the slave plantation South denoted a preserve of pastness. As it industrialized, the North regarded itself as the torchbearer of the modern over and against an obsolescent South. A distance in space was transposed with a distance in time. As industrialism ramped up in the Northeast in the mid-nineteenth century, Northerners freely deployed this rhetoric of difference, which had been in use at least since Crèvecœur's American farmer encountered "Southern" slavery outside Charleston in 1782 (even though Crèvecœur himself used enslaved labor at his Hudson Valley plantation).[36] Northern abolitionists resorted to a metaphor of feudalism when depicting the slave plantations of the South. In *Uncle Tom's Cabin* (1852), for example, to portray the ne plus ultra of plantation slavery in Simon Legree's estate, Harriet Beecher Stowe expresses the cognitive dissonance of a medieval South within a modernizing America through a language of ruin. In the chapter "Dark Places," she describes Legree's estate as having "been left to go to utter decay," before using adjectives such as "forsaken," "slovenly," "mildewed," "grown over with weeds," "mouldering," and "desolate."[37] Frederick Douglass was far more explicit when he used this trope in his second narrative, published in 1855. "In its isolation, seclusion, and self-reliant independence, Col. Lloyd's plantation resembles the baronial domains during the Middle Ages in Europe. Grim, cold, and unapproachable by all genial influences from communities without, *there it stands*; full three hundred years behind the age, in all that relates to humanity and morals."[38] By the 1860s those registers of spatial and temporal difference had become thoroughly fused, characterizing the plantation and, by extension, the South itself. The slave plantation was turned into a historical and territorial excrescence in abolitionist discourse, one whose removal would require the surgeries of civil war. In actuality, plantation slavery was not precapitalist—always having been grafted into the world market—nor did it interfere with industrial capitalism in the North, with which it was articulated—quite the contrary.[39] But there was rarely any affirmation of just how intertwined the Northern and Southern economies were.[40]

These distancing tropes imposed a temporal break so that modernity—and so legitimacy—accrued to the Northern system of democratic industrial capitalism by casting the plantation South as that outermost antagonist of the modern: the feudal. This was the alchemy that turned slavery into freedom, with bondage on the South's "feudal" plantations pitched as *the* regime of unfreedom that defined, by opposition, the "true" freedoms of Northern contract labor. The Union victory in the Civil War also spelled victory for these discursive strategies of periodization. The rationalization of U.S. sovereignty and its expansion of powers *coincided* with the discovery of an American feudal past in the South, as its alibi. That discovery was made empirical and popular in the wake of a total war, as actual ruins became ever more visible on the Southern landscape—now an important stop for Northern tourists in the postwar South—such that these remnants of the built environment reified that prewar discourse of backwardness.[41] After 1865, the indistinguishable monotony of a feudal plantation prehistory was rent asunder by the locomotive acceleration of Northern, which is to say American, progress.[42] This ideology still shapes the telling of our national history.[43] The periodizing break of 1865 supposedly signals a watershed in national history, dating the birth of modern America.[44] In turn, that break enables the compartmentalization of slavery's vestiges and legacy within a "backward" South. But the connotations of 1865 are more a triumph of abolitionist discourse than a triumph of abolition itself, if that's to be defined as slavery's uprooting.

FROM THE VERY FIRST, slavery supplied the skeleton that supported American nationalism—in New England, in the West, and obviously, in the South. Yet by weathering the Civil War, the nation and the nationalist ideology built atop this infrastructure came to be seen as absolved of this history, rather than as this history's continuation.[45] The quilt of the American nation is stretched and constructed on the frame of antiblackness. Our national culture has long been rooted in specious narratives of its exceptionalism, as the world haven of equality and freedom, ensured through democratic citizenship. But the lack of a total abolition, *that* unredeemed history, left its traces everywhere. To rip apart the seams of this official narrative of the United States is to reveal uglier and more long-standing presuppositions about who belongs and who doesn't, whose lives matter and whose don't, who will be in control and who will be kept prone.

If the culture of a nation is organized through commodity spectacle, as the feminist scholar Anne McClintock argues, then in the United States, the national fetish sine qua non has been and remains the black body, blackness itself.[46] Neither were placed beyond commerce, or beyond the realms of production and circulation in 1865. Though no longer chattel, blacks in America weren't relieved of the commodity's mark. Blackness is realized in a historical matrix of economic exchange and cultural production, a real abstraction.[47] It is the stamp of a long and ongoing history of violence, which is transmuted into and through culture in ways that are both obvious and obscure.[48] In the words of literary historian Bryan Wagner, "To be black is to exist in exchange without being a party to exchange."[49] As a historical category, "black" designates an empty set. Conceived in Europe, by those identifying as Europeans, "the Negro ... substantially eradicated in Western historical consciousness the necessity of remembering the significance" of African civilizations within the development of "the West," as Cedric Robinson explained in *Black Marxism*. "From such a creature not even the suspicion of tradition needed to be entertained. In its stead there was the Black slave, a consequence masqueraded as an anthropology and a history."[50] Black racialization specifies one who is subject to being exploited, expropriated, and annihilated.[51]

This book conceives blackness through a lineage of black radical thought that includes Cedric Robinson and Sylvia Wynter, Hortense Spillers and Saidiya Hartman, Ida B. Wells and W. E. B. DuBois. Through their writings, blackness (and whiteness) designates a formation at once durable and historically contingent, reproduced and reiterated across time.[52] The captive black body indicates the repetition of a pattern at the heart of slave racial capitalism, an apparent stasis beneath and beside a history of eventful progress.[53] While scholars in critical race studies speak of racis*ms*, of processes of racialization, which are proxies for historical change, there is also a durability that obtains for blackness in the American context. Tracing this constancy has been one of the offerings made by the school of thought that has come to be known as Afro-Pessimism, but Afro-Pessimists go awry when they confuse that durability with ontology. Too often they render blackness, under the sign of the slave, a fixed and unchanging essence, set outside the conflicts and contradictions of history.[54] The writings gathered under the heading of Afro-Pessimism tend to depict white supremacy as an airless and synchronic totality. In contrast, black radical imaginaries acknowledge the murderousness of the given social order of white supremacy *and* acknowledge the reality and the potential of black life and its knowledge of freedom. Despite the state's lethal antagonism, despite being consigned (and confined) to spaces and conditions rendered uninhabitable, black life persists.[55]

Antiblackness is sustained, in part, by a narrative that posits the U.S. nation-state as the means of realizing universal freedom. Another name for this narrative is liberalism, and it aids and abets the supremacy of white people. Structured around an outside and an inside, liberalism continuously enfolds its others, but never fully. A more perfect freedom, a more perfect belonging, for those others is the demesne of "progress," and because always in process, so always in the offing, belonging permanently to the future. (And on behalf of that project, as a shibboleth of American liberalism, the year 1865 does some heavy lifting, a trophy to the state's glorious achievement.) "*Race* as a mark of colonial difference is an enduring remainder of the processes through which the human is universalized and freed by liberal forms," the critical race theorist Lisa Lowe writes, "while the people who created the conditions of possibility for that freedom are assimilated or forgotten."[56] In a sense, race is the trace worn by those not covered by liberalism's original dispensation, the sticky residue of liberalism's constitutive outside, of the less-than-human. Race is the vestige of this structure of power and its movement across time, as "history."

The liberalist order of things has been enshrined in the legal form of the contract. Contract has been conceived as a near-panacea against racism's attributes of domination, coercion, and objecthood. As a legal form, it has stood as irrefutable evidence of free will's exercise, an ironclad guarantee of the law's efficacy, and a talisman against material inequalities.[57] To enter into and honor a contract was to reiterate one's willing subjection within the polity—the individual contract a replica of the social contract—in a kind of synecdoche. Public and private, contract was the paper tiger supposed to devour the remains of chattel slavery. From one direction, this has meant that the work of *emancipation* has eclipsed the work of *abolition*. Whereas abolition is an extinguishment (*OED*: "suppression, destruction, annihilation"), emancipation is a setting free that entails a political relation. One isn't simply emancipated, but rather emancipated *into* the nation-state.[58] Crucially, these are freedoms with two different horizons, one of rights and assimilation, the other without domination or usurpation.[59] In the United States, emancipation secured the *formal* abolition of slavery by nominally including the bondsperson within the social contract as a citizen, which was then reiterated and affirmed through their individual labor contracts as workers. So conceived, emancipation-as-abolition has affirmed the law's plenipotentiary power and magnified the state's resplendent sovereignty. Once it was imagined to have accomplished its end of legal inclusion, abolition became a kind of nullity, a fulfilled prophecy.

National culture gives the lie to the legerdemain of the law. "Although the law is perhaps the discourse that most literally governs citizenship, U.S. national culture—the collectively forged images, histories, and narratives that place, displace, and replace individuals in relation to the national polity—

powerfully shapes who the citizenry is, where they dwell, what they remember, and what they forget," Lisa Lowe writes.[60] The law's universals (freedom, equality, citizen, progress) disavow the forces of history still extant in society, still pressing on lived experience, and which contradict such abstract ideals. But that material reality will not be denied and, like magma under pressure, history's contradictions erupt into public life and harden in the objects of our shared culture—images, figures, genres, styles. These objects and forms are, let's say, the petrified resolutions to history's irrepressible contradictions, and in their various shapes, in their diverse crystalline organization, we can determine the stuff of and the process by which they are made. Moreover, history's eruptions and culture's appearances might occur at times and places that are unexpected, seemingly far removed from their source—like a slave in a Western, as the third chapter will argue. *Black Market* is one inventory of this debris, a survey of the stony field of national culture that discloses slavery's unabolished systems of exploitation, expropriation, and domination.[61] While the totality of slavery's remains can never be fully grasped—whether in a Southern scene of bondage or through a dossier of empirical evidence—that totality *can* be glimpsed through representations.[62] The shifting tectonics of slavery's political economy after formal abolition surface, partially and momentarily, through contradictions that are worked out in the realm of cultural production. In other words, this book's critical attitude is, by and large, that of cultural materialism.[63]

Black Market offers a synthesizing account of American cultural history between the mid-nineteenth and the mid-twentieth centuries, but not by means of a straightforward historical narrative. Instead, its arguments move laterally, even obliquely, following the ripples that expand outward from each chapter's primary subject, by reading and historicizing a set of texts—court cases, paintings, performances, photographs, stories, and novels. Catching the culture's flotsam and jetsam, those ripples often arrive on unexpected shores. Objects of culture are sometimes the *only* way to get at the materiality of history. In this way, reading becomes a mode of critical historical analysis, by articulating how concepts, images, narratives, genres, and words themselves—culture, for the sake of this project—are linked together within history's matrix and how this repertoire is transmitted and transformed across space-times, principally through the circuits of capital.[64]

To focus on slave racial capitalism, rather than simply racial capitalism, is to insist on the centrality of the slave as a form of value within the American project.[65] The slave signifies both a concrete individual and an abstract category—a worker, a type of property, a status in law, a unit of value. "Slavery is not simply an antebellum institution that the United States has surpassed but a particular historical *form* of an ongoing crisis involving the subjection of personhood to property," the literary scholar Stephen Best argues.[66] Under capitalism, social relations are abstracted from their concrete specificity—rendered comparable and formally equivalent via the medium of abstract labor power. This is the work of the value-form, according to Marx, which imposes similitude on the unalike and eclipses situated particularities. The literary scholar David Kazanjian points out: "Crucially, Marx is not claiming that commodity production and exchange are the only social relations transformed by the value form. Rather, it seems as if he makes the commodity the exemplary instance of the value form in action to help his readers," because they encountered commodities all the time in their day-to-day lives and so would be most prepared to grasp that example. Actually, Marx suggests that "all social relations are subject to the value form." For example, *equality* and *freedom* in liberal nation-states are always articulated with and through the logic of the market. And, on the American scene, their meanings have been routed through the slave market. In the United States, equality and freedom have always stipulated the slave: slaves as property, slaves as money, slaves as fungible goods, slaves as objects and subjects of accumulation.[67]

"As an object, the commodity has a material form; as a social mediation, it is a social form," the philosopher Moishe Postone writes. That same dual structure applies to the slave, which has both a "material form" and a "social form." To reckon the slave as a form of value requires comprehending the violence necessary to produce humans as concrete and alienable objects of commercial exchange. Such a reckoning also requires comprehending how the slave abstracts and determines a widespread system of social relations, particularly given its status as a general equivalent. The historian Stephanie Smallwood has detailed the destructive processes (captivity, starvation, social death) necessary for "turning African captives into Atlantic commodities" on the brink of the Middle Passage, and Walter Johnson has done much the same in his analysis of how "the chattel principle" governed the lives of the enslaved in the nineteenth-century U.S. South. Both histories also reveal the totalizing logic of market relations, a market omnipresent and inescapable and uncontained—a bitter truth known to those with a price stamped on their heads, however much it was disavowed and ideologically obscured by their trader-enslavers. Historically, that stamp specifies blackness itself: Blackness brands certain humans as objects to be expropriated and expended, with social sanction, and is genetic to the capitalist mode of production. Blackness mediates and is reproduced by the political economy of the

Atlantic world and, by extension, that of the American project. And since the remedies proposed to slave racial capitalism (a system regional, national, and transnational in scale) were merely statutory in the United States—a matter of moving furniture around, changing title, while leaving the house itself undisturbed—a fungible and captive black personhood continued to mediate U.S. social relations after 1865. The nation-state still cohered as a black market. The following chapters uncover and analyze some of the chattel principle's operations in American life up through the middle decades of the twentieth century: a mortar for the structures of citizenship, a catalyst to capital's spectacular subsumption of society, a key to the symbolically loaded mythology of the frontier, and a glue in the binding of "American literature."[68]

As a critique of political economy, which takes culture as its primary object of analysis, *Black Market* adds to the growing field of studies of capitalism. These new studies, usually histories, have tried to make sense of the totality of that overarching global system by collecting data and fitting it to the shape of a linear narrative. Slavery has been a central problematic for the field, and it has laid to rest the antique notion that slavery was precapitalist and premodern.[69] But unlike Du Bois's *Black Reconstruction*, their prototype, these histories of slavery and capitalism tend to regard 1865 as a moment of rupture.[70] They likewise tend to regard culture as supplemental, supernumerary, a fog above the hard ground of data.[71] *Black Market* takes a different tack. The following chapters train attention on those national structures of law, economy, and culture that have debased black life by defining its value in terms of use and exchange, preserving and reproducing the episteme of chattel slavery.[72] Full of returns, repetitions, and echoes, *Black Market* regards historical time more as a spiral than an arrow.[73] Each chapter's narrative strategy grows out of its particular problematic, and in each instance, from unanticipated angles and in unforeseen ways, what's made visible are slavery's remains.[74]

THE TITLE *Black Market* focuses on a few associations. First and most obviously, the title refers to the trade in illicit goods. Slavery might have been declared unconstitutional in 1865, but the practice of bondage was far from over. Black bodies were still bought and sold through the buying and selling of personal debt, and an enslaver would even be pardoned in 1903 because no criminal law forbade him from holding slaves.[75] The twilit commerce examined in *Black Market* has as much to do with the veiled specters of the slave as a value-form as it does with the concrete bodies where that value congealed. Explicitly forbidden and driven underground after 1865, the institution of slavery still sabotaged the vehicles of freedom and tampered with the mediums of public life.

Second, the title names the fusion of racial capitalism and slavery in the American project. Alongside the open and regularized market, which itself produces racial differences to exploit, a "black market" is grafted—one more naked in its violent and thoroughgoing subsumption of human life—that is imagined to precede it and to be set apart from it, but that in fact allows it to function. That is to say, there is an ongoing system of more blatant theft and overmastering that is racially organized, whose operation normalizes the liberalist illusion of freedom and equality. "The commodification of laborers and the commodification of labor power came to be understood as two entirely separate and, indeed, opposite things—slavery and freedom, black and white, household and market, here and there," Walter Johnson argues, "rather than as two concretely intertwined and ideologically symbiotic elements of a larger unified though internally diversified structure of exploitation."[76] The conditions of enslavement clearly exposed capitalism's exploitation and coercion, through the position of slaves as both producers and the means of production, their status as workers *and* capital, machines *and* money, objects *and* subjects of accumulation. Slavery accents the domination fundamental to capitalist exploitation, which, in the United States, has been seared into black skin. ("Labour cannot emancipate itself in the white skin where in the black it is branded," according to Marx.)[77] That brand was the mark of being owned, the mark of disgrace and dishonor—and soon enough, in a logic the second chapter excavates, *that* brand was transmuted into brand as name and image.

Third and last, the title points to the abstracted reiteration of the literal market in black bodies after 1865. If formal abolition banned the commerce in chattel slaves, it nevertheless left in place the chattel principle—the commodity logic of slavery—along with a market culture that continued to define the value of blackness through exchange.[78] That historical reality suggests the perils of conceiving, as liberalism does, the project of freedom as the project of the law. Total abolition would require far more. "The slaves destroyed tirelessly," the historian C. L. R. James wrote of Haiti's revolutionaries. "[T]hey were seeking their salvation in the most obvious way, the destruction of what they knew was the cause of their sufferings; and if they destroyed much, it was because they had suffered much. They knew that as long as the plantations stood their lot would be to labour on them until they dropped. The only thing was to destroy them." Toussaint Louverture commanded, "Leave nothing white behind you."[79]

The first chapter of this book is an attempt to make sense of slavery's remnants in material terms, to come to grips with the structural transformation of the "peculiar institution" triggered by emancipation. Chapter 1 reassembles the immediate and concrete history of abolition after 1865, from the counter of the Southern country store to the international trade in cotton, as it sorts out the mechanisms of law and arrangements of political economy that chaperoned the tremendous value incarnated in slaves across the gulf of the Civil War. Chapter 2 explores how this history spoiled the subjecthood of the freed. It begins by looking at a trompe l'oeil painting of a black boy playing soldier, which teeters between portrait and still life, before crossing the river to Brooklyn to survey the grounds of a public park remade into a cotton plantation, populated by black workers from the South. Focusing on the logic of realism as it intersects with the racial ideology of Jim Crow, the second chapter exposes how free black personhood was turned into a commodity spectacle.

The first two chapters attend to the renovation and reproduction of blackness, drawing out the ways that "the chattel principle" remained a salient feature of the racial formation of the freed. Whiteness, or rather white supremacy, supplies the center of gravity for the third and fourth chapters, which offer accounts of the institutions of national culture—canons, genres, characters, styles, considered essentially "American"—that slavery built, decades after it was deemed a dead letter. The book pans westward in chapter 3 to investigate a single novel, Owen Wister's *The Virginian*, regarded as the beginning of the Western, an origin story for that national mythology. *The Virginian* and the Western would seem to have nothing to do with slavery, but as this chapter reveals, slavery supplies the scaffolding for that most American of heroes, the cowboy. Set against the backdrop of Southern land grabs in the 1830s and again in the 1930s that were meant to sustain the cotton economy, the fourth chapter studies the literary representation of the poor whites who were sidelined by the slave plantation's expansion and modernization, and who were then remade into a national folk by literary elites. Facilitated by these Southern enclosures, the ambivalent canonization of poor whites as the nation's folk would have a decisive and determining influence on the constitution—and the racial covenant—of American literature, and not only on its Americanness but also on its literariness. Slavery was the condition of possibility for this literature, but its role, along with that of the enslaved, was silenced. These enclosures of the South, coupled with racist violence, propelled many black sharecroppers out of the Southern states, north and westward, and the conclusion turns to the trap of the ghetto where black Americans found themselves caught in the wake of the Great Migration, on the brink of another reformation in U.S. slave racial capitalism.

The problem of slavery didn't, and doesn't, belong only to those with black skin. It is hardwired into the American project—the motherboard of the nation's economy and culture. The literary scholar Leigh Claire La Berge has argued that "representation does more than represent, it constitutes the value that it is supposedly representing."[80] Beyond the claim that the "actual" value of the slave is represented in cultural texts, *Black Market* insists that cultural texts, in representing that value, also materially reproduce it—in other words, that the relationship between value and text is dialectical.

Behind the scrim of formal equality attached to free black personhood in 1865, there remained the obdurate edifice of slavery's declensions of humanity. Liberalism's discourse of legality and rights has swallowed and entombed the irruptive meanings of abolition. The impoverishment of abolition and the foreshortening of its political horizon *under the cover of an accomplished freedom* is liberalism's handiwork, or rather its sleight of hand. These essays into the culture of slave racial capitalism—which might as well be called American capitalism—are surrounded on all sides by the wreckage of lives broken and wasted because of the willful blindness and dissembling of that ideology, which has served to secure and placate white power. Abolition is no friend of liberalism. And the law is no ally of the ex-slave. "The law guarding the gates of slavery, segregation, and neosegregation has not forgotten its origin; it remembers its father and its grandfather before that. It knows what master it serves; it knows what color to count," writes legal scholar Maria Grahn-Farley.[81] Too focused on locales, or physical abuses, or capitalists themselves, or literary figurations, or the façade of 1865, we have not paid enough heed to what Hortense Spillers calls the "dominant symbolic order" as itself a source of the material destruction of human life. "We might concede, at the very least, that sticks and bricks *might* break our bones, but words will most certainly *kill* us," Spillers writes.[82] Her claim isn't metaphorical, it's historical. And it's most definitely not in the past tense.

CHAPTER ONE

Freedom as Accumulation

How, after the war, triumphant industry in the North coupled with privilege and monopoly led an orgy of theft that engulfed the nation and was the natural child of war . . . and delivered the land into the hands of an organized monarchy of finance.
—W. E. B. Du Bois, *Black Reconstruction*

For years longer than we can remember, cotton has been our companion; we travel down the plantation road with debt holding our left hand, with credit holding our right, and ahead of us looms the grave, the final and simple end.
—Richard Wright, *12 Million Black Voices*

Let's begin with the debts, which already couldn't be repaid. Near Helena, Arkansas, someone told Ann Ulrich Evans that a man in that state, or Alabama, or Missouri, wanted "a gang of niggers to do some work and he pay you like money growing on trees." But then after bringing in the "fine big crops" on those "great big farms," she was told she owed more than when she arrived.[1] In the Brazos Bottom of Texas, a storekeeper promised Laura Smalley anything she'd like, any kind of money, any dress her daughter desired, if she'd just open an account before Christmas and stick around another year.[2] Henry Blake got such offers in Arkansas, too—twenty dollars in food, a gallon of whiskey, whatever clothes he wanted.[3] "They'd let you go jus' as far in debt as you wan' to go." "Anything that kept you a slave." "We never did git out of debt."[4]

These were the voices of former slaves and their descendants as they recalled standing before the counter of the country store, facing the white merchant on the other side. That scene, fraught and repeated, was a cornerstone of the South in the decades surrounding the turn of the twentieth century.

While one of the merchant's hands might relax its hold on necessities, proffer some small comforts, and thus extend a brief reprieve in a world of forced privation, *all for a price*, everybody knew his other hand gripped a pistol. Such was the consumer's choice, the contract's consent. "He cussed me, hit me with the pistol and broke two teeth. He told me he had learned I was planning to move on Mr. R. C. Nichols place . . . and that he would kill me before he let me work for anybody else. He made me get in his automobile and"—let this sink in—"go to his store and get a month's supply of groceries."[5] And after that white merchant put down the gun and handed over the seeds, the shoes, the bacon, the bolted meal, the bolt of cloth, the suit, the dress, the overalls, he grabbed a leather daybook and a pen to note those debits and mark them against an individual's account. Pistol and pen, both weapons in the so-called New South: the first threatened a quick death, reinforcing the slow one promised by the second.[6] In our mind's eye, the red we imagine is probably the blood fresh on Jake Dunwoodie's bashed mouth, shy two teeth, rather than the red ink that fills those store ledgers. But after 1865 in the South, it's hard to tell the hues apart.

This chapter is about that red ink, and what it symbolizes—about national and international flows of racial capital, and the ongoing circulation of slavery's economic value in modes of finance after 1865. One can begin to follow the arithmetic in the receipt for those groceries. The ex-slave Bayley Wyat does the math in a speech he gave in 1866: "And den didn't we clear the land and raise de crops ob corn, ob cotton, ob tobacco, ob rice, ob sugar, ob ebery ting? And den didn't dem large cities in de North grow up on de cotton and de sugars and de rice dat we made? ... I say dey has grown rich, and my people is poor."[7] A similar calculation was made a century later by Stokely Carmichael and Charles V. Hamilton in *Black Power*, in their polemic against an institutional racism that enmeshes black Americans in an unending colonial exploitation by whites. In the unfinished ledgers of our unfinished Atlantic world, the conventions of slavery's double-entry bookkeeping remain in force: *white life is written in black*.[8]

This chapter puts forward a few distinct but related propositions: first, that the slave remained a form of value after the developments of 1865; second, that freedom names a metamorphosis of the slave in terms of political economy; and third, that the political economy of slavery continued to implicate the entire United States in the late nineteenth and early twentieth centuries. A number of unresolved questions, which are often repressed in historical accounts of the long Reconstruction era, stand behind these propositions: What attributes of slavery did abolition disestablish? Does slavery designate a status that can be summarily reversed by law? And is it then the law's failed execution that must be blamed for the persistence of slavery's attributes? Or should we also understand slavery as an entrenched institution in American political economy and culture, one so entrenched that its supposed legal meliorations—a rights-bearing personhood, for example—only further secure its bonds? As an institution central to "the making of American capitalism" as a recent book has it, does slavery transcend the immediate circumstances of captivity, of physical domination and confinement? And if so, did the implementation of abolition dismantle slavery's vast fortune-making machinery, or did it instead preserve and refurbish it? To put the matter plainly: What exactly was accomplished by the developments begun in 1865 that we deem "abolition"? Which features of slavery were eradicated and which were left intact?[9]

To describe freedom as accumulation disputes emancipation as a simple admission into a postwar rights-bearing subjecthood. The personhood that was constitutionally secured by the Union's victory also enabled new modes of accumulation, on both an individual and global scale. Achieving salience through the functions of commercial exchange, personhood was a conceit of law fashioned into a means of acquisition—and of dispossession.[10] Late in the century, the Supreme Court would fix this conception of personhood through a bold-faced interpretation of the Fourteenth Amendment, conferring personhood's rights and liberties on corporations. The court supplied that new gloss, as we will shortly see, in a case directly tied to the American plantation economy, one that centered on bales of cotton. All this jurisprudence turned on interpretations of that amendment, which defined birthright citizenship and affirmed the rights of due process. Often overlooked in accounts of slavery's afterlives, which tend to focus on the Thirteenth Amendment and its infamous loophole that legalized enslavement "as a punishment for crime," the Fourteenth Amendment instituted a notion of freedom rooted in an ideology of contract. It also tethers the definition of citizenship, and the rights of personhood, outlined in Section One, to the "validity of the public debt of the United States," in Section Four, which "shall not be questioned." *Freedom* names here the status and process incumbent to the mendacious work of *formal* abolition, rather than *total* abolition. *Freedom* indicates a transformational process within slave racial capitalism—not the antithesis to the political economy of slavery but rather its modification. It comprises here a metamorphosis in the value-form of the slave. "In a money culture ... value survives its objects," the theorist and historian Ian Baucom writes, and that fact, one affirmed by the object's loss, "confirms the system-wide conviction that that value was *always* autonomous from its object."[11] And liberated capital needs someplace to go.[12]

FORMAL ABOLITION DIDN'T so much dissolve the fact of bondage as it amended the terms of the bond. There were no revolutions in 1865, no permanent razing of factories in the field, no backbreaking coup de main against the profit regimes of black captivity, no seizure and return of the coin minted from the sweat and blood of those captives. And while the general strike by the slaves won major legal concessions—their bodies safe against being bought and sold, their families safe against being sundered by such sales, their departures safe against charges of self-theft—these bulwarks of freedom could and would be overtopped.[13]

The substance of these amended bonds was financial. A black North Carolina congressman in 1880 encapsulated the new arrangements this way: "A [landlord] has land which he rents to a tenant; the tenant desires to run his crop; he comes to town and must make a mortgage, either directly with the merchant or indirectly through his landlord, to have his supplies furnished. . . . [T]hat gives him credit, and that is all there is in that matter."[14] Abolition amounted, in other words, to a financial arrangement. And that financial arrangement amounted to the bailout of an institution that was too big to fail: the plantation, the site of slavery's production. In the decades after 1865, the plantation was reconstituted and revitalized.

While the Civil War caused vast damage to real estate and industry, far worse for planters was abolition itself, which vaporized the overwhelming capital accumulated in and circulated by slave bodies. By 1860, slave property's value amounted, conservatively, to three billion dollars—a figure worth more than investments in manufacturing, railroads, and banks; worth more than gold; worth more even than land. By 1860, slaves were the collateral of credit relations, the antichresis pledged in mortgages. This "new black flesh coin" was the general equivalent, the "real" currency *not* just of the Southern economy, but of the national economy.[15] And of course slaves were not just *objects* of accumulation; they were also *subjects* of accumulation.[16] They were commodities who labored and produced other commodities, ever more capital. When abolition eradicated white wealth by nullifying the slave as a commodity form, numerous white Southern planters and merchants found themselves deeply in debt.

Rich white Southerners looked to two legal maneuvers to help navigate their postwar loss of property and its value. First, the legislatures of the former slave states almost immediately passed crop-lien laws. These laws simultaneously compelled the freedperson to work "willingly" on a planter's stated terms and under a regime of contract, and allowed the planters to secure credit from merchants based on their workers' future labor. The cotton crop's projected profit was promised in advance for liquid credit in the present. Second, the federal government passed a Bankruptcy Act in 1867 intended to restore Southern wealth. This act expunged the debts and obligations of those who were insolvent, and through property exemptions, it allowed them to hold onto much of what they owned. Controlling the land meant the owners also had political and social control of the region, as the historian Elizabeth Lee Thompson has shown.[17]

This act preserved the plantation as a geographical entity, an integer under central control, and unbound the plantation from the debts that threatened to sink it. With one hand, the Bankruptcy Act wiped away the planters' debt, and with another, crop-lien laws dispersed and atomized future risks by subjecting the freed to the enclosures of credit.[18] Because they no longer held collateral in slave bodies, planters now relied on the value of their acreage (secured by the Bankruptcy Act) and their coming crop (secured by state lien laws) to obtain the credit that would refinance the postwar plantation. This meant that the crushing debt that war and abolition had placed on planters' and merchants' shoulders no longer rested so squarely on them. Instead, the maneuvers forged from freedpeople themselves new links in that chain of debt.

The law's full recognition of personhood in the ex-slave was a Trojan horse that trapped such persons with the liability for a financial debt they literally incarnated. The gift of freedom opened to reveal the inheritance of slavery. At once contriving the consent of the freed and encumbering them with debt, the contract system reanchored the value of the slave's *body* in the freed's *person*. To use a chemical metaphor, it is as if the value-form of the slave underwent a phase change, a kind of sublimation. Although exchange value was technically no longer engraved in black flesh as a commodity form, this value reattached to a number of those bodies in the red ink of merchants' ledgers—like a kind of ghost conjured by law and capital, constantly haunting the freed and compelling their labor. Ex-slaves were, in a sense, never fully in control of the property in themselves, which was almost immediately held against them as debt. Formally, ex-slaves had been ushered into a regime of contract, which was conceived as the very denouement of freedom, but unlike most waged laborers, contract's entitlement to selfhood and to any consequent property or wealth had not been granted to them outright but instead was held in perpetual abeyance.

To say that slave capital was vaporized by abolition, then, does *not* mean that such capital was destroyed, only that it was transmuted and then transmitted elsewhere, into other hands. On those ledger pages, the ex-slave's debits for purchases at unconscionably high "time prices"—exorbitant amounts charged for items to be purchased later, on "time," not cash—were the mark of usury's magical profit for white lenders. What the freed were forced to buy at credit's discrepant prices was the lost exchange value of their own bodies. And as planters sought to manage their own exposure, the risk of the entire Atlantic economy in cotton was rolled down onto the backs of sharecroppers. What the Bankruptcy Act and the crop-lien laws enacted was the mortgage of freedom.

The scope of this financial metamorphosis in the South was immense, and it marked a shift from the traditional and established financial networks of banks to their newer and less formal replacements, general stores. In part, this change was impelled by the National Banking Act of 1863 that standardized and nationalized a paper currency. This paper money was secured with U.S. bonds, bonds that were being marketed by the financier Jay Cooke to the general public as a means of supporting the Union war effort. As many as "1 million Northerners ended up owning shares in a national debt that by war's end amounted to over $2 billion," Eric Foner writes. "But most bonds were held by wealthy individuals and financial institutions." (And after the war, it was they "who reaped the windfall from interest paid in gold at a time when depreciating paper money was employed for all other transactions.")[19] The Banking Act set up a "system of correspondent banking"—a three-tiered pyramid of local banks, beneath eighteen city reserve banks, beneath the apex of New York banks. This system channeled resources from the nation's hinterlands into the financial markets of New York.[20] Consolidating a national capital market, enabling future investment in commerce and industry, the system also handed over control to Wall Street.[21]

Given that the enslaved had functioned as the general equivalent for the nation's economy, its true "gold standard," one cannot help but note that the National Banking Act was passed in 1863, the same year as the Emancipation Proclamation, which began the process of decommodifying slave capital. The Banking Act, whose provisions inhibited the development of banks in agricultural regions, and the war, which had ruined the South's old factor system of state banks and cotton brokers, together incited the proliferation of general stores in the South, the region's new lenders. For example, while forty-nine state-chartered banks were located in Georgia and South Carolina in 1860, just four remained after 1865. By 1868, only twenty of 1,688 national banks were located in Southern states. Five of the twenty would close within the following year.[22] By contrast, at the turn of the twentieth century, general stores in the South had reached a tally of 150,653, a number that reflected their exponential growth since the war's end.[23] "Destruction of the southern banking system" contributed, as historian Richard Bensel succinctly puts it, to "the rise of debt peonage as the major form of labor organization in cash crop agriculture."[24]

In part, these numbers of stores versus banks also represented an unfolding history of technological change. Cotton once had to be shipped to factors in ports because ports were the hubs of market information and commerce, of pricing and export. With the advent of improved cotton compresses, the railroad, the telegraph, the transatlantic cable, and through bills of lading, cotton buying began to move inland. Every community now had its own compress, whose well-packed bales could be off-loaded onto rail cars, as the railroads' steel vines spread across the South. And where the rails spread, hundreds of new markets flowered. Telegraph wires now supplied inland sellers and buyers with immediate access to cotton's going rate on the world market. Any Southern town could now be a cotton market, and there—distant from any port—buyers could sample, class, and compress the crop. Northern and British mills now dealt with brokers who had representatives stationed across the inland South. Direct buying of cotton reduced costs all around, and on through bills of lading, cotton hardly stopped its transit at ports and no longer needed to pass through the hands of factors, whose business began to vanish.[25]

As a result of all of these structural changes, an altered, and much more expansive, web of finance was being spun over Southern states, and this web was composed less of banks and factors than of general stores and merchants. These stores became the new financial circuits in an increasingly nationalized market—nationalized as cotton prices were standardized through instantaneous communication and as the same brand name goods were stocked on different shelves across the South. Just as railroads could now take cotton out of inland markets, so railroads could bring consumer goods in. And just as centralized markets in seaports gave way to atomized markets across the interior South, so the capital and credit controlled by seaport factors began to flow through the hands of merchants at general stores. More markets equaled more credit, and more credit equaled more consumers.

As a consequence of formal abolition, planters were no longer the only purchasers of goods. The store and its merchant reflected the legal extension of will and personal sovereignty to millions of ex-slaves throughout the South. Before 1865, only white masters and their factors could claim full legal status as sovereign individuals, and their contracts with one another formed the South's financial matrix. For the master, such sovereignty implicated all of his property, including slaves, and even as his slaves' labor constituted his personhood, his personhood occluded and absorbed his slaves. Formal abolition shattered and dispersed these master–slave relations of sovereignty. In the liberalist terms that framed U.S. abolition, what the master had owned now the slaves themselves owned: their bodies, their labor, their persons. Possessive individualism comprised freedom's endowment—*freedom* naming that thin etymological shade that falls between *own* and *owe*.

Once the freed themselves became the legal proprietors of their own labor, the networks of finance that had previously supported the plantation underwent a structural transformation as well. In other words, the redistribution of sovereignty necessitated the redistribution of finance. War and abolition had decimated antebellum networks of credit. According to a Mobile businessman, everybody wanted to buy in the years following the war, but nobody had any money.[26] And by April 1867, the South's leading financial advocate and commentator James De Bow declared that the credit shortage problem had "already reached the point where business becomes paralyzed."[27] Enter the rural merchant, that little territorial monopolist who controlled the commodity of credit.[28] All across the Southern states, almost without exception, a wage system was quickly abandoned, replaced—following the passage of crop-lien laws—with what's euphemistically called the "share system." Credit supplanted wages. And this change was, as explained simply by one landowner, "because of more profit in share system to landlord."[29] Much like the system of slavery, sharecropping was not merely a system of labor but also a system of capital accumulation. The formerly enslaved were conscripted by law to make recompense, endlessly, for the lost exchange value of their own bodies, a process crystallized and reproduced each time they were debited for obscenely priced goods by their white lenders. Indebtedness specifies the interval between the "no longer" and the "not yet," between slave and free, an ongoing moment where the engine of history stalls out.[30] A freedom arrived, a freedom deferred. As the editor of the *Progressive Farmer* put it in 1904, "The pathos of the lien-farmer is that he is always only 12 months away from freedom."[31]

The Northern victory that realized the formal abolition of slavery also implied the victory of long-standing Northern principles, which yoked the entitlements of freedom with the rights of contract. From one perspective, the freed were now persons with full legal standing who elected to contract their labor. But from another angle, with black flesh shorn of its exchange value, black life was being forced into the red, press-ganged into debt. The line distinguishing these two interpretations was the length and shape of the counter at the Southern country store, in that it determined whether one stood on the side of copious supplies or on the side of contrite supplication. The deposition of chattelism was hailed as the coronation of contractualism, as the end of an era defined by status.[32] To contract freely with another was to perform, quintessentially, the freedom of the individual will: "One of the greatest privileges of a freeman is to *choose* for himself. Slaves must do as they are commanded, but freemen *choose* for themselves" for whom they'll labor, one freedmen's primer noted.[33] But behind the words and the politics were the actual experiences of the new contract: here we find Jake Dunwoodie, for example, with his lost blood and lost teeth, pistol-whipped and kidnapped in order to buy a month's supply of groceries at the store—of his own free will.

In the efflorescence of credit and the entanglements of debt, in the financial relations that conscripted and coerced the freed across the South, in the scope and scale of the plantation and in the vectors of its capital flows, one doesn't witness the contravention of the personhood and citizenship conferred by the Fourteenth Amendment in 1868, one witnesses their fulfillment. When scholars narrate the aftermath of formal abolition, the law and its interpretation by the courts tend to appear in the ensuing years to pervert freedom's entitlements, both in the public law that governs the individual's relation to the state and in the private law of torts and contracts. The ex-slave appears to be abandoned legally, as freedom's legal safeguards are slackened to give business a free rein. But that narrative misunderstands the law's function. Abolition's framing as freedom of contract and the subsequent rise of laissez-faire economics, both of which relied on the Fourteenth Amendment, were born of the same legal philosophy.

If contract names the lawful means of acquisition, or dispossession, in a market society, then personhood appears as market society's preferred technology of expropriation. The formal admission into full legal standing of the slave's person after 1865—that is, citizenship—was really only the entrée into a more thoroughgoing subsumption by racial capitalism. Personhood operates here as liberalism's cover story, as it intensifies colonialism, a legal prism through which heteronomy appears as autonomy, extortion as volition, hierarchy as equality, and hunger as choice. The needs of one's flesh and the desires of one's spirit, the idiosyncrasies of a life cobbled together as a self, get translated through personhood into the formal and deracinated equivalence of contract (whether realized in the wage of economics or in the identity of politics). It acts as the legal rail switch in political economy for capitalist accumulation at the scale of the body.[34] And any presumptions that the circulation of the capital extracted and accumulated through the work of personhood was neatly contained within "the South," sequestered at the scale of the regional, must be promptly dismissed. This was not true prior to the Civil War and formal abolition, and it becomes even less true in the many long decades afterward.[35]

A LETTER MAILED ON 3 OCTOBER 1894, from New Orleans to New York, brings this history into sharp relief. This letter was, in itself, nothing but a bit of economic dross, some paperwork. Yet it's all there, slavery's blood money and the plantation's grisly map, once we see what it concerns, and note where it comes from and where it goes.

This letter reads: "Insurance is wanted by E. Allgeyer and Co., for account of same, loss, if any, payable at Paris ... For $3400.00, on one hundred b. c.

[bales cotton] on board of steamer —,—— master, and to be insured at and from L. Rock to N. Orleans per R. R., and thence per steamer to Havre."[36]

The letter writer, Charles Emile Allgeyer, was partner in a New Orleans exporting firm, and he had an open marine insurance policy in New York, with the Atlantic Mutual Insurance Company. This particular letter notified Atlantic Mutual of a shipment of cotton, coming from Arkansas and destined for France. One hundred bales of cotton were to be loaded onto a train at Little Rock, to be off-loaded onto a steamer at New Orleans, to be shipped to the French port of Le Havre. A hundred bales of Arkansas cotton, grown, tended, and harvested by workers such as those whose voices introduced this chapter: by Ann Ulrich Evans cheated of her earnings, by Henry Blake cajoled to take on more debt, by Jake Dunwoodie hustled off in a red terror.[37] So much was, and would soon be, at issue in that letter mailed that day in 1894. Soon enough that letter would come into the hands of the justices of the U.S. Supreme Court, and their reading of it would redefine the endowments of freedom.

A few months earlier, the state of Louisiana had passed an act that forbade "any person, firm, or corporation" from contracting with any marine insurance company that didn't have a footprint within the state—such as Atlantic Mutual—because such firms couldn't be taxed.[38] Louisiana fined E. Allgeyer & Co. one thousand dollars for violating this new law. Asserting its power to regulate corporations that were engaged in business within its territory, the state claimed that the contract contained in Allgeyer's letter was made within Louisiana and that it contravened the statute. Allgeyer claimed that the contract was made in New York and rejected the act's constitutionality. The company then appealed its way to the U.S. Supreme Court. That little economic formality of contracting marine insurance contained in that slip of paper that Allgeyer posted from New Orleans to New York became the center of the case.

A commercial form nearly identical to thousands upon thousands of others, Allgeyer's letter was one datum in the plantation's network of finance. Nevertheless, the case can be read like that network's map, a guide to the plantation's resurgence and expansion and to the changes in its structure. More precisely, through the court's interpretation of the Fourteenth Amendment in the *Allgeyer* decision, the plantation's expanding regimes of accumulation would find anchor in the legal recognition of free black personhood. The institution of slavery would remain tightly intertwined with the institution of freedom. In *Allgeyer v. Louisiana*, the Fourteenth Amendment's language of formal equality would be made to guarantee, not the autonomy of the ex-slave, but the liberties of the plantation and a laissez-faire corporate capitalism.

Contrary to many planters' fears, and contrary to contemporary historical memory, the Civil War didn't wipe out the Southern plantation economy. Indeed, by the time Allgeyer's letter arrived before the court in the mid-1890s, the cotton economy in the South had made up for the losses in production from the war and from abolition, to say the very least—a fact that the letter itself, seeking to insure a hundred bales of cotton for export to France, only serves to corroborate. Within two decades, American farmers began exporting more cotton than they had at the Civil War's start, and within three decades they were producing twice the cotton of 1861.[39] Meanwhile, miles of rail were being built more quickly in the South than in any other region in the country in the final quarter of the century (often by leased black convicts), and these new railroads opened more remote lands to cotton's cultivation, now profitably transported where previously it hadn't been.[40] Between the war's end and the century's end, the national acreage devoted to cotton production increased more than threefold; by 1930, sixfold.[41]

Cotton's economic importance had always been more than regional.[42] Well before the Civil War, cotton secured the base of financial operations in New York City: "Cotton, the fuel of the industrial revolution, remained at the center of the city's trade relationships," writes Sven Beckert, "and a growing number of merchants committed themselves to this line of business."[43] He adds, "The export of cotton also secured the nation's credit on the European money markets and thus kept the city's banks afloat."[44] Not least through the mechanism of the national debt, the Civil War consolidated New York's hold on ever more of the capital in the cotton economy, including that which had circulated between the South and Britain. (It was primarily Southern cotton, of course, that fed the enormous British textile industry.) Raising tariffs on imports and developing its own factories (with ever more of those factories located in Southern states), the United States challenged the British market, and by century's end, it had become the second largest cotton manufacturer in the world after Britain.[45] With exports of raw cotton continuing to expand, this was a recipe for tremendous capital accumulation, not least in New York where so much of that capital circulated.[46] The city built on cotton before the Civil War was assuming its mantle as the world's financial capital by the turn of the century.[47] And in 1870, at One Hanover Square, a few blocks off Wall Street, just as these transitions were gaining steam, the New York Cotton Exchange opened. It was the first in the country and the second in the world, and only the second commodities exchange in the United States.

Two features increasingly defined a new pattern in the cotton trade by the 1880s: consolidation and speculation. The family-owned plantation—the big house surrounded by fields—began to disappear after the Civil War and was replaced by an agribusiness model of absentee ownership and extensive infrastructure.[48] The change was even more dramatic as the harvest left the fields. A handful of American and European firms now controlled cotton buying, with representatives stationed in nearly all Southern markets.[49] As Richard Wright noted, "The Bosses of the Buildings now own almost one-third of the plantations of the South, and they are rapidly converting them into 'farm factories.'"[50] Along with technological developments, these new forms of organization enabled Southern cotton to dominate the world's markets even after 1865.[51] Meanwhile, speculation in the cotton market ballooned.[52] Short selling of futures contracts abounded—that is, contracting to sell cotton one didn't own to be delivered at some later date.[53] As a consequence, large firms across the South began building enormous warehouses to stockpile cotton, hedging it against fluctuations in the commodity's price.[54] These futures markets were a means of managing and distributing risk—as was the entrapment of the freed in the meshes of credit, with the vulnerabilities always falling heaviest on the sharecroppers. This is all to say that the institution was changing, with a colossal restructuring and expansion of the plantation underway, as commanded by Northern finance capitalists.

As interior markets opened across the South thanks to new technologies—railroads, the transatlantic cable, through bills of lading—in New York sales of actual cotton fell off after the Civil War. Whatever cotton did go to New York was mostly used to cover futures contracts.[55] But New York's share of the finance capital that floated the postwar cotton trade only got larger. This was due in no small part to the boom in commodity speculation in these years.[56] A more direct lineage of finance capital can also be traced, as it was by a Georgia planter in his testimony before a federal commission in 1899:

Q: How do they [Southern farmers] get supplies?
A: Through merchants.
Q: And the merchants?
A: Through the banks.
Q: And where do the local banks get their money?
A: New York.[57]

The sentiment remains in a Southern editor's complaint in 1910: "The new gold which cotton brings from foreign lands is of such vast sums that it is absolutely unwise to permit it to be returned to New York instead of to [the South]."[58] And again in a government survey of 1922, which declared flatly, "New York is the most important source of cotton loans."[59] Put simply, the plantation had gone corporate, and its headquarters had been relocated to New York.

Through the *Allgeyer* case, one glimpses an alternative history of the corporate form's emergence on the American scene, yoked to plantation slavery. According to the theorist Giovanni Arrighi, the history of capital can be arranged into systemic cycles of accumulation, with each cycle anchored in and bounded by a sovereign territorial formation. Around 1870, as Arrighi theorizes it, global capital underwent a structural change, a moment of transition between a British cycle, which had begun in the late eighteenth century, and a U.S. cycle, which was just starting and would dominate the long twentieth century.[60] Shifts from one cycle of accumulation to the next are marked by a sovereign territory's capture of the capital set free by its predecessor—in this case, the capture within New York of the tremendous capital circulating in the prewar cotton trade between the South and Britain, which had anchored the Industrial Revolution.[61] Moreover, what has marked the U.S. cycle are precisely those innovations that restructured the cotton industry: the process of vertical integration, shortening the chain between production and distribution, the absorption and reduction of transaction costs within a corporation. Without question, this global shift registers in the plantation's reorganization during this same moment. But considering that plantation capital forms the submerged foundation of New York finance, couldn't one also claim, more brashly, that the initial elements of this global shift can be traced back to the plantation's reorganization? And that the chronology of Arrighi's U.S. cycle begins five years earlier than he contends, in 1865?[62] Whatever else it signifies, the destination of that letter mailed by E. Allgeyer & Co., seeking marine insurance for an international shipment of cotton, must not be interpreted as coincidental or trivial.

Allgeyer v. Louisiana reveals how liberalism and colonialism are knotted together on the American scene. We bear witness to that entanglement as we follow the chains of credit forged out of black indebtedness that snake a path beyond and outside the South and that tether the plantation to the foundations of corporate capitalism in New York. As individual personhood is transposed into corporate personhood, and as the latter arrogates to itself the supposed rights of the former, we again confirm the tight bind that yokes them. Personhood enacted a geographical form of capital accumulation at the national level, as it was legally codified after 1865, reinstating the program of the plantation, and as we can now see, at the global level, too. In its authorizations of personhood in the scenes of plantation finance, whether the counter of the country store or a marine insurance firm in New York, the law enables us to grasp the modes of accumulation installed in the wake of formal abolition meant to preserve slavery's value-form and allows us to jump scales, from the ragged confines of an erstwhile estate to an ascendant metropolitan world capital. Or, to restate the proposition: capitalism is never *not* racial capitalism. As James Baldwin put it, "White is a metaphor for power, and that is simply a way of describing Chase Manhattan Bank."[63]

Issues of territoriality formed one crux of the *Allgeyer* case—specifically, whether Allgeyer's mailing of notification constituted a new contract and, if so, whether the agreement that letter contained had occurred within the state's jurisdiction. Yes, the Louisiana attorney general argued, regulating commerce between its inhabitants and foreign corporations fell within the purview of the state's police powers.[64] The state's attorneys reiterated the philosophy espoused by the Louisiana Supreme Court. That court had insisted, ruling against Allgeyer, "Individual liberty of action must give way to the greater right of the collective people in the assertion of well-defined policy, designed and intended for the general welfare." This was the rationale that lay beneath all police power: general welfare, *salus populi est suprema lex*—the safety of the people is the supreme law. The exercise of police powers had long been the levy that states exacted from corporations in exchange for issuing these organizations' charters that granted them a long list of benefits (a legal personality, monopoly rights, limited liability, eminent domain).[65] And police power had supplied Louisiana's rationale just a year earlier in 1896, in the landmark case *Plessy v. Ferguson*. Argued before the U.S. Supreme Court, the state successfully fought to uphold its segregation laws under the "separate but equal" provision, despite the well-planned efforts of Homer Plessy to see them overturned. Police power appears in these moments as the avatar of states' rights—constituting jurisdiction by regulating foreign bodies, whether that denoted corporations in New York or black passengers in New Orleans.

Issues of personal freedom formed another focal point of the case, and the arguments made on behalf of E. Allgeyer & Co. on that score were no less troubling. Allgeyer's defense claimed that the statute was depriving him of his liberty—that the law was "violative of the 14th Amendment of the Constitution" because it divested him of his liberty and his property without due process. "In the present case the defendants are denied the right of doing in Louisiana so innocent an act as the mailing of a letter to a party in New York, with whom they have made a contract," their lawyer pleaded with disarming simplicity. "It is difficult to conceive of a more naked, unauthorized invasion of liberty." The defense claimed that the state's regulation on marine insurance companies was interfering with a right to contract, much vaunted and federally guaranteed by the Fourteenth Amendment. He was prohibited from communicating with his New York business associates, after having entered a perfectly legal contract with them in that state. "A party having the free right to contract anywhere in the world, finds that he is prohibited from doing so by the act of a foreign corporation, with whom he desires to contract. What protection under the law is enjoyed by such a prohibited person?"[66]

The argument was twofold: as it argued on behalf of an individual's civil rights, it simultaneously sought the commercial rights of the corporation. It invoked the charged language of status ("a prohibited person") to insist on a redefined freedom and a deregulated market. The rhetorical force of a question challenging the state's police powers, which seems to have been cribbed from the pitched legal struggle against Jim Crow, is here pressed into the service of commercial freedom and the corporation's extraterritoriality. ("What protection under the law is enjoyed by such a prohibited person?") A New Orleans cotton broker and, by proxy, an insurance corporation could adopt the posture of stigmatic racial injury in appealing to the court to bleed *freedom* of any lingering antislavery reference. And Allgeyer's defense proposed a truly capacious definition of liberty, one untethered from abolition, to be protected by the Fourteenth Amendment, which "includes more than mere freedom from physical restraint; it includes the right to use and enjoy all the energies, physical and moral, with which man is endowed; the right to use the faculties to engage in or follow any lawful vocation or business, by which a livelihood may be gained."

And property, too, denoted more than might have been readily apparent. As the defense reckoned it—and appropriate to a case that involved the complex credit economy of the cotton market—the amendment's protection of property would henceforth denote both present wealth and future accumulation: "property imports the idea not only of possessing and enjoying, but of acquiring, and to this end, engaging in business, and making contracts, for the purpose of emolument or gain."[67] In some sense, Allgeyer was returning "substantive due process" to its proslavery origins, a doctrine first elaborated by John C. Calhoun in 1836 to protect slaveholders' human property within the nation's capital, against abolitionists' campaigns to outlaw slavery in the District of Columbia.[68] Here, the languages of a formal equality and a formal liberty are revealed to be the very script of racial capitalism.

The court couldn't have agreed more, and it ruled for Allgeyer. In its opinion of 1897 it lifted, more or less wholesale, the redefinition of freedom proposed by his defense.[69] For the first time, the Supreme Court in *Allgeyer v.*

Louisiana codified the liberty protected by the Fourteenth Amendment as primarily economic. Its decision initiated what has since been labeled the "*Lochner* era," a forty-year stretch of laissez-faire jurisprudence at the beginning of the twentieth century.[70] Abolition's legacy had long since been abandoned by the courts, but here it withered to a "mere freedom from physical restraint," its connection to racial slavery attenuated, enslavement rendered but a vestige. The logic of the court's decision marked the beginning of a deterritorialized existence for the liberated corporation, as well as for Plantation, Inc. A state could now only regulate a corporation if it chose to have a footprint within its territory; it could not police any foreign corporation's commerce with its citizens. *Allgeyer* was an accomplice to the plantation's persistence at the turn of the twentieth century. The case and its verdict ushered in ever more complicated arrangements of finance capital and ensured that the real "freedoms" of late capitalism—that is, the fluidity of commodities, the liquidity of credit, the flows of capital itself—redounded the institutional apparatus of the plantation.

Through the smallest exercise of the imagination, one could reconnect this newfound freedom of commerce, now guaranteed constitutionally and soon ramifying through a fat corporatocracy, to the bondage that underwrote it. Beside and beneath the economic abstractions in *Allgeyer*, the more frictionless transit of goods and value, the linchpin of more corporate freedom, stood those hundred bales of Arkansas cotton in all their hard materiality. Those bales and the value they represented, their circulation within a global economy, were *produced*, and were produced by *someone* under conditions of impoverishment and uncertainty and privation. Beside and beneath the machinations of white finance in *Allgeyer* stood the entrapments of black debt.

GENERALLY SPEAKING, CREDIT KNIT TOGETHER one's management of money with one's moral standing. And in the increasingly abstract economy of nineteenth-century America—where credit was a step removed from cash, or many steps in the case of commodity futures, and money itself appeared ever more untethered from any intrinsic value—morality often seemed to be the presence of some perceptible meaning that could stand in for its many mystifying absences in an advanced money economy. Character compensated for the confusion of finance. "If the [money] ethic assumed a notion of the Good, which was character, it also assumed a notion of the Bad, which was weakness, slavery, and the loss of self-control," the historian Lendol Calder writes. "If credit was a reward for character and therefore an emblem of the Good, debt symbolized ... 'the middle class hell,' a state of moral and literal bankruptcy brought on by the inability to face down desire."[71] Debt represented the ultimate moral failure. It was a homologue of slavery. (In the words of Benjamin Franklin's Poor Richard, by far the century's most trusted economic counselor, "the Borrower is a Slave to the Lender"—words bluntly reiterated in 1893 by one I. H. Mayer, who wrote in his *Domestic Economy*, debt "makes a man a slave. Avoid it!")[72] Nowhere were these issues of money, credit, and character brought into sharper focus than in public concern over the formerly enslaved. Slavery proper was imagined by white abolitionists to have destroyed the character of both the enslavers and the enslaved. To cross the line from status to contract, to assume the mantle of citizenship, would require of the freed, at minimum, an education in the bourgeois virtues of financial responsibility. Their self-appointed teachers were a group of Northern white philanthropists, and the institution founded to instruct them was the Freedman's Savings and Trust Company.

The Freedman's Savings Bank was a moral crusade, not an attempt to invest in poor black communities.[73] Abraham Lincoln signed a charter authorizing the bank in 1865 to operate as a nonprofit institution that could only invest in government securities. It was, furthermore, *private* and had neither the backing nor the guarantee of the federal government. Beginning as a repository for black soldiers' pay, the bank soon expanded its purview and encouraged civilians to deposit their money. The bank's literature was a compilation of parables and admonishments that equated savings with moral rectitude and public respect. By saving, one piece counseled: "All people will trust you. Men will point you out and say—'There's a sober, hard-working, honest man, with money ahead; you can trust him.'"[74] The parables told and retold stories of temperate and provident men who resisted momentary pleasures, putting the money they might use to pay for their vices instead into their savings accounts. Thus, one man "put in the bank the exact amount which he would have spent if he had gone out to drink" with his colleagues on each occasion. "He kept to his resolution for five years. He then examined his bank account, and found that he had on deposit $521.86." Not only that, but following his colleagues' descent into alcoholism, the "water drinker then bought out the printing office, went on enlarging his business, and in twenty years from the time he began to put by his money, was worth $100,000." Many pamphlets sought to school the freed in this extraordinary magic of accumulation. That magic could be harnessed even without self-denial through the wonders of interest. Sowing fear in those who preferred to keep their money at home, another piece suggested: "Or suppose it isn't stolen or eaten up by mice; if safe hid away it would be making nothing for you.... Instead, then, of hiding your savings... put it in the bank, where it will be making money for you." Under the heading "REASONS WHY YOU SHOULD ALL PUT MONEY IN THE SAVINGS BANK," one pamphlet from 1867 gave as reason Number 4, "*You should use this Bank* because it is conducted entirely by your best friends . . . and being authorized by Congress, and approved by the President of the United States, it is the safest place you can find for your money."[75]

The bank fell under the auspices of Jay Cooke and Company, which effectively controlled the bank between 1870 and 1873.[76] But Jay Cooke and his firm had another, larger concern during and after the war. It was he who had helped to underwrite the massive war debt accrued by the Union. Debt and character weren't just paired rhetorically in the era's economic self-help literature. Credit and citizenship were warp and weft of the U.S. nation-state that emerged from the Civil War. That fact is codified, as noted earlier, by the Fourteenth Amendment itself. While Section 1 defines birthright citizenship for the first time in the nation's public law, enshrining rights of due process and equal protection, Section 4—less familiar to us—reads, "The validity of the public debt of the United States, authorized by law . . . shall not be questioned." The section also nullifies "any debt or obligation incurred in aid of insurrection or rebellion against the United States, or any claim for the loss or emancipation of any slave." Within the text of the Constitution, national citizenship is tethered to the national debt—a discursive link with its own material history. In macroeconomic terms, no less than in the case of the individual before the counter of the country store, that link in the Fourteenth Amendment set in motion an engine of accumulation whose motor was primed by slave capital.

"War is expensive," as the historian William G. Roy notes, and the Union "had to find a way to pay for supplies, not out of its puny revenues but by borrowing as much as it could and inventing a national currency."[77] The government turned to public financing, commissioning a half-billion dollar issue of bonds in 1862. But without the means to market and sell them, Secretary of the Treasury Salmon P. Chase called on the financier Jay Cooke to act as the government's investment banker. The Union also established a uniform national currency of bank notes through the National Banking Act. These notes were drawn on nationally chartered banks and secured by U.S. bonds. Public finance was partly socialized as many Americans, not just the rich, invested in these securities. But this also concentrated financial control in a few hands. "Financing the war effort brought the federal government into the heart of Wall Street," Roy writes. "By the end of the war, the federal government and its debt were a major concern and would continue to be so, with a total war debt over $2.5 billion." The national debt—and the national currency that was yoked to it—functioned to consolidate irrevocably the wealth and influence of New York's finance capitalists. "Wealth flowing into New York and invested in securities generated profits that could be reinvested in the corporate system, leading to its further growth," as Roy points out.[78] Further, the war-making powers of the state had now been aligned with the interests of capital—no small point when contemplating the succession of imperialist wars the United States would, and yet does, instigate in the name of freedom. Following the example set by the Civil War, U.S. warmongering would be justified hereafter by high-minded moralizing about democratic liberation that worked to conceal the thievery committed on behalf of a small coterie of the nation's most rich and powerful. It was, Du Bois writes, the birth of "a system by which a little knot of masterful men would so organize capitalism as to bring under their control the natural resources, wealth and industry of a vast and rich country and through that, of the world."[79]

The Fourteenth Amendment's guarantees both of black suffrage and of the national debt were meant to subjugate loyal Confederates, to smash the political power of the planter bloc. The Civil War effected the permanent transfer of citizenship from individual states to the nation, whose new governmental powers had been epitomized by the Emancipation Proclamation and the creation of a national currency.[80] The Fourteenth Amendment legitimated the Union war debt to cut off at the root any Southern protests about being made to pay for their own defeat or any efforts to repatriate the confiscated value of their slave capital. But codifying "the validity of the public debt of the United States" and enshrining a system of public credit that "shall not be questioned" fundamentally altered both the function of the state and the social relations of its subjects. "Reducing governmental stability to financial prosperity, public credit transforms the relations of citizenship—both the relations between government and its citizens, and those between citizens themselves—into relations of credit, relations between debtors and creditors," as Stephen Best puts it.[81] A national debt represents "the alienation of the state," according to Karl Marx. That is, it forces a shift in the state's raison d'être, from serving the ends of its citizens toward serving the ends of capital, operating not for the good of all but for the profits of a few. "The public debt becomes one of the most powerful levers of primitive accumulation," Marx writes. "As with the stroke of an enchanter's wand, it endows barren money with the power of breeding and thus turns it into capital without the necessity of its exposing itself to the troubles and risks inseparable from its employment in industry."[82] With the creation of a sovereign war debt, the new market in government securities fostered this "power of breeding," which manifested as the interest due, in perpetuity, on billions in federal bonds, bonds mostly held by a new and emerging class of financiers.[83]

Public debt operated as such a lever of accumulation in the postwar South too. These financiers had little patience for the vision of radical Reconstruction—those federal programs that aimed to redistribute power and wealth from the plantation regime to the newly freed. They wanted to get paid, and they wanted arenas where they could reinvest their capital. Recall that cotton was the nation's primary international export and that New York was central to the financial and commercial infrastructure of the cotton trade. For Northern capitalists with an interest in that trade, including New England textile manufacturers, Southern plantations couldn't get back in working order fast enough. These men were becoming a rentier class supported by income from their investments, and their firms were now producing more surplus capital than could easily be plowed back into those same enterprises.[84] They had money to spare. One lucrative venue was bonded debt, both that of the United States and, more and more, that of railroads.[85] ("We think the railroad enterprises are one of the conduits through which the excess of capital in the North is to flow into our nearly exhausted coffers," wrote the Richmond *Dispatch* in 1871.)[86] The railroads accompanied the insistent push into new cotton-growing territory in the South and West, particularly the 1848 cessions of Mexican land, driving the displacement of indigenous populations. Infrastructure projects cemented the incorporation of these territories, and so "cotton bloomed alongside the railroad," as historian Sven Beckert puts it. For example, miles of rail were being laid at an astonishing pace in Oklahoma and Texas in the late nineteenth century, and once laid, cotton production went through the roof, increasing 465 percent in a single decade in the case of Dallas County.[87]

Northern finance capitalists opposed radical Reconstruction because it would impede the reboot of cotton production, and they cared about cotton production because it was through the international commerce in cotton that they got their gold.[88] (Responding to their pressure, Congress passed a Public Credit Act in 1869 that obliged the Treasury to pay creditors in gold. The act's stated purpose was "to remove any doubt as to the purpose of the Government to discharge all just obligations to the public creditors." The interest paid was also tax exempt.)[89] Seeking what the geographer David Harvey famously termed a "spatial fix," these Northern capitalists wanted to reinvest their gold in expanding industry, finance, and territory. The American state functioned in the late nineteenth century to facilitate just the expansion these financiers desired. Following the abandonment of Reconstruction, this led to the more far-reaching withdrawal of investment by the federal government in the Southern states. Cotton was the only asset the South brought to this Northern project of capital expansion, and even without government assistance, capitalist markets efficiently converted what the crop earned through foreign exchange into lines of credit and bullion that serviced the national debt.[90]

Rather than a triumph of humanitarian principles, formal abolition enacted an elaborate money-laundering scheme. Thanks to the alchemy of the Fourteenth Amendment, through the crucible of the national debt, the cotton produced under coercion by the nation's new black "citizens" was magically transformed into the golden interest due to those Northern financiers who had guaranteed the Union's war to "free" them. The national debt was the driver—a word I choose carefully—of the postwar plantation regime. The nominal freedom of the "formerly" enslaved was really just the diktat to grow ever more cotton, or else to starve and die, or to be incarcerated, which amounted to the same thing. The national debt scripted the function of the ersatz citizenship conferred on ex-slaves, propelling their entrapment in personal debt, mortgaging their freedom. The national debt assumed the role that had been played before the war by slave capital, the aggregate exchange value affixed to black flesh. The national debt was the final guarantor of cotton's matchless value as a commodity. And it indemnified Northern capitalists against the heavy losses of abolition, since in ways both figurative and literal the national debt represented their confiscation of slave capital from the Southern planter regime.

The ex-slaves worked for the North now. Beneath all the convolutions of American finance capitalism, and thence of American industrial capitalism, ex-slaves' personal debts forced them into the cotton fields: the red ink in merchants' ledgers that supervened any substantive black freedom only gained coherence *because* of the national debt, which was underwritten by corporate profiteers. The Civil War served as a "forcing-house" for the national debt, to borrow Marx's phrase, and once established, it could magically bestow on "barren money" that "power of breeding" that would render it capital. That capital then fed Northern industry and finance. One historian estimates that "half of the rise" in the rate of capital formation after the war can be attributed to the debt's repayment. And by the time the debt had been substantially repaid, Northern industry was well founded.[91] Historians often speak of how slavery, by way of cotton, financed the Industrial Revolution in Europe before the Civil War.[92] But, in like manner, it was "freedom," by way of cotton, that financed the industrial revolution in the United States *after* the Civil War.[93]

Plainly put, the national debt was a lever for the continuing accumulation of slave racial capital, based in the unfree labor of black "citizens" on cotton plantations in the South and West.[94] With regard to the freed, the national debt is precisely the alienation of the state: it operates as a life-support apparatus for the prewar system of enslaved labor. It ensures that the state *does not* exist for the benefit of these new citizens. That particular claim is a banality of Reconstruction history, but here, a deeper truth is revealed. We see the Reconstruction program of black abandonment and white accumulation fixed within the very mechanisms of the state, which is built anew on ex-slaves' stooped backs and picked pockets. Indeed, organized through the national debt, the relation between black producers in the South and white capitalists in the North *names* the state. It would be more apt to say that these "citizens" exist for the state's benefit, as the true guarantors of its financing and of its sovereignty. The Union war debt—taken on in their name, as they would be told again and again—was to be held against them not only rhetorically but also literally.

Codifying the personhood of the freed and locking the shackles of contract, the Fourteenth Amendment enables expropriation at the scale of the individual. We can connect the dots: ex-slaves' labor, under contract, produced cotton, and that cotton was then traded through New York on international markets. There cotton became the debt-servicing interest paid to Northern financiers who held the bonds that underwrote the federal state, a state produced by the Civil War. Through the material and discursive work of the Fourteenth Amendment, prewar systems of enslaved labor were rebranded as "freedom" rather than "slavery." But what can "freedom" possibly mean under such historical circumstances? What does the capacity of "citizen" designate except the conscription of the freedperson as a "slave of the State"?[95] With its exception of "punishment for crime," the Thirteenth Amendment isn't abolition's only loophole. Indeed, from this vantage point, the Fourteenth Amendment appears to be a loophole large enough to have driven the whole slave South through.

THE RELATIONS OF formal abolition were relations of credit. The articulation of liberal personhood in the freed through notions of contract was simultaneously the articulation of a network of finance capital. After 1865, the relations of finance capitalism supplanted slavery's flesh standard, and those relations also subsumed slavery's relations of racial domination. Credit became the cornerstone that buttressed the plantation, at once articulating race and personhood in the ex-slave—through laws against false pretenses, vagrancy, and enticement—and expanding the institution's regimes of accumulation. Implicated and overdetermined, credit and black personhood were mutually constitutive of each other.

Formal abolition spelled the perfection of the plantation's colonialism. Its colonization was rendered *intensive* as well as *extensive*—not only laying claim to new lands for cash crops such as cotton, but also to the needs and desires of black laborers. It involved the very modes of existence. It was articulated with forms of personhood, such as those delineated in this chapter's first half. It establishes a relation with "desires, forms of living, and intentions," with subjectivity, writes philosopher Jason Read.[96] One gleans the flavor of Read's point in a report from Edward King's Southern travelogue of 1875. Writing about merchants, King notes, "they always manage to retain a profit, rarely allowing a freedman to find that his season's toil has done more than square his accounts with the acute trader who has meantime supplied him and his family with provisions, clothing, and such articles of luxury as the negro's mind and body crave."[97] Any such "cravings" for "articles of luxury" aren't *sui generis*; they're articulated with a mode of production. As Read puts it, "Classes and subjectivities do not preexist their particular material conditions."[98] Nor are such desires all-encompassing or inescapable. One hears a defiance in accounts such as Henry Blake's and Laura Smalley's, which began this chapter. In this model, credit itself becomes a form of subjection that is mediated through the terms of both law and custom.[99] Now black life's necessities and its fleeting luxuries accrued to white profit, as did the black labor that underwrote the plantation's production of commodities. After 1865, that profit streamed northward into the coffers of corporate capitalists without delay.

In *Allgeyer*, the scales of credit that sustain the postwar plantation can be seen to coincide—macro and micro, global markets in commodity futures and predatory lending at the local crossroads store. If one zooms out so as to perceive the sprawling web of capital flows, then one zooms in to comprehend the "elaborate micropenality of everyday life," in Saidiya Hartman's words.[100] Blacks' existence in the South was marked by a kind of tyrannical localism—theirs was not the freedom of capital but rather the intensification of territoriality. Southern laws against vagrancy and enticement, the involuntary servitude enforced through false pretenses laws, the whole diffuse system of Southern incarceration and convict leasing, segregation itself—all of these were the modern means of immobilization and the refurbishments of captivity. All ensured that black labor led to the accumulation of white wealth, whether in the fields or at the counter of the crossroads store. "Freedom" proves itself, through *Allgeyer*, to be the consort of the plantation complex, seemingly forged against slavery but ever yoked to it. This was the culmination of a freedom borne of slavery and aligned with contract. "Rather than view the Court's economic interpretation of the 14th Amendment as a move away from morality, we need to see it as implementing the moral victory of Northern principles," warns legal scholar Brook Thomas.[101] And "freedom" in the law came to equal free trade and contract rights *not* in some case wildly tangential to that concept's origin, but rather in a case set in Louisiana, a case about unrestrained commerce in *cotton*.

The scandal of slavery's value trespasses outside whatever zone is imagined to be its proper area, and so too does that value communicate beyond the period imagined to be its crypt. To recognize freedom as mortgaged, to claim freedom was tantamount to primitive accumulation, to understand it as a theft and an enclosure: these notions deform the slave plantation's geography, and they also deform its history. The antebellum South is not slavery's sepulcher, and 1865 erects no cordon sanitaire that neatly quarantines its political economy within the past. The truth of that claim registers less in the continuity, after abolition, of the barbarous treatment inflicted on black bodies—rape, beating, starvation, captivity, murder, the whole infamous inventory of slavery's punishments, which endured unabated—than in the systematic preservation and continued production and circulation of the slave as a form of value, which licensed the ongoing domination and disposability of black life.

What is the political economy of the afterlife of slavery in the United States? And is this word, *afterlife*, the best way to describe slavery's ongoing scandal? What does the year 1865 signify to our historians? As a matter of *historicity*, 1865 marks a moment when the enslaved seized their own freedom.[102] As a matter of *historiography*, though, 1865 marks an ideological cover-up that erroneously calls slavery's time of death. "[T]his is just what the manumission of the black people of this country has accomplished," black editor and author T. Thomas Fortune wrote in 1884. "They are more absolutely under the control of the Southern whites; they are more systematically robbed of their labor; they are more poorly housed, clothed and fed, than under the slave regime; and they enjoy, practically, less of the protection of the laws of the State or of the Federal government."[103] This was the point W. E. B. Du Bois made in 1935 when he titled the penultimate chapter of his magnum opus *Black Reconstruction* "Back Toward Slavery." And, more recently, if perhaps less emphatically, one can find the point being made in the new social history and the new institutional economics of the 1970s and early 1980s. It is in these accounts of Reconstruction and its aftermath—written after the wave of revisionist histories in the 1960s that honored the accomplishments of the freed and of black politicians—that the phenomenon of "planter persistence" began to receive attention. Scholars working in the late 1970s and early 1980s reached the consensus that there had been no revolution and that antebellum planters had retained both their wealth and their power. This meant that antebellum planters were not hindrances to the industrializing "New South" but rather its midwives.[104] Dedicated to a different sort of historical empiricism, this new crop of social historians and new institutionalists saw beneath the changed wardrobe of Southern circumstances, holding up an x-ray that revealed that the skeleton of slavery's political economy had remained intact after the Civil War.[105] In the words of a 1936 article cited by historian Pete Daniel in his book *The Shadow of Slavery*, "Slavery was too integral a part of the social life of the South and too vital to the interests of certain classes to be suddenly eliminated by a mere constitutional amendment, although the [Thirteenth Amendment] did make necessary the finding of new ways of perpetuating the Negro's enslavement."[106]

These dire conclusions were tempered in the majestic sweep of synthetic histories such as Eric Foner's *Reconstruction: America's Unfinished Revolution* (1988) and Edward Ayers's *The Promise of the New South: Life after Reconstruction* (1992). The narrative model for these stories was tragedy (revolutions unfinished, promises unfulfilled) and their framework, which abandoned the Marxist underpinning of the new social history, was a liberalist one. It would be the detonation of Saidiya Hartman's *Scenes of Subjection* (1997), which used many sources cognate to an earlier social history, such as slave narratives and plantation diaries, albeit with a wildly different method, that would illuminate and rattle that liberalist framework and reclaim and amplify the bleak prospects of her antecedents. Hartman's subtitle—"Terror, Slavery and Self-Making in Nineteenth-Century America"—embraced the whole of "nineteenth-century America"; she narrated across the breach of 1865, deeming it a nonevent, so that the very form of her book stands as a radical assertion of continuity between racial domination before 1865 and after. Slavery and its badges were not so easily discarded in her historical reckoning, nor were acts of resistance sure-footed paths to freedom. As the legal scholar Guyora Binder argues, slavery as an institution might persist without a single individual being held as a slave. If abolition amounted to universal manumission, then slavery need not have been disestablished to carry it out; manumission was already a feature of the system.[107] (Furthermore, it was perfectly legal for private individuals to hold slaves after 1865, and we might want to recall again, as a point of historical order, that a man in 1903, after undergoing a federal trial, received a presidential pardon for being a slaveholder. In 1903, being a slaveholder was not against the law.)[108]

Recently, the new histories of capitalism have returned to questions of political economy and have done much to remap the once vexed affiliation of capitalism and slavery, revealing the modern and systemic character of slavery and its means of production.[109] But the effects of formal abolition on this extensive system remain unclear. Historians of Reconstruction and its aftermath often tend to neglect the vast scope and scale of the transformations in racial capitalism after 1865. Their vision, instead, narrows upon regions; their focus tightens upon incidents of captivity and deadly violence.[110] Such acts of violence against the ex-slave are symptomatic, though, of an entire social ontology, one in which black death is the precondition of white life. And *nothing* that happened in 1865 altered this. Without sufficient explanation, it is as if slavery's systems of circulation and production, *which survived formal abolition*, no longer comprehended and incorporated the whole United States and had instead become magically restricted to "the South."[111]

In the end, this history is also a history of captivity, and it shows no movement. As an engine of change over time, it coughs and sputters and stalls.[112] When ex-slaves report again and again that freedom was a harder deal than slavery; when James Baldwin insists, "I picked the cotton, I carried it to the market, I built the railroads under someone else's whip for nothing"; when George Jackson writes, "I recall the very first kidnap, I've lived through the passage, died on the passage, lain in the unmarked, shallow graves of the millions who fertilized the Amerikan soil with their corpses"; when Jamaica Kincaid asks, "what should history mean to someone who looks like me?" then asks, "Should it be an idea, should it be an open wound and each breath I take in and expel healing and opening the wound again, over and over, or is it a long moment that begins anew each day since 1492?" what are we being told about the times proper to slavery? Or about the event—or nonevent—of abolition?[113]

"Finance represents the production of time under capitalism," Leigh Claire La Berge has written, and that time is produced unevenly.[114] Further, that unevenness expresses racial difference. To have ready access to finance capital is to have ready access to a planned future. That is how finance is meant to operate in a capitalist economy: it bridges the troubled waters of capital's turnover cycles. It papers over the rifts and lags, the fluctuations and shortfalls, in profit making, forestalling imminent—and immanent—crisis. So at the level of the individual, to be a merchant in the South, or to be a trader in New Orleans, or to be a businessman in New York was to possess the prospect of a better tomorrow, the promise of some dependable momentum for oneself and one's family across time. Money, stocks, bonds, loans, mortgages: these have been the paper and ink on which one would write that quintessentially American narrative of the self whose saga moved toward stability and prosperity.[115]

But this was not a narrative to be written by the sharecropper or the tenant farmer. Their lives and those of their families were to be plotted not as a line, like an arrow, but as a circle, like a cell. The horizons of their expectations were the breadth of a cotton field and the length of its growing season, hemmed in by the annual cycles of having credit furnished and having debt tallied, and of never having that arithmetic add up to another future. Here the quagmire of debt becomes the inertia of history—flagged by Baldwin, Jackson, and Kincaid—and it is all still the stalled time of slavery. That stuckness also gets limned as blackness. To be or to become swamped in poverty and debt is to be or to become black. An obscure proposition from 1874 makes that crystal clear: in "The Problem of Poverty and How to Deal with It, through Immediate Colonization," John H. Keyser, a member of Boss Tweed's corrupt Tammany Hall political machine, recommended sending New York City's urban poor and unemployed to Southern plantations "with or without their consent, to work for their food and shelter."[116] Meaning, in other words, for Keyser at least, that the white-skinned and free urban poor could be rendered black slaves a decade after abolition. In the United States, debt, poverty, stasis have been the features of a political economy that formulates race.[117]

Partial and incomplete, "freedom" became a theft and an enclosure. Whites robbed blacks without cause or concern all over the South. In 1880, a discharged Union soldier from Shreveport named Henry Adams testified before the Senate:

> I also saw many colored people in that part of the State who told me that the white people would not pay them for their work, and would take all their crops every year, and had been doing so ever since the surrender. They, the colored people, told me they had tried to live upon government land but it all had been taken away from them, and they could not live on any land but what they would buy from white people. They told me all the colored people that were or are living on government lands was every two or three months put in jail, and the land taken away from them and the whites claimed the land themselves. Those colored people who still lived on government land had no stock, and had to hire horses or mules at five and ten dollars per month.

Adams also testified to blacks being swindled, cheated, robbed, whipped, murdered, starved, and run out of town. Whites would come to them holding contracts and "bring in old bills and say to the colored people, you owe me this, and I want it paid; the whites would then take all the colored people had, horses, mules, cows, hogs, chickens, beds and bedding, and then run them off the place or kill or shoot them."[118] Legislatures began to pass game laws and fence laws to reestablish private property.[119] And meanwhile, commercial interests in the Northeast and Midwest were purchasing vast tracts of public land in the South, cementing its colonial situation after the Civil War.[120]

Perhaps most egregiously, the freed were encouraged by government officials to invest all of their money into the Freedman's Savings Bank, which had at its height 72,000 depositors who had saved $57 million.[121] The charter of the bank was altered, permitting those savings to be used in real estate speculation in the nation's capital. Black depositors across the South suspected that their local branches of the bank were just "a 'drag net' to bring the money into Washington." They were right. "As soon as possible every cent that the institution could command was loaned to private individuals and corporations," writes one of the bank's historians. "Loans were made rapidly and recklessly, on bills against the District government, on District securities issued without warrant of law, on second mortgages, on stock in promotion companies, and on other paper of doubtful value."[122] Stated plainly, the development of the nation's capital was financed through the stolen savings of former slaves. And the architect of the swindle was none other than Henry Cooke, associate and brother of Jay Cooke, financier and underwriter of the U.S. government.[123] Here, a national debt supposedly incurred for slaves' freedom revealed itself to be, clearly, materially, a national debt owed to those freed slaves. One recalls the pamphlet "REASONS WHY YOU SHOULD ALL PUT MONEY IN THE SAVINGS BANK," which offered up, as reason Number 4, "*You should use this Bank* because it is conducted entirely by your best friends ... and being authorized by Congress, and approved by the President of the United States, it is the safest place you can find for your money."[124] The "vaults of the bank were literally thrown open to unscrupulous greed and rapacity," in the words of Frederick Douglass, and when the bank collapsed in 1874 the "toilsome savings of the poor Negroes ... melted away—vanished into thin air."[125] Most of them never saw a dime.[126]

Across rural store counters of the South, what was being lent and bought was not just credit, not only dresses. The stakes were higher. Loaned was something more like a title to the black body itself, and bought was the mortgage of freedom this chapter has described. The political economy of abolition determined that ex-slaves would be forced to subsidize the lost exchange value of their own flesh and the lost future surplus of their issue. Under these relations of freedom—"freedom" figured as freedom of contract, freedom of commerce, as economic liberty—even under these already compromised terms, the ex-slave could not be said fully to possess herself.

After so thoroughly explaining systems of credit, I need, finally, to state an emphatic corollary, and to return to where we began: *finance* is just another word for other people's debts.[127] Those systems of credit preserved as their fundament the condition of black indebtedness. The point is not meant as a tautology. Credit offers a heuristic for the flawed inheritance of abolition, but debt—not credit—fills the testimony given by the ex-slave and her descendants. Credit abstracts the harm that manifests itself in debt. Credit renames the violence of ownership, blurs it; debt is the fix and the feeling that accompanies the violence of being owned. The "freedom" entailed by abolition did not denote an account that was to be marked as "paid in full" by the state to the ex-slave in 1865, and much less did it denote an account centuries in arrears (in such arrears that it could never hope to be repaid). Indeed, the account books of the state accorded nothing owed to the slave; quite the opposite. Not only was the ex-slave cast in a condition of *moral* indebtedness to a white nation for the blood and treasure spent in a Civil War on her freedom, but the arrangements of law—the Bankruptcy Act of 1867, the states' crop-lien laws, the statutes against false pretenses, enticement, and vagrancy—were bent to cage her in actual indebtedness as well.[128]

The plantation names this trap of debt and its compulsions. It also names the whole wide and growing network of credit and finance capital that preserves the slave as a form of value; the law of the state that is the firm ground on which its system is built; the contradictions between the easy commerce of white capital and the hard lockdown of black and brown bodies; and the difference between the reasoned economics of derivatives trading and the open theft of subprime loans that have continued to define capitalism in America. It is, at last, such contradictions that plait together the legal tethers of debt binding Jake Dunwoodie and Henry Blake and Laura Smalley and Ann Ulrich Evans with the lawful lines of profit commanded by the corporate form—that disembodied person, manifold and unrestricted—which were disclosed through the fate of Emile Allgeyer's letter. *Law* must be understood not as the solution to such contradictions but as their outgrowth; the law continually inclines its face, like a heliotrope, toward the sun that nourishes it, which is racial capitalism. The untrammeled shipment of E. Allgeyer & Co.'s bales of cotton from New Orleans to France or the transit of that cotton's speculative value through the commodities markets of New York or Liverpool *at the same time* guided a merchant's hand in Pleasant Hill, North Carolina, or Red Bay, Alabama, or Little Rock, Arkansas, as he wrote down in his leather daybook twenty-five cents for a pound of bacon—its "time price" and quadruple the going cost—against the account of a farmer and ex-slave held captive by a rigged game of red ink and some future reckoning never yet made in her favor.[129]

Mt Vernon Ill Mch 24 21
Hon Warren G Harding
President of these U.S.
Dear Sir I just beg forgiveness for taking this liberty in Writing you sir But feeling After Reading of your Inauguration and the chapter in the Bible where your hand rested when you taken the oath I feel that you will consider my plea for Justice and right Born a Slave And after being set free Went to work As instructed by those who was impowerd by An act of congress to establish Banks that the Negro might become Thrifty And saving Mr President we did as we was told not knowing at the times our a b c And then in seventy four to loose every dollar that we had earnestly earned to loose all Congress has paid us 62 per cent of that money But for 30

The first page of a letter from Henry L. Thomas, a Freedman's Savings Bank depositor, written in 1921, addressed to President Warren G. Harding (National Archives and Records Administration, Washington, D.C.).

Mt Vernon Ill
Mch 27–21

Hon Warren G. Harding
President of these U.S.

Dear Sir
I first beg forgiveness for taking this liberty in writing you sir but feeling after reading of your inauguration and the chapter in the Bible Where your hand rested when you taken the oath I feel that you will consider my plea for justice and right Born a slave and after being set free went to work as instructed by those who was impowered by an act of congress to establish banks that the negro might become thrifty and saving. Mr President we did as we was told not knowing at the times our abc and then in seventy-four to loose every dollar that we had earnestly earned to loose all congress has paid us 62 percent of that money but for 30 odd years we have prayed for our balance Their has been in the past about 3 bills past for our relief in the senate but never could get through the House Mr or Senator McNary in the last congress had a bill four our relief but it was burden with two many other things to insure us success. Mr President I pray you to consider us old People after all these years our best life spent in slavery and sir our bal of 38 percent coming to us now in our old age would be a God send to us old one who lives after all these years. We thought our money safe I have my book to day audited by the Treasure Department with a Balance of $631.91 due at 38 percent. Mr President that would be a God send to me in my old days and also for the hundreds of others who lives many have died some in want where there little balance of 38 due would have made their last days brighter. Mr Nary has promised to reintroduce the bill for the depositers of the Freedman Saving Bank alone and sir could you consider to help us We can not reward but God in his power will It has seemed we have not many in the past 30 years to help us But we still believe that help will come through all these years Just asking for what we worked for and lost Because we knew not how to protect our Just freed and thought the Government was looking for our interest But

(*Continued*)

since informed was not so now sir Your Honor I beg forgiveness for writing But I can not but ask and may be that through the Guidance of the supreme you may consider and gives us your assistance at this next session Before we all die of [off] and thousands of negroes now old an some unable to work who would get their bal of 38 percent will prais you and never forget your Help I pray I have not erred

Resp

Henry L Thomas
Claiment Freedman Savings & Trust Co. Box 343

PS Sir I am writing this my self not a days schooling

Freedman's #394

April 1, 1921.

JFD

Mr. Henry L. Thomas,
   Box 343,
      Mt. Vernon, Illinois.

Sir:-

Your letter of March 27, addressed to Hon. Warren G. Harding, President of the United States, has been referred to this office for consideration.

You are advised that the matter of the Freedman's Savings and Trust Company, after paying 62% to creditors who have proved their claims according to law, has been entirely closed as the funds belonging to that institution have been completely exhausted and no further payments can be made or claims proven.

It is not within the province of this office to take up the matter of any relief to the creditors of this institution on account of them not having been paid in full. The only relief that may be obtained is through legislative action by Congress.

Respectfully,

Commissioner.

The letter sent by the Office of the Comptroller of Currency in reply to Henry L. Thomas's letter (National Archives and Records Administration, Washington, D.C.).

William Harnett, *Attention, Company!* (1878) (Amon Carter Museum of American Art, Fort Worth, Texas).

CHAPTER TWO

The Spectacle of Free Black Personhood

"Oh, certainly, I will be told, now and then when we are worn out by our lives in big buildings, we will turn to you as we do to our children—to the innocent, the ingenuous, the spontaneous. We will turn to you as to the childhood of the world. You are so real in your life—so funny, that is. Let us run away for a little while from our ritualized polite civilization and let us relax, bend to those heads, those adorably expressive faces. In a way, you reconcile us with ourselves."
—Frantz Fanon, "The Fact of Blackness"

The spectacle then would coincide with the moment when sign-value takes precedence over use-value. But the question of the location of this moment in the history of the commodity remains unanswered.
—Jonathan Crary, "Spectacle, Attention, Counter-memory"

Consider the painting *Attention, Company!* from 1878 by William Harnett. A black boy stands in front of a green wall, made of horizontal planks. Plastered with torn posters and notices, this green wall is a jumble of letters, some printed and some carved. At least one handprint is stamped there in yellow paint. And the wall is pushed close to the picture plane, so close that were it not for this boy's body, the two would seem to coincide. Without him, only the most subtle signs of depth interrupt its flatness: the planks' gaps and missing splinters, the dog-eared fold of a poster, the jagged tear of a notice. These are the generic codes of trompe l'oeil painting. Most prominent among them is the wall, which is the horizontal table of still-life painting—where its fruit, meat, and books, its objects, would be arranged—vertically flipped.[1] The wall is the sign of still life, which amplifies the realism of still life's objects and exacts the viewer's contemplation of them.

Trompe l'oeil flowered in late nineteenth-century America, thanks in part to a cultural preoccupation with skepticism and illusion. This preoccupation coincided with technological innovations such as the cinema and the phonograph that enabled a new verisimilitude in representing motion and sound. Many found pleasure in deceptions that might leave them undeceived. "Which is which?" asked an advertisement for the Victor Talking Machine Company about live versus recorded sound.[2] That question was also posed by the apparent cracks and folds in trompe l'oeil paintings. Were objects pasted on the canvas or were these just painted depictions? Real or represented: which is which? The genre's elements meant to trick the viewer and solicit a confirming touch. And no one in the nineteenth century would achieve more renown for these effects meant to deceive the eye than the painter of *Attention, Company!*, William Harnett, who lived and worked in Philadelphia and New York. He could flawlessly render, with photographic detail, tattered money, rusty hinges, Colt revolvers, and *cartes-de-visite*.

With trompe l'oeil, to see is to touch—the splintered gap by the boy's right elbow, the iridescent gleam of mother-of-pearl on his clasped top buttons, the curling paper of the poster behind him. But mostly, him: the smoothness of his skin, the sheen of his lower lip, the glittering impasto of his hair beneath the newspaper cap. Harnett's "pictures made one's eyes feel surfaces," in the words of art historian Michael Leja.[3] Or, as a contemporary critic wrote of Harnett's paintings: "The wood *is* wood, the iron is iron, the brass is brass, the leather is leather. The fur of the rabbit and the feathers of the birds tempt the hand to feel their delicate softness."[4] The desire to touch in trompe l'oeil arises out of a compulsion "to slip a finger between the brute matter of the painted canvas and the powerful illusion it contains."[5] To touch would be partly to feel for texture, but just as much, to feel for some substantiation of the real versus the represented.

When Edith Halpert exhibited Harnett's work in 1939 at her Downtown Gallery in New York, according to the familiar story, she pulled him out of the obscurity that had claimed him almost immediately after his death in 1892. *Attention, Company!* demonstrates Harnett's innovative use of the wall as a compositional device to amplify his paintings' illusions, forcing a shallow background to achieve eye-tricking effect.[6] That innovation may well be the condition for our knowledge of the genre. The show at the Downtown Gallery resituated trompe l'oeil painting within art history as a step in the progressive march forward of the picture plane's impassable flatness that characterized modernism. Subsequently, the influential critic Clement Greenberg established the modernist reading of trompe l'oeil painting by positioning it within a historical current of painting that flows toward abstraction.[7] The discursive association that links trompe l'oeil and modernism remains in force, even if Greenberg's outmoded account has been supplanted.

My concern is less with Harnett though, than with this figure.[8] What can we say about him? Very little, it seems. A black boy wears shabby clothes that pretend to be a uniform and a hat made of folded newspaper, tacked with a straight pin and colored ribbon. A pole whose end is notched with a loop of twine is nestled against his right side. The hems of his vest and jacket are frayed; the elbow is patched. He is illuminated from the left. Beyond this, the painting appears opaque. What is his name? How old is he? Is he even a living subject? That his clothes seem too threadbare and his lips seem too exaggerated certainly mark him, in 1878, as "black," yet he isn't presented as caricature. In a frontal half-body pose, he is turned fully toward the viewer, observed coolly and closely. This painting presents a still and insistently silent black figure, a subject who stares back, a stare that puts up some resistance and affirms an honesty.[9] A realist portrait? But almost immediately he seems *too* closely observed. There's too much of the real, the picture seems surcharged with it. We also perceive the lifelessness of a paper doll. Human figures are exceptionally rare in trompe l'oeil, and except for this painting, black figures are nonexistent. And none are presented in this manner, against a wall, which causes the figure to oscillate between flatness and depth.[10] A confusion of genre situates *Attention, Company!* between portrait and still life, signaling—thirteen years after formal abolition—an ontological confusion between subjecthood and objecthood that still attends blackness. Is this black figure the person of portraiture or the thing of still life?

Crushed to a silhouette, blackness is situated here at the limit of the real.[11] Trompe l'oeil strives to bring objects into being, to turn an absence into a presence. Conjuration obsesses it. Here, paint transubstantiates what it depicts, and in this painting what it depicts most emphatically are the signs of blackness. The picture renders surface as subject. *Attention, Company!* locates the sensuousness of pure form in blackness, which it remakes into an aesthetic figure, an art object, a fetish.[12] In it, race and realism become conjoined. Whether depicted here as "black" skin or staged elsewhere as "black" personality, blackness becomes realism's figure par excellence in this era, the fetish that would perfectly delimit and figure, at their boundaries, imitation and authenticity. In this regard *Attention, Company!* is less exceptional than exemplary.

Images of blacks proliferated in Northern popular culture in the decades after the Civil War, mostly as stereotype and caricature, on stage and in print, circulating through sheet music or advertising goods. Northern whites yearned to suture the wounds of war following the end of hostilities, and they grew cold and impatient with political demands for racial equity.[13] Reconstruction's ameliorating projects capsized in the becalmed seas of such white indifference, as meanwhile a new and piratical machine was built by planters and merchants across the Southern states. Even as white Northerners withdrew their political attention along with their occupying forces, they held an awareness of their black countrymen that remained and expanded. Alongside familiar and deforming comic images, another impulse also grew, a desire for "realistic" depictions of the freed. Only rarely was that impulse not corrupted by defaming stereotype. Still, such realistic representations emerged with a different impetus.

IN THE UNITED STATES, the slave has designated a commodity, a particular form of value. "A commodity appears, at first sight, a very trivial thing, and easily understood. Its analysis shows that it is, in reality, a very queer thing, abounding in metaphysical subtleties," Marx wrote. The commodity doesn't name the fungible object but the entire system of transient value that is temporarily congealed there. In other words, the commodity of the slave isn't identical to the body of the slave. Value "converts every product into a social hieroglyphic," according to Marx. "Later on, we try to decipher the hieroglyphic, to get behind the secret of our own social products; for to stamp an object of utility as a value, is just as much a social product as language."[14] Formal abolition didn't dismantle slavery's entire system of value, though it did force that system's reorganization, such that the alienable body of the slave found its substitute in the alienable person of the freed. Exchange value in black flesh was rescinded in 1865, but the exchange value of *blackness itself*—as image, personality, mask—remained in force. Free black personhood bore the residue of slavery's chattel status. Objecthood continued to plague the freed subject, or to put it in the grammar of *Attention, Company!*, still life determined the portrait.

In the urban North of the late nineteenth century, that social hieroglyphic stamped a series of paintings and illustrations, a stage production, and a Mark Twain novel, which this chapter gathers and analyzes. Mostly produced by and for Northern whites, they exemplify a telling confusion in their attitude toward the freed, who are situated somewhere between liberal subjects and consumable objects. Riven with contradictions, these cultural productions reveal how thoroughly the commodity logic of chattel slavery still superintended a "free" personhood. As had been the case before the Civil War, northern cities were at once deeply connected to and yet seemingly distant from the crushing realities of the new plantation economy. First abolitionism and then the war itself had forced a reckoning by Northern whites with a plantation region that many would have preferred to ignore, exposing all of its cruelties, its poverty, and its luxury. The South appeared like a foreign land, a distant colony, albeit one within the geographic boundaries of the United States. During this same time, plantation capital traced a line of flight to the growing world metropolis of New York City. The concrete connections that financially linked the North to the Southern plantation region contradicted the imaginative distance that kept that region separate and unknown.[15]

The personhood of the freed was a token—at once an emblem and a literal trace; a specter of value—of the financial infrastructure that reproduced and sustained the plantation as a means of production after 1865.[16] Like a ghost, both at hand and absent, in the present but of the past, their personhood was one symptom of this space-time that was out of joint. As a technology of credit and debt, of accumulation and incrimination, personhood was more like slavery's tether than liberty's lifeline. In the North, the center of so much deterritorialized capital from the plantation region, the personhood of the freed appeared as the flickering signal of this geographical and historical contradiction, of an elsewhere and a past haunting the here and now.

That contradiction shapes the array of white Northern cultural productions assembled here, a handful of white portrayals of black subjects that eschew the comedy and horror that set the terms for black representation as mammy or wench, buffoon or beast. Minstrelsy and its stereotypes are well known to us. But what about the obverse of minstrelsy's tradition, a kind of portraiture that pretends toward dignity, or at least neutrality, where that neutrality is the mark of their realism? How do these representations function, whose tendencies are most notable for the absence of caricature's malice? What would it mean to consider the maintenance of a pathological blackness not through caricature and infamy, where its presence is keenly felt, but through portraiture and personhood? This chapter's portraits ponder the status of blacks as political subjects by rendering them as aesthetic subjects.

Especially in the confused trompe l'oeil of *Attention, Company!* and in the immersive stage production *Black America*, these texts are marked by an innovation of style, a sort of hyperrealism. These texts' incipient modernism registers the colonial relation that linked the rural South with the urban North. Modernist innovations in style can be ascribed, in part, to the spatial breach of empire that divides metropole and colony, Fredric Jameson argues. The situation of colonialism "means that a significant structural segment of the economic system as a whole is now located elsewhere, beyond the metropolis" and this "spatial disjunction has as its immediate consequence the inability to grasp the way the system functions as a whole."[17] The life, the suffering, the exploitation in the colony is the missing complement and the condition of possibility for daily life in the metropolis. In the late nineteenth century, New York was no longer in New York, and these texts feverishly attempt to conjure what's absent, namely, an extensive and ongoing system of unfree labor whose cornerstone was an ersatz black personhood. That absence is both concrete and abstract. Concretely, as plantation laborers, those persons are literally located elsewhere, at a distant remove. Abstractly, the exchange value attached to those persons is fugitive—a specter of finance capital and a flickering inscription on black skin. The mark of blackness remained the mark of fungibility after 1865. Continuously invoking the slave as a form of value, these Northern texts struggle to represent a fractured social whole, and as ever, white sociality takes its shape around the kernel of a blackness that it has itself created. As a "white man's artifact," Frantz Fanon reminds us, blackness demands white adjudication, sparks white sensation, solicits white guilelessness and perspicacity.[18] The discourse of aesthetics that unites these cultural productions strikes a coin, then, whose sides fuse a black sensuousness and a white enjoyment (enjoyment in terms both of pleasure and of possession). These white representations constitute that which they pretend to describe—decorating, designating, *fabricating* certain bodies. In these decades, one byword of this blackness is realism. Another is spectacle.

The Subject of Blackness

Attention, Company!'s title immediately registers in the uniform of its subject and in his about-face pose: a black boy playing soldier in 1878. He stands neatly dressed, as if for military inspection, his bearing stiff and direct. This painting seems to index concern over the Civil War and the spilled blood of soldiers—white and black soldiers—and the meaning of that blood. "They are not dead," one heard in Northern memorializations of the fallen; "the early manhood of this nation retains its majesty by their fall, and the black stain of slavery has been effaced from the bosom of this fair land by martyr blood." The descendants of the fallen were "no longer strangers and foreigners, but are, by this baptism of blood . . . , consecrated citizens of America forever."[19] Martyr blood, baptism of blood—in this rhetoric, blood is transubstantiated into the new nation-state purified of slavery's sin. It transfigures the stranger into the countryman, yielding a citizenry now unified across differences of ethnicity and class. These remembrances bear witness to the renewal, if not the creation, of both national community—the populist "we"—and the righteous power of the state to lay claim to citizens' lives for its survival. This is the justifying blood of sacrifice, which in preserving the old order makes it new.

But the fallen remembered here are not black, a fact that reflects the intentional white erasure of the legacy of emancipation, a forgetting that forged national reconciliation. In this light, the painting might be understood to in-

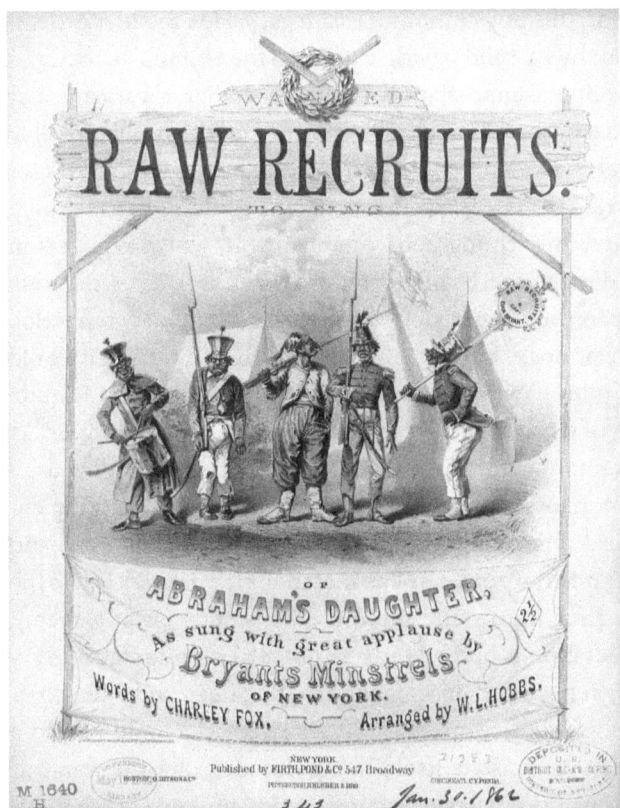

Raw Recruits (1862) (Library of Congress, Washington, D.C.).

fantilize the black soldier, to participate in minstrelsy's use of that character during these years as one of pomp and buffoonery, an iteration of the effete black dandy. "Beginning during the war with 'Raw Recruits' [1862] and reaching full development in the 1870s, minstrels created a series of popular farces centered on blacks who were ludicrously inept at 'playing soldier,'" the historian Robert C. Toll writes. "Like children who imitate without understanding, these uniformed blacks captured part of the form of the military but none of the substance."[20] (Indeed, strong lines of resemblance connect the second of these "raw recruits" and the boy in *Attention, Company!*: the former's wide-eyed posture of fear and vertical musket translated into the latter's cool stare and upright mopstick.) Alternately, from a more liberal historical angle, a black boy playing soldier in 1878 becomes a reminder of the war's true legacy, a reminder of slavery and its abolition. Under this historical reading, slavery's injuries are repaired and black citizenship is made salient through the more inclusive work of memory.[21] By enacting through make-believe the role of those who fought, this boy embodies that legacy. He's the first generation after emancipation; he's a child paying tribute to the Union's victory.

Critical appraisal or liberal appreciation, the black soldier as caricature or the black soldier as citizen: these two options seem to mark out the possible engagements with what *Attention, Company!* depicts. The thread that ties together the following pages runs between those options while also lacing them together, explaining how the iconography of enlistment, which registers in *Attention, Company!*, defines the terms of black citizenship. This painting does more and less than the properly cultural work of, by turns, refracting and affecting power relations. In terms of influence and audience, it could only be considered a "minor" work. Its material history as an object is quite murky; the conditions of its creation, exhibition, and sale remain unclear. As with a role played by a minor actor, however, its anonymity might allow us to see better and to see more of its prismatic qualities. In fact, this painting enacts a theory of political representation for the freed. That is, its form and iconography carry over *into* the political. The metaphor for its work is less the reflection of some dynamic mirror and more the transmutation of alchemy. Here, aesthetic representation is bodied forth in political representation.

If the war ultimately renewed a sense of nation—that deep and wide comradeship secured through shared memory—it also served as midwife to a new modern incarnation of the state itself. In the decades after the war, this state arrogated to itself broad powers of administration and police over persons, both physical and corporate.[22] Liberalism, as an ideology, negotiated this balance between the individual freedoms secured through the state and the state's demands on the individual's freedom. That these "freedoms" denoted *not* the ongoing work of abolition and emancipation after 1865, the more complete unfettering of those nominally freed, and instead suggested the unfettering of markets and the unhanding of "economic man" casts together liberalism's competing strands: the humanitarian and the laissez-faire. Liberalism strives toward both the inclusion of those not clothed with the rights of the propertied self and the exclusion of those who interfere with increasing the value of the self's properties. Here, as outlined in the first chapter, one need only consider the legacy of the Fourteenth Amendment, ratified as an extension of formal equality to freed slaves and then codified, in *Santa Clara v. Southern Pacific Railroad* in 1885 and in *Allgeyer v. Louisiana* in 1897, as a further extension of those rights and freedoms to the "persons" of corporations.[23]

So what did the war *abolish*? Consider next the first of two triptychs, both of which surely influenced the painting of *Attention, Company!* In Thomas Waterman Wood's *A Bit of War History* (1865–66), another black subject in

The Spectacle of Free Black Personhood 59

The Contraband, from Thomas Waterman Wood, *A Bit of War History* (1865) (Metropolitan Museum of Art, New York).

uniform shifts from *The Contraband* to *The Recruit* to *The Veteran*.[24] In the first a black man in stained and rumpled clothes doffs his hat to the viewer, dried tobacco spilling from his pocket, while he clutches a stick and kerchief, items that mark him as a runaway, a slave who has crossed Union lines and has, as enemy property, been "confiscated." A new musket and a soldier's effects are propped near him, beside a chair that holds a newspaper, and behind him through a cracked door, we can see a tasseled U.S. flag and a drum. Pasted on the wall are two notices: "Provost Marshal's Office" and "Volunteers Wanted." In the second, holding a stance nearly identical save for his proud posture and his turned gaze, he has been clothed in a new blue uniform, as if—given the repeated pose—by magic. He now wears the gun and the effects, the newspaper is open and cradles a cigar, the "Volunteers Wanted" sign has been pulled down and a flag posted in its place. In the final panel, he offers a salute, and his uniform is again stained and faded, as is the strap of the musket, which has

The Recruit, from Thomas Waterman Wood, *A Bit of War History* (1866) (Metropolitan Museum of Art, New York).

returned to its original position along with its effects. Returned, too, is the "Volunteers Wanted" sign. Missing are the drum, the newspaper, and, of course, this soldier's leg.

What I want to point up here is the suspect narrative this triptych unfolds. If we are meant to read this character as a "wanted" volunteer, the agency behind his volunteerism is immediately undercut by the painting's title. Here, "volunteer" becomes indistinguishable from "contraband." In terms of agency, the two are janiform: The negated will of the "contraband," named as property, is implicitly bestowed only as the gift of the state, while what the volunteer "volunteers" is precisely his own illusory will that, along with his body and his life, is yielded up to the state to be canceled by it. Both monikers signify, in the guise of freedom, only a transfer in the deed of personal ownership. Both figures have become, in fact, someone else's property, and that someone else is the state.[25] It is the state's power that appears to transform

The Veteran, from Thomas Waterman Wood, *A Bit of War History* (1866) (Metropolitan Museum of Art, New York).

the contraband, to make him new and whole as a recruit, which means the picture voids the prospect of self-emancipation, erasing a claim such as Frederick Douglass's after defeating Covey that "however long I might remain a slave in form, the day had passed forever when I could be a slave in fact."[26]

The triptych's plot suggests freedom's evolution, a freedom won by the slave who has taken up arms against his master as a soldier. Yet the figure is fixed in place. The triptych, despite its wont, finally bespeaks a continuity of status, not its rupture. The third panel reiterates the first: the return of the rifle, the return of the "Volunteers Wanted" sign, the return of the stained and rumpled clothes, the return of the deferent gesture, the return of the kerchief, now worn beneath his cap. Not to mention the soldier's own stance of return: this looking backward, in the painting's logic, can only be a looking backward toward slavery. The deep blue of the recruit's uniform has become the dull gray of the veteran's, a color change that signals some profound ambivalence about the war's meaning. (What is the difference between the Union and the Confederacy, really?) The paintings affirm slavery's preservation, not its abolition. And the price that has been exacted for a freedom that now seems insubstantial is nothing less than a leg. The leg's absence is the triptych's ultimate focus. If the veteran's amputation is meant as the sign of a hard-fought freedom, that sign reads as easily as the state's deed on this man's life. (Where do we locate personal will in the constellation of contraband, volunteer, and recruit?) The state's mortgage of his body dissembles as the nobility of sacrifice. His amputation becomes a branding by the state, the mark of possessive control, the *fruition* of its property interest in the contraband, rather than that interest's invalidation. In the circularity and stasis of Wood's paintings, the slave ends up just where he began. Freedom, it counsels, is not something like mobility gained, but something like a leg lost.[27]

Ostensibly, though, like *Attention, Company!*, *A Bit of War History* foregrounds the Civil War's emancipationist legacy. (Wood was himself an ardent abolitionist from Vermont. *His First Vote*, painted in 1868, lionizes a freedperson casting his ballot.) As Wood's painting plots it, the meaning of black soldiers' blood sacrifice is trained to fit the shape of the state. Indeed, *The Recruit* is only the more realistic reproduction of an allegory drawn by Thomas Nast the previous year. In *Pardon and Franchise*, a two-page illustration from 1865, Columbia ponders the fate of white rebels in one panel ("Shall I trust these men?"), while laying her hand on another uniformed black soldier with an amputated leg in the next ("And not this man?"). In the first, she and her throne block the movement of the Southern supplicants at her feet. In the second, Columbia offers the veteran, as her charge, to a hidden assembly, while a carpet runner lays open before him—his star-studded path down into the people. Nast makes glaringly explicit what Wood strongly implied: the telos of the war is emancipation, and the telos of emancipation is inclusion within the state. With a requisite air of tragedy about the "failure" of that inclusion, the plot still holds in most contemporary histories of Reconstruction.[28]

In its equation with emancipated citizenship, this trope of soldiering also only designates male-bodied persons, which can't be overlooked. That masculinity signals, at least in part, the altered position of black women after formal abolition. No longer the belly of the world, their labors no longer generating for their enslavers the profits that one dare not designate *their children*, black women had been divested of literal and symbolic value as the wombs of future slave capital. Under the regime of a nominal freedom, burdened by the privations of enforced debt and a liberal rhetoric of individual

Thomas Nast, *Pardon* and *Franchise* from *Harper's Weekly* (5 August 1865) (Library of Congress, Washington, D.C.).

responsibility, black women were to be recast as figures of liability, economically and socially—or, as often, outcast: now figures of superfluousness rather than of superabundance.[29]

Accounts by black soldiers themselves, however, especially slaves, reject the arc of that narrative of inclusion.[30] A soldier's letter found in the streets of New Orleans, written in September 1863 by the anonymous signatory "A Colored man," makes the point:

> liberty is what we want and nothing Shorter. . . . Sure the Southern men Says the are not fighting for money the are fighting for negros the northern men Say the did not com South to free the negroes but to Save the union very well for that much what is the colored men fighting for if the makes us free we are happy to hear it And when we are free men and a people we will fight for our rights and liberty we care nothing about the union we heave been in it Slaves over two hundred And fifty years we have made the contry and So far Saved the union.[31]

The writer here assumes a line of dissent that can be traced back to David Walker and Henry Highland Garnet. In this tradition, the freed are not consecrated to the nation-state; they are consecrated to the divine. Their blood is spilled as that prayer that would bring about the miraculous—the rupture of an ongoing history of death and violent dispossession. It is the divine, not the state, who hears the appeal in such sacrifice and intervenes, often through those who rise up together, in force. In Garnet's advice, "If you must bleed, let it all come at once."[32] Ordained insurgency, not patriotic soldiery, is the applicable framework, for "we care nothing about the union." White "northern men" give up their lives to "Save the union," because it is *their* union, a white Union, and that's the only reason they give up their lives. But, in the words of "A Colored man," a former slave, "we have made the contry." It is the abject blood and tears of slaves that underlay the country, which have been turned into white wealth, which shadow the "native soil" logic of citizenship. This writer's critique deflates the noble emancipationist rhetoric of the Union cause, which still triumphs in most histories. In this writer's account, for black soldiers the state exists only as the most pragmatic means toward abolition and toward advancing "our rights and liberty."

Consider now, alongside Wood's painted series, the second of the triptychs that hang a question mark over the war's objectives, which appeared in *Harper's Weekly* in 1863 (on the Fourth of July, no less.) The images of an illustration for an article titled "A Typical Negro" reveal the trajectory of "the negro Gordon... as he entered our lines," "under medical inspection" and "in his uniform as a U.S. soldier." The article glosses the images:

> We publish herewith three portraits, from photographs by McPherson and Oliver, of the negro Gordon, who escaped from his master in Mississippi and came into our lines at Baton Rouge in March last. One of these portraits represents the man as he entered our lines, with clothes torn and covered with mud and dirt from his long race through the swamps and bayous, chased as he had been for days and nights by his master with several neighbors and a pack of blood-hounds; another shows him as he underwent the surgical examination previous to being mustered into service—his back furrowed and scarred with the traces of a whipping administered on Christmas-day last; and the third represents him in United States uniform, bearing the musket and prepared for duty.[33]

Like *A Bit of War History*, the triptych of Gordon narrates a tale of enlistment, one not entirely dissimilar. And the military iconography and drama of both Wood's painting and Gordon's engravings resurface (playfully? parodically?)

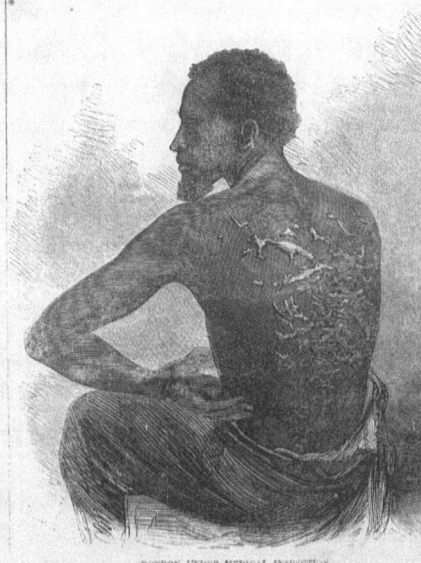

A Typical Negro, from *Harper's Weekly* (4 July 1863) (Library of Congress, Washington, D.C.).

in *Attention, Company!*. In Gordon's triptych, the slave's tattered clothing again becomes the crisp uniform of the armed and accoutered soldier; the state's magic is again seen at work. But the plot's points have changed, with an ending in recruitment and with the insertion of a middle term of "inspection." The typesetting leaves no doubt that this middle image should be the viewer's focus.

To what ends? Most obviously, his image is offered up as proof of slavery's evils. As the article notes, a photograph subtends the triptych's wood engraving, endorsing its truth claims. A homology instantly emerges between Gordon's image and Gordon's body, too. Both the photograph and the body itself are mediums ideologically suffused with truth. As mediums (Latin: intermediary, middle term, intervening substance), both the photograph and the body are self-effacing, disavowing their substance as conduits—mediums that are *immediate* and utterly transparent, mediums that *aren't*. They transcribe and speak fact, imagined to be capable only of veracity. Gordon's own skin and the "skin" of the image come to seem conflated and confused here, maybe even consubstantial.[34] Abolitionism required its proofs against slavery to be physical, embodied, *visible*, for such proof requires "inspection"; it demands exposure to the public's white eye.³⁵

A second purpose of this image, then, was to affect whites, ideally to elicit their sympathy for Gordon but also to flatter their critical faculties. Whites were meant to read, not just react to, Gordon's image and his body, partly to determine the image's believability and partly to determine Gordon's. The historian Walter Johnson has explained a version of this skilled exegesis, which took place on the auction block. "Looking at the scars, slave buyers created whole stories for the people who stood stripped in front of them: perhaps if the scarring was very light the offense had been minor," he writes, "perhaps if it was very old the vice had been whipped out of the slave. The buyers thought they could read slaves' backs as encodings of their history."³⁶ The image of Gordon's back not only suggests proof, it suggests a biography. His scars are meant to be read as though they offered both a story about slavery's ravages and a narrative about him—to be read, at once, as history writ large and as *his* history.

Those narrative possibilities weren't lost on white Northerners, either. Holding a *carte-de-visite* with Gordon's picture, Samuel K. Towle, a Union surgeon stationed in Baton Rouge, wrote about his image in a letter, "Few sensation writers ever depicted worse punishments than this man must have received, though nothing in his appearance indicates any unusual viciousness—but on the contrary, he seems INTELLIGENT AND WELL-BEHAVED."³⁷ Clearly, the knowledge of how to read a slave's scars wasn't confined to the auction block, and for Towle, this image works precisely because it subverts the expectations suggested by Walter Johnson. That Gordon appears "intelligent and well-behaved," that he appears innocent, his whipping undeserved, *doesn't* warrant Towle's sympathy, but as his emphatic capitalization signals, it does make all the difference because it warrants his credence and indubitability. Abolitionism preserves Gordon's status as a thing, a piece of evidence in the public trial against slavery, and "his appearance" reads like a caption that proclaims that evidence to be untainted, and therefore damning. Gordon is merely an example, a particular sacrificed as an instance of the general—in *Harper's* words, "A Typical Negro." That image, in its consubstantiality with his flesh, functions in at least one other way. The photograph that entranced Towle borrows its force from the violence recorded in Gordon's scars: the veracity of the body amplifies the veracity of the photograph. Through his wounds, the photograph gets surcharged with the real. In the same movement, though, the photograph casts his body as artifact ("an object made or modified by human workmanship, as opposed to one formed by natural processes" [*OED*, 2nd ed.]). That is, the aesthetic effects of each recapitulate to the other.

All of this resulted in the image going viral. With his letter and its description, which was mailed to the surgeon general of Massachusetts, Samuel Towle enclosed a *carte-de-visite* of Gordon—from the photograph taken by McPherson and Oliver and reproduced in *Harper's*. McPherson and Oliver had begun churning out the small cards, responding to demand and stoking it, and soon photographers' houses in Philadelphia, New York, Boston, and London began printing the picture, including the famed studio of Matthew Brady. Gordon's likeness was carried in soldier's pockets, thrown up on broadsides, and distributed in pamphlets, all in the name of abolitionism.[38] As an anonymous writer in the *New York Independent* put it: "This Card Photograph should be multiplied by 100,000, and scattered over the States. It tells the story in a way that even Mrs. [Harriet Beecher] Stowe can not approach, because it tells the story to the eye."[39] In a sense, those wished-for effects of multiplication took place. Whites fighting for the Union, on the battlefront like Samuel Towle or on the home front, could hold a piece of cardstock named "Gordon" and, staring at this endlessly replicated image of his scarred naked back, feel again the righteousness of their efforts and, further, feel again that sense of unified political community that bound them together across great distances in a common and noble cause. In other words, the circulation of Gordon's broadcast nakedness, his display, affirmed the North's nationalist sentiment.

This circulation sparked in whites a fellow feeling for Gordon, *and* it revealed a particular hunger for this image. This public fascination surely had much to do with the apparent evidence of slavery's violence, but to end with that assertion only recapitulates the photograph's false transparency as a medium. Their fascination also had a lot to do with the synchronizing of the facticity of the photograph and the facticity of the black body, like two waves that merge and amplify. The scars on Gordon's back also redounded to the nascent art—or more aptly, artlessness—of photography. In this exchange, it isn't the photograph that appears to bear the marks of human facture; it is Gordon himself. Ideologically, the photograph posits the scarred flesh on his back as the sign of a thing made by another's hands. That registration, by the photograph, of workmanship in the slave's flesh purchases the photograph's own immediacy, its transparency, the disavowal of *its* workmanship. It is, literally, exceptional, in that it helps to establish photography's rule, and this might explain why Gordon's photograph became such a sensation.

On the one hand, Gordon's body as image is remade into a kind of serial souvenir for a white audience. He is reduced to their affecting memento, conscripted for the public work of abolitionist sentimentality. And that reduction is the very business of sympathy—imaginatively to void another's subjectivity by substituting one's own. On the other hand, the photograph confers to his body the status of artifact so that it might then perform narrative work. One of those narratives relates slavery's evils and affirms a righteous Northern nationalism. The triptych in *Harper's* relates quite another narrative, however. That image resides at another level of remove from Gordon's body. If the original photograph's transparency casts *him* as an artifact, as an object marked by human intention and encoded with meaning, then the *Harper's* image further abstracts his body as mere illustration when it renders him as a wood engraving, one carved by an artist's hand to then be mass produced and widely circulated in a national newspaper—a literal act of manufacture. The engraving of the image augments his body, through the forcible display of the scars on his back, as an engraving in itself.

There's an epistemological violence at work here. Abolitionists maintained an investment in the objecthood of the slave, who was made a salacious curiosity toward their liberal ends. "I was generally introduced as a *chattel*—a *thing*—a piece of southern *property*—the chairman assuring the audience that *it* could speak," Frederick Douglass writes of his tours "to secure subscribers to the 'Anti-Slavery Standard' and the 'Liberator.'" After noting his advantage to the cause by "being a *brand new fact*," he writes: "During the first three or four months, my speeches were almost exclusively made up of narrations of my own personal experience as a slave. 'Let us have the facts,' said the people.... 'Give us the facts,' said Collins [a 'general agent of the Massachusetts anti-slavery society'], 'we will take care of the philosophy.'" Douglass affirms the abolitionist investment in the black body's facticity, explicitly yoking his status as a slave in the South with his status as evidence in the North, where he was compulsively introduced as an object that was then compelled to narrate its making. His narrations were not primarily meant to establish his humanity but to verify his "thingliness"—personal history cast as material history. "It did not entirely satisfy me to *narrate* wrongs; I felt like *denouncing* them," Douglass writes, but his history was to be unembellished by thought or reasoning, as Collins made clear. A runaway slave, self-emancipated, Douglass finds himself in a strangely "mechanical" (his word) scenario where his spoken narrative is meant to describe, to specify, *to conjure* the very body producing that account. The slave's body as artifact must speak itself. It must articulate the preconditions of its articulation. His narrative re-sounds his body. What precisely does this mean? It is the bewildering constellation conveyed in the dictate of "the people": "Let us have the facts," since "facts" simultaneously names Douglass's story, Douglass's body, and a distillate of verifiable truth. His story is meant to expose, describe, and verify his body, *not* the converse. "Be yourself... and tell your story," Collins insists, but what advice is this exactly? The congruence of the statement's halves is deceptive, as if one flowed into the other, but in actuality his "telling" acts to arrest his "being." ("It was said to me, 'Better have a *little* of the plantation manner of speech than not; 'tis not best that you seem too learned.'") His subjectivity is suspended by and *suspended in* his objecthood, at once frozen and embedded there. What the abolitionists want is not a dynamic human but a static artifact, and any recognition of the former requires the repetition of the latter.

The repetition of the slave's story must re-present the slave's body, and the success of that representation is the final arbiter of truth and recognition. As soon as Douglass began to "seem too learned," he recounts, "People doubted if I had ever been a slave. They said I did not talk like a slave, look like a slave, nor act like a slave, and that they believed I had never been south of Mason and Dixon's line.... [H]earing the free spoken Yankees saying, repeatedly, *He's never been a slave I'll warrant ye*, I resolved to dispel all doubt, at no distant day, by such a revelation of facts as could not be made by any other than a genuine fugitive."[40] The style of Douglass's account fractures his appearance. His words remain audible as autobiography only insofar as they speak the truth of his body as an artifact of slavery. So consider for a moment the animating force of suspicion in his account, the work done by that free-spoken Yankee incredulity. Arising from what they hear, the audience's disbelief in his appearance—the grain of his voice, his countenance, his comportment, the signs of his body—seats Douglass's resolve to publish his *Narrative of the Life* (1845), meant "to dispel all doubt" through an incontrovertible "revelation of facts."

The *Narrative* functioned to write Douglass into history as a political being. It "gave the world assurance of a MAN," as William Lloyd Garrison states in the *Narrative*'s authenticating preface. Henry Louis Gates Jr. offers the canonical assessment: "Douglass is our clearest example of the will to power as the will to write. The act of writing for the slave constituted the act of creating a public, historical self."[41] But as should be clear by now, his *written* "revelation" of "facts" implicated the *visible* exposure of the flesh. (Thus, in the introductory chapter of his written *Narrative*, he is obliged to portray "the blood-stained gate": his intensely visual "witness" of Hester's whipping, at once a vivid "exhibition" of "horrible" details and a "terrible spectacle" he must watch while hiding in a closet.) Not only did the *Narrative*'s success depend, once again, on the slave body's authentic re-presentation; the *Narrative* itself is partly a *symptom* of the slave body's authentication.[42] When Frederick Douglass avows in chapter 5, "My feet have been so cracked with the frost, that the pen with which I am writing might be laid in the gashes," his writing performs some complicated maneuvers.[43] Like the disciple Thomas before the body of the resurrected Christ, it is the moment when the doubting reader can somehow feel his broken skin. It also manifests as what the art historian Michael Fried, after Gustave Courbet, labels a "real allegory": the pen anchors in the gashes, the writing furnishes the body, the public self incarnates the wound.[44] Just to be clear, my point is not that a petty desire to overcome white cynicism motivates Douglass to publish his narrative, but rather that the reception of his narrative and the concomitant recognition of his humanity (or at least the potential for that recognition) *require* this bodily exposure, and even this woundedness. Disclosing white liberalism as tantamount to white suspicion, Douglass reveals a black subjectivity constituted through the exhibition of the captive's afflicted body. "I was a 'graduate from the peculiar institution,' Mr. Collins used to say, when introducing me, *with my diploma written on my back!*"[45]

A similar dynamic shapes Gordon's triptych in *Harper's*. Both his image and Douglass's account raise a question: What *kind* of object was the slave for white abolitionists? When William Lloyd Garrison comments on "the multitudes . . . melted to tears by his pathos" or the "extraordinary emotion [Douglass's speech] excited in my own mind—the powerful impression it created upon a crowded auditory, completely taken by surprise," such that Garrison himself "never hated slavery so intensely as at that moment," how is Douglass being characterized? Of interest is not just the intensity of affect ("extraordinary emotion," "powerful impression") that surrounds him but its crosshatching with disbelief ("completely taken by surprise"). Consternation complements sentimental discourse; it is shadowed by a hermeneutics of suspicion. The multitudes' tears are indissoluble from their "free spoken Yankee" doubt. Ultimately, the slave represents an object of aesthetic value—that is, an object that solicits both sensuous perception *and* critical evaluation (*aisthetikos*: "things perceptible by the senses, things material as opposed to things thinkable or immaterial, also 'perceptive, sharp in the senses'" [*OED*, 2nd ed.]). Gordon's image, like Douglass's staged body, is meant to galvanize a public through sensation, but as his image makes even clearer, that sensation is framed by inspection. The triptych's plot charts the development of the ragged slave into the uniformed soldier, a movement that includes and requires the middle circuit of exposure, where Gordon bares his scarred back.

At the least, the triptych plots assimilation and incorporation for the slave, if not citizenship. Such inspection bespeaks the white public's skepticism, and this skepticism toward the slave's body continues to afflict the freed as "citizens" after 1865, too.

So two narratives comprise the warp and weft of this triptych's plot. In one, the iconography of enlistment ensconces the power of the state. The magic that transforms the slave's degradation into the soldier's repletion is the display of the state's unassailable warrant, literally, to dismantle its subjects (here, in an allegorical stripping of vestment; in Wood and Nast, through the stripping of a leg). In its other narrative, the triptych gives voice to white suspicion. If the triptych's plot proposes that it's Gordon the slave who comes "under medical inspection" as part of his own progress, this narrative of suspicion countermands the forward movement of that emplotment. It arrests his transformation. As with Douglass "the man," Gordon the soldier also requires bodily verification. As its pyramidal layout suggests, the triptych can be read both forward and backward, its middle image as much the baring of Gordon the soldier as the baring of Gordon the slave. Why does this matter? In the triptych, the appeal for political recognition—the position of the soldier—stipulates something like an always-unconsummated writ of habeas corpus. Just as a demand to "have the body" is what's heard in the people's cry to Douglass, "Let us have the facts," so too is that demand made manifest through Gordon's naked inspection.

These are the conditions of political recognition that would accompany emancipation, its terms set by this white abolitionist discourse. Tellingly, aside from its advertisement of his own physical tortures, the accompanying *Harper's* article verifies Gordon through a litany of graphic—and completely unrelated—cruelties suffered by slaves named Charlie Sloo, Overton, Tom, Margaret, and Rose Ann. The printed insults to *their* bodies are needed to make *Gordon's* body fully legible. Like Douglass, Gordon functions as a metonym—"An American Slave," "A Typical Negro." A well-worn rhetorical figure in white abolitionism, metonymy affirms a particularity only to designate a generality. The article indicates Gordon's name precisely to substitute others. Gordon is Charlie Sloo is Overton is Tom is Margaret is Rose Ann. The political recognition of the freed—their emancipation within the state—would not thereby confer on them the disembodied universality of citizenship.[46] The fungibility of the slave object was translated into the fungibility of the freed subject, and the alienability of the black body into the alienability of black personhood. It is a mistake to assume that liberalism confers majority identity when it confers minority rights. It confers difference, a difference that is embodied, permanently and irrevocably. (Such members don't belong to the polity so much as they belong to a set.) The logic of the *Harper's* triptych denies the possibility of disembodiment for the formerly enslaved and instead obsessively conjures that body, demands to "have the body," remarking on its injuries, remarking injury's obdurate materiality.

With its logic of exchangeability, ever re-marking blackness as the sign and vestige of exchange, the value-form of the slave would also superintend the personhood of the freed. Identity is equivalent to exposure and interchangeability, a stripped back and a misnaming. An ersatz singularity is made the surrogate of a denied universality. Necessarily physical rather than psychic, injury is catalogued not for the purposes of redress, but to allay white suspicion about slavery's harm. Impressed on the bodies of Douglass, Gordon, Wood's and Nast's veteran, and the formerly enslaved en masse, "blackness" stipulates injury, and within liberalism's paradigm, it's an affliction to be ignored or administered to by a white public. Subjected to white suspicion, the slave's political recognition ultimately designates *blackness* as a state of publicity. The rights of Man are extended on the basis of an open wound, a wound *kept* open. The pen must rest forever in the gashes. Both state power and white suspicion are encoded *in* and *as* liberalism, which plots freedom as the subjection of individuals within the state. Here, exhibition—or rather, commodity spectacle—is that freedom's prerequisite.

The Spectacle of Blackness

A portrait connotes—if it doesn't explicitly denote—the existence of an actual individual toward whom its likeness offers fidelity. At the same time, the portrait exceeds that mere likeness (or perhaps more deeply fulfills it) by also intimating the inner truth of its subject, the genuine self. And because of its realist assumptions, the portrait also elicits scrutiny in its execution of a likeness, something between an empirical and an aesthetic judgment: Is it a "good" portrait, or a "bad" one? The stronger its realism, the more the portrait amplifies that mode's innate tendency to put its own medium under erasure, to suggest that it presents a substitution for the original.[47] In contrast, still-life painting has tended to depict objects meant to imply and affirm the subject who would view them. In the early nineteenth century, still-life painting enshrined Republican virtues of possessive individualism, a fiction of selfhood couched in the terms of the market. The quantity and quality of the things one owned demonstrated whether and to what degree one owned oneself.[48] Generically fused and confused as it is, *Attention, Company!* gathers portraiture's concerns for naming and authenticity together with trompe l'oeil still life's notions of possessive individualism and consumer desire.

Closely related to the "rack pictures" painted by Harnett and his contemporaries John Haberle and John F. Peto, *Attention, Company!* substitutes a black boy into the genre's iconography of guns, pipes, miniature photos, and money. Given a patina of age and use, the genre's worn objects suggest a specifically masculine yearning for a simpler time, before the era of industrialism and consumerism, when encounters with things were supposed to be authentic and uncorrupted by commodity relations. "Objects need not actually have been old to have conveyed a comforting sense of age and permanence; they need only to have appeared enduring and stable in contrast to the unsettling flux of the present," the art historian David Lubin writes.[49] So, as a genre's codes, this boy is also cast as an object, one saturated with nostalgia for "calmer, less hurried times," in Lubin's words. Paradoxically, as a machined illusory surface, the picture plane in these still lifes comes to resemble the display window of a store, depicting objects that are inaccessible and implanting a consumerist desire to possess them.

Such was the aesthetic function of blackness in the urban, industrial milieu where *Attention, Company!* was painted. This figure is on display not to exhibit a human likeness but to affirm the authenticity of a fetish: black skin. Take the subject's gaze, that phrase intended to secure most firmly the reality of the portrait. Here, the boy's fixed intent look wavers between being merely paint (the gleam in his eyes divulged as only peaked impasto) and suggesting something "located *beyond appearance*," in Roland Barthes's words, beyond the surface of face and skin—a fetish of the real.[50] And yet, simultaneously, its trompe l'oeil style places the identity of the painting's subject/object "under suspicion." In other words, as with Douglass's audience and Gordon's inspectors, the painting constructs a viewer marked by dubiety and discernment. Fidelity is negotiated here as a question of the real versus the counterfeit.[51]

NOW, CONSIDER the advertisement for a show staged in 1895: "Every newspaper in New-York and Brooklyn enthusiastically declares it to be The Greatest Novelty Ever Seen in America! Real living scenes in the life of the real Southern negro, amidst real cotton fields and in real cabins."[52] The name of the novelty was *Black America*. It went up in a Brooklyn park that summer, something of a sequel to *Buffalo Bill's Wild West Show*. The two shows shared a promoter, Nate Salsbury, and where there now was a plantation, there had been a Western frontier in the same park the summer before.[53] *Black America* covered three acres, one of them planted with cotton. One hundred fifty cabins housed at least five hundred black performers, perhaps nearer seven, who were "on consignment," in the *New-York Tribune*'s words, from plantations across the South.[54] Some worked a century-old cotton gin that operated continuously and that pressed the same cotton into the same two bales over and over. Giving exhibition drills was the all-black Ninth Cavalry, which three years later would find itself with Teddy Roosevelt on San Juan Hill.[55] And each day there was also a show with minstrelsy's staples—Stephen Foster songs, cakewalks, buck-and-wing dancing.[56] The show ended with patriotic anthems sung on stage by the entire cast beneath enormous electrified portraits of abolitionist heroes—Harriet Beecher Stowe, Frederick Douglass, John Brown, Abraham Lincoln.

Minstrelsy and its stereotypes were on full view at Ambrose Park. *Black America* also traded in a kind of plantation nostalgia that, while already well established by minstrel songs prior to the Civil War, was no longer just the imagined sentiment of the homesick slave.[57] It became a sentiment openly experienced by whites across the nation following Reconstruction. (And the claim could be made that it stitched the nation together again; one white family romance became another.) But something else, something besides mythic romance and anachronistic caricature, was also going on at *Black America*. "Mr. Salsbury is particularly anxious that the public understand that 'Black America' is not a minstrel show," wrote one reporter. "It is not a 'show' at all; it is an exhibition."[58] Salsbury's particular anxiety registers in his promotion: *real* living scenes, the *real* Southern negro, *real* cotton fields, *real* cabins. Once again we encounter a concern with authenticity, an insistence on the "real."[59]

The plantation resurged on the minstrel stage in the middle of the 1870s, not least because the minstrels on that stage were now all black. Southern settings displaced the traditional opening semicircle on stage, and the stage itself began to resemble a simulacrum of the plantation. One Boston show took place in a field with "overseers, bloodhounds, and darkies at work."[60] One troupe, according to Robert C. Toll, "promised to use real logs, tree stumps, moss, and a cypress tree to add realism to the plantation opening."[61] And minstrel promoter J. H. Haverly increased the number of his company to more than one hundred.[62] The magnitude of the company and the realism of the scenery meant to envelop spectators in a virtual world. The shows were imitations that sought to disavow themselves as representations—not performances, but exhibitions. And not reenactments, so much as simply *enactments*, which collapsed time and place, with the spectator in Ambrose Park in 1895 suddenly enfolded in a Mississippi plantation four decades earlier. (Three years later, in 1898, the Columbia Phonograph Company Orchestra's recording of

"Down on the Swanee River." was advertised to include not just songs and dances, but also the atmospheric sounds of location, "pulling in the gangplank, the sounds of a steamboat engine, and ... the chiming of a steamboat bell.")[63] A discourse of genuineness and immediacy surrounded these performances. These trends would culminate in *Black America* in 1895—and *The South before the War* in 1892 and *The Old Plantation* at the world's fairs of 1895, 1897, 1901 and 1904—but this discourse yielded more than these performances, and it meant more than it said.

From one angle, this plantation show was nothing more than an enhancement of the minstrel show, meant, in the words of a reviewer, "to show the darky in all sorts of situations in real life, ranging from song-and-dance and fisticuffs to a military parade and active labor on the cotton press."[64] *Black America* just presented one more black company required to perform as the white man's Negro. It aimed to "show the labors that the negroes of slavery days engaged in, and the happy, careless life that they lived in their cabins after work hours were over."[65] But from another direction, it heralded a new kind of "plant show," with its hundreds of black performers living in cabins spread across three acres.[66] Opening each day at 11 A.M. in New York and an hour before showtime in Boston, the "arena in which many of the features will be given has been constructed to represent an actual plantation"—which spectators were encouraged to explore—"and here field hands will be seen in the work of gathering and sorting the cotton, and preparing it for market in a cotton press and gin, which as far back as 100 years ago was in actual service on a plantation in Georgia."[67] The performers had been recruited—though under what auspices we don't know—as working field hands from Southern plantations. Their provenance provided the capstone for the production's emphasis on scenic realism. "There is little art, in the dramatic sense, shown by the performers," the Boston *Daily Globe* wrote. "The negroes merely appear as natural as possible. There are all sorts of temperaments, from the lively and mischievous to the sedate. Men, women, and picaninnies act as they would on the plantation."[68] The production advertised itself in the *New-York Tribune* as comprising "500 real negroes from the South (none from the North), as they are in their own plantation life."[69] The performance proper, with its minstrel staples, took place on a stage 160 by 190 feet, and behind the stage were "scenic effects of prodigious size": "These scenes will picture Southern landscape plantations, town and city, in a realistic way."[70] The show's grand finale included the entire all-black cast of six hundred, singing patriotic songs on a stage beneath those portraits of abolitionist heroes. The portraits were gigantic—ten by twenty feet—and electrified, and they formed the backdrop for the massive renditions of "Tramp, Tramp, Tramp, the Boys are Marching," "Marching through Georgia," "John Brown's Body," and "America."[71] In the words of Nate Salsbury, "'Black America' tells a story and an interesting one."[72]

The show aggregates, apparently for the first time, a number of representational shifts. First, without superseding it, an insurgent mode of realism overlaps that of caricature. The frame of "natural" appearance, the notion that the performers show "little art," coincides with minstrelsy's vision of the slave's "happy, careless life." Salsbury told one newspaper that *Black America* "has an ethnographic value [from] a scientific standpoint as well as its amusing side."[73] The coincidence of realism and caricature in *Black America* might be explained, too quickly, as precisely what is seen through the lens of scientific racism—a contemporary discourse that interchanged nature with culture, grounding artificial caricature in empirical reality. It was scientific racism that legitimated the cultural deformations of ethnography as the given "nature" of race. In that context, minstrelsy's perversions of blackness only played out biology's predestinations.

But this is too simple. As its grand finale suggests, *Black America*'s realism also articulated a political program. The show's scenic realism was borrowed and amplified from the extravaganza *South before the War*, its direct predecessor that opened in 1892, and from which it also took its finale. ("The Scenery is simply excellent, the cotton field true to nature," proclaimed *South before the War*'s promotional materials, "actual cotton plants, 'jes from de Souf' being plentifully placed upon the stage. The steamboat landing and steamboat, a piece of perfect realism seldom equaled in scenic effect.")[74] In fact, *Black America*'s finale was partially drafted as a third act for *South before the War* by Billy McClain, who, along with his wife Cordelia, worked for that earlier show and who is credited as the creative genius behind both productions.[75] McClain and his wife were also black, and their position on the color line might suggest another reading of *Black America*'s realism and its politics. McClain himself clarified those political stakes; he said he meant "to show the colored man's advancement since the war, introducing him as the citizen, soldier and statesman."[76]

The mode of realism tends to wear its liberal affinities on its sleeve. It's the empirical affirmation of a shared humanity, and its trained focus on the quotidian in others' lives seeks to reveal the commonplace. In realism, another's differences are vitiated through assimilating their experiences as the parallel to one's own. Karl Marx drafts this same equation as liberalism's formula of

Black America, broadside (Nathan Salsbury Papers, American Literature Collection, Beinecke Rare Book and Manuscript Library, Yale University, New Haven, Connecticut).

political recognition in "On the Jewish Question." Marx argues that a schism lays under the liberal state, dividing political community from civil society. "In the *political community*," he writes, the citizen "regards himself as a *communal being*; but in *civil society* he is active as a *private individual*, treats other men as means, reduces himself to a means, and becomes the plaything of alien powers.... In the state..., on the other hand, he is an imaginary member of an imagined sovereignty, divested of his actual individual life and endowed with an unactual universality." In other words, political emancipation within the state succeeds by alienating the individual's particularities within society (i.e., "emancipating" one from them). And realism might be understood precisely as the survey of the social realm created by that split, the aesthetic complement to political emancipation—realism's paradigmatic character resembling nothing so much as "a *private individual*, [who] treats other men as means, reduces himself to a means, and becomes the plaything of alien powers."[77] Marx's words could serve as its credo. Realism's advocates and practitioners understood it to be producing portraits of the American people, an aesthetic mode that yoked the nation together in fellow feeling and pointed the way toward progressive social change. "After all, what can realism produce but the downfall of conventionality?" a commentator asked in *Century* magazine. "Just as the scientific spirit digs the ground from beneath superstition, so does its fellow-worker, realism, tend to prick the bubble of abstract types. Realism is the tool of the democratic spirit, the modern spirit by which truth is elicited."[78]

Billy McClain must have understood this. *Black America*'s finale only amplified the implicit agenda of the show's realism, which, as McClain avowed, meant to introduce African Americans as citizens and statesmen, as part of the demos. In a sense, that finale hijacked the minstrel show format and attempted to offer in its guise a progressive and evolutionary narrative of what he called "the colored man's advancement since the war."[79] McClain attempted to accomplish on stage what Frederick Douglass had attempted in his autobiography: assuming an institutional performance that might enact the recognition of black humanity. And in fleeting and contradictory moments, it seems to have done just that. One white reviewer wrote about the finale in the *New York Times*, "It is impossible to listen to 'America' as those 500 negroes sing it before the picture of Abraham Lincoln and observe their appeals to his mute but benign countenance, and not feel for the time being that he made a country for them of that which had formerly been but an abiding place."[80] Still caught in the trappings of scientific racism and minstrelsy,

McClain hoped to clear their webs long enough to fulfill the promise of the show's title: the eponymous portrayal of black America. Through the show's claims to realism and patriotism, McClain scripted the Civil War's legacy as one of emancipation and pluralism.

But the show's staging overwhelmed McClain's scripting. And this wasn't because caricature subordinated realism. One thing *Black America* demonstrates is how caricature can adopt the very grammar of realism. The scholar Henry Wonham has argued that the fin de siècle exponents of American realism—William Dean Howells, Mark Twain, Henry James—showed an affinity for and reliance on ethnic caricature in their works. (Even Joel Chandler Harris, author of the Uncle Remus stories, voiced his artistic philosophy as that of realism.)[81] The two modes correspond. Despite "all their theoretical antipathy," Wonham writes, "realism and caricature pursue strikingly similar aesthetic aims. Indeed both programs understand their function in terms of 'penetration' and 'exposure,' and both claim a unique capacity to lay bare the 'essence' of the human subject."[82] The former does so through mimetic fidelity, the latter through the ideal deformity. Through deformity, caricature aims to "reveal the very essence of a personality," wrote its namesake Annibale Carracci. "A good caricature, like every work of art, is more true to life than reality itself."[83] That correspondence clearly bears on a show that proposes to represent the anodyne plantation of minstrelsy as the reality of black America in 1895. Still, this isn't meant to suggest that the *correspondence* is a *conflation*: the realism employed by *Black America* isn't just caricature in a kinder, gentler disguise. Its realism bears its own political force.

At *Black America*, crowds didn't encounter the plantation as a representation, or as a reproduction, or as a replica. In Ambrose Park, Brooklyn, and at the Huntington Avenue Grounds in Boston, and in Chicago, Atlanta, and Washington, D.C., they encountered an aspect of the plantation itself—its intrinsic display function having been riven from its basic industrial function. At *Black America*, the plantation realizes production's dual meanings: it becomes a zone where production as manufacture merges with production as staged exhibition. How else are we to understand this small posting in the *New-York Tribune*? "Reinhard Seidenburg, president of the New-York Cotton Exchange, on behalf of the Board of Directors and the resident members, has accepted the invitation of Nate Salsbury, director of 'Black America,' at Ambrose Park, to visit that exhibition on Friday evening in a body. Seats on the grandstand will be reserved for their special use and they will see the old-fashioned cotton press, the cotton gin, the acre of planted cotton and all the other attractions of the outdoor exhibition."[84] Salsbury's invitation to Seidenburg seeks the legitimation of his show. It is fanfaronade about *Black America*'s sparkling realism—good enough to entertain industry professionals. And one imagines the investors' acceptance of the invitation was their endorsement of a kind of advertisement for the plantation offered in *Black America*. Salsbury's perverse vision amounts to good marketing. But what a strange scene: the very Northern factors discussed in chapter 1 who had long financed the plantation regime in the South, before and after 1865, now officially visit a show in Brooklyn to watch conscripted Southern field hands work a plantation that only produces and reproduces its own valuable image. These financiers might well provide the capital for the Southern plantations that ensnare these same men and women to grow and gin cotton, and here the "president of the New-York Cotton Exchange, on behalf of the Board of Directors and the resident members," along with his colleagues, observe them tending an acre of cotton and repetitively pressing and dismantling two cotton bales. Salsbury presents Seidenburg with the flickering double of the institution that fills the coffers of the cotton exchange. It seems wholly likely that this would be as close as many of those board members would ever get to a Southern plantation. *Black America* inverts (or does it maintain?) the plantation's dynamics, as the production of cotton is made incidental to the "production" of blackness as spectacle, whether in toil or in merriment.

Black America conjoins the commodity value of black bodies and of their "free" labor in the form of its spectacle. On its three-acre stage, and not least in its rousing anthems sung beneath the mammoth electrified icons of abolition, *Black America* welds the public sphere of the nation to the public sphere of capital. Political representation as free persons and citizens—the show's titular purpose—is indistinguishable from representation as commodity. What *Black America* capitalizes on is the very spectacle of free black personhood itself. That personhood is cast as illusory, magical, mechanical. Note that the frame for *Black America*'s quite tangible reality—its cabins, its cotton, *and* its performers—is one of expert imitation. Perhaps it is easy to forget that the show is meant as a convincing deception: "Real living scenes in the life of the real Southern negro, amidst real cotton fields and in real cabins."[85] The advertising copy protests too much and so suggests the show's fakery. And this hint of fakery attaches not just to the show's reenactment of the plantation, but also, in complicated ways, to its black workers.

THE MODE OF REALISM here establishes a literal relay between the production on Southern plantations and the "production" of *Black America*. Con-

Photographs of *Black America* from *The Illustrated American* (29 June 1895), including "Way Down South in Dixie" and "Leisure Moments."

sider the account of one white reviewer who, adopting a kind of New Journalistic stance, narrated his visit to *Black America* in a tone of wry familiarity that bears quoting at length:

> "Where are you from?" the writer asked of an old darkey who was passing up baskets of cotton to the man on top of the cotton press. "North Car'lina, sah," said the old man.... "How old are you?" The old man was evidently approaching that period of life in which a negro lasts for thirty, forty, or even sixty years, without any change in his apparent age. "Fifty-fo', sah, the tenth day of nex' Augus,'" said the man. "Were you a slave?" "Yes, sah."
>
> All the men about the cotton press looked as if they belonged to the age of the press itself. And that was a hundred years old, the manager said. It looked it. In order to get it for exhibition, the managers had to give the owner of it a modern machine, and promise to bring the old one back as well. Very slowly and deliberately the old men, who had thin beards, that looked as if a coating of cotton had collected on their faces, filled their baskets from a pile twenty feet off, brought them over to the press, and passed them up to the men on top. Very slowly and deliberately, the men on top, with apparent coatings on the tops and backs of their heads, emptied their baskets into the press.
>
> Slow as they were the pile was gone after a time, and the press was full, and a younger colored man sang out: "We are now about to press and bind up this bale of cotton." Somebody slapped the mule, and it walked around and around the press, while the big wooden weights came down and down till the mass of cotton was only half its first size. Then the old men laboriously passed the iron straps around the bale and hooked them, and the job was done. Anybody who expects a new bale of cotton to be made every time is most unreasonable. The show would have to get several cargoes of cotton as the summer went on. There are two bales of cotton on hand, and each of them is repeatedly pulled and pressed and baled over again. The cotton ought to be well squeezed together by the end of the summer.[86]

The relay between the industrialized production on Southern plantations and *Black America*'s stage production is made obvious, if nowhere else, in the cotton gin, "which as far back as 100 years ago was in actual service on a plantation in Georgia," according to another report.[87] The antique model in use and on display in Ambrose Park doesn't stall production at its Georgia home.

On the contrary, its loan comes with the purchase of a newer model. And that newer model isn't a replacement; the one borrowed will be returned. So this "simulated" Brooklyn plantation doubles, at the very least, the output of a functioning plantation somewhere in Georgia. *Black America* peddles a mythic "Old South" that directly finances the New South's construction. The New South's mouthpiece, Henry Grady, had said six years earlier: "Before the war, when the southern planter had a little surplus money he bought a slave. Since the war, he buys a piece of machinery."[88] And not just the Georgia plantation, but (reflecting Grady's telling equation of slaves and machines) *Black America* itself manifests that mechanization. Its display of plantation labor undercuts any vision of a "happy, careless life" for its laborers. It mirrors, perhaps inadvertently, the entirely modern nature of the plantation it helps to finance. Even as F. W. Taylor was refining his principles in Philadelphia, and sixteen years before he would publish *The Principles of Scientific Management* in 1911, Taylorism is diagrammed at this cotton gin. Ginning cotton employs the assembly line, its component actions broken down, specialized as tasks. Labor is rendered repetitive and utterly meaningless. Two bales worth of cotton are ginned, pressed, and hooked, only to be pulled apart to be ginned again.

Before 1865, as Grady's quip implies, machines and slaves were equivalent.[89] What *Black America* suggests is—thirty years after abolition and well into an age where contract is supposed to supplant status—they still are. "All the men about the cotton press looked as if they belonged to the age of the press itself." The antiqued look of the machine is reflected in the "antique" faces of its black workers. Three years later, in 1898, a Missouri politician bluntly reaffirmed the equation; he deemed blacks "mere existing human machines."[90] In myriad ways, this reviewer's narration reminds us that "labor" as a concept is inapplicable to the plantation in the United States. The reviewer's application of the trope of black agelessness links these workers to machines even as it also explicitly casts them as artifacts, in the same manner as the bodies of Gordon and Frederick Douglass. The ubiquitous figure of the "old darkey," or the black "uncle," is critically presumed to operate mostly as the neuter of the bestial figure of the black rapist. But here, himself insensate, the "old darkey" is primarily an artifact who speaks, a kind of talking machine who at once embodies and narrates the history of "the old plantation." (One is reminded of the Uncle Remus stories, whose first volume Joel Chandler Harris introduces this way: "If the reader not familiar with plantation life will imagine that the myth-stories of Uncle Remus *are told night after night* to a little boy by an old negro *who appears to be venerable enough to have lived during the period which he describes*—who has nothing but pleasant memories of the discipline of slavery.")[91] Just as it was for Northern abolitionists, this artifactual nature is the preservation of the slave's condition, posed between the means of production and the commodity produced. The commodity form has changed, though. The age of these men defines their value for *Black America*. An authenticity registers in the body and countenance of the formerly enslaved; they render *Black America*'s plantation scenery unimpeachable. (One wonders just how much is being asked and answered in the exchange: "Were you a slave?" "Yes, sah.") And that commodity status accords with the reviewer's uncertainty as to whether these elderly workers most resemble the gin or the cotton they feed into it: "the old men ... looked as if a coating of cotton had collected on their faces ... the men on top, with apparent coatings on the tops and backs of their heads."

These men "on consignment" from Southern plantations are not laborers.[92] At this slave plantation replica, they are still offered up as commodities—presented, however, in the frame of portraiture. According to Nate Salsbury, the show's promoter, those hired were meant "to represent the different phases of life" in the South.[93] He advertised the show as "500 real negroes from the South (none from the North), as they are in their own plantation life."[94] And the newspaper reviewers validated his claims. From the *Boston Daily Globe*, quoted earlier: "There is little art, in the dramatic sense, shown by the performers. The negroes merely appear as natural as possible."[95] A *Washington Post* reporter: "After the numerous burnt cork caricatures of negro life it will be pleasant to hear the old plantation songs as they appear in this entertainment, rendered true to life by people to whom the parts assigned are natural, and not the result of stage tuition."[96] In this regard, *Black America* shares something of the midway sensibility of the world's fairs. Indeed, "The Old Plantation," a similar attraction, also opened in 1895 at the Atlanta Cotton States and International Exposition, and would return to the fairs of 1897, 1901, and 1904. As historian Robert W. Rydell notes, just like "the villages depicting the Chinese, Japanese, and Mexicans, the Old Plantation conferred colonial status on its inhabitants."[97] At once foreign and domestic, Southern blacks were no less subject to the imperial gaze of the United States in the 1890s. Amidst paeans to scientific progress, the ethnological exhibits of the midway were racial narratives of human evolution crystallized for the white gaze. But this doesn't fully explain that midway affinity. Such fairs and expositions, in Walter Benjamin's words, "were training schools in which the masses, barred from consuming, learned empathy with exchange value. 'Look at everything; touch nothing.'"[98] By this, he means that the commodities viewed there were appraised not for their usefulness or for their worth. Rather, an "empathy with exchange value" suggests a further abstraction of the commodity's value, which becomes a symbol, its fungibility appreciated as pure sign-value. In such displays at these expositions and at *Black America*, crowds encountered capital's emergence as spectacle.

BLACK AMERICA TAKES its frame as a simulacrum of reality largely from the panorama's American renaissance, which reached its zenith between the years 1872 and 1885 and still could be seen after 1900. These panoramas were of two types. In stationary panoramas, viewers would ascend to an elevated vantage point where they were surrounded by a 360-degree painting of stunning illusionism, able to take in both the foreground and the distant horizon. For moving panoramas, viewers were themselves stationary, as a painted canvas was unscrolled before them, simulating the view from a boat or train with deceptive realism. As cinema's antecedent, the panorama collapsed for the viewer distances of space and time, bringing close the foreign and the historical. The panorama depended on and delivered the shock of a perfectly realized substitute reality. Like its contemporary of trompe l'oeil still life, or like the commodity itself, the panorama also depended on obfuscating its own means of production. *Black America* combined elements of both panoramic forms. Its spectators were cast as both active and passive, wandering through the show's three-acre grounds and among its performers prior to showtime, then sitting motionless in the grandstand before a stage background with "scenic effects of prodigious size" that "picture southern landscape plantations, town and city, in a realistic way."[99] Like the panorama, *Black America* sought to envelop its spectators and to overwhelm their senses. Counterintuitively, *Black America*'s success required that its materiality appear to viewers as a flawless image. All its tangible aspects had to be subverted as representation. The show didn't set out, nor would it succeed, as merely "presenting" its plantation scene. This was a vicarious and twice removed "reality": the reality of a representation of reality.[100]

As a technology of vision, the panorama yielded, in its moving form, "the transformation of space into an image of time," in art historian Angela Miller's words, and trained the eyes, in its stationary form, for imperialism's geography and its power relations, surveying from above distant lands brought close. These effects structure *Black America*. Certainly in its confused rendition of an antebellum plantation, *Black America* strives for nothing so much as "the transformation of space into an image of time." And its panoramic allusions, no less than its echoes of the midway's ethnological exhibitions, suggest an imperial relation of North over South and of white over black. Obliquely (or not), the show anticipates the reinvigoration of American imperialism three years later, in 1898, as "black Americans" stand in for future colonized subjects. Here, for the moment, the South and its black workers are the focus of the imperial gaze of a re-United States. Very soon, "the South" would again designate a space that wasn't just national but hemispheric and global.[101] (The Ninth Cavalry, posited as the success story of black America's racial evolution, provides the thread that would stitch it all together: embodying the iconography of enlistment, as the first African American regiment, these men represent degraded slaves transformed into soldier citizens by the magic of the state, just like the triptychs of Gordon and *A Bit of War History*. No surprise, then, that they should appear as part of *Black America*'s exhibition, but telling that they should do so between themselves fighting the Indian Wars of an "old" imperialism and charging up San Juan Hill on behalf of the "new.") "As the cinema would later do," Angela Miller writes, the panorama, and by extension, *Black America*, "offered a sensationalized simulacrum of the real—rendering the newly colonized regions of the world both accessible and visible, glorifying the imperial state, and imposing the illusion of order onto the fabric of the rapidly urbanizing cities of Europe and America."[102] That is to say, *Black America* was symptomatic of the ideological rift that seemed to separate "the North" from "the South," as noted at this chapter's outset, and of the economic ties that connected them.

Like the panorama and *Attention, Company!*, *Black America* sets out to trick the eye, and nowhere more insistently than with its black cast. The show recapitulates the dynamics of Harnett's painting—portrait fused with trompe l'oeil still life—in its depiction of black personhood. And black personhood becomes something of a phantasmagoria here. Consider the words of that same reporter for the *New-York Tribune*:

> What the spectators want, after all, is a show, and the most of the show of "Black America" is in the inclosure where the music and variety programme is carried out. The unfortunate difference between doing things naturally and doing them on purpose is again apparent here. Nobody who feels himself to be on exhibition can help showing the feeling a little, till he has had great experience. These poor people from the plantations have not had great experience, and they feel all the time that people are looking at them. It is curious to note the different effects that this feeling

has on them. A few keep their eyes painfully to the front and count their steps. But in general there is a deep love of show in the darky nature that cannot be altogether suppressed.[103]

Through this reporter's eyes, we watch black agency transmute into a fetish on display. If the spectators want a show, what exactly is the show that's being offered? What fascinates about this scene, if not the specter of black agency? *Black America* occupies the space "between doing things naturally and doing them on purpose," between a "real Negro" and a fake. That dichotomy also registers, though, a sinister mix-up about animation itself. All those questions of artifice, deception, and authenticity were applied primarily to the cast, not to the background scenery. And the question that truly fascinates seems to regard the nature of black personhood: What animates "these poor people from the plantations" who are fellow citizens? Is it culture or is it nature? Do they most resemble agents or automatons?

The frame of the spectacle willfully intends the questions because it seeks to eclipse agency as autochthonous. Which is to say, despite appearances (or rather, because of them), *Black America* offers no space for self-representation. Yet the show seems to eschew script and narrative in favor of the unmediated realism of self-portrayal. (Recall that earlier quote: "There is little art, in the dramatic sense, shown by the performers. The negroes merely appear as natural as possible.") Ultimately, these "real Negroes" are meant as magical effects of the show's apparatus, something between ghosts of the past and images on a screen. What *Black America* insists on most fervently, then, is the conjunction of black personhood and publicity. Agency is allied with exhibition. If, in Michael Warner's words, "To be public in the West means to have an iconicity," then iconicity for African Americans names a condition of commodity spectacle.[104] The show renders it a matter of amusement whether that condition—of becoming pure sign-value, a fetish on display—is dreadful or natural, whether it is painful or whether it reveals the "deep love of show in the darky nature." Once again, as with the slave, personhood is seen to be the counterpart of dehumanization, the very means of commodification, rather than its opponent. It abetted slavery's violence; it didn't safeguard against it.[105]

Black America parodies black citizenship. Here, entrance into the public sphere confuses the promised formal equality of citizenship with the interchangeability of the commodity. That public sphere doesn't secure the individual's sovereignty; instead, it anchors fungibility in the identity of blackness. And in this way, *Black America* also parodies black emancipation. In its borrowings from the panorama, the show prioritizes a simulation of white mobility (to move through the grounds and to watch the production is to travel through the South) at the expense of black mobility (as the cast are converted into captive objects on display). But in the trip North for the show and the spectacle's tour from city to city, there *is* a freedom of movement that's made proper to "black America." Emancipation becomes the freedom to move as commodities move, through capital's circuits—the "freedom" of circulation. The residue of slave personhood tars the citizenship bestowed on the freed, and the logic of that personhood remains the accomplice and the signatory of slave racial capitalism. And its profit motive continued to superintend black personhood long after 1865.

Black America supplied a plantation scene absent of any master. The spectator was to fill that vacant role, as a process of subjectification also took place on the other side of the color line. "Spectacle is not primarily concerned with a *looking at* images but rather with the construction of conditions that individuate, immobilize, and separate subjects, even within a world in which mobility and circulation are ubiquitous," according to the theorist and art historian Jonathan Crary. "Spectacle is not an optics of power but an architecture."[106] Spectacle is insistently geared toward cellularization. Separation is its watchword. It generates individuals. Here, too, *Black America* bears the mark of the cinematic. Its technology at once aggregates and divides. In its audience it composes a community, even as it insistently singles out and hails each viewer. (So too, in this era, power diffuses and cellularizes; the ultimate figure of racial violence and white supremacy is no longer the capricious despotism of the master but the concerted acts of the lynch mob.) And while Crary's words describe *Black America*'s white subjects, his distinction about the spectacle's innocence doesn't hold; it is both an optics *and* an architecture of power. Collapsing production as staged exhibition with production as labor's output, this show yields a white viewer who is subject to new values of imperialism, consumerism, and privacy.[107]

SPECTACLE INTEGRATES THE REALM of politics and the realm of economy, spheres whose seeming separation is foundational to liberalism's social order. In spectacle, power and capital operate through images. These images crystallize force and value, and they maintain a system of relations by obfuscating both how that system came into being and how it is reproduced. "The spectacle," as Guy Debord famously defined it, "is *capital* accumulated to the point where it becomes image."[108] Spectacle emerged in the United States within a racial capitalism whose locus of value was the slave. Writing in and about the mid-twentieth century, Debord conceived spectacle as capital's thoroughgoing colonization of everyday life, a transformation within capitalism that created a feedback loop between the abstract figments of ideology and the concreteness of social reality. It is a "dictatorship of illusion" that represents capital's real subsumption of society.[109] Spectacle comprises a technological and cultural shift toward forms of consumerist entertainment—toward capital's advertisements for itself and for the world of its own making.[110] And in turn, these advertisements become reality. According to Crary and the art historian T. J. Clark, who both focus on Europe, spectacle originates in the late nineteenth century, and since, by and large, theirs is a Europe without colonies they, like Debord, conceive spectacle without regard to race, although racism has always been intrinsic to capitalism.

The capital accumulated through the system of slavery wasn't destroyed or redistributed in 1865 but was instead preserved through the machinations of contract and debt that defined sharecropping. As described in the first chapter, slave capital was financialized. And once financialized, "capital itself becomes free-floating. It separates from the concrete context of its productive geography," as Fredric Jameson writes.[111] The workings of finance autonomized the slave as a value-form, further abstracting it. Along with the bodies where that value had congealed, that value was itself set free by formal abolition. With slave capital's flight northward to be incorporated in New York, it was deterritorialized. Although Jameson describes a different historical context, not concerned with these questions of racialization and exchange value, his words help illuminate what's underway. Once "objects have become equivalent as commodities," he writes, once

> money has leveled their intrinsic differences as individual things, one may now purchase as it were their various, henceforth semiautonomous qualities or perceptual features; and both color and shape free themselves from their former vehicles and come to live independent existences as fields of perception and as artistic raw materials. This is then a first stage, but only a first one, in the onset of an abstraction that becomes identified as aesthetic modernism.... Modernist abstraction, I believe, is less a function of capital accumulation as such than of money itself in a situation of capital accumulation.[112]

Here, black bodies constitute those objects, slave capital that money, and blackness itself that abstraction. Spectacle designates their emergent and articulated formation.

Through the commodification and consumption of blackness as image, and blackness as a catalyst for what Crary calls a "larger organization of perceptual consumption," we begin to grasp the coalescence of this spectacle. These are the dynamics of representation that structure the synesthetic painting of *Attention, Company!* and the immersive performance of *Black America*. Still tethered to the slave as a value-form, blackness as a commodity achieves a semiautonomous character during the decades after 1865, as it is alienated and abstracted. These developments ramified across U.S. culture. Take, as examples, the black stereotypes that proliferated to advertise mass-produced consumer goods that defined and expropriated the attributes of blackness (stove polish, cleaning products, prepared foods); the ubiquity of those stereotypes in the burgeoning sheet music industry, which allowed whites to perform vaudeville's signature "coon songs" in their own homes, at their own pianos, and in their own voices; the central role of "black" sounds for early phonographs; the importance of blackness to the technological-perceptual schema of early cinema, from the kinetoscope to *The Birth of a Nation* to *The Jazz Singer*; and soon after, the popularity of segregated urban venues such as the Cotton Club or Plantation Club where white patrons chased dissolution through the erotics of jazz and possession of its "cool."[113] Blackness was the accomplice to—indeed, the medium that facilitated—the multiplication of these new media entertainments in the late nineteenth and early twentieth centuries.[114] This spectacular commodification of blackness goes far beyond blackface, itself a residue and a symptom of these dynamics.[115] Rather, what I am describing here is akin to a logic of blackface that becomes, a social universal, almost completely subsumed within the culture of American capitalism—no longer a play of masks but precisely that "larger organization of perceptual consumption" Crary references. Along with *Attention, Company!*, *Black America* offers us a blueprint for this all-encompassing structure of racial spectacle.

This totalizing structure and the ways it warped "the souls of black folk"— how this racialization was internalized by black people as it stamped the external world—were just what W. E. B. Du Bois invoked in his concept of "the Veil" in 1903.[116] For whites, to be unable to pierce the Veil was to see only the false scrim of racist culture, to mistake this pervasive racial capitalist *representation* for the actual lives that proceed "behind" it, so to speak. It is to be unable to see the lives of "black folk" shaped and constrained by human desire and necessity. That humanity, *their* humanity, is occluded and made culturally invisible. In America, the spectacle is precisely this Veil, this screen of culture, a pandemonium of images that is mistaken for and reproduced as material reality. Black personhood and the commodity spectacle of blackness now form a Möbius strip. Under chattel slavery, personhood was the public-facing aspect of the enslaved, that garb that allowed the slave to be apprehended by the law, both literally and figuratively. After formal abolition, black personhood is reconfigured as alienable, as persona, and blackness as a surplus liable to be appropriated—a commodity to be consumed *as experience*. To borrow Debord's words, "For one to whom the real world becomes real images, mere images are transformed into real beings."[117]

The dynamics of spectacle signal a sea of change for slave racial capitalism: if its system of accumulation could no longer as easily proceed through the ownership and dissipation of black bodies, then it would proceed through the ownership and dissipation of black personas. If, theoretically, the law conceived of the formerly enslaved as a "total person" with a public aspect, that publicity would be resubjected to the needs of racial capitalism as a commodity. (Consider the appearance in this era of the "spokesservant"—Aunt Jemima, the Gold Dust Twins, and countless others. "Lithographed and printed images worked only for their white masters. 'Spokesservants' served their products, their companies, and all white consumers who bought their products," as historian Grace Elizabeth Hale notes.)[118] Contemplating spectacle's periodization, Crary writes: "The spectacle then would coincide with the moment when sign-value takes precedence over use-value. But the question of the location of this moment in the history of the commodity remains unanswered."[119] One wonders, how could history's most salient, formative, and violent history of commodification be absent from the conception of spectacle? How could a commodity that is genetic to capital and that is vaporized by law in 1865 not trigger some crisis in racial capitalism, some turning point in its mode of production?[120] So perhaps it is the moment when that *ur*-commodity is emancipated (*which is not to say abolished*) in formal personhood. "The black is the apogee of the commodity," writes critical race theorist Anthony Paul Farley. "It is the point—in time as well as in space—at which the commodity becomes flesh."[121] And spectacle is the point, in time as well as in space, at which that flesh becomes image.

The Segregation of Blackness

The logic of segregation also infuses such realistic spectacles in soliciting a viewer's discernment and adjudication, constructing their whiteness by fabricating blackness. Besides offering up one of the nineteenth century's most trenchant exposés of race, Mark Twain's *Pudd'nhead Wilson* goes some way toward spelling out that logic, *especially* as it generates white identity. In the story, published in the 1890s and set in 1853 in the Missouri town of Dawson's Landing, an enslaved mother named Roxy swaps her infant son with her white charge, the son of her master, also seven months old. "To all intents and purposes Roxy was as white as anybody, but the one-sixteenth of her which was black outvoted the other fifteen parts and made her a negro. She was a slave, and salable as such. Her child was thirty-one parts white, and he, too, was a slave, and by fiction of law and custom a negro. He had blue eyes and flaxen hair like his white comrade."[122] Roxy's son grows up believing himself to be her white owner, under the name Thomas á Becket Driscoll, while she raises the white child as a slave, under the name Valet de Chambre. The balance of the novel addresses the consequences of their mistaken identities. Tom becomes a cruel gambler, whose crimes escalate with his debts. He robs houses; he sells his manumitted mother downriver; and finally, he murders his uncle. He frames a pair of Italian twins for this last crime, and the novel reaches its denouement in the final chapter's courtroom scene. Celebrated as the preeminent realist of the nineteenth century, Twain created in *Pudd'nhead Wilson* a novel that has been hailed for its humane portrayals of black characters. "Mark Twain, in his presentation of Negroes as human beings, stands head and shoulders above the other Southern writers of his times," Langston Hughes wrote. "And that he makes them neither heroes nor villains is a tribute to his understanding of human character.... In 1894 *Pudd'nhead Wilson* was a 'modern' novel indeed. And it still may be so classified."[123] Twain's work seems to expose race ("a fiction of law and custom") as a cultural construction at the moment of its scientific verity and of Jim Crow's entrenchment. His narrative tone has been critically understood to skewer racism, even while his voice shows its influence.

Appearing fifteen years after the painting of *Attention, Company!* but a contemporary of *Black America*, Twain's novel distills a logic shared among them by more fully revealing the white subject each invokes. His novel is interesting, in part, because its story seems largely unconcerned with its eponymous character. Rather, it is Tom Driscoll and his mother, Roxy, the novel's two black characters, who draw most of the narrative's attention. Known to the locals as "Pudd'nhead" for his foolish ideas and predilections, particularly his inventory of every townsperson's fingerprints, the white lawyer David Wilson remains largely out of sight once he is introduced, until the final chapter where he provides the plot's courtroom conclusion. Representing the framed Italian twins, Wilson procures their innocence and sets identities to rights, through a dazzling comparison of the fingerprints left on the murder weapon with the records in his inventory. More crucially, though, he exposes Tom as a changeling and Chambers as, in Twain's words, an "imitation nigger." Having concealed their identities for the effect of his revelation, Wilson declares in court, "*A* was put into *B*'s cradle in the nursery; *B* was transferred to the kitchen and became a negro and a slave ... but within a quarter of an hour he will stand before you white and free!"[124] As Twain writes in the conclusion:

> The real heir ["Chambers"] suddenly found himself rich and free, but in a most embarrassing situation. He could neither read nor write, and his speech was the basest dialect of the negro quarter. His gait, his attitudes, his gestures, his bearing, his laugh—all were vulgar and uncouth; his manners were the manners of a slave. Money and fine clothes could not mend these defects or cover them up; they only made them the more glaring and the more pathetic. The poor fellow could not endure the terrors of the white man's parlor, and felt at home and at peace nowhere but in the kitchen.[125]

With the revelation made, "Tom" again becomes a slave and is sold away.

Meanwhile, the identity of "Pudd'nhead" Wilson also undergoes a transformation that lays bare the property interest in whiteness. The change undergone by his character is depicted as a problem of privacy versus publicity, a legal matter just outlined in 1890 by the jurists Samuel Warren and Louis Brandeis. "It is the unwarranted invasion of individual privacy which is reprehended, and to be, so far as possible, prevented," they wrote in the pathfinding article, "The Right to Privacy," which defined the concept, adding that the emphasis on *unwarranted* "in the above statement is obvious and fundamental." The right to privacy can be abrogated; it doesn't apply equally to all. "There are persons who may reasonably claim as a right, protection from the notoriety entailed by being made the victims of journalistic enterprise. There are others who, in varying degrees, have renounced the right to live their lives screened from public observation." Warren and Brandeis give as examples legislators and public officials. "Matters which men of the first class may justly contend, concern themselves alone, may in those of the second be the subject of legitimate interest to their fellow-citizens." In the character of Pudd'nhead Wilson, Twain epitomizes such a figure of privacy, a man most always portrayed inside his home and "toiling in obscurity at the bottom of the ladder."[126] His privacy is emphasized, if not prompted, by his notoriety as "a damn fool" and "perfect jackass": "The first day's verdict [by the townspeople] made him a fool, and he was not able to get it set aside, or even modified."[127]

The novel's title underscores Wilson's primary role in the plot's courtroom resolution, but it also stresses a parallel plot that tends to be overlooked. The bombastic courtroom scene at the end doesn't only mete out justice to the other characters; it's also David Wilson's legal vindication for twenty years' worth of slander as a "pudd'nhead." He had been astute and judicious all along. In other words, the plot that exposes the racial imposture of Tom Driscoll and Chambers interlocks with the plot that absolves Wilson of the injurious reputation he suffered. (In the novel's conclusion, the townspeople realize: "'And this is the man the likes of us have called a pudd'nhead for more than twenty years. He has resigned from that position, friends.' 'Yes, but it isn't vacant—we're elected.'")[128] Nor does such a seemingly minor infraction slip beneath Warren and Brandeis's radar. "To publish of a modest and retiring individual that he suffers from an impediment in his speech or that he cannot spell correctly," they write, as example, "is an unwarranted, if not an unexampled, infringement of his rights." So the finale's scene of law restores two sets of identities: those of the changelings and that of Wilson himself.

In the former case, race is clearly intrinsic to identity's resolution, leading to a "white" man being sold away as a "black" slave. Perhaps less apparently, race also governs the clearing of Wilson's name. In his argument on behalf of Homer Plessy just a few years later, the lawyer and author Albion Tourgée made a claim strikingly resonant with Warren and Brandeis's innovative article.[129] Tourgée pleaded that by being removed from the train's whites-only coach, the light-skinned Plessy had been deprived of the reputation of being a white man—in other words, radically claiming that reputation as property, to which Plessy had rights. Whereas much early privacy case law staked out claims against unwarranted intrusion from prying eyes, protecting a private citizen's right to retreat from public life, and thus orienting itself around a figure not unlike that of "Pudd'nhead" Wilson, Tourgée's defense of Plessy came at the issue from the other direction. Arguing not for a right to privacy but for a right to publicity, Tourgée claimed that Plessy had property rights in his reputation, property rights that "essentially add up to a right to stake out a claim to a public persona," as literary and legal scholar Stephen Best notes.[130] Such a right wouldn't be worked out in the law until well into the twentieth century.

In the Supreme Court's majority opinion in *Plessy v. Ferguson*, Justice Henry Billings Brown disagreed with the defense, unable to see how Plessy had been wronged. "If he be a white man, and assigned to a colored coach, he may have his action for damages against the company for being deprived of his so-called 'property,'" Brown wrote. "Upon the other hand, if he be a colored man, and be so assigned, he has been deprived of no property, since he is not lawfully entitled to the reputation of being a white man."[131] Brown's reasoning borders on tautology, but the majority opinion is framed around two implicit assumptions. First, it depends on the unremarked privacy of whiteness: to be white in a white train car is to preserve a norm of imperceptibility. In 1896, on the heels of Warren and Brandeis's article, whiteness has no truck with a right to publicity. Indeed, that claim seems discursively silenced, as though Tourgée's argument could not, in fact, be *heard*. The property of whiteness included title to the enjoyment of privacy (not least a freedom from "enforced commingling"). Second, explaining that inaudibility, the opinion affirms the publicity of blackness. Perhaps the majority cannot assent to *white* reputation as property because of the articulation—still in force after 1865, and so unremarked—of property and *black* reputation. Black publicity names a vestige of chattel status, where the character of personhood (i.e., reputation) was put on and taken off precisely as the mantle of public accountability.

Implicitly, the court affirms exactly the inverse of Tourgée's argument: that blackness, rather than whiteness, includes the ambiguous "right" to a public persona. In this historical moment, though, such a conjugation of reputation and property could not be understood as a "right." That coupling could not be seen to fulfill or extend the logic of possessive individualism because it still inscribed the stamp of possession by another. Entitlement (if this is the correct word) to any conjunction of personhood, property, and value, or to its possible inheritance, still named the taint of chattel status and the degradation of blackness in the 1890s. One hears as an undertone in Brown's framework a strict equation of privacy and reputation-as-property. For the court, such "property" becomes visible only through its divestiture. One would be deprived of his "property" because he would be disallowed from enjoying the "properness" of his racial reputation in the privacy of the appropriate coach. The logic of separate-but-equal structures Brown's reasoning here, too. He assumes, for the sake of argument, that property inheres in both white and black racial reputations, and that Tourgée only argued one of the two possible sides of the case. Reputation-as-property becomes an abstract category, evacuated of history, bestowed upon and enjoyed by both races. This can only be accomplished by the court's willful disregard of the category of the slave who marks the point of collapse of property and personhood, the historical figure who embodies the history of their consolidation. Put differently, to reach its verdict on this matter, the court could not and did not address the issue of "pecuniary value" raised by Tourgée, which comprises that history.[132]

The color line effects an architecture that constitutes the privacy of white personhood through the production of black personhood as spectacle. We must not forget that the decision in *Plessy* comes down as it does precisely because segregation isn't considered an issue of *public* space but rather of *private* sentiment, of "natural affinities" in Brown's words. What the court also affirmed in *Plessy* was the pseudosovereign right of the conductor to assign the racial identity of passengers. A certain dubiousness is personified in the conductor in this role of policing the color line. This quality links him to Pudd'nhead Wilson, who unmasks racial imitators, and no less to the spectator at *Black America* who scrutinizes "real Negroes"—and to the viewer facing the trompe l'oeil figure of *Attention, Company!*, and to Frederick Douglass's chary Yankee audience. "Convicting the black man of imposture as a white gentleman, Wilson's miraculous revelation of Tom's identity restores the community's subverted aristocratic order and saves it from mongrelization by the monstrous double" of the mulatto, writes literary historian Eric J. Sundquist, "much as the overturning of Reconstruction and its accompanying civil rights legislation and antimiscegenation theory restored an antebellum racial hierarchy in the new dress of Jim Crow."[133] And thus Wilson himself is cleared of notoriety, permitted to resume an unremarked—a *private*—life. The entertainment of *Black America*, too, was meant to train its spectators in the discernment of racial authenticity. Even the show's managers weren't exempt; meal tickets were distributed to the cast "to prevent miscellaneous negroes from outside coming in and living on the management."[134] What we witness in each instance, to varying degrees, is the decoupling of race and biology toward a more "liberal" association of race and culture. But instead of race's deconstruction, each performs its reification. In some way, race is recognized as more mutable only to then be reaffixed. Each example reveals that policing the color line requires a white hermeneutics of suspicion. In the case of *Attention, Company!*, that requirement delves deeper and fabricates more than the superficial confusions of trompe l'oeil.

IN LATE JANUARY 1864, only a few months after it ran Gordon's image and story as "A Typical Negro," *Harper's Weekly* published a letter from a member of the National Freedmen's Relief Association named C. C. Leigh. Leigh's letter related the details of a trip—a tour, really—through New York and Philadelphia by a group of freed slaves. The company had come from New Orleans in their capacity as students because the Louisiana schools for the freed were in dire need of aid. One year before, the same month that the Emancipation Proclamation took effect, General Nathaniel Banks had established Louisiana's first free schools, and within a few months over fourteen hundred students had enrolled. They were being taught by twenty-three teachers.

Support through taxes and by the Union army filled in the ranks of teachers as more and more students began to attend, but more financial backing was needed. So the American Missionary Association (AMA) lent its assistance and its members, recruiting teachers and philanthropists. The AMA decided that its fundraising efforts would be made easier if abolitionists in the North could see the faces of the students they would be helping. So the AMA arranged this tour, with the help of the letter's author, Mr. Leigh, and the Freedmen's Relief Association.[135] The group's chaperones were two white men: one a colonel, and the other a teacher named Philip Bacon, who "established the first school in Louisiana for emancipated slaves," according to Leigh, "and these children were among his pupils." These formerly enslaved students were likely among the first legally educated blacks in the South. He closes his letter with the notice: "A large photograph of the whole group . . . has been taken, and *cartes de visite* of the separate figures. They are for sale at the rooms of the National Freedmen's Relief Association. . . . The profits to go to the support of the schools in Louisiana."[136]

Their lot as needy students in those photographs was not, however, what was meant to draw the attention either of *Harper's* readers or of Northern abolitionists. Accompanied by a full-page image that preceded the article, the letter ran under the same title "White and Colored Slaves." The emphasis fell on the three white children, supposed to seize the viewer's notice. Leigh describes them in his letter: "Rebecca Huger is eleven years old. . . . To all appearance she is perfectly white. Her complexion, hair, and features show not the slightest trace of negro blood"; "Charles Taylor is eight years old. His complexion is very fair, his hair light and silky"; and "Rosina Downs is not quite seven years old. She is a fair child, with blonde complexion and silky hair." Their images were meant as a shock that would incite the viewer's imagination. After the relentless expansion of slavery had been read in their faces (*even whites were enslaved!*), that implication took the shape of a threat (*even I could be enslaved!*). The pictures grounded an identification by viewers with these children in an apparently shared whiteness. These children then functioned mostly as empty ciphers that allowed viewers to assume their place, to imagine themselves or their families as slaves. And those faces were a riddle about how to see blackness; one was encouraged to scrutinize their countenances to identify its sign. The letter says that their appearances show "not the slightest trace of negro blood," even as the letter says that those appearances lie.[137]

Leigh's story continues, "These three children, to all appearance of unmixed white race, came to Philadelphia last December," where they lodged at

Emancipated Slaves, White and Colored from Harper's Weekly (30 January 1864).

a hotel with "their protector, Mr. Bacon.... Within a few hours, Mr. Bacon informed me, he was notified by the landlord that they must leave. The children, he said, had been slaves, and must therefore be colored persons, and he kept a hotel for white people."[138] Thirty years prior to *Plessy*, this episode in wartime Philadelphia is a reminder that segregation was no postwar Southern invention. Leigh's letter, but even more so the *carte-de-visite* made for the occasion, literalize the publication of blackness. "THESE CHILDREN," reads the caption beneath the image of Rebecca, Charles, and Rosina, "Were turned out of the St. Lawrence Hotel, Chestnut St., Philadelphia, on account of Color." The photograph isn't a commentary on the capaciousness of white identity (or the lack of it), but on the potentially elusive nature of blackness, an alarm about the spectral sign of slavery and its steady creep. The caption's slightly indignant tone would seem to distance it from the insistently neutral logic of colorblindness in *Plessy*. But both are lessons in what the scholar Robyn Wiegman calls "the visible epistemology of black skin," that economy of white privacy and black publicity.[139] These children's images figure the myth of blood, that greatest of American mystifications, whose legal inheritance here was property status and commodity life. On the basis of blood,

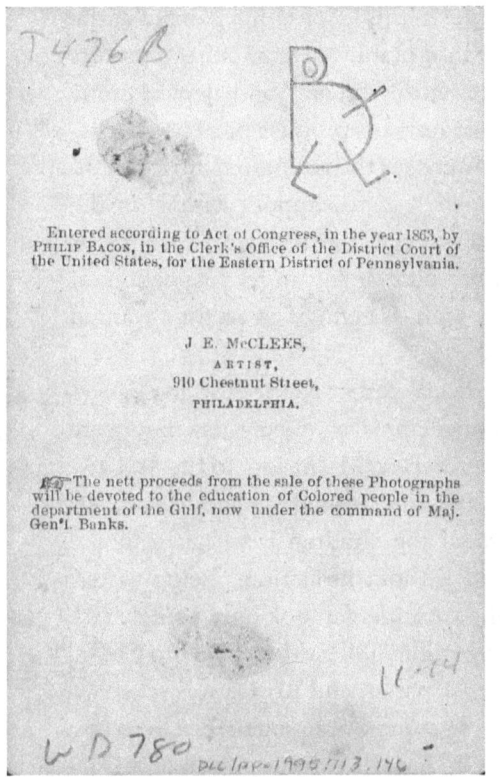

These Children, carte-de-visite (verso and recto) (Library of Congress, Washington, D.C.).

Hortense Spillers writes, "American Africanity was assigned to the axis of 'thingness,'" and for the person with blood so tainted, the law was bound to "recognize only his blackness, in which property is not self-possession or identity but a sign of the rights of others," as Sundquist notes.[140] Here, no less than in *Plessy*, the logic of segregation confirms not only that whites enjoy the property of *their* racial reputation but that they also enjoy a property right in blackness—in its meanings, its disposition, and its enjoyment. To inherit the taint of blood is, legally, to inherit the taint of slavery, its "thingness." Segregation reproduces this ideology of slave racial capitalism and, in the words of Martin Luther King Jr. "substitutes an 'I-it' relationship for an 'I-thou' relationship . . . and ends up relegating persons to the status of things."[141]

And what does any of this have to do with the painting of *Attention, Company!*? Perhaps one can see these circumstances reflected, however obliquely, in its composition. Behind its figure there churns a sea of letters, written, carved, printed, with not one legible word. One banner is askew, and the folded newsprint is vertical and miniscule. In this black child, painted at the close of Reconstruction, surrounded by inscrutable writings on torn posters and as graffiti, *Attention, Company!* dramatizes literacy and depicts some scene of education, though whether of education's promise or of its folly remains unclear. Its wild lettering somehow evokes the mission of those photographs of freed students, as *cartes-de-visite* sold to support schools in the South. Perhaps we also see the signs of publicity: in the figure's frontality, which echoes that of the freed children—on display, up for inspection, at "attention," in the boy's newspaper hat, with its echo of an ad for a wanted fugitive.

And then there is William Harnett's own apparent connection to this history. When these children came to Philadelphia on their tour, they were taken, according to the letter, "by their protector, Mr. Bacon, to the St. Lawrence Hotel on Chestnut Street," where they were turned out because of their race. "From this hospitable establishment the children were taken to the 'Continental,' where they were received without hesitation," Leigh writes. Their walk from the St. Lawrence to the Continental took only a single city block. It took them past the photography studio of J. E. McLees at 910 Chestnut Street where the portrait of Rebecca, Charles, and Rosina was taken.[142] For the few days they were in town, staying at the Continental, they lived just around the corner from a widow named Hannah Harnett, listed at 7 Garwood Place.[143] It's nearly impossible to imagine that her son William—who was then working as an engraver but would later lose his job to a machine, and who would go on to become a painter whose life's work as an artist shows a deep and contentious engagement with photography—could be unfamiliar with the nearby studio of J. E. McLees. He might well have bought one of these *cartes-de-visite* or seen the children themselves passing by on his block. It's also hard to imagine that he would not have known about the large procession of black volunteers who filed up Chestnut Street six months earlier in June 1863. General Robert E. Lee had threatened to invade the city, but white Philadelphians hesitated to take up arms. They also refused to recruit and arm black soldiers, and a parade formed in protest. According to a local diarist: "several hundred colored men in procession march[ed] up Sixth to Chestnut, and up Chestnut Street. They were not uniformed nor armed, but were a good looking body of men. They had a drum and fife, and [were] carrying inspiring banners."[144] They were headed, he wrote, to drill at a camp of black troops on the city's outskirts. And don't we want to see in a painting with the title *Attention, Company!* some record of these wanderings along Chestnut Street, of black soldiers, of freed children, whom William Harnett might have seen entering the Continental Hotel in 1863?[145]

But, as I said before, Harnett concerns me far less than does the figure in his painting. What can we say about him? The painting does not intend to be about *this* child, who has remained nameless. Its composition narrates a contradiction of subject and object, and suggests its consequences. It is not merely that his name has been lost; it has been scrubbed away as immaterial. The figure is a fetish—a precipitate of commodity logic and spectacle—such that his actual biography must transmute into some fantasized material history. A real boy becomes a mock artifact.

But a name *has* been erased. This child is Isaac White. He accompanied the three whiter children on the tour, mostly it seems as a foil *for* their whiteness.[146] His photographic image is meant only as a sign that points to the horrors of "white slavery." *His* story of enslavement is a commonplace. To be white and unfree is the exception that startles; black unfreedom merely establishes the rule. And so Isaac's slight existence in the historical record comes to us as its own eclipse. Leigh's letter gives his biography in two sentences: "Isaac White is a black boy of eight years; but none the less intelligent than his white companions. He has been in school about seven months, and I venture to say that not one boy in fifty would have made as much improvement in that space of time." Harnett undoubtedly painted from Isaac White's *carte-de-visite*. But once finished, in 1878, the painting forgot its context, its subjects, its names. These were willfully misplaced. The work of this painting is the work of abstraction. To suggest otherwise, to suggest that these details were merely lost over time ignores how this painting stages what might as well be called the violence of allegory. As in slavery, it abstracts the human as an object of accumulating value. Scrawled along one preserved portrait of Isaac White and Rosina Downs, a handwritten caption reads, "Proceeds for benefit of colored people in the Department of the Gulf Louisiana," and "1863 Relic of the Civil War."[147]

What begins here under the auspices of liberal sympathy colludes with the logic of slavery. The objectives of formal abolition—an end to the selling and owning of black bodies—presages the accumulation of capital through the selling and owning of images of black bodies, as "relics," as artifacts, as spectacle. These photographs propose that the black image be made into a repository of value that the black body will no longer be. This might be conceived as a shift in the slave's form of value from flesh to skin after 1865, which was kith and kin of that concurrent shift in political economy, tied to contractualism

Isaac and Rosa, Emancipated Slave Children, carte-de-visite (Library of Congress, Washington, D.C.).

Isaac & Rosa, Slave Children from New Orleans.
Photographed by Kimball, 477 Broadway, N. Y.
Ent'd accord'g to act of Congress in the year 1863, by Geo. H. Hanks, in the Clerk's Office of the U.S for the So. Dist. of N. Y.

and finance, from the slave's body to the freed's person that the previous chapter termed "the mortgage of freedom." In 1859, Oliver Wendell Holmes wrote about photography using this metaphor of skin, as though the camera peeled a membrane from the world to make its images:

> There is only one Coliseum or Pantheon; but how many millions of potential negatives have they shed—representatives of billions of pictures—since they were erected! Matter in large masses must always be fixed and dear; form is cheap and transportable. We have got the fruit of creation

now, and need not trouble ourselves with the core. Every conceivable object of Nature and Art will soon scale off its surface for us. Men will hunt all curious, beautiful, grand objects, as they hunt the cattle in South America, for their skins, and leave the carcasses as of little worth.[148]

Not black flesh but black skin—as image, as voice, as personality—designates one afterlife of slavery; matter yields to form.[149] The barred slave market is reconstituted around another traffic in blackness, a kind of black market. Impressed in black skin are notions of authenticity and a lure to desire, which ground white subjectivity, and continually redound to it.

This painting diagrams the economy of the fetish: the givenness of the material is eclipsed so as to produce the truth of an illusion—a portrait into a still life, a living boy into a nostalgic relic. The real Isaac White into the "real" figure of trompe l'oeil. Skin into paint. Skin as representation. All these declensions of the indexical are not without consequence. And once again what comes into view are characters such as Aunt Jemima or Uncle Ben or the Gold Dust Twins, those public faces of commodities who helped forge a national market while also creating a culture of segregation. As white marketers portrayed such figures as "real" and "authentic," blackness became a trusted brand. And white consumer desire for it and stoked by it would often turn back violently, through dismemberment and literal commodification as souvenirs, onto the black body itself in spectacle lynchings.[150] Through an ongoing enmeshment of personhood and property, slave racial capitalism calibrates its mode of production and augments its strategy of accumulation. The circulation of "blood" remains layered with the circulation of pecuniary value. Its calamity moves through time, as racial inheritance, and through space, as commodity. Perhaps, too, the painting remarks enigmatically on this diffusion, on the expanding circuits of the slave as a form of value. Behind its figure, once named Isaac White, is pasted a long white poster, artfully torn, so that one can hardly decipher its message. The banner reads "Grand Excursion."[151]

CHAPTER THREE

Cowboys and Slaves

Dreams are merely novels, they are made with every sort of literary trick; a word stands for a year, if it is the right word, equally with the reader and the dreamer.
—Robert Louis Stevenson, letter to Owen Wister

The real impulse of the bulk of the American people toward their former slave is lethal: if he cannot be used, he should be made to disappear.
—James Baldwin

About halfway into Owen Wister's *The Virginian*, the novel long regarded as the first Western, the protagonist breaks into a minstrel song apropos of nothing. "Dar is a big Car'lina nigger / About de size of dis chile or p'raps a little bigger, / By de name of Jim Crow [. . .] Dat what de white folks call him. / If ever I sees him I 'tends for to maul him."[1] It's a bizarre moment, if not a surprising one. A white man entertaining others through antiblackness—that's certainly minstrelsy's calling card, and a keystone of American culture. But it is a moment strange for its incongruity. It appears without context in a book that otherwise barely acknowledges blackness, a book that will define a genre that likewise barely acknowledges any black presence in the American West. It's all lily-white cowboys and vanishing Indians out there on the mythical frontier of the Western. And of course, the whole matter might just be left at that, a fleeting and not particularly meaningful recurrence of minstrelsy's tropes. Although one hesitates to set it aside so quickly, recollecting that this racist ditty is being sung by a character named "the Virginian." That it's a *Southerner*, "his head tilted at an absurd angle upward at the sky," belting this tune in this place casts the scene in a changed light, makes it signify differently somehow.

By verse's end, the song reveals itself to be about reputation: "Jim Crow" will be mauled "Just to let de white folks see / Such an animos as he / Can't walk around the streets and scandalize me." Race, violence, reputation—the song names clear and recognizable tropes for the Western. (Just recall the plot of John Ford's *The Searchers*.) But here, those tropes remain inchoate. In this moment of the genre's emergence, its rules haven't yet been codified, its tropes haven't yet crystallized. Some adulterating residues remain visible in these lyrics and this novel that will become more submerged in later

Westerns—the hero's Southernness and, relatedly though less prominently, a "signing Africanist presence," as Toni Morrison puts it.[2] These residues bear witness to historical functions of the Western genre that have gone unexamined. With respect to this genre's origins, the West is not in the West. *The Virginian*'s title, and the titular character, and thus the novel itself, are recruiting their energies from a grid of associations tied to "Southern" slavery, and in fact, antiblackness is exceptional in its formal importance for *The Virginian*. Beyond a reinterpretation of Wister's novel, or even a new understanding of the genre it founds, what is brought into focus in the following pages is the hidden seam that connects the American frontier and American slavery, and in the ongoing history of American imperialism, the white sovereignty that is generated through that coupling.

Slavery and its economy would seem to have no place in the Western, which locates itself beyond slavery in a land and a time untouched by it and untainted by blackness. After all, what is the frontier of the Western if not the white populist dream of Free Soil, viewed with the hindsight of Union victory? In this West, North and South are reconciled, and the Civil War, regarded as a gratuitous conflict of brother against brother, is buried. But the absence of blackness in the West is a fiction. Up to one in four cowboys was black, according to some historians' estimates, and beginning in the late 1870s, black Exodusters surged westward to escape the malevolence of Southern whites.[3] There was, too, a *South*western frontier in the decades before the Civil War that was cleared by and for slave labor to create an empire of cotton, a history that has been almost entirely repressed in the national consciousness. Wister himself erased the black cowboys from one of his early Western stories, "Pilgrim on the Gila," after he had recorded them in an episode in his journal on which that story was based.[4] This is all to say that the whiteness of the fictional West is a white*washing*. This imagined frontier grounds a fantasy of white autonomy, wherein that material ground of land, wealth, and the property of whiteness itself will be passed down from father to son through the generations. The final sentence of *The Virginian* suggests as much, establishing the family's fortunes (the hero now "able to give his wife all and more than she asked or desired") and introducing the Southerner's "eldest boy" who has been given his father's prized horse, Monte (293).

The Western projects a fantasy of law and order across space (sovereignty, settlement) and across time (historical progress, patrilineal inheritance). It battles chaos and anomie at every turn. As a depiction of the frontier in North America, it also draws on a long tradition of other representations, other histories, which disclose an interface between the figures we define as "West" and "South"—a needful association between the figure of the white settler and the black slave too, then, which we have consigned to those spaces. By the mid-twentieth century and after, one can barely glimpse that connection— say, in Ethan Edwards's faded gray trousers in *The Searchers*, a man who still keeps his oath of allegiance to the Confederacy and declares, "I don't believe in surrenders," or in the absurd genre mash-up of Quentin Tarantino's *Django Unchained*. But earlier, that link had been less obscure.

In 1651, for example, when Thomas Hobbes wrote the final words of *Leviathan*, the magnum opus of English political philosophy. There, Hobbes transmutes the colonial expropriation of land into the distribution of a legal order. The genesis of property *is* the genesis of sovereignty. In *Leviathan*, this process has its proper verb: "to plant," or nominalized, "plantation." And it has a location: Virginia is the laboratory where one *sees* the alchemy of sovereignty taking place; the plantation, which Hobbes calls the child of the commonwealth, taking possession of the voided land along its frontier.[5] This "planting" amounts to the original performance of law itself, the birth of history; the plantation is a perceptible demonstration of the spatial and temporal incursion of England's legal order into wilderness.[6] Such philosophical speculation was indexed to another kind of speculation for Hobbes, who was himself a shareholder in the Virginia Company, who attended thirty-seven of the company's meetings in two years and held title to a grant of Virginia land. In *Leviathan*'s political philosophy, the space-time of law and history articulates the space-time of imperialist speculation.

Or much later, in 1821, the link was apparent when Henry Meigs, a New York congressman, proposed a motion in the House of Representatives to set aside a fund of "five hundred millions acres of public lands west of the Mississippi," which would be surveyed into 640-acre sections and 160-acre quarter sections, with every other quarter section to then be sold for "certificates of the value of slaves"—all this as a scheme for "gradual emancipation." By this plan, slaveholders would voluntarily exchange captive black bodies for free western lands. The other half of that land fund would be sold at large, and the proceeds would subsidize the removal of the emancipated from the United States, colonizing them in Africa. (Because to be free of slavery meant to be free of blackness.) Meigs's scheme had the sheen of a Jeffersonian fantasia, the frontier as an "empire for liberty." Scratching the surface revealed, within this fantasy, the overmastering logic of finance capital, wherein territory becomes property and a human life becomes a slave. Everything abstracted, made measurable, fungible, saleable at a distance, and, ultimately, equivalent: lands = slaves.[7] That equation was prescient, since the surveying work that turned Western territory into acred parcels begat a feverish market in land speculation, which then begat dreams of cotton's white gold, which then begat feverish speculation in slaves, which then begat the brutal market in the million bodies abducted through the "domestic slave trade."

Or take the summer of 1864, when a sixteen-year-old Missouri boy named Jesse James rode out to join a party of Confederate guerrillas whose leader threatened the state's Unionists: "I will hunt you down like wolves and murder you. You cannot escape"—which they did. James came from a family of recalcitrant slaveholders, on whose farm emancipation never seemed to arrive, and as a young man after the Civil War, as a vigilante bent on thwarting Reconstruction, he continued such raids and murder sprees. He was an outlaw who studied money's ebb and flow between metropolitan New York and the farmlands of the South and West, and he knew that if you hopped a train in Iowa, blew a safe, and severed the artery of frontier accumulation, you'd be a rich man. In 1873, now making national headlines with his daring robberies and already becoming an icon and folk hero of the frontier West, Jesse James held up one of these trains while "masked in full Ku-Klux style."[8] Through him, we get close to the onset of the amnesia that obscures the link connecting the frontier "West" to the plantation "South."

Of a piece with these predecessors, the genre of the Western is birthed in a novel fixated on market speculation. Distinct from the long tradition that aligned the frontier with agrarian virtue (from Crèvecœur to Jefferson to the Free Soilers to Turner), *The Virginian* codifies the frontier as an economy of risk, a culture of finance. Its hero is not a farmer but a cowboy—a manager. One in charge of laborers and commodities, he produces nothing and only safeguards expropriated values, instituting and preserving capitalist rule and order. In an act exemplifying his dogmatic attachment to economic order, the protagonist lynches his best friend Steve for the injudicious decision of "putting his iron on another man's calf" (232). As a novel, *The Virginian* is preoccupied with the prospect of economic *disorder*, intent on getting the better of risk and speculation amid boom and bust markets. Just after the text names the horse "Monte," after the eponymous card game, we learn that "steers had 'jumped to seventy-five' . . . a great and prosperous leap in their value" and locals "had been jumping over the moon for some weeks, all on account of steers." The novel is set in the midst of a bonanza in cattle, where steers are live commodities that function as a form of currency. In back of all this, behind this new frontier façade of cowboy-lawmen and ranches, there subsists the same logic of accumulation and fungibility tied to plantation slavery that animated the imaginations of Thomas Hobbes, Henry Meigs, and Jesse James.

THE WESTERN REITERATES problems central to the genre of the novel itself. The novel emerged from eighteenth-century market culture and served a pedagogical function. It imparted a sentimental education that offset the market's cold acquisitive logic, and it instructed readers to discern the many types of people they might encounter in cities—places increasingly populated by rootless strangers knit together by commercial transactions.[9] The novel offered readers a heuristic for comprehending an anonymous market society. Itself preoccupied with the problems of an urban society that's defined by financial markets, the Western takes shape against the new historical backdrop of corporate capitalism.[10] (Take, as a ready example, the genre's affiliation with the "West cure"—the masculine version of the popular "rest cure"—which was prescribed to all those well-off pencil-pushing young men enervated by office jobs, sent packing to Wyoming for the summer. One young man so diagnosed and treated was Owen Wister.) In his opening "Note to the Reader," Wister writes that *The Virginian* is a "historical novel," a "colonial romance." Just as good-versus-evil functions in the historical romance, what the Western's hero-and-villain binary teaches readers is that someone who might otherwise be a peer must also be realized as a rival—a threat to professional advancement, financial security, and personal autonomy.[11] As it encodes the market relations specific to corporate capitalism, the Western construes one's fellows as one's competitors in a zero-sum turf war where personal independence is conflated with territorial independence, where free rule over oneself becomes confused with the freedom of self-rule. When the rival threatens the hero's good standing in the community, he also threatens the rule of law and the practice of government in a given territory. (This becomes most clear when the Western hero is the literal embodiment of sovereignty, a lawman.) These generic tropes are a means of rendering concrete, abstract competition for status and authority, one specific to the urban milieu of management: the struggle for position within the upper echelons of a growing executive class.[12] If the Western is a romance, it is a romance of political economy.

In any contest with such a rival, one's prospects are put on the line, whether in the form of one's livelihood or of one's life. Think of the gambling table and the duel, central tropes that also shape *The Virginian*. In the Western's games of chance—say, poker or Monte—players are compelled to be "all in," their life's fortunes put at stake. The only limit to the stakes in these games is life itself, as one might be made rich or laid waste, cut down by chance or gunfire. And what solicits such violence is not loss but insult. In the frontier's space of migrant labor and market speculation, as a stranger among strangers in a land of get-rich-quick schemes, one must trade on one's personality, on how one appears to others. The genre's scenes of gambling are just that: scenes, miniature performances of the self in the theater of public opinion. In this economy of credit, as in others, reputation is on the line, but here, to impute cheating is to court murder. In the same vein, the genre's duels are battles of prestige and of position, undertaken by two ostensible equals. That is to say, as moments when fate and the future are suddenly reckoned, those duels are also about personality and speculation. So it is worth noting that *The Virginian*'s introduction of its hero and of his rival, Trampas, occurs while they sit gambling on a game of cards. Trampas first addresses him, "Your bet, you son-of-a—." The Virginian responds by drawing his pistol, saying, "When you call me that, *smile*." Then the reader is told, "it seemed as if somewhere the bell of death was ringing." The situation de-escalates, having foreshadowed their coming duels, but the scene establishes the trope of the high-stakes gambling match, both for this novel and for the larger genre. The scene comprises a setting of speculation, an insult to personality, and a mortal rivalry.

And what do Jim Crow and blackness have to do with these issues of speculation, personality, and rivalry in the Western? Another novel published in the same year as *The Virginian* and also set in the American West offers some clarity. Although Pauline Hopkins's *Winona: A Tale of Negro Life in the South and Southwest* is set in the 1850s, decades earlier than *The Virginian*, she also uses the historical situation of the American West to explore racial hierarchy and slavery's legacies in her contemporary moment. The novel centers on the story of Judah and Winona, whose enslaved mothers escaped via the Underground Railroad. Raised free by a Native American father near Buffalo, New York, Judah and Winona are kidnapped by Missouri slave-catchers, after which they join the battles in Bleeding Kansas, alongside Free State militiamen and "Old John Brown himself."[13] Like *The Virginian*, a meditation on social equality in 1902 ("But is there such a thing as social equality? Who is my social equal?"), *Winona* is organized as a territorial rivalry between slavery and freedom, "a terrible struggle between the two great forces—Right and Wrong" (377, 412). At the narrative's end, Judah and Winona emigrate to England, which is aligned not with white racial purity (as it was for Wister) but with abolitionism and the black liberation struggle. There, "American caste prejudice could not touch them in their home beyond the sea" (435). For Hopkins, slavery still impinges on her present through the injuries of blackness, and the fate of freedom still hangs in the balance. Through *Winona*, "Hopkins explicitly reminds her readers that, as all of her protagonists' suffering under slavery parallels that which African Americans currently experience under Jim Crow, that system represents a fundamental affront to a nation committed to [an] ideal of progress," in one scholar's words.[14] Hazel Carby is even more pointed: "*Winona* is transparently a call for organized political resistance against contemporary persecution displaced to a fictional history"—and displaced to a fictionalized geography.[15] What *Winona* reveals, in relation to *The Virginian*, is that repressed connection between the West and the South.[16] Hopkins's "melodramatic adventure shows how intimately the western movement was intertwined with North-South relations, especially in terms of the extension of slavery," literary scholar Christine Bold writes, and it is precisely this dynamic that the era's more conventional Western "disguises in its insistence on the East-West axis as the foundation of the nation." As Bold notes, in *Winona*, "the action insistently moves back and forth between frontier and plantation, and the characters' heritage is a mixture of both regions."[17]

A mixture that also holds true for the character of the Virginian, lest we forget his eponym—and true, too, for Wister himself. Wister's grandfather was Pierce Butler, scion of one of the largest slaveholding families in the United States and a descendant of the U.S. senator from South Carolina who drafted the Constitution's fugitive slave clause.[18] Butler inherited the family's plantations on the Georgia Sea Islands, and he also owned a palatial residence outside of his birthplace, Philadelphia. Wister spent much of his childhood at this Pennsylvania estate, Butler Place, which was reminiscent of a Southern plantation. It boasted three hundred manicured acres of lawns and gardens as well as a driveway lined with oleander, lemon, and citron trees brought from Georgia by Butler's wife and Wister's grandmother, the famed actor Fanny Kemble.[19]

In this family, the conflict of the Civil War was quite literally and locally domestic. Kemble and Butler divorced in 1849, in no small part because Kemble despised his slaveownership. She had written *Journal of a Residence on a Georgian Plantation in 1838–1839*, which was published in 1863 and received by abolitionists as an excoriation of plantation slavery. One of their daughters, Sarah, would adopt her mother's stance on abolition and would give birth to Owen Wister. The other, Frances, would venerate her father and, after the war's end and his death, would devote herself to reviving the family's plantation on

Butler Island. Frances published her Southern apologia *Ten Years on a Georgia Plantation since the War* in 1883 as a rejoinder to her mother's *Journal*. And that apologia's frontispiece happens to be a poem titled "Brothers Again"—a bit of nationalist treacle, white fraternal heroes clasping hands across the sectional divide—by one "O. W." In fact, her young nephew "O. W." made a number of visits to his Aunt Fan's Georgia plantation. In the family's civil war, Wister clearly sympathized with the sentiments of its Southern half. ("I was brought up to revere my grandfather.")[20] The house that he and his wife bought in the South would be the place where he finished *The Virginian*, and the note "To the Reader" that prefaces the novel bears the dateline "Charleston, S.C., March 31st, 1902."

Wister wrote *The Virginian* during a watershed moment in American political economy. As he notes in the novel's preface, "A transition has followed the horseman of the plains; a shapeless state.... I shall not dwell upon it here." The project of settler colonialism that had subdued the Western lands of North America and brought them under the sovereign rule of the United States had culminated, and the great wealth generated by that project was being aggregated in ever-larger corporations—as in the case of the railroads, which enabled the continental commerce of raw materials and manufactured goods. Finance capital assumed an outsize place in the nation's economy, the elusive work of speculation as legitimate a path to profits as the manual labor of production. Alongside such changes came the last of the American Indian Wars and the end of formal slavery, as well as the dwindling dream of cheap and profitable lands where white men presumed to fix their own destinies. The "incorporation of America" was well underway, as Alan Trachtenberg termed it. Within the context of corporate organizations and industrialization, white men found themselves being pulled into bureaucratic structures and managed under someone else's thumb. The naked domination and expropriation enacted by Indian removal campaigns and by the slave plantation no longer offered these men the occasion to seal their identities in blood and sweat exacted from Natives and blacks. The ground that had so long supported their fantasies of autarky and supremacy was now shifting beneath their feet. Wister points out in his introduction that the cowboy had vanished so recently and so quickly that he had to change his novel's verb tenses—"Time has flowed faster than my ink." Nevertheless, *The Virginian* is far more than just an epitaph for the "closed" frontier. By the end of his "Note to the Reader," one gets the sense that Wister is writing feverishly to fill up the space of that "transition."[21] He is scripting a character from the past for the present historical conditions and what the novel contains are Wister's stage directions for the next act.

FOR CONTEMPORARY READERS, there is no figure more closely aligned with the Western than the cowboy. This is one of the genre's codes set in place by Wister's text.[22] But from one angle, the cowboy is an incongruous set piece. As noted above, he represents a sharp departure from the agrarian tradition usually associated with the frontier. The cowboy is a nomad, not a settler. If the farmer is a producer, then the cowboy is a manager and a broker, a middleman. He tends another's property and delivers it to the market.

Wister's Virginian finds his place in a genealogy of the Western hero that begins with James Fenimore Cooper's Natty Bumppo, the military aristocrat who polices the raced borders of civilization and savagery. Like Natty Bumppo, the Virginian is a lawkeeper who is willing to resort to violence. But whereas Natty Bumppo represents "a one-man *precapitalist* utopia," as frontier historian Richard Slotkin puts it, in which the "great promise of the Frontier is that of absolute escape from one's competitors and rivals," the Virginian rewrites Bumppo for the turn of twentieth-century America.[23] The Virginian is instead a one-man *capitalist* utopia in which the great promise of the frontier becomes the *vanquishing* of his competitors and rivals.

Competition and rivalry in *The Virginian*, despite the Western setting, isn't necessarily over land. As a zone of territorial expansion by a new population, contested or uncontested, the frontier—the unvarying backdrop for the Western, the setting for its cowboy stories—has come almost solely to denote land. But this is a category error. If the frontier is, in part, the violent incursion of a new spatial order, where land changes its status as territory, the frontier is just as much a dynamic of market speculation. In the past, from the Virginia Company's beginnings to the mid-nineteenth century, the American market was based on stolen land, the great fortune-making engine for the colonization of the Americas. The agrarian frontier of land diminishes in importance in the second half of the nineteenth century as the industrializing American economy comes to depend increasingly on trade and capital accumulation. This process is exemplified in the *bonanza*, or speculative bubble. "Beginning with the California Gold Rush of 1849, the 'bonanza' became the characteristic theme of each new frontier enthusiasm," Slotkin writes. "Where agrarian profit depends on the steady rise of population and land values, bonanza profits derive from the opportunity to acquire or produce at low cost some commodity that has a high commercial value."[24] Gold, silver, cotton, wheat, oil—all were bonanzas in the West from 1849 until the early twentieth century. As, of course, were cattle. The beef bonanza was reaching its peak when Owen Wister first stepped from the train into Wyoming in 1885, a territory where cows outnumbered humans 17 to 1.[25] *The Virginian* occupies a moment when the frontier was becoming uncoupled from any actual territory on the North American continent. This was the wake of Frederick Jackson Turner's thesis, whose central claim was that by 1890 the frontier no longer referred to a geographical place.[26] It had become instead a space in the white American imagination (as it had always been).[27] But as much as in myth, that imaginative frontier once again found its creative outlets in the market.

Wister wrote and published *The Virginian* during a moment marked by the aggrandizement of the corporation and the ascendancy of consumerism. For much of the nineteenth century, owing to the importance of both agriculture and industry, producers stood at the center of the political economic system. In the white republican tradition of the United States, wages had long been conceived to be one's rightful dividend for actually productive labor. It was the "real" value produced by one's labors that validated one's consumption. Under this view, revived by populists in the late nineteenth century, capitalists, speculators, bankers, managers, and middlemen were *not* genuine producers. Rather, they were just siphons of productive labor, vampires feasting on the lifeblood of farmers and skilled laborers who created value. These populists were responding to rapidly changing and deleterious circumstances. Agriculture's share of the national economy was declining and so was the number of farmers. Mechanization was leading to the deskilling of labor. Capitalists began to argue that their enormous outlays on fixed capital magnified their economic importance (their vital role as "job creators," in contemporary parlance). At the same time, greater efficiency had resulted in a perceived problem of overproduction, and prominent intellectuals began to place an emphasis on new markets and new consumers. Scholars such as Thorstein Veblen and Simon Patten were reconceptualizing consumption as central to the national economy, not as parasitic but as generative.[28] Taking shape in the 1870s in Europe, economic theories of marginalism reconceived the relations of production to the benefit of capitalists, largely by redefining value.[29] In marginalist theories, which took root in America in the 1890s, the best measure of value wasn't the cost of labor production but the amount of consumer satisfaction. This utility theory of value didn't just apply to consumer products, according to the American marginalist economist John Bates Clark, "but also to such 'commodities' as the physical labor of the working class and the mental labor of capitalists," writes historian Kathleen

Donohue. "In Clark's view capitalists received so much not because they expropriated the labor of the working class but because their contribution to the production process was worth so much."[30]

These changing ideas were attended by the rise of the "trust movement"—large-scale corporate enterprises that integrated separate industries and consolidated competing firms. From 1898 to 1902, an avalanche of corporate consolidation swept up between "one-fourth and one-third of the nation's entire manufacturing plant," which "culminated twenty-five years of intense intercapitalist as well as class conflict," the historian Jeffrey Sklansky writes. Out of this cascade, there "arose a new economic order" dominated by the large business corporation, which was now "owned by absentee shareholders, managed by a hierarchical bureaucracy, [and] producing a diverse and integrated array of goods and services for a national and international market."[31] Capitalists became legitimate producers, according to marginalist theories, just as farmers and skilled workers were producers under the dispensation of republicanism. These dramatic changes also catalyzed a cultural revolution in the conception of white selfhood. The paradigm of the freeholder and the proprietor—the framework of the white settler—was on the wane.

This political economic context begins to explain why *The Virginian*—that canonical first modern Western—resembles nothing so much as a bildungsroman of management. The novel charts the ascendance of its protagonist from sly cowhand to corporate titan, ending with the Virginian being promoted to partner in the firm. That is to say, the hero triumphs not via independence on a staked claim, but by cannily maneuvering within a business structure. And the parting shot of the protagonist, who has climbed still higher on the corporate ladder, shows him as "an important man, with a strong grip on many various enterprises" (293). He is a monopolist, a miniature robber baron with a "strong grip" that calls to mind the hand of J. P. Morgan gripping his armrest-cum-dagger in Edward Steichen's famous portrait of him—a man whose portrait Wister admired while in Wyoming.[32]

TURN-OF-THE-CENTURY political economic concerns sit at the heart of *The Virginian*, both figuratively and literally, the focus of a linked set of stories that comprise the novel's center. The climax of those central chapters is a joke. Part of a lying contest, this joke represents the most important duel in *The Virginian*, one that does not rely on guns, but on wits. Because this Western is preoccupied with control rather than force, violence is scarce.[33] Indeed, the novel's final showdown takes place in a single sentence. But the joke and its setup are spread over four of the novel's middle chapters, grouped in three acts and one intermission as "The Game and the Nation." The joke confirms the Virginian's prowess as a manager and a businessman. But it also roots his success in the durability of slave racial capitalism—the joke being a tall tale about the plantation South—a fact that has so far gone unnoticed.[34]

The Virginian's boss, Judge Henry, has appointed him the foreman of a crew of cowboys for a trip by train to deliver a herd of cattle to Chicago's livestock markets and, while there, to barter with the railroad for lower transportation rates from Wyoming in the future. Once he has completed the job, he is to bring all the judge's employees safely back to the ranch. Among his subordinates is the villain Trampas, who bridles against the Virginian's authority during the trip. During their return, Trampas convinces a number of men that they should mutiny and defect to a town named Rawhide where gold has been discovered. Feeling smug, Trampas gets the better of the Virginian with a tall tale of his own. He manages to pull the wool over the Virginian's eyes with a bogus vignette, and the Virginian is made to look the fool in front of his subordinates. "I'd thought yu'd be afeared to try it on me," he tells Trampas, and soon sets off on a joke that will outwit his rival (106).

An impressive display of the Virginian's managerial abilities, his joke wouldn't seem to have anything to do with the slave plantation. But, as Sigmund Freud would argue a few years later in *The Joke and Its Relation to the Unconscious* (1905), the logic of the joke, like the dream, isn't literal. When their train is stopped, behind at least four others, and Trampas begins rousing the men for an exit, the Virginian sees an opportunity both for profit and for revenge. Passengers from the other trains have spilled out along the tracks, and they are starving after being stranded for four days. The Crow have been selling the passengers food at inflated prices, and a bystander tells the Virginian: "Them Eastern passengers has just been robbed. I wisht I had somethin' to sell!" The Virginian replies: "But all you folks has forgot one source of revenue that yu' have right close by, mighty handy. If you have got a gunny sack, I'll show you how to make some money" (108). Recalling a weird tidbit he's learned about the delectability of frogs' legs in New York City, he capitalizes on the knowledge. They're going to be supper for everyone he declares, to the bewilderment and consternation of all.

It is the Virginian's yarn about the origin of frogs' legs in American cuisine that constitutes the joke. As Trampas's men are tempted by a gold rush (a bonanza), and while surrounded by and en route to cattle country (a bonanza), the Virginian embarks on an unlikely firsthand story about another bonanza, in *frogs*. As the travelers turn up and open their pocketbooks, they're astounded that the Virginian could enter a situation and so quickly size it up to advantage where others floundered. "'That's right easy explained,' said the Virginian. 'I've been where there was big money in frawgs, and they 'ain't been. They're all cattle hyeh. Talk cattle, think cattle, and they're bankrupt in consequence. Fallen through.'" Not so long ago in Tulare, California, there was quite a market in frogs, and the Virginian tells his audience—with an eye toward Trampas—the spot they're standing on in Montana is "'just waitin' to be a frawg ranch.'" They would have a monopoly in the market; there would be no competition, given all the cattle. "'And you folks would be sellin' something instead o' nothin'" (111). During the Tulare frog bonanza, he tells them, "'there was millions'" of frogs in the county, and "'the money rolled in!'" As the Virginian lends embellishments to the story, his audience (now all men) "edged close, drawn by a common tie" (114). But Trampas remains aloof. The Virginian continues spinning his yarn:

> There was a man named Saynt Augustine got run out of Domingo, which is a Dago island. He come to Philadelphia, an' he was dead broke. But Saynt Augustine was a live man, an' he saw Philadelphia was full o' Quakers that dressed plain an' eat humdrum. So he started cookin' Domingo way for 'em, an' they caught right a hold. Terrapin, he gave 'em, an' croakeets, an' he'd use forty chickens to make a broth he called consommay. An' he got rich, and Philadelphia got well known, an' Delmonico [the originator of frogs' legs] in New York he got jealous. He was the cook that had the say-so in New York. (115)

Augustine and Delmonico embark on a furious bidding war, driving up the price of frogs. They become infuriated with each other, and each heads to Tulare, California, vowing to vanquish the other and gain control of the California market. Delmonico strikes out on a train from New York, and the "very same day Saynt Augustine he tears out of Philadelphia. He travelled by the way o' Washington, an' out he comes a-fannin' an' a-foggin' over the Southern Pacific" (115). When they arrive at the same time (indeed, on the same train, the two having linked up in Mojave), they "'started in to screechin' what they'd give for the monopoly'" (116). But the men of Tulare begin (defensively?) firing at them. Augustine and Delmonico flee the ranch

> "and soon as they got to a safe distance they swore eternal friendship, in their excitable foreign way. And they went home over the Union Pacific, sharing the same stateroom. Their revenge killed frawgs. The disease —"
> "How killed frogs?" demanded Trampas.

"Just killed 'em. Delmonico and Saynt Augustine wiped frawgs off the slate of fashion. Not a banker in Fifth Avenue'll touch one now if another banker's around watchin' him. And if ever yu' see a man that hides his feet an' won't take off his socks in company, he has worked in them Tulare swamps an' got the disease. Catch him wadin', and yu'll find he's web-footed. Frawgs are dead, Trampas, and so are you." (116)

And so the Virginian claims victory. Trampas is his dupe. "'Rise up, liars, and salute your king!'" yells the Virginian's compatriot, and he finds himself accepting hugs and shaking hands with his audience (116).

This is a parable of the Civil War and the war's legacy seen through the distorting lens of the joke. Augustine is a French expatriate who "got run out" of the Spanish (i.e., "Dago") island of Domingo. That is, he was expelled from Santo Domingo/Saint-Domingue, the island long divided between French and Spanish colonial powers—divided, that is, until the Haitian Revolution, when uprising slaves compelled the French to flee. In fact, many of the French fled to Philadelphia, like Augustine, and many arrived there as he does, "dead broke."[35] Into this Quaker city, Augustine brings his old ways, "an' they caught right hold." Philadelphia was a refuge for proslavery whites—some of them French expatriates, many of them Southerners from the Carolinas—and they were welcomed by the city's upper classes.[36] (Wister knew this history. As noted earlier, his grandfather Pierce Butler was one of these Carolinian slaveholding aristocrats who made his home in Philadelphia.)[37] Then, the ways of this Southern-identified Augustine begin to rile Delmonico, his Northern counterpart. They spar over "frawgs," especially the issue of "frawgs" in California. Each desires a "monopoly" over that Western territory, which blooms into a "disaster" that should "never have occurred" (115–16). California was *the* plum of contention between the North and the South leading up to the Civil War, intensifying sectionalism amidst a boom in the prices of gold and of slaves.[38] And the joke's "disaster," its civil war, takes place against the background of skyrocketing prices on "frawgs." Once the calamity is over, despite their adversity, this pseudo-Southerner and pseudo-Northerner "swore eternal friendship." And while Augustine had arrived via the *Southern* Pacific, both men "went home over the *Union* Pacific, sharing the same *state*room." This stateroom is the dream of white national reunion in which radical Reconstruction sank. (Meanwhile, the value of "frogs" plummets, and while trade in their flesh is made taboo, the *desire* to buy and sell their bodies clearly remains: "Not a banker in Fifth Avenue'll touch one now if another banker's around watchin' him.") By joke's end, little room is left for the Virginian's auditors, or Wister's readers, to question the actual referent of these frogs. It concludes with a skewed rewriting of the tragic mulatto trope: "And if ever yu' see a man that hides his feet an' won't take off his socks in company, he has worked in them Tulare swamps an' got the disease. Catch him wadin', and yu'll find he's web-footed." The Virginian figures frogness as a genetic pathogen that's communicable to humans (read: blackness as a contagion in the blood of whites) to be one hazard that befalls the flesh-trading profiteers of the "Tulare swamps" (read: the Southern plantations). Any remaining doubt about the parable's true subject surely vanishes when Wister refers to one of Trampas's men, now reconciled again to the Virginian's authority, as "a *reconstructed* mutineer" (117). And, of course, all of this takes place in chapters titled "The Game and the Nation"—that is, the Civil War and the United States.

So the joke and the novel share the backdrop of a speculative bubble in a live commodity, frogs and cows, respectively.[39] When the Virginian declares, before launching into his joke, "They're all cattle hyeh. Talk cattle, think cattle"—a joke told among *cowboys* who have just delivered *steers* to market— the effect is to bring those two animals, frogs and cows, into equivalence in the reader's mind. ("And same as cattle trains, yu'd see frawg trains tearing acrosst Arizona—big glass tanks with wire over 'em—through to New York, an' the frawgs starin' out" [113].) Cows are the explicit referent of this funny allegory. So when the joke ultimately equates frogs and slaves, which are its more implicit referent, a syllogism takes shape: slaves are like frogs, and frogs are like cattle, therefore slaves are like cattle (as the shared etymology of *chattel*—linking cows and slaves as property—hovers just outside the frame).[40] In the first chapter of this sequence, the Virginian walks the railyard among the train cars, "each car packed with huddled, round-eyed, gazing steers," headed for slaughter in Chicago. "'Yu' might suppose they know somehow what they're travellin' to Chicago for,'" he says, "while the terrified brutes stared . . . through their slats" (88). And later, he declares:

> This hyeh is a mighty cruel country. . . . To animals that is. Think of it! Think what we do to hundreds an' thousands of little calves! Throw 'em down, brand 'em, cut 'em, ear mark 'em, turn 'em loose, and on to the next. It has got to be, of course. But I say this. If a man can go jammin' hot irons on to little calves and slicin' pieces off 'em with his knife, and live along, keepin' a kindness for animals in his heart, he has got some good in him. (155)

The almost perceptible sentience of these "cattle" threatens to blur the lines that order the chain of being, which sustains the ranch's profit and the ranch-hand's authority. Are these "brutes" more like animals or more like humans? What do the incitements of terror reveal in these creatures? In the end, according to the Virginian, it's irrelevant. What matters is what the incitements *to* terror reveal in the cattle's owners. The practices of cruelty are unavoidable in this system; the trick is not to let one's absolute power over the life and death of another corrupt one's morals. The man with the glowing iron and the bloodied knife must yet keep "a kindness for animals in his heart," a sign that "he has got some good in him." This is the sentimental ideology of paternalism. And there is another forgotten history that haunts these lines: "You notice ... that every train going south has just such a crowd of slaves on board, and a 'nigger car.' ... You notice also that these slaves whom you constantly meet going south in the trader's hands ... are for the most part apparently picked slaves, boys and girls or young men and women," wrote a traveler to Virginia in 1856. And in his first trip South in 1859, J. Pierpont Morgan noted, "1,000 slaves on train." The historians Ned and Constance Sublette write, "As railroad cars extended their reach, captives were packed like cattle into freight cars, shortening the time and expense to market considerably."[41]

Wister's grandmother, Fanny Kemble, laid out the actual logic that yoked the plantation and the frontier in 1838 and, indeed, would seem still to yoke them in her grandson's novel. Kemble wrote of the "vital importance to [planters] to command an unrestricted extent of [frontier] territory" because "in the course of a few years" of unrelenting tobacco and cotton production, the planter will "see his estate gradually exhausted and unproductive." She writes that the planter, faced with such spent land, "who can move a 'gang' of able-bodied negroes to a tract of virgin soil is sure of an immense return of wealth." Other inland planters who remain stuck with exhausted plantations, their soil "refusing its increase," will opt for a different course, though. With his "black population, propagating and multiplying [such a planter] will be compelled, under penalty of starvation, to make *them* [slaves] his crop, and substitute, as *the Virginians* have been constrained to do, a traffic in human cattle for the cultivation of vegetable harvest."[42] On Wister's utopian frontier-plantation, agriculture has vanished to make way for the cultivation of a more perfect livestock, a commodity that produces only its own exceptionally profitable and entirely consumable flesh. Wister's Virginian trafficking his cattle approaches the near-perfection of his grandmother's vision of "the Virginians" trafficking their "human cattle," a book he surely knew well, as a bonanza in cows hearkens back to a bonanza in slaves. On his train journey as foreman, Wister notes, the Virginian has been given "the care of several thousand perishable dollars and the control of men." ("Moreover, Chicago finished up the steers" [88].)[43]

THE JOKE'S SUCCESS commends the Virginian for a partnership in the ranch. This is partly because his management of his men and "of several thousand perishable dollars" is shown to be unimpeachable. But it is important to note that this is also because his business acumen is demonstrated by the performative force of his narrative. The Virginian doesn't just relay a tall tale about a bonanza in frogs; the tall tale itself *becomes* a bonanza in frogs. When "the Southerner let[s] loose his heaven-born imagination," the divine power of his mind inspires value into rubbish, the refuse of frogs. ("'Well, my gracious!' said the enthusiast. 'What fool eats a frog?' 'Oh, I'm fool enough for a tadpole!' cried the passenger. And they began to take out their pocket-books" [110].) The Virginian creates demand. He creates a bonanza economy just by imagining one. He is a speculator who bets on the difference between a commodity's current price (frogs are worthless) and its future price (frogs open pocketbooks).

When he returns from the swamp with his assistant, he only partly empties his own sack, to make just that point regarding the value-creating powers of his own imagination: "'There,' said he, very businesslike, to his assistant, 'that's all we'll want. I think you'll find a ready market for the balance'" (110). And, of course, the fantasized commodity about to be traded in this rough-and-ready frontier market isn't frogs, as the joke soon makes clear, but black slaves. In this arid locale populated by travelers stranded and "under penalty of starvation," Wister's Virginian seems the very incarnation of Fanny Kemble's Virginian, discerning this amphibious "black" "population, propagating and multiplying"; seizing a chance for wild profits, he makes "*them* his crop"—this Virginian, too, enacting a "substitute" for "a traffic in human cattle."[44] The slave market has ended, says the joke, says history—black bodies and black life stripped of value—meanwhile, the Virginian hangs out his shingle, and traders and buyers line up to purchase his symbolic "crop."

In the midst of a revolution in political economy, marked by rampant speculation and corporatization, and set against a backdrop of populist revolt that valorized producers, Wister deploys his hero to redeem the capitalist.[45] Under the earlier dispensation of white republicanism, the historian James Livingston writes, "Those who consumed without producing were parasites on civil society, on those who, by mixing their labor with their property, made it productive and themselves free." Republicanism ordered a division of manual and mental labor—that is, of productive and unproductive labor. "The typically American fear of 'middlemen,' bureaucrats, bankers, lawyers, and all other forms of apparently unproductive mental labor ultimately derives from the assumption that they consume the wealth created by productive labor," writes Livingston. "In the nineteenth century, this fear extended to, or rather focused on, capitalists, the modern-industrial version of a many-layered aristocracy that consumed and controlled wealth without producing anything."[46] This rhetoric began to lose its hold in the late nineteenth century, thanks partly to the emerging theories of marginalism and to economic thinkers such as John Bates Clark. "Mental labor was crucial to the creation of wealth because if 'one class of laborers' [i.e., farmers, skilled workers, etc.] produced 'specific useful commodities' with the attribute of utility, the other 'general class' [i.e., capitalists, lawyers, etc.] produced laws, principles, and procedures that gave objects the 'attribute of appropriability,' in effect by bringing them to market, or simply by naming them, as consumable commodities," Livingston writes, summarizing Clark.[47] Enter the Virginian. He does precisely this: brings frogs to market, and through "his heaven-born imagination" and the mental labor of speculation, names them consumable commodities. Such mental labor is here redeemed, in a new scene and on another stage, by Wister's title character from "old Virginia" who hails from a family of "farmers and hunters not bettering [their] lot and very plain" (6, 217).[48]

At the scene of the joke, people gather to admire the Virginian's commercial greatness, mental prowess, and the powers of his "heaven-born imagination." And here, civil society is not a balance struck between production and consumption but is instead a scene of capitalist profits—that is, a scene of overproduction and surplus populated by consumers. People consume the dreck the Virginian has convinced them to purchase. Ideological relations of parity have been recoded as relations of hierarchy. Critics often mention "The Game and the Nation" because it contains *The Virginian*'s most didactic moment. It is Wister's unequivocal affirmation of elitism. "There can be no doubt of this:—All America is divided into two classes," he writes, at the very beginning of "The Game and the Nation" (as if echoing that earlier republicanist producer/consumer schism before obliterating it), "—the quality and the equality." Here and in other writings, Wister demonstrates his commitment to "let the best man win" because "true democracy and true aristocracy are one and the same thing" (85). For Wister, meritocracy privatizes the conditions of possibility for success or failure. These possibilities are to be shouldered now by the citizen-worker, who is no longer one among many producers (the member of a class) but instead an individuated consumer (a free agent). Democracy does not redistribute power and foster autonomy so much as it preserves a "level playing field." Wister retailors the ideology of the American Dream so that our corporate overlords deserve their dominant places.

And Wister employs a flesh-trading Southerner in the new guise of the cowboy on a relocated Western frontier to do this cultural work, which sanctions the paradigmatic shift from settler colonialism to an ascendant corporate capitalism, from the dream of a white republic of freeholders to that of a mass society of consumers. Wister's idealized figure of the frontier isn't a white settler or a landed proprietor; it's a manager who is climbing the corporate ladder. "The notion of freedom as a form of managerial control... understands property not as tangible and physical possessions [but]... as a form of knowledge or information," writes scholar Bryan Wolf. And after the Civil War, Wolf notes, "the foreman functioned increasingly as the agent of an imperial management in the work space."[49] The Virginian, as a manager, is that capitalist operative meant to ensure the pliability and productivity of workers. Thus, the desire for mutiny that Trampas stokes among the men, which springs from the promise of a gold rush, is precisely the desire to escape these corporate relations of control. The difference between a frontier of gold and a frontier of cattle is the difference between working for one's own wealth and working for someone else's. Despite the nostalgia for a passing West that seems to occasion its writing, *The Virginian* isn't oriented toward some bygone idyll of freeholding settler propriety but rather toward a future that will be ordered by rational corporate control.

An earlier proprietarian order had founded selfhood in the productive ownership of private property (especially land) and its socially necessary labor. Now, not only would workers be denied ownership of the means of production, but corporate capitalism would also reclaim the terms of *value* as profits rather than as wages—that is, redefine value as the capitalists' dividend. This entailed a crumbling of the foundations for white selfhood and self-determination: "For where in the name of sanity have all the courage, foresight, initiative gone to, what has happened to all the rugged virtues that are supposed to be inherent in the magic of property?" Walter Lippmann would ask a decade later in *Drift and Mastery* (1914). "They have gone a-glimmering with the revolutionary change that the great industry has produced. Those personal virtues belong to an earlier age when men really had some personal contact with their property. But to-day the central condition of business is that capital shall be impersonal, 'liquid,' 'mobile.'"[50] The

Western would appear, superficially, to arise as a jeremiad wailing the demise of that "magic of property." But really Wister just wants to resecure "courage, foresight, initiative" and "rugged virtues" in the new conditions where capital is "impersonal, 'liquid,' [and] 'mobile.'" He wants to clear this proving ground of individuality so as to reestablish an elite authority, because the compromise of that earlier system also meant the compromise of paternalist power.

Wister wasn't alone in his search for a new order.[51] The year before *The Virginian* appeared, the sociologist Edward Ross published his major work, *Social Control: A Survey of the Foundations of Order* (1901), which addressed the radically shifting conditions of American life at the turn of the twentieth century. Social control "meant essentially a system of power founded upon control of human instincts, desires, and habits rather than upon ownership and rulership as they were conceived in political economy," writes Jeffrey Sklansky.[52] This new kind of control was oriented less toward the flesh and more toward the mind; its operations were less manifest and more insidious. The Virginian embodies this sort of soft control. As mentioned earlier, despite expectations for the genre, the novel depicts almost no physical violence. Instead, it trades the force of terror for the force of persuasion. The single sentence that captures the final showdown between the Virginian and Trampas makes the argument in both its abbreviated form and in its content: "A wind seemed to blow his sleeve off his arm, and *he replied to it*, and saw Trampas pitch forward" (280). Language, more than the gun—a reply, rather than a shot—is the prime instrument of power in the novel.[53] "The Game and the Nation" hammers home this point, too. It is *this* duel where the Virginian literally replies to Trampas, rejoining the mutineer's joke with one of his own that carries the most weight in the narrative. The joke can be understood as more brutal than any bullet because it wounds not the body of its mark but its victim's personality, his appearance to others. It unmasks as fraudulent the features on which he trades. The victory of the Virginian's joke predicts, and may even trump, his lethal victory later in the showdown, and he knows it: "Frawgs are dead, Trampas, and so are you" (116). If the Virginian's tall tale about frogs produces market value, just as importantly it also produces his authority. Awe and obedience accrue to the Virginian less because of who he is than because of what he projects. His narrative and its effects turn his auditors into willing subjects:

> Indeed, the male crowd now was a goodly sight to see, how the men edged close, drawn by a common tie. . . . All eyes watched the Virginian

and gave him their entire sympathy. Though they could not know his motive for it, what he was doing had fallen as light upon them.... Even the Indian chiefs had come to see in their show war bonnets and blankets. They naturally understood nothing of it, yet magnetically knew that the Virginian was the great man. And they watched him with approval. He sat by the fire with the frying-pan, looking his daily self—engaging and saturnine. (114)

One's self-determining character was to be supplanted by an externally mediated personality under the new conditions of corporate capitalism, and Wister uses this shift to edify the aristocratic subjectivity idealized and embodied by the Virginian.[54] This cowboy proves his mettle as a leader not through muscle, but through charm, through wiles rather than violence: "All eyes watched the Virginian and gave him their entire sympathy." What the minstrel song makes clear, when the Virginian belts it out in the chapter after he routs Trampas in their lying contest, is the unmistakable racialization of this personality. When he sings, "Dar is a big Car'lina nigger.... By de name of Jim Crow...," he is, in fact, naming his rival, dishonoring him, blackening him. "If ever I sees him I 'tends for to maul him. / Just to let de white folks see / Such an animos as he / Can't walk around the streets and scandalize me" (125). This authoritative personality is adamantly white, and it achieves its coherence through the degradation of blackness.

As a form, the joke bolsters these stratagems. In his theories of the joke and the unconscious, published three years after Wister's book, Freud would reveal the pertinence not merely of the joke's content but also, and even more, of the joke's logic. Freud identifies two main categories of the joke: the innocuous, which dwells in word play, and the tendentious, which possesses a purpose, a tendency. The Virginian's tall tale falls into the latter category, what Freud calls a "hostile" joke, meant to make "our enemy small, mean, contemptible, comical."[55] Its telling forges and reveals a social bond among its listeners. The joke "is the most social of all the psyche's functions that aim to obtain pleasure," Freud argues, and "laughing at the same jokes is evidence of far-reaching psychical compatibility."[56]

Pleasure is the aim of the tendentious hostile joke, which allows one to "*get around restrictions and open up sources of pleasure that have become inaccessible.*"[57] Given that this is Freud, who set his life's work toward decentering the rational ego, one should not be surprised that it is the *ir*-rationality of pleasure that orders the joke's psychic economy. "Reason—critical judgment—suppression—these are the powers it fights one after the other;" he writes of the tendentious joke, "it holds on to the original sources of pleasure in words."[58]

And for Owen Wister, there was indeed an original source of pleasure in words, peculiar perhaps to his upbringing as a Butler family scion. Here is a journal entry written by a family friend of the Wisters about a young Owen, nicknamed Dan, on a trip to the family's Southern plantations:

> Dan, some weeks ago, went with his mother to pay a visit to her father at his plantation in Georgia. Before she went, Dan's father told him that the Negroes would not call him Massa now, but Bub, at which Dan was very indignant. The morning after they arrived in Savannah, Dan went out into the entry, where two clean, well dressed Negro women met him & immediately exclaimed "Oh what a nice young Massa, good morning young Massa." "That is the way," said Dan, "in which I always expect to be addressed."[59]

This was a lifelong preoccupation. Quoting from a letter he sent his mother in 1903, the year after *The Virginian*'s publication, his biographer Darwin Payne notes Wister's displeasure about two decisions made by Wister's friend Theodore Roosevelt: first, his decision to invite Booker T. Washington to dinner at the White House and, second, his decision to appoint a black man, Dr. William Crum, as port collector in their new hometown of Charleston:

> Wister thought he could discern another deleterious effect of Roosevelt's unpopular recognition of the two black men: an adverse effect on servant-master relationships. An incident in his own household reaffirmed his convictions. Molly [his wife] had called in a new housemaid upon her tenth day on the job to assess her performance. "You have taken no interest in your work," Molly complained. "No, mum, I have not—not until to-day. To-day I have begun to take an interest." There had been no mockery in the new maid's voice; she had spoken in a "perfectly respectful and candid" fashion. Wister was amazed at such behavior. "It seems new. Quite new—to me." What the ultimate impact of such attitudes would be Wister could not guess. One thing was certain: he was not pleased.[60]

So we would be mistaken—and indeed, in wagering the very "nation" on this "game," the bombast of the chapters' titles becomes nonsensical if we do—to assume that the primary enemy nominated by the Virginian's joke is the villain Trampas. The joke reveals an even more fundamental motivation: the desire to rewrite history by positing a counterfactual narrative about the consequences of 1865. The logic of the joke is such that the Civil War ends slavery by exterminating the slaves themselves. The *enemy*—for the joke, for the nation—is the ex-slave.

The pleasure produced by the Virginian's joke is the fantasy of black annihilation combined with white joint profits. Fighting for Western monopoly, "Their revenge killed frawgs"—that is, the revenge of whites, North and South, upon each other. No black presence interferes with the good feelings of national rapprochement that resolve his tall tale, of becoming "Brothers Again" (nor, unsurprisingly, do slaves appear in Wister's poem memorializing this fraternal war), of journeying together "home over the Union Pacific sharing the same stateroom." Instead, their war "Just killed 'em" and "wiped frawgs off the slate of fashion" (116). *This* holocaust is the joke's animating fantasy. And as a parable in which one's inferiors are *eaten*, it exemplifies almost perfectly the apogee of power's irrational pleasure described by the author Elias Canetti: "He is their leader, and they cluster around him in thousands and thousands. But they do not merely remain gathered about him like a people about its leader . . . they are reduced by him. . . . He, compared with them, is a giant, while they are tiny creatures striving around him. But that's not all: the great man swallows them. They literally enter him and vanish. His effect on them is annihilatory. He attracts and collects them, reduces and devours them. Everything they once were now benefits his own body."[61] Canetti's fantasy reveals the integral connection between the figure of absolute power and a figure of absolute degradation. (Consider here Olaudah Equiano's first sight of a slave ship: "When I looked round the ship too and saw a large furnace or copper boiling, and a multitude of black people of every description chained together . . . I no longer doubted of my fate; and, quite overpowered with horror and anguish, I fell motionless on the deck and fainted. When I recovered a little I found some black people about me. . . . I asked them if we were not to be eaten by those white men with horrible looks, red faces, and loose hair." Or Ottobah Cugoano: "I saw several white people, which made me very afraid they would eat me."[62]) In other words, the joke is a fantasy of complete authority, of ultimate sovereignty.[63] It adamantly reaffirms what the art historian Alexander Nemerov calls "the ongoing whiteness of the mythic West."[64]

That massacre seeks to extinguish blacks from the "free" space of a postslavery history of the modern nation. (And what else *is* the episteme of "the West"?) It is this annihilation that forges a society from the Virginian's listeners, a comradeship fed by enmity. This is the "nation" produced by the "game" of his joke. "A joke with an aggressive tendency transforms the initially indifferent audience . . . into accomplices in hate or scorn," Freud writes, "and creates an army of foes for its enemy, where once there was only one."[65] The joke disappears blackness from the time and space of the nation, as the condition of that nation's emergence and unity. For many whites in the North and South before, during, and after the Civil War, the freedom of emancipation meant freedom from blackness. Whether the colonization schemes of Thomas Jefferson or those that provide the deus ex machina in Harriet Beecher Stowe's *Uncle Tom's Cabin*, this meant the displacement of free blacks outside the United States and outside its body politic.[66] In its purer forms, this fantasy foresaw a genocide. One Southern physician succinctly outlined that vision, writing, "all things point to the fact that the Negro as a race is reverting to barbarism with the inordinate criminality and degradation of that state. It seems, moreover, that he is doomed at no distant day to ultimate extinction."[67] In such white imaginings, black bodies were ravaged by disease and by crime. These were the manifest symptoms of a coming racial extinction. For whites, under the conditions of slavery, black bodies had possessed and accumulated value; for whites, under the relations of legal freedom, black bodies designated surplus and waste.

But it is the capacity of the Virginian to conjure wealth from nothing, from waste. This is the desideratum of the frontier, not least the frontier plantation, according to political theorists such as Thomas Hobbes and John Locke: to change the void of nature into profitable commodities and meaningful time. The law of the market is conjoined to the law of history, and so it is through Wister's work as well. The frontier as history is merged with the frontier as speculation. In this origin story for the genre of the Western, the nation is tantamount to a market, where black life is captive to white profit. And here, in this central narrative of the joke, we view the despotic irrationality and epistemic violence on which this logic feeds. Waste enters history only as it is turned toward a profit, imbued with value. When the white man's bonanza is over, once again it assumes for him the condition of shit. In this case, that waste is a surplus population.

THIS CHAPTER OPENED with observations about the Western's trope of gambling—all those high-stakes card games, hands of poker where fortunes are made and reversed. Perhaps we can now recognize those recurring scenes as miniature dramas of boom and bust. They are vignettes of the antic financialized economy of the frontier, tableaux of its bonanzas, where commodity prices balloon and pop. A bettor playing at cards mimics an investor grubstaking a venture or a stockholder playing the market. "Modern economic development as a whole tends more and more to transform capitalist society into a giant international gambling house, where the bourgeois wins and loses capital in consequence of events which remain unknown to him," writes

Paul Lafargue, whom Walter Benjamin cites in *The Arcades Project*. "The 'inexplicable' is enthroned in bourgeois society as in a gambling hall.... The capitalist whose fortune is tied up in stocks and bonds, which are subject to variations in market value and yield for which he does not understand the causes, is a professional gambler."[68] Gambling in the Western foregrounds this ascendance of risk, a modern capitalist society awash in rising tides of contingency, just as the genre's admiration of management skills in its cowboy protagonists targets the mitigation of that risk. Captains in uncharted waters, the Western's cowboy heroes evince the cool-headed resolve of capable and confident decisionmakers. Theirs is an ethos of direction and supervision. Beginning with the Virginian, the cowboy resembles those late nineteenth-century men of empire described by Hannah Arendt in *The Origins of Totalitarianism*, white adventurers who are no longer outside the system, but who are instead brought within society's pale. These formerly liminal men became the functionaries of colonial capitalism. Part gentleman and part criminal, such men showed a contempt for the human; they were scoundrels who evinced an aristocratic hauteur, "irresistibly attracted by a world where everything was a joke"—players in what Rudyard Kipling called the "Great Game" of imperialist history.[69]

As such a game, the Western's fatal environment of contingency—along with the capacity to prevail despite it—becomes untethered from history. The genre depicts apparent laws of nature. Speculation transcends the domain of the economic in the Western, attaining a status that is almost ontological. That aspect achieves a cold clarity in one of the genre's limit instances, Cormac McCarthy's *Blood Meridian*, written in the 1980s, set in the 1850s. Near the novel's end, Judge Holden, the baleful philosopher-king, expounds on this universe of "will or nill" as he calls it:

> Suppose two men at cards with nothing to wager save their lives. Who has not heard such a tale? A turn of the card. The whole universe for such a player has labored clanking to this moment which will tell if he is to die at that man's hand or that man at his. What more certain validation of a man's worth could there be? This enhancement of the game to its ultimate state admits no argument concerning the notion of fate. The selection of one man over another is a preference absolute and irrevocable and it is a dull man indeed who could reckon so profound a decision without agency or significance either one. In such games as have for their stake the annihilation of the defeated the decisions are quite clear. This man holding this particular arrangement of cards in his hand is thereby

> removed from existence. This is the nature of war, whose stake is at once the game and the authority and the justification. Seen so, war is the truest form of divination. It is the testing of one's will and the will of another within that larger will which because it binds them is therefore forced to select. War is the ultimate game because war is at last a forcing of the unity of existence. War is god.[70]

Speculation becomes cosmology. The competition for survival is framed by the judge as a wagered game of chance, and the game's outcome renders the final verdict on its players' right to exist. More than individual success is at stake here. Given that the game's apotheosis is war, also implicated in this existential gamble is some larger faction—one's tribe, one's people. From here—from speculation annexed to war—it is but a short step to the domain of the economy annexed to the domain of biology, such that the free market administrates the life of the species. And in fact, according to the theorist Sylvia Wynter, this is precisely the dispensation that orders our contemporary era. In our secular scientific age, it is a Darwinian logic of natural selection that rationalizes who falls within and without the protected category of the human. Throughout the nineteenth century, that evolutionary logic had been overlaid with a discourse of racism—constituting "the break between what must live and what must die," in Michel Foucault's words—but over the course of the twentieth century that logic would become more and more affixed to a discourse of class difference, which did not displace racism but was rather grafted onto it.[71] With this shift, the jobless, the homeless, and the "underdeveloped"—those inhabiting the inner city, the global South, the racialized and inhuman spaces that geographer Katherine McKittrick calls "the lands of no one"—came to be understood as "dysselected" by evolution, and slated for ultimate extinction, just as certain races once had been.[72] Superfluous, the economically "disadvantaged" have been made derelict to capitalism and humanity, and have been abandoned. Our own episteme naturalizes their fates and resigns them to the category of the damned.

McCarthy's judge looks both backward and forward, exposing an older Hobbesian ethos of all against all within a newer rhetoric of risk, contingency, and speculation. On this nineteenth-century frontier, the emergent language of corporate capitalism recuperates a residual worldview in which the state of nature is a state of war (and in *Blood Meridian*'s fights between whites and Natives, it is very much a race war). The judge's philosophy also animates *The Virginian*, given those chapter titles under consideration here or such thinking's paler iteration in Wister's decree, "Let the best man win!" And the novel insinuates that its hero is no less engaged in warfare. In the Virginian's letter to his darling Molly's grandmother, he writes of his family: "We have fought when we got the chance, under Old Hickory and in Mexico and my father and two brothers were killed in the Valley sixty-four. Always with us one son has been apt to run away and I was the one this time" (217). Under the banners of Andrew Jackson, James Polk, and Jefferson Davis, his family has fought for Indian removal, for American imperialism, and for slavery (for which his father and two brothers died), and the implication is that he, too, is part of this warmongering lineage for white supremacy in the South/West.

In *The Virginian*, that drive for racial dominion is folded into a quest for economic superiority. The central chapters of "The Game and the Nation" are set up by some germane observations on luck in the preceding chapter, titled "Quality and Equality." Near its end, sounding like the cousin of McCarthy's Judge Holden, the Virginian takes issue with Molly's egalitarian (and feminist) notions that all are born equal:

> I know a man that mostly wins at cyards. I know a man that mostly loses. He says it is his luck. All right. Call it his luck. I know a man that works hard and he's gettin' rich, and I know another that works hard and is gettin' poor. He says it is his luck. All right. Call it his luck. I look around and I see folks movin' up or movin' down, winners or losers everywhere. All luck, of course. But since folks can be born that different in their luck, where's your equality? No, seh! call your failure luck, or call it laziness, wander around the words, prospect all yu' mind to, and yu'll come out the same old trail of inequality." He paused a moment and looked at her. "Some holds four aces," he went on, "and some holds nothin', and some poor fello' gets the aces and no show to play 'em; but a man has got to prove himself my equal before I'll believe him." (83)

As a concept that yokes fate and fortune, "luck" conceals and subsumes differences of circumstance, differences that may disadvantage certain people for sociohistorical reasons (say, disabilities, fewer material resources, membership in an oppressed group). Such differences are quietly dissolved as "chance," as mere accident. Then these historical differences, denominated "luck," are reasserted and revalued as "inequality." Failure in one's dealings (whether at "cyards" or at "work") is rendered as failure at life, and as an *inborn* inability to master one's environment. Luck voids out history, which is recast as biology: "folks can be born ... different in their luck, [so] where's your equality?" By the Virginian's lights, one succeeds despite one's luck, and de facto, winning legitimates one's inherent *biological* superiority. Life is cast as a gamble, and luck—or rather, the making of luck—becomes the joint between market competition and evolutionary competition. Difference is not social but genetic. Or, as Wister put it in a letter in 1902, "Inequality is the first law of the Universe one meets, and it is inexorable."[73]

Immediately, we find ourselves returned to the discourse of racial inferiority and to the logic that animates the cowboy's minstrel song about Jim Crow. "Dat what de white folks call him. / If ever I sees him I 'tends for to maul him. / Just to let de white folks see / Such an animos as he / Can't walk around the streets and scandalize me" (125). It is a fantasy of conquest, the crushing of a rival for no reason other than to prove his supremacy—a peer whose sameness cannot be abided. The other exists as an "animos," a coinage suspended between animus and animal, a dishumanized enemy. *The Virginian* is pieced together from old Virginia cloth. A thread of antiblack racism holds together this first Western, gives it shape, but it is a garment fitted to the form of a new corporate era.

Here, the logics of evolutionary biology and managerial capitalism merge and amplify. *The Virginian* considers a far more elaborate dream of management than that concerning the cowboy and his recalcitrant underlings. Hot on the heels of 1898, that dream may have played out most obviously as another way "in which the Western frontier was violently exported," in Amy Kaplan's words, "to the New Empire in Cuba and the Philippines (and in later imperial wars of the twentieth century): in the form of soldiers (many of whom were veterans of Indian wars); as social policy (the resettlement of native Filipinos according to the plans of Indian reservations); and in vibrant symbols—Roosevelt's Rough Riders."[74] If the joke at the center of *The Virginian* establishes the cowboy's administrative talents, then it also projects an extensive vision for how to manage subject populations, who, rendered as something other than human, are therefore expendable. But, all importantly, *The Virginian* routes that dream through the plantation, that other frontier institution whose original mission was to extend "civilization" and its legal order. The "frogs" are both profitable commodities and infectious hazards. They must be cultivated like a crop *and* isolated like an illness. These are the modi operandi of exploitation and segregation. The Virginian's joke fantasizes that black bodies might once again "feed" white prosperity as a "crop" of profitable goods or, otherwise, that they might be made to disappear. Blacks amounted to an invasive species, a plague on (white) American society; in its multifaceted operations, the police powers that animated Jim Crow sought to identify, quarantine, and exterminate this pestilence.

These are not metaphors. Published a year before *The Virginian*, a year when one hundred blacks were lynched, W. E. B. Du Bois's *The Souls of Black Folk* also voices the stark reality of these relations of power: "The . . . thought streaming from the death-ship and the curving river is the thought of the older South: the sincere and passionate belief that somewhere between men and cattle, God created a *tertium quid*, and called it a Negro . . . foreordained to walk within the Veil."[75] The Virginian, with his tall tale's animal figuration of the enslaved, epitomizes that "thought of the older South." One is reminded of an anecdote Du Bois related to President Woodrow Wilson in an open letter written a decade later to protest the policy of segregation being enacted against black civil servants. "In the Treasury and Post Office departments colored clerks have been herded to themselves as though they were not human beings," he writes. "We are told that one colored clerk who could not actually be segregated on account of the nature of his work has consequently had a cage built around him to separate him from his white companions of many years."[76] This encapsulates a logic of slave racial capitalism that corresponds at every point with the regime of Jim Crow. Blacks are made into a captive reservoir of value, liable to be tapped for white profit at any time, but must remain set apart, denied prestige or affluence or honor, and marked by stigma.[77]

Management, writ large, becomes a schema of racialization—a matter of who *manages* and whom, or what, is being *managed*. In the worldview of the first Western, which is the worldview of the West, black existence persists only at the whim of white enjoyment. This logic produced small cages such as the clerk's as well as the larger cages of ghettos, where perhaps this clerk lived. Beginning to assume a more rigid shape in this era, the ghetto, too, is a scheme of population "management," where *management* approaches eradication.[78] The ghetto is a holding pen from which low-wage labor can be extracted to the benefit of the larger (white) economy, even as its legal and economic structure ensures that inhabitants are kept in place. And, kept in place, those black inhabitants were left susceptible to massacre. With its dream of black life as a source of riches and as an object for annihilation, the Virginian's fable contains the crux of this logic of racial management, which blossomed into full flower in historical events that took place after its publication.

Consider just one example, from 1917, in East St. Louis, Illinois, which presaged more violence to come—in Atlanta, Chicago, Philadelphia, Tulsa, and elsewhere. Of the atrocities that destroyed hundreds of thousands of dollars of black property, that killed up to 150 black residents, and that drove six thousand blacks into exile, Ida B. Wells wrote in a pamphlet: "The assaults and murders were cold-blooded, deliberate and incredibly brutal. They were not the mob infuriated against particular offenders. They were the work of groups of men and women who sought out and burned out the Negroes and then shot, beat, kicked and hanged them. The work was done in a spirit of flippant, relentless barbarism." She adds, with chilling concision, "The black skin, without regard to age, sex or innocence, was the mark for slaughter."[79] Du Bois offered an even more graphic account of the carnage. "The white men ... killed and beat and murdered; they dashed out the brains of children and stripped off the clothes of women; they drove victims into the flames and hanged the helpless to the lighting poles. Fathers were killed before the faces of mothers; children were burned; heads were cut off with axes; pregnant women crawled and spawned in dark, wet fields; thieves went through houses and firebrands followed; bodies were thrown from bridges; and rocks and bricks flew through the air."[80]

This is the horizon, however fleeting, that one glimpses in *The Virginian*. This same veiled logic sits at the novel's center. Frogs: "for the frogs were all gone." "Their revenge killed frawgs ... Just killed 'em." Cows: "'Yu' might suppose they know somehow what they're travellin' to Chicago for,'" says the Virginian, among railway cars filled with cattle, bound for a slaughterhouse, "while the terrified brutes stared ... through their slats." "Think what we do to hundreds an' thousands of little calves! Throw 'em down, brand 'em, cut 'em." Ex-slaves: other-than-human populations, possessed of superfluous life, except when managed for white profit. The foreclosed black futures in the West, about which Wister dreamt, also assumed the brute historical materiality of corpses and rubble. That violent dream was a point of communion for white nationalism, North and South, East and West.

It is worth mentioning one final historical scene that lurks behind this joke, an event in which a surplus captive population was liquidated wholesale to resecure the crumbling foundations of white life. In early March 1859, in Savannah, Georgia, 436 souls valued at $303,850 were sold to cover a white family's mounting debts. It constituted the largest recorded slave auction in U.S. history.[81] "The human assets were brought to a racetrack ... where they were put in stalls for horses as they awaited buyers."[82] Those slaves were owned by none other than Wister's grandfather, Pierce Butler, and that auction was, in some material sense, the condition of possibility for Owen Wister to sit down at his desk in his fine home in Charleston, South Carolina, to write what would be recognized as the first novel of the Western genre. "Everything they once were now benefits his own body."[83]

GENRE ENCODES THE IDEOLOGIES of a social order at a particular historical moment. An individual work derives from and replenishes a repertoire of literary forms, while corresponding with its own concrete historical situation. If the Western has survived the moment of its emergence at the turn of the twentieth century and evolved as a form, that is because we continue to live in the shadow of its history. The historical predicaments that provided the conditions of possibility for the Western are still ours. That penumbra still covers us. And to say that we live in the shadow of its history also means that we continue to resort to the ideologies that the Western articulates in attempting to resolve those historical predicaments. The solutions it proposes retain for us the charm of common sense.

The Western surfaced out of an urban Eastern milieu of market volatility and of burgeoning corporate enterprise. (The Panic of 1893 had not yet faded, and Wister was himself training as a lawyer in a Philadelphia firm specializing in corporate law and railroad law when he first escaped to Wyoming in 1885.)[84] The genre also emerges against a rhetorical background rooted in late nineteenth-century populist revolt that tarred speculators, capitalists, managers, and middlemen as parasites who survived by leeching the "real" value created by the working masses. Against an agrarian populist discourse that defined property and its attendant rights as the concrete products of physical labor, Wister's Western novel addresses itself to the contradictions of the industrial corporate era, to the corporate form's abstraction, to speculative property's immateriality, and to the illegitimacy of the capitalist's profits and authority. It attempts to resolve these contradictions through the symbolic figures, respectively, of the ranch, of livestock (cattle, frogs), and of the cowboy. And the novel transpires within the historical space of the frontier, a cultural symbol that dovetails with American sovereignty, a historical space that *The Virginian* recodes—recovers—as a zone of speculation. By doing so, in part, it articulates a mode of individualism newly fit for the corporate age.[85] But behind each of the Western's symbolic figures stands an obscure double, a historical counterpart. These concealed pendants derive from another time and place, from the homeland of the author's family, from the homeland of the titular hero—a usable past where such contradictions must have seemed, to Wister, ironed out. Behind the ranch stands the plantation. Alongside the livestock stand the enslaved. Beside the cowboy stands the overseer. The far Western frontier driven by cattle speculation is haunted by that earlier

Southwestern frontier driven by slave speculation. And *that* frontier had been the prelude to a certain order.[86] Wister longed to resurrect it.

In the development of its hero's career from cowboy manager to business executive, *The Virginian* charts a trajectory from landed settlement to corporate oligarchy. For the ex-slave in, ostensibly, an era of freedom, it charts no life at all. The ex-slave becomes the object of a fantasy of massacre, erased from the time of the nation, disappeared at the level of discourse—rendered an invisible man. After the formal abolition of slavery in 1865 and after the formal closure of the frontier in 1890, what was to be the foundation of white sovereignty in the United States, if no longer the cardinal claim on black flesh or Native land? *The Virginian* was, in part, Owen Wister's meditation on how to renovate white subjectivity, paternalist power, and political authority in his moment of profound change. In *The Virginian*'s mythology of the West, it is the slave, more than the Native, whose ongoing subjection, whose exclusion and death, will constitute the renewal of white sovereignty in an era of property's abstractions. And in this regard, *The Virginian* signals a change in the prevailing racial schema, in that space where slave racial capitalism and settler colonialism intersect, because here it is the slave who *also* becomes the object of genocide alongside the Native.[87] To be black is to be named in the market only as its surplus; that is the joke's crux. The first novel Wister would publish after *The Virginian* brought much of its racism to the surface, and it turned explicitly from the West to the South. Set in a barely fictionalized Charleston, South Carolina, the best-selling *Lady Baltimore* (1906) would parade its antiblackness and white supremacy unabashedly.

We usually consider the Western genre as the apotheosis of an obsession with land and the frontier as a moving marker of territorial acquisition. The Western appears as a primal scene of capitalism in America, the genesis of landed property and national territory. But through this return to the genre's beginnings in *The Virginian*, what is revealed is that the Western is not even in the West. Its epicenter isn't Wyoming, so much as New York or Charleston. The genre is less concerned, at its outset, with accumulating landed property than with mitigating the cultural shifts of an emerging corporate capitalism, which it proposes to accomplish by redeeming and extending the project of slave racial capitalism. Heir of a slaveholding dynasty, Owen Wister stands in the West and looks to the South trying to plot a course through a revolution in political economy that also poses a crisis for the structure of white selfhood and authority. Profits without power won't suffice. So Wister conceives the character of the Virginian, a Southerner in the West, as a way to navigate both the end of domestic settler colonialism and the end of chattel slavery. In

The Virginian, he plays the chords of the original harmony that unified plantation and frontier—that zone where the delay of profits in a speculative economy rhymed with the promise of progress through a colonizing law and order.[88] The American project demands that the generation of surplus value be wedded to racist exploitation and domination, whose object remains the slave. Under that ongoing system, the time of markets is again elided with the time of history, and the despotic white profiteer assumes the mantle of an ordained sovereignty.

CHAPTER FOUR

Southern Enclosure as American Literature

For some time now I have been thinking about the validity or vulnerability of a certain set of assumptions conventionally accepted among literary historians and critics and circulated as "knowledge." This knowledge holds that traditional, canonical American literature is free of, uninformed, and unshaped by the four-hundred-year-old presence of, first Africans and then African-Americans in the United States. It assumes that this presence—which shaped the body politic, the Constitution, and the entire history of the culture—has had no significant place or consequence in the origin and development of that culture's literature. Moreover, such knowledge assumes that the characteristics of our national literature emanate from a particular "Americanness" that is separate from and unaccountable to this presence.
—Toni Morrison, *Playing in the Dark*

The faces of the white world, looking on in wonder and curiosity, declare: "Only the Negro can play!" But they are wrong. They misread us. We are able to play in this fashion because we have been excluded, left behind; we play in this manner because all excluded folk play. . . . But every powerful nation says this of the folk whom it oppresses in justification of that oppression.
—Richard Wright, *12 Million Black Voices*

White people in this country will have quite enough to do in learning how to accept and love themselves and each other, and when they have achieved this—which will not be tomorrow and may very well be never—the Negro problem will no longer exist, for it will no longer be needed.
—James Baldwin, *The Fire Next Time*

1. American: 1930s

Owen Wister had dedicated *The Virginian* to his friend and former classmate Theodore Roosevelt. And on White House stationery, a quaint note to Wister commended him on his "remarkable novel": "If I were not President, and therefore unable to be quoted, I should like nothing better than to write a review of it. I have read it all through with absorbed interest."[1] A year after his term ended, Roosevelt mailed another letter of praise to the author of another book on the American West, an anthology of Western songs, which was also dedicated to him. Roosevelt praised the animating instinct to collect and preserve shown by this author, John A. Lomax, but with an air of foreboding. Noting that it was "very curious" that the same "conditions of ballad-growth which obtained in medieval England" should appear in the United States, Roosevelt goes on to sound an alarm. "Under modern conditions, however, the native ballad is speedily killed by competition with the music hall songs; the cowboys becoming ashamed to sing the crude homespun ballads, in view of what Owen Wister calls the 'ill-smelling saloon cleverness' of the far less interesting compositions of the music hall singers." Lomax placed Roosevelt's letter as the preface to his *Cowboy Songs and Other Frontier Ballads* (1910), clearly pleased with the imprimatur.[2]

If an ancient "Anglo-Saxon ballad spirit" survived in the American West, that was thanks partly to its rural geography and partly to its backward inhabitants, Lomax argues. "Illiterate people, and people cut off from newspapers and books, isolated and lonely—thrown back on primal resources for entertainment and for the expression of emotion—utter themselves through somewhat the same character of songs as did their forefathers of perhaps a thousand years ago." Deprivation turned these people into archives of premodern tradition, human hard drives storing the old ways. Lomax emphasizes his own acts of transcribing and recording these songs—"jotted down on a table in the rear of saloons, scrawled on an envelope while squatting about a campfire, caught behind the scenes of a broncho-busting outfit"—recited to him orally by the folk themselves and "never before in print," presaging the methods that would make him famous in coming decades. Unlike his own bylined work ("collected by John A. Lomax"), the expressions of the folk would remain anonymous, considered organic outgrowths of a collective soul. "In only a few instances have I been able to discover the authorship of any song. They seem to have sprung up as quietly and mysteriously as does the grass on the plains." Lomax deemed the songs themselves to be a "vital, however humble, expression of American literature."[3]

Before long, Lomax found an even deeper reservoir of the "isolated and lonely," of "people cut off from newspapers and books," of—as he identified his folk performers for his second anthology, using plain language—"poor people."[4] One part of the country had revealed itself as home to the lion's share of the nation's poor, illiterate, isolated, lonely people in the interval between his first two books: the South.[5] When Lomax chronicles in his preface "some of the best singers that we have met" and where they live, the first seven in the list are Southern, half of the total. Well, half of the *first* list—because Lomax then offers a *second* list. This one also chronicles "some of the singers who have moved us beyond all others," and these sixteen named singers, too, all live in the South. The singers are, however, separately classified as "the Negroes," the logic of Jim Crow spelled out on the page.[6] We might wonder why exactly the South should have become such a privileged location for the American folk. And if both (unmarked) whites and "Negroes" comprise an American folk tradition—an otherwise undifferentiated and populist national heritage—what is signified by these segregated lists? And what, if anything, does this have to do with "American literature," as Lomax insists?

The economic condition of these singers and of their region was not, of course, a fact of nature, poor people having been made poor. The apparatus of "freedom" that was set in place in the Southern states after 1865 had snared both blacks and whites in its meshes. That system had been—and was still—bleeding them dry and leaving them derelict in fields of chopped cotton. The Great Mississippi Flood of 1927 laid bare the dire conditions afflicting Southern farmers for those outside the region. The economic crash of 1929 only upped the contrast on this bleak view. Six years later, having just assumed the presidency, Franklin D. Roosevelt (FDR) passed the Agricultural Adjustment Act (AAA). The AAA was meant to rationalize farm production, with the federal government paying landowners not to grow cotton on their lands, so as to restrict supply and thus increase and stabilize prices. But that policy also rendered the sharecroppers and tenants who had been working those lands superfluous, turning them into liabilities on the ledger sheet. Despite formal protections within the act, thousands of farmers were summarily evicted from their farms. The Lords of the Land, as Richard Wright called them, didn't use their government checks to subsidize their unemployed tenants. Instead they purchased tractors and permanently replaced those tenants.

Kicked off the land, many farmers moved to towns and cities across the South; many others moved even farther. And many just had to keep moving, season after season, becoming migrant laborers.[7] "Just about the time of the panic the tractor come in strong.... In just a few years the tractor improved so much it put the mule out of business. The landowner was quick to take a likin to the tractor. With it he would have no people to feed, no doctor's bills or houses to repair, and no mules to feed. He could buy fertilizer with the money he used to pay hands," the black sharecropper Ed Brown told Jane Maguire in his biography. "Men started walkin the roads lookin for a farm, for a dry place to sleep, and a place to raise somethin to eat. Mr. So and So, they'd tell me, has got a tractor and I got to move. Some would walk weeks lookin for a farm."[8] Mostly black but also white, the Southern poor had beneath them none of the new social safety nets that might break their fall.[9] Along with the arrival of the boll weevil and wartime labor shortages, this Great Removal was one trigger for the Great Migration, which urbanized the majority of the country's black population, who were also fleeing disenfranchisement, lynching, police brutality, and segregation.

The New Deal policies that pushed farmers off the land to enable agricultural "modernization"—rationalizing production, mechanizing labor, aggregating competing interests into large-scale industrial agribusiness firms—were by-the-book acts of enclosure, quite literally "the forcible expropriation of the people from the soil."[10] And these enclosures signaled a sea change in the political economy and social makeup not just of the Southern states but of the nation as a whole. Southern farmers were being relieved of all means of production. Millions would be internally displaced in these decades, a seismic demographic shift as the South's rural peoples moved into cities across the United States. After the Great Flood of 1927, certain contradictions were being exposed in the system of slave racial capitalism that still ordered the American nation-state. According to historian Pete Daniel: "conditions in the flood area suggested a way of life not very different from slavery days. The flood emergency had simply washed the system into the open."[11] Two contradictions in particular were brought into sharpest relief: the uneven development that had produced and maintained a geographical entity identifiable as "the South" and the failure of Jim Crow culture to sustain the privileges of whiteness. Suddenly, the colonial situation of the Southern states had become visible, as had the region's grinding poverty, which afflicted both blacks (the unsurprising norm) and whites (the startling pathology).

Meanwhile, another vast program was simultaneously underway, underwritten by the state, to *represent* these dispossessed. By the 1930s, the South and its poor could symbolize the nationwide depredations of capitalism for public officials and cultural producers.[12] When Roy Stryker's photographers fanned out across the nation to take pictures of the downtrodden everyman for the Farm Security Administration (FSA), they photographed the South more than any other region.[13] The FSA produced images meant "to conciliate public opinion," in mission architect Rexford Tugwell's words, not to educate its audience or to offer context for the harms suffered by its subjects, as in the earlier social photographic work of Lewis Hine. That conciliation enabled the state to further its mission of rural industrialization, enlisting middle-class support for the federal projects of modernization. Through framing, composition, and captions, the subjects of the FSA's photographs were rendered a deracinated American folk, "symbols of ideal life" in the words of photography scholar Maren Stange. In some sense, the FSA's subjects became a commons, a public domain. These people were remade into touching art objects for a bourgeois audience who were wistful for a bogus halcyon past and were saddened at the sight of what Tugwell called the "most friendless, hopeless people in the whole country."[14] Meanwhile, to document a certain black folk history, the Works Progress Administration had also begun recording interviews with former slaves. These interviews were usually conducted by whites and transcribed in the deformed speech of minstrelsy. And alongside these records, a shadow archive hidden to the public eye was growing ever larger, one stuffed with letters written by black farmers across the South who were still manacled by debt and coercion, still terrorized, missives begging for the federal government's intercession on their behalf. What these captive sharecroppers received in reply most always was a cold bureaucratic form letter that defined peonage and then maintained that the law didn't apply to them—a demurral and a silence.[15]

In 1938, the *Report on Economic Conditions of the South* was released, commissioned by President Roosevelt. At the conference inaugurating that report, FDR famously declared: "It is my conviction that the South presents right now the nation's No. 1 economic problem—the nation's problem, not merely the South['s]. For we have an economic unbalance in the Nation as a whole, due to this very condition of the South." That statement's second half, though less well remembered than the first, is no less important: the South is cast as the nation's backward, colonial other. The *Report* etched that sentiment in stone and largely faulted Northern corporate avarice for the South's situation. A contemporary article from 1939 put this in boldface. "The South, as much as any British colony of old or today, is a colony, with headquarters in New York. There live the Privy Lords of Trade and Plantations, who ... govern the South by remote control," wrote Maury Maverick, a former Democratic congressman from Texas and a staunch supporter of FDR's New Deal programs. "The South actually works for the North: mortgage, insurance, industrial, and finance corporations pump the money northward like African ivory out of the Congo." The title of his piece was its own polemic: "Let's Join the United States." Maverick pointed out the black and white impoverishment this situation had caused. He even insisted that "a unanimity of opinion should demand that the Negro obtain economic justice," but quickly added that this demand "should be considered as largely selfish for the protection of the white people themselves." Selfish because, economically speaking, Jim Crow had not guaranteed white prosperity, and since—and *only*

Dorothea Lange, *Cotton Sharecropper Family Near Cleveland, Mississippi* (June 1937) (Library of Congress, Washington, D.C.).

Arkansas sharecropping family evicted over membership in the Southern Tenant Farmers Union (January 1936) (John Vachon, Library of Congress, Washington, D.C.).

Ben Shahn, *Poverty on the March, a Destitute Ozark Family, Arkansas* (October 1935) (Library of Congress, Washington, D.C.).

since—black and white poverty were inextricably linked, black poverty had to be addressed.[16] Cue modernization.

RIGHT AROUND the time that John Lomax published *Cowboy Songs* in 1910, a nationalist rhetoric began to surface among cultural producers, who were craving a special "Americanness" in the nation's cultural creations. This nationalist urge animated many of the arts during this period: the Ashcan School in painting, the Prairie School in architecture, the musical compositions of Charles Ives, Aaron Copland, and Henry Cowell. Many of these modernists turned to the national landscape to campaign against a corrupting and pervasive market that they believed to be threatening the ideals of American democracy.[17] All were seeking—producing, inventing—an American tradition.[18] And by the 1930s, the South and its peoples had emerged as the most valuable repository for whatever it was that made America most American.

The same impulses animated U.S. literary critics. Literature had become the arid preserve of elites, both among its scholars and its practitioners, according to certain insurgents of the 1910s and 1920s.[19] Critics such as Van Wyck Brooks, Lewis Mumford, and Waldo Frank sought to restore to American literature some kind of use value. In "American literature something has always been wanting," Brooks wrote in *America's Coming-of-Age* (1915), "a certain density, weight, and richness, a certain poignancy, a 'something far more deeply interfused,' [that] simply is not there." Critics like Brooks wanted a literature—and a criticism—that might symbolize American democracy, and redeem it. If "literature really does record the spirit of a people," then Brooks believed that the American writers who had been canonized in the late nineteenth century—Henry Wadsworth Longfellow, Oliver Wendell Holmes, James Russell Lowell, John Greenleaf Whittier—were no longer representative of the nation these insurgents imagined, being too genteel, too provincial, too *British*.[20] Plus, those writers had begun to smell of the lamp.[21] To mine the grit and slang of the masses and then to burn away its dross to yield society's golden image—*that* was the task of the artist. "There was a growing feeling that 'To be refined is to be 'goody-goody,'" that had taken hold of the arts, according to one contemporary scholar, whereas "gutter slang is 'so actual.'"[22] This entailed the quest for an American language, distinct from the British—one that was simple, demotic, virile.[23] They wanted to reclaim literature from the bourgeois gentlemen of the urban North who sat ensconced in their Victorian parlors, and to locate it instead among the vibrant people in the street and in the countryside. In doing so, these critics hoped to light a path toward a different future. Their impetus was no less modernist.

By the 1930s, new Americanist trends in literary criticism were at full steam, with the publication of a series of landmark books—Vernon Louis Parrington's *Main Currents in American Thought* (1927), Constance Rourke's *American Humor* (1931), Bernard DeVoto's *Mark Twain's America* (1932), and F. O. Matthiessen's *American Renaissance* (1941).[24] All of them were after what Matthiessen called an "organic style"—"the fusion between the word and the thing"—in American letters.[25] Most locked onto the 1830s as the birth*date* of a national literature, but its birth*place* was a bit more contentious. One strand of scholarship identified the source of that tradition in the urban East, in the more refined work of Hawthorne, Emerson, and Melville.[26] Another strand, tracing its genealogy back through Mark Twain, who was just then achieving his apotheosis, located it in the rural West.[27] More accurately, these origins were located in the *North*east and the *South*west. In the former case, "It became possible to have an American literary history (and also cultural history) that begins with the Puritans and culminates with the [American] Renaissance without including an Afro-American writer," as literary scholar Ronald A. T. Judy writes.[28] Slavery "could be banished from the page, erased from the story," creating a sacred Northern democracy. In the latter case, far from overlooking slavery, the ribald stories of the Southern frontier that had been written amidst a boom in land, cotton, and slaves in the Mississippi Valley were being recovered and anointed for their native originality.[29] The political economy of slavery provided the setting and the occasion for these stories, a genre also known as "the humor of the old Southwest." For critics in the 1930s, not unlike the FSA photographing the South's poor farmers, these crude stories seemed to provide (and why shouldn't they?) something peculiarly "American."

Writing of Twain in 1927, Parrington set the tone: "Here at last was an authentic American—a native writer, thinking his own thoughts, using his own eyes, speaking his own dialect—everything European fallen away, the last shred of feudal culture gone, local and western yet continental." Twain was "the very embodiment of the turbulent frontier that had long been shaping native psychology, and that now at last was turning eastward to Americanize the Atlantic seaboard."[30] (Incidentally, FDR would lift the phrase "the new deal" from Twain's *A Connecticut Yankee in King Arthur's Court*.)[31] In his study of Twain five years later, here's how Bernard DeVoto put it: "The importance of this [Southern frontier] literature for criticism is that, humble as it is—a sort of rudimentary art on or just below the threshold of literature—it finally ripened in Mark Twain.... From his earliest days he read books which were a continent away from the damned shadow of Europe and, a continent away from the shadow, he lifted the *genre* into immortality." Its antecedent of oral storytelling "declare[s] unanswerably the assurance that his roots go down deep into the common life of America and are nourished by the native blood of the folk," DeVoto writes.[32] These stories "were enormously popular in the quarter century during which most of them appeared, from 1835 to 1860," notes Constance Rourke. Of the tall talk and tall tales of the Mississippi Valley, a region of the South identified as the West in that era, she writes, "It was in the West that these tales took on their final inflation; and from the West they spread over the country," asserting the frontier's importance in that genre's full realization. It offered a sacred spring of the vernacular, she suggests. "Passing so soon into the wilderness as to preserve their habits of speech, and to be uninfluenced, presumably, by the later stability of the English language," the backwoodsman was a fly in amber.[33] When he opened his mouth, out poured the speech of the Elizabethan age, cut and mixed with Americanisms. Describing the Sut Lovingood stories of George Washington Harris, F. O. Matthiessen simply declared: "He brings us closer than any other writer to the indigenous and undiluted resources of the American language, to the tastes of the common man himself."[34]

At a surface level, these literary critics were taking some small part in the flurry of cultural representations of the South that enjoyed a mass audience and achieved national influence during these years: D. W. Griffith's *The Birth of a Nation* (1915), the craze for country blues records (1920s–1930s), the Bristol Sessions that produced the Carter Family and Jimmie Rodgers (1927), *Gone with the Wind* as both novel (1936) and film (1939). These critics were acting partly to represent a South whose remoteness as an internal colonial other had begun to dissolve as its residents migrated outward to the North and West in the years during and after World War I. Improvements in transportation and communication were also further collapsing the distance that allowed the South to remain, abstractly, an isolate for and from the rest of the nation in the half century following Reconstruction. Multiple crises that crescendoed in the upheaval of the New Deal's farm evictions had constituted the South's rural poor as a class and had commanded a reckoning with the region's relation to the U.S. nation-state.

THE LITERARY CRITICISM of the 1930s perpetrated and abetted the ongoing work of Southern enclosure. Poor white Southerners and the specific contradictions they embodied were apprehended—both understood and arrested—during that decade as fundamental to a national literary tradition, as a unique wellspring of the American voice, the font of an American style. A cadre of cultural nationalist critics conceived through them a historically situated "voice" and "style" that then assumed a deracinated national character. Rooted in the mid-nineteenth century literature of the Southern frontier, these aspects became the transhistorical mark of "American" literary expression. In this same moment, the formalist New Critics theorized poetry as the manifestation of an unchanging Anglo-American tradition—a continuous and common tradition that was actually, if obscurely, grounded in a particular time and place, the preindustrial plantation South. The parochial provenance of this tradition became dissolved within an aesthetic and abstract formalism that the New Critics proclaimed to be universal. The cultural coding of the "authentic" Americanness of the Southern "folk" variously undertaken by these critics produced the ideological grounding for the emerging discipline of American literature. Grasping the conditions and causes that produced "the South" and this "folk," but grasping them only partially and imperfectly, literary critics of the 1930s also, albeit inadvertently, expressed the historical circumstances endured by the displaced black and white rural population in the region, as it interpellated them within its disciplinary field. The operations of this disciplinary project disclose that project's concealed foundations in the long and unfinished history of slave racial capitalism in the United States. By the end of World War II, not only the *Americanness* but also the *literariness* of America literature had its deepest roots in the slave south.

Despite its reifying work, the concept of the folk also intimates a real continuity and commonality of historical conditions among the dispossessed, a union that disregards the color line that was consistently made to overlay and divide it. And for brief moments around the 1830s and especially the 1930s, that latent unity was made manifest. But the mass of poor whites in the early nineteenth century, like the mass of slaves, are lost to the historical archive, which precludes any recovery of the ties that yoked them. That fact isn't incidental; it is integral. Only through the division of these two groups and through their silencing could this "American" voice and style emerge. The process of Southern enclosure and the narration of it in this literary critical discourse offer one episode in the hostile making of the Human, that most uneven of categories. The following pages attempt to return some of this violent history to "the humanities." Translated by literary critics, the grammar of the folk concept attests to the material historical conditions that produce—and are shrouded by—"American literature." Style's timelessness and literature's universality emerge from the predicaments of forgotten human lives.

2. American: 1830s

Conjunction rather than coincidence explains the nationalist critics' turn in the 1930s toward the 1830s. That earlier moment was, too, defined by the enclosure of "the South" and by the attendant ramping up—the modernization—of its factories in the fields.[35] Through state and nonstate violence, American Indians were driven from their Southern homelands, or simply killed, in order that "wilderness" could be turned into private property. This theft kickstarted a market revolution in America from 1815 to 1845 as men, goods, and money were set in motion. Surveyed, commodified, and divvied into sections and quarter-sections, that stolen land was remade into an empire of cotton, produced through the machinery of slaves, which "provided the key impetus to the market revolution," political theorist Michael Rogin notes, as "much northwestern development depended on southern expansion."[36] Crucial to the national economy, those plantations were thoroughly modernized and rationalized. "A sophisticated literature of plantation management [compelled a greater level of] labor discipline than northern factories had achieved; and plantation ledgers provided for daily, quarterly, and annual accounting of yields, costs, profits, and individual worker productivity," historian Charles Sellers writes.[37] By 1836, nearly half of the country's economic activity stemmed from the cotton grown by forced slave labor on the Southern frontier.[38]

The market revolution underway in the United States was being consolidated through a market in slaves.[39] This was precisely the argument being made by the nascent white abolitionist movement in the 1830s. Outlawing the international slave trade in 1808 had "actually created the internal slave trade as one of the first entirely *domestic* forms of U.S. commerce," writes literary historian Trish Loughran.[40] And the literature of immediate abolition was the first to compel a spatial imagination of the states united as a singular nation, as a "United States." During the 1830s, articulated and distributed in the publications of the American Anti-Slavery Society (AASS), Loughran argues, this abolitionist literature was committed "to a geopolitical critique of the nation as an integrated space ... as federalism's most canny, if unrecognized, antebellum other."[41] As it critiqued the nationwide commerce in enslaved bodies—the commerce both of the domestic slave trade and of Northern fugitives forcibly returned to the South—this abolitionist discourse also conceptualized the United States as a thoroughly unified entity: the nation *as* a market in slaves. The AASS rendered that abstraction concrete by papering the nation with pamphlets sent through the U.S. postal service, like tracers injected into the bloodstream, materializing the nation through its routes of commerce and communication, inundating the mail with vivid accounts of slavery's horrors and sparking so much Southern rage that postmasters impounded them. Faced with the embargo of their pamphlets and with a gag rule on their antislavery petitions in Congress, the AASS proceeded to deluge the Capitol with more petitions "by waggon loads," in John Quincy Adams's words, "filling a twenty-by-thirty foot room to its fourteen-foot ceiling."[42]

The ideologies that underpinned abolitionism also underpinned Northern literary production more broadly, not least a fervent political theology of freedom made to sync up with this emergent market culture. An egalitarian individualism rejected institutions for a bold and romantic embrace of the common man. That individualism was germinating in the soil of free market capitalism, however, and it would not reject *that* institution. Individualism's leveling of hierarchies animated radical claims for the equality of women and slaves (and hence, spurred immediate abolitionism), but this doctrine of liberal selfhood also denied the violence and power innate to capitalism. As a "free" worker, one was never victim to circumstances, to institutions, to history, one was the victim only of personal shortcomings according to these lights. The common man was expected to fan the flames of his own divine spark, to take responsibility for his own improvement and advancement, his education and success—or his utter failure—in this new discourse of what Emerson termed "self-reliance." If such workers suffered, "theirs is the fault," as preeminent abolitionist William Lloyd Garrison bluntly put it. The solution to their problems was "an internal rather than an outward reorganization."[43] Sanctifying freedom and equality, abolitionism sacralized the free market.[44] So defined, as many have noted, "freedom" achieved its coherence in opposition to slavery. In parallel, attendant virtues of character and interiority were being enshrined in the North's literary culture, virtues that supplied bourgeois alibis for the practices of class exploitation. And to the extent that Northern literature articulated the cultural program for this free market ideology, it too depended on slavery. Sometimes that dependence was quite direct: the first and foremost literary journal in the United States, the *North American Review*, was edited between 1835 and 1843 by John Palfrey, the scion of enslavers in Louisiana's sugar country, and Palfrey often received funds from his family to keep the magazine afloat. Slavery's profits paid for the paper and ink that printed the words of William Cullen Bryant and James Fenimore Cooper.[45]

COUNTERPOISED TO THIS well-studied Northern print culture and its worldview stood the emergent literary genre of humorous writing from slavery's Southwestern frontier. "A new vein of literature, as original as it is inexhaustible in its source, has been opened in this country within a very few years, with the most marked success," wrote William T. Porter in 1845, in the preface to *The Big Bear of Arkansas*, the first anthology of "characters and incidents in the South and Southwest."[46] Thomas Bangs Thorpe, the author of the story that gave *The Big Bear* anthology its name, would later introduce his own collection by noting, "Here, in their vast interior solitudes, far removed from trans-Atlantic influences, are alone to be found, in the more comparative infancy of our country, characters truly *sui generis*—truly American." Thorpe's sentiment could serve as the slogan for this genre and the place it would assume within a national literature.[47] Hewing close to the grain of an imagined American voice, more proximate to homespun customs of storytelling and music making, these tales exemplified a realist tradition and a vernacular idiom.[48] Their writers were praised for a prowess in transcribing country manners of speech and converting oral tales into printed matter; they were deemed the inheritors of a project in colloquial literature begun centuries earlier by Geoffrey Chaucer. William T. Porter and his paper *Spirit of the Times* "brought out a new class of writers, and created a style which may be denominated an American literature—not the august, stale, didactic, pompous, bloodless method of the magazine pages of that day; but a fresh, crisp, vigorous, elastic, graphic literature, full of force, readiness, actuality and point," an obituary later claimed.[49] Rather than romantic transcendentalism, this fiction expressed a sensuous immanence. Sex, shit, violence, death—these were its purview.

Or more accurately, these were the purview of its subjects, who were almost invariably poor Southern whites. The authors themselves were professional men, occasionally planters, but more often doctors, lawyers, or editors. They had been drawn to Alabama and Mississippi and Arkansas by the boom economy in cotton, slaves, and land, the trifecta of the Southwestern frontier. Coming from the East, many of these professional men found themselves to be strangers in a strange land, immersed in a foreign local culture, and they took special interest in it. When, for example, lawyers in these locales would gather annually for regional meetings of the Bar, "the members, who often lived in remote isolation, joined in bouts of story-telling as after long drouth," Constance Rourke writes. "The strangest, most comic experiences, quiddities, oddities, tales, and bits of novel expression were treasured and matched one against another."[50] Within that small milieu, these oral anecdotes knit together their speakers and listeners, circulating as a kind of professional currency. Men were spinning the golden thread of their regional reputations from the straw of the impoverished locals. Once these professionals began writing down their humorous sketches—which usually featured the antics of those poor white backwoodsmen—and then publishing them in Eastern papers, their audience became a national and international one.

Their sketches operated partly within the register of ethnography, like travelogues that documented the curious inhabitants of an alien world. What those stories registered was not the local subjects' identity with the narrator or reader, but rather their difference. In their speech and their manners, the frontier's white squatters and homesteaders were the occasion for humor because of their debasement. Formally, this difference precipitated the genre's frame narrative, a feature of nearly all the stories. The frame narrative sets the corrupt speech of the sketch's subjects apart from the polished voice of the narrator, whose intro and outro usually bookend the tales. Stylistically, what most defines and unifies this literature is the counterpoint between a demotic voice (attributed to the backwoodsmen) and a hieratic voice (attributed to the professional). These works interpose the vernacular and the authoritative, a formal innovation within U.S. literature with a peculiarly modern flavor that, over time, would ramify widely—through the work of Mark Twain, William Faulkner, James Agee, Charles Portis, Barry Hannah, Cormac McCarthy, and John Jeremiah Sullivan among others. On the page, this tension between the common and the genteel, the slangy and the erudite, reads as a type of playfulness, a learned narrator being put through his paces on an unlettered ambit. This tension performs as a sign of the authentic, electrifying the text with the charge of "true" language, stripped of cliché, shorn of parlor pieties, gritty, wild.[51] One finds in these frontier works the seed of that later modernist preoccupation with "voice" in written style, which is—both as it emerges here, and as it remains in the later authors just cited—adamantly masculinist.

The genre's sketches were widely distributed in magazines such as New York's *Spirit of the Times*, a self-styled gentlemen's sporting paper, with a like-minded readership that extended North and South, East and West. That imagined community is legible within the form of the stories themselves. "The structure of narration carves out a position the reader shares with other readers such as himself... a reader who travels, bets, and swaps stories along the way; a reader who knows his place as well as he knows the place of others," literary scholar Lloyd Pratt writes, noting that the paper "fancied itself... the party organ of a transatlantic community of literate enfranchised men."[52] Unlike the one projected by the literature of immediate abolition, this imagined community was no nation stained by the sin of slavery, but instead a proud fraternal order *founded in* the slave racial capitalism of the Atlantic World. That order carried the ambitions of its white male subjects, both readers and writers, who were aspiring professional gentlemen. It sustained their identities and would be defended tirelessly; the Southern frontier—a speculator's market built on black and brown bodies and populated by the dispossessed white poor—was its animating fantasy. There was little, if any, disagreement about the virtues of the slave South among the genre's coterie of authors. Two anthologists of the genre offer a composite portrait of these writers as fierce Southern sectarians, even if they were born elsewhere, who fervently supported slavery and later secession.[53] Generally speaking, they and their readers were not aligned with President Andrew Jackson and his "Democracy," but rather stood up for the "interests of men of character, breeding, and position against domination by the new political machine."[54] These men were Whiggish and preferred a hierarchy based in culture, a fact made plain by their stories' frame narratives. But the stories were nonetheless Jacksonian in spirit, given their subject matter and voice.[55]

These men also found themselves standing on shaky social ground. "The rise of the professions, the decline of the trades, the emergence of the 'clerk' . . . all of these contributed as much (or more) to the unsettling of these men's modes of self-understanding as it did to the lining of their pockets," Pratt writes.[56] Caught in the flux of the market, experiencing its uprootedness, these authors and their readers perceived a stasis in the South's poor whites that was unavailable in their own lives. The fiction they wrote depicts this stasis ambivalently, with a mix of wistfulness and disdain. On the one hand, it registers nostalgia for an organic community and an agrarian way of life supposed to exist prior to the corrosive effects of a capitalist free market. As the anthologists note, "One of their strongest motivations was to preserve."[57] On the other hand, that stasis becomes a testament to the sheltered lives led by poor whites and to their backwardness. Ultimately, it produces them as a people who stand in the vestibule of history, without a story of progress, a status they share with women, blacks, Natives, Asians, and Mexicans. Unlike those groups, because of a shared whiteness, the stasis of poor whites could seem familiar, common, but also precious, at once adjacent and alienated—like a lost heirloom. More mannered and cosmopolitan, these authors regarded their subjects from a distance, as inhabitants of a "local" space-time in Pratt's terms, a space-time different from their own, which was so enmeshed with the cultures of print and the market. That distance was coded as *pastness* and *authenticity*.

Missing from prior accounts of this literature are the racial and class antagonisms that accompanied the enclosures of land in the Mississippi Valley—land forcibly expropriated from Natives, populated largely by a marginalized group of nonslaveholding whites, and developed by capitalist landowners through their enslavement of blacks. Between 1814 and 1830, following defeats of Natives, the British, and the Spanish, an enormous public domain had been created in the Mississippi Valley and a new continental conception of the nation blossomed. Once the General Land Office decided to auction this newly acquired territory, the resulting land market was straightaway overwhelmed by speculators. Ultimately, planter-capitalists took ownership of the most and the best land, seeding the cotton kingdom that would make, by 1860, "more millionaires per capita in the Mississippi Valley than anywhere else in the United States," historian Walter Johnson writes. "White privilege on an unprecedented scale was wrung from the lands of the Choctaw, the Creek, and the Chickasaw and from the bodies of the enslaved people brought in to replace them."[58]

Their privilege was laced with terror. The boomtime cotton economy in these years "sharpened conflict between planter elites and the white South's small-farmer majority."[59] When defined as owning twenty or more slaves, planter status couldn't be claimed by even one in a hundred white families in the South.[60] "Slaveholders feared that the slaves upon whom the Cotton Kingdom depended, as well as the nonslaveholding whites whom it shunted to the margins of a history they had thought to be their own, might rise up and even unite in support of its overthrow," according to Johnson.[61] By creating the Southwest's cotton kingdom, the expansionism spearheaded by Andrew Jackson also became the guarantor of the market revolution across America. The market's metastasis also widened the wealth gap and opened a yawning chasm between the rich and poor. Class differences became more severe during this era than ever before.[62]

Nonslaveholding Southern whites occupy a pivotal—and conflicted and tragic—place in this history. According to national lore, the "common man" of the South swept Andrew Jackson into the presidency, following the extension of universal white male suffrage. That constituency had been organized by frontier elites who supported Jackson, the first candidate ever to campaign for the office.[63] Jackson sometimes referred to his party simply as "The Democracy," as against a genteel aristocracy, an egalitarian body of which he was the executive head. It was a democracy in name only, however. The extension of suffrage as well as the move to state nominating conventions had shifted power toward anonymous men of ambition, men who didn't necessarily enjoy the privileges of family standing and social class. "Jackson's frontier strength initially derived from the ambition for power of frontier elites, and not from a mass democratic uprising against local leaders," Michael Rogin writes.[64] Much as they would a century later for the FSA, common white men supplied "symbols of ideal life" for the Jacksonian era, opportunities for grandstanding, electioneering, and usurpation. The market revolution meant that economic class increasingly supplanted social class. New money came with new access. Given a mass electorate of unpropertied white men, politicians could now legitimate their personal ambition by citing the voice of the people, identifying themselves as expressions of a newly expanded popular will. Wrangled by a specialized party apparatus, this enlarged voting bloc really just fed the growth of executive power and political bureaucracy.[65] Even Jackson's signal political victory, the dismantling of the Bank of the United States, a campaign that was undertaken in the name of the everyman against an elite "moneyed power," served the interests of wealth rather than the common good. In fact, the campaign to destroy the Bank deflected attention from a more insidious and pervasive force. "A power distant from [white] men's lives was growing in mobile capitalist America, and [white] men encountered it as they sold crops, bought land, and joined promotional schemes," Rogin notes. "That power was the power of the market." Before long, the Jacksonian ideology of entrepreneurial independence would generate structures of power that would oppress the majority of such men, in the forms of the factory, the corporation, and the militarized corporate state.[66]

Some won, most lost. The acts of enclosure in the Mississippi Valley sidelined white nonslaveholders, who were ignored by an extending plantation regime. Many left. Early in the 1800s, countless white farmers fled. A long "caravan of emigrant wagons rolled north to the free soil of Ohio, Indiana, and Illinois," while another "rolled west to populate the Gulf plains thickly with farmers before many plantations overtook them," Charles Sellers writes. In the Northwest, prior to the Civil War, families from the South outnumbered those from the North.[67] Farmers who stayed behind were shunted onto less desirable land—wherever cotton couldn't be profitably grown, in the Southern mountains or the piney woods. Farm labor in the black belt became degraded through its association with slavery, racialized as "nigger work."[68] While those nonslaveholding whites who fled were likely more inclined toward abolition (though still harboring antiblack racism), those who remained frequently became foot soldiers for the empire of cotton— merchants, overseers, patrollers—slavery's ardent and often forgotten defenders, who would die en masse decades later on the Confederacy's front lines.[69] Aside from whiteness itself, which can't be discounted, these men and their families enjoyed few of slavery's material dividends. Nouveaux riche at its center, the Jacksonian ideology nonetheless won (partly through coercion, as ever) the consent of the frontier riffraff, a group whom it did and did not represent politically.[70] Of poor Southern whites, Du Bois writes, "the labor movement ignored them and the abolitionists ignored them; and above all, they were ignored by Northern capitalists and Southern planters. They were in many respects almost a forgotten mass of men."[71]

THEY WERE NOT FORGOTTEN by the writers of the Southwest's frontier stories, however. The contemporary popularity of this new genre, centered as it was on the japes and capers of poor whites, likely owes to the larger absence of this population from public discourse. The sketches must have electrified readers with the charge of discovery: *Who are these people?* Widely distributed, these stories helped establish a new grammar for their cultural representation. Rude, ignorant, and uncouth as they appeared, they represented an invented agrarian tradition that counterbalanced the culture of commerce and the cosmopolitanism of the market, so identified with a corrupting Northern industrialism. Poor whites were protagonists for a fairy tale whose emblem and apogee was the plantation. They occupied the starting point on an ideological course that culminated in the plantation's ease, refinement, gentility, and wealth. They possessed the crude ore that, fired in the kiln of the Southern slave "tradition," yielded a purer whiteness. Living anachronisms, part derelict and part relic, poor whites became symbols of the Southern plantation's common past, the raw materials for its cloud-castles of precapitalist freedom.

As slaves were dishumanized by the plantation regime, so too, albeit less absolutely, were poor whites. These were "landless white men in a landscape being remade by black slavery and private property ... [and] they were woefully out of place," Johnson writes, as class differences among whites could be translated "into other sorts of difference: historical difference, which made poor whites seem like men from another time; racial differences, which made them seem not quite white."[72] These were also men and women who entered into all manner of intercourse with slaves—not least the obvious sexual sort, but also the commercial kind—which undermined the rigidity of status in the South. "Slaves and poor whites conducted a thriving illicit trade throughout the antebellum era," according to historian Jeff Forret, often exchanging stolen plantation goods for liquor or clothing.[73] This massive and potentially restive underclass also posed a danger to the plantation regime, if one less vivid than that of slave revolt. Consorting with slaves, breaking racial etiquette, possible co-conspirators in a feared uprising, these men were under suspicion for their loyalty by the slaveholding elite, as in Mississippi in 1835 when a feared plot involving them ended in executions of both blacks and whites. As "incomplete members of a society in which privilege was defined by slaveholding even more than by race," they threatened the established order. These were persons who could be asked in all earnestness by the South's aristocracy, "Were you to witness a bloody conflict between the slaves of this country and the white people, on which side would you be?"[74]

3. Literature: 1830s

It is *this* history that is essential to the formation of American literature. This history of ostracism and division produces the quality of authenticity that is so fundamental to the fiction of the Southwestern frontier. Formally, Southwestern humor roots "American literature" only through its new representational inclusion of poor whites. Just as importantly for its discursive success, this fiction also ironizes literary discourse. It pokes fun at highfalutin codes of politeness, gentility, and deference, but it also *sustains* them. When compared to the measured Northeastern literature of the American Renaissance, this new voice and style can be properly understood as a modernist innovation. But this genre's inclusion of poor whites is vexed. Avatars of popular democracy and frontier independence, nominally represented by the state but never actually included (another paradox of "we the people"), these whites were a site of contradiction. Their abject status exposed the universalizing creed of the liberal democratic state as nothing but hot air. At the same time, they represented outsiders who were in the process of being made free by that state.[75] Through its frame narratives and its counterpoint of high and low registers, this literature formally articulates a configuration of whiteness that is *assimilative*: these poor folks are, or can become, white. Here, literary form *itself* is a narrative of progress that is also a testimony to difference. Formally speaking, the liberal project instantiated through this genre imagines these poor whites becoming its authorial subjects and bridging the divide of the frame narrative. (And this is precisely why Twain is so revered.)

What earmarks this literature and what primes it for appropriation by the critics of the 1930s is how this tense and particular history congeals within the language itself. In their conceit of transcribing the speech of their subjects, including their orthography of dialect, these stories already formally adopt the pose of immediacy. And yet, as the critic Richard Bridgman pointed out long ago in his study of colloquial style in American literature, "Intensification of the illusion of reality is inseparable from the intensification of artifice."[76] Representing the language of these poor whites, the printed word is made to express something more than its actual meaning, a floating tone of naked presence. Of a piece with this language's "thingliness," while apparently defying it, this tone resembles the "aura" described by Walter Benjamin, a

> 176 SUT LOVINGOOD'S SERMON.
>
> menyfeld tribulashuns nur anuther this side the place whar murd'rs, 'dult'rs, hook-nose Jews, suckit-riders, tavrin folk, an' sich like cattil go tu arter they's swep frum the face ove yeath by death's broom, tu cumfort tharsefs drinkin bilin tar, an' eatin red-hot casiron sassengers. Hit is durn'd infunel single slay'd, pewter spoon, fly-blown, one hoss, half stock'd, single trigger, smoof bore tavrins, an' railroad feed troffs. They's shorten'd my days, they's lainthen'd my nights, they's poperlated the hole territory ove my cackus, clear'd lan' an' wood lan', wif all breeds ove dredful insex, they's gutted my pockid, they's disturb'd my dreams, they's 'stonish'd my stumok, they's skeer'd my appertite, they'se spilt my smellin tools, they's deafen'd my years, they's 'sulted my eyes, an' they's lef a marster stink all over ontu me furever an' ever more, an' more so too ay—men. Oh, my dear yearers, 'keep the dus' ove thar dinin-room ofen yer foot, an' the smell ove thar bed-room ofen yer close, that yer days may be longer in the lan' what yer daddy's tuck frum the Injuns.'
>
> "I seed a well appearin man onst, ax one ove em what lived ahine a las' year's crap ove red hot brass wire whiskers run tu seed, an' shingled wif har like ontu mildew'd flax, wet wif saffron warter, an' laid smoof wif a hot flat-iron, ef he cud spar him a scrimpshun ove soap? The 'perpryiter' anser'd in soun's es sof an' sweet es a poplar dulcimore, tchuned by a good nater'd
>
> SUT LOVINGOOD'S SERMON. 177
>
> she angel in butterfly wings an' cobweb shift, that he never wer jis' so sorry in all his born'd days tu say no, but the fac' wer the soljers had stole hit; 'a towil then;' 'the soljers hed stole hit;' 'a tumbler,' 'the soljers hed stole hit;' 'a lookin-glass,' 'the soljers hed stole nit;' 'a pitcher ove warter,' 'the soljers hed stole hit;' 'then please give me a cleaner room.' Quick es light cum the same dam lie, 'the soljers hed stole hit too. They buys scalded butter, caze hit crumbles an' yu can't tote much et a load on yer knife; they keeps hit four months so yu won't want tu go arter a secon load. They stops up the figgers an' flowers in the woffil irons fur hit takes butter tu fill the holes in the woffils. They makes soup outen dirty towils, an' jimson burrs; coffee outen niggers' ole wool socks, roasted; tea frum dorg fennil, an' toas' frum ole brogan insoles. They keeps bugs in yer bed tu make yu rise in time fur them tu get the sheet fur a table-cloth. They gins yu a inch ove candil tu go tu bed by, an' a littil nigger tu fetch back the stump tu make gravy in the mornin, fur the hunk ove bull naik yu will swaller fur brekfus, an' they puts the top sheaf ontu thar orful merlignerty when they menshuns the size ove yer bill, an' lasly, while yu're gwine thru yer close wif a sarch warrun arter fodder enuf tu pay hit, they refreshes yer memory ove other places, an' other times, by tellin yu ove the orful high price ove tuckys, aigs, an' milk. When the dveil takes a likin tu a feller, an'

Pages from *Sut Lovingood's Yarns* by George Washington Harris (1867). While Harris began publishing in *Spirit of the Times* in the 1840s, his *Sut Lovingood* stories did not appear until the 1850s, but they are an apex of the genre's tropes and its use of dialect.

"strange tissue of space and time: the unique apparition of a distance, however near it may be," which here attaches to the "authentic" speech of the "folk."[77] These stories dissemble as plain talk, face-to-face conversation. In their efforts to make the printed word "speak," as it were, these stories work to deny the mediating effects of the print culture and market society in which they are produced and circulated. Ironically, they end up reinforcing that objectification. Words themselves assume a "thingly" aspect, registering this reifying process.

The alienation of aspiring and middle-class white men, which is the backdrop for this literature, seeks an ersatz remedy on the page through certain techniques of realism. At the same time, "Orthography reminds the printer's gentlemen subscribers that their class is a natural feature of language," as Michael Warner writes.[78] Written and consumed by snobbish Whigs, this fiction bears witness to an emergent culture of taste and sensibility that unites author and reader, a culture that achieves coherence through those whom it excludes. Fostered by contemporary and future criticism, this literary culture increasingly becomes a "tradition" that defines itself as "national," as "American."[79] It is not simply that a romantic note of agrarianism creeps into the content of these stories, along with frank racist speech. The historical setting of racialized class conflict solidifies within the *form* of these stories. This becomes the imprint of *style*. This fiction's humor, as well as some of its immediacy, derives from a practiced contrast between the low and the high, its oscillations between slangy and formal diction. By means of this style—coded as the epitome of a genuine national literary expression, deemed exceptional for its exemplary folk character—"ordinary" language amplifies and demarcates "literary" language.

The particular style that emerges matches perfectly what Theodor Adorno would later describe as the "jargon of authenticity." Adorno argued that this jargon pretended to offer a philosophical critique of alienation while actually mystifying human domination.[80] Authenticity, Adorno writes,

> can support itself on the fact that over a long period of time literal as well as figurative mobility, a main element in bourgeois equality, always turned into injustice for those who could not entirely keep up. They experienced the progress of society as a verdict: a pawned-off remembrance of their suffering, under that system, brings authenticity, along with its jargon, to a ferment. Its bubbles cause the true object of the suffering, the particular constitution of society, to disappear. For the selected victims of the feeling against mobility have themselves been condemned, ever since the sphere of circulation was fused into the sphere of production. The jargon strives to turn the bitterness of the indigenous, of the mute, into something like a metaphysical-moral verdict of annihilation against the man who can speak out; and the jargon has had so much success only for this reason, because this verdict in question has already in effect been spoken, and has been carried out in Germany against innumerable people—because the gesture of rooted genuineness is at one with that of the historical conquerors. That is the substantial element in authenticity, the holy fount of its strength.[81]

In other words, those whom capitalist transformation leaves behind, those whom it disempowers and dispossesses, those whom it causes suffering, those whom history hurts—these injured become the repository of the real. The jargon of authenticity exalts their destitute condition as more simple and true, and so damns them to continuing deprivation. The jargon is the notary of this fait accompli of "progress." Authenticity reifies dispossession as a hallowed anteriority, only in and of the past, which is also a "verdict of annihilation," a belatedness that is sacred and touched by pathos. Once objectified, the customs and language of the impoverished can be revalued and reappropriated—just as "the vernacular and its still vital sources of production ... are reappropriated by the exhausted and media-standardized speech of a hegemonic middle class," according to Fredric Jameson.[82] Adorno continues: "Allegedly hale life is opposed to damaged life, on whose societalized consciousness, on whose 'malaise,' the jargon speculates. Through the ingrained language form of the jargon, that hale life is equated with agrarian conditions, or at least with simple commodity economy, far from all social considerations." He writes: "This life is in effect equated to something undivided, protectingly closed, which runs its course in a firm rhythm and unbroken continuity.... Past forms of societalization, prior to the division of labor, are surreptitiously adopted as if they were eternal. Their reflection falls upon later conditions which have already been victimized by progressive rationalization, and in contrast to those the earlier states seem the more human."[83]

It is as if, at least in the context of the Southern frontier of the 1830s, the first enclosure of land and markets, which displaces and disables certain populations, is succeeded by a *second* enclosure in the domain of culture that coopts and commodifies the modes of life and speech of these populations. This second enclosure renders them a "folk" burdened by "authenticity." These poor whites' spoken language expressed their historical situation, having been cast aside and excluded by a voracious market that counted them extraneous. Their dialect was nothing but the watermark of this exclusion, evidence of their removal to the periphery of a society now entirely oriented around the fortunes to be made from stolen lands planted with cotton worked by enslaved labor.[84] They became a kind of living archive that could be pilfered indiscriminately by cultural producers, raw material that could be mined and refined into cultural capital. It is this history and ideology that predicates the authentic Americanness of the style forged in these stories. And the style itself borrows profligately from this created fund of the genuine to sponsor the individuality of its authors. When one of these authors writes in his book's preface, "Wherever it has been possible we have let our characters use their own language in portraying their *individuality!*" he expects to reap a similar dividend.[85] Style, as Jameson writes, "is the very element of individuality itself, that mode through which the individual consciousness seeks to distinguish itself, to affirm its incomparable originality."[86] Through this Southern frontier style, which becomes a pretender to national American style, "The formal gesture of autonomy replaces the content of autonomy," in Adorno's words.[87] Aestheticism supplants agency. The folk represents a cultural commons of humanness that is tragically mismanaged by the folk themselves and will supply the raw material to repair commodified personhood within a market society that can now appear unified rather than fragmented, idiosyncratic rather than cookie-cutter. Style amounts to private property produced by that second enclosure.

Although it emerges to remediate voids of alienation, instead this style of authenticity accentuates and calcifies that alienation, setting language at a temporal and spatial remove, further objectifying it. Language isn't regarded as living speech that constitutes particular and material social relations or as the historical manifestation of such relations—not, in other words, as a mode of practical consciousness.[88] Instead, it is instrumentalized. Style expressed a contradiction, bearing the insignia of the timelessness and autonomy, even as it is determined within a market culture, amid a glut of surplus value underwritten by racial slavery. Specifically, in the print culture and market society coalescing in the 1830s, these stories respond in counterpoint to two other types of writing, two other forms of circulating printed matter: namely, paperwork and paper money. Both paperwork and paper money reached a high-water mark in the Mississippi Valley of the 1830s, achieving a level of predominance heretofore unknown in U.S. history. Both provide a sort of negative example of rationalization and alienation against which this literary genre assembles and defines itself. And the influence of each leaves its mark on these stories.

"IN THE FULNESS of time, the new era had set in—the era of the second great experiment of independence: the experiment, namely, of credit without capital, and enterprise without honesty," Joseph Glover Baldwin writes of the 1830s slave frontier in *The Flush Times of Alabama and Mississippi*. Beneath the feverish bidding wars around slaves and cotton was an enormous real estate bubble, an insatiable hunger for the land the federal government had violently seized from Natives and was now selling off in regular surveyed parcels. Through legal machinations, those parcels could actually be traded on before they were sold, fueling wild speculation in land claims. That rapacious accumulation of acreage—and of finance capital—also generated an avalanche of land patents and, in tandem, as Walter Johnson notes, "an army of clerks," such that "the boom years of 1831–1835 brought a sort of bureaucratic apocalypse to the district land offices of the Mississippi Valley. In Mississippi, a few beleaguered clerks were dwarfed by towering stacks of field notes ... in Arkansas, an overwhelmed and dismissed Surveyor General left behind him more than 5,000 miles' worth of unprocessed reports, more than twice the length of the Mississippi River itself. Despite spending much of December 1832 personally signing land patents," Johnson writes, "President Andrew

Jackson fell so far behind that he convinced Congress to appropriate money to pay a full-time clerk with the sole responsibility of signing the president's name to land patents."[89] All of these tasks fell under the aegis of the General Land Office, a bureau within the Treasury Department.[90] At points during the 1830s, there was such a backlog that it would have required almost eight years of work to get up to date, and simply signing patents—just *signing them*—would have absorbed the whole attention of the bureau's commissioner literally for years.[91]

The terra firma of the frontier that was being surveyed and parceled, sold, and traded, found its imaginary complement in the land patent, which formed the crux of the bureaucratic apocalypse Johnson describes: sectioned acres of land that were abstracted in a paper avalanche of forms. And avalanche isn't too far off the mark. "Records of the land districts filled every corner of the General Land Office; adding to the crush were the new 'Chickasaw business,' the unending labor of the draftsmen, and the procession of patent books. . . . The thirteen rooms on the lower floor of the State Department Building were no longer adequate to hold the records of the land business, much less provide working area for the several clerks," according to another historian. The time lag and its frustrations filtered into applicants' daily lives, too. The backlog was such that the commissioner estimated that at least 5,500 applicants would die before they got their patents.[92] Nothing like this had transpired before in a fledgling United States.

The files of land patents that were proliferating on the State Department's ground floor were the *official* version of the frontier, as it was being transformed from natural features into denatured information, from a given terrain into a plotted territory, from commons into commodities—as it was being metabolized by and incorporated within the United States. The frontier on the ground was always simultaneously a frontier on the page. The labor of the "pioneer," of the settler, paralleled the labor of the clerk, the bureaucrat. The paper pushers would get no heroic ballads or romantic treatments, however. Indeed, it is fair to say that they've been banished from the nation's cultural and historical memory, and that a vast—and disavowed—state apparatus of administrative machinery operates behind our vaunted apparition of the frontier's absolute independence. (That forgotten reality coined the idiom of "doing a land-office business.") But, from a certain angle, the clerks and their ilk *did write* those tales and legends. The authors of frontier humor far more closely resembled desk jockeys than they did any axe-swinging, muzzle-loading backwoodsmen. These writers were not, on the whole, to-the-manor-born; they were neither heirs nor planters. Even by many of them, their efforts were framed as something akin to ethnography, as though they were producing surveyor's reports on the *human* topography of the Mississippi Valley. And the shape and tenor of these "fictional" pieces are actually decorated with the furniture of documentary—the firsthand auditor, the objective witness, the story as "sketch"—that replicates the official report and the bureaucratic record. Produced by professionals, these sketches share something of that virtual world of patents, records, and reports.[93] This system of paperwork pushes writing toward automation, reducing it to a sterile information technology that extinguishes the writer's personality. "Business writing rested on an insistently utilitarian ethos, self-consciously shorn of stylized gesture," business historian Michael Zakim has written of the rationalization of handwriting in paperwork. "Facts were to speak for themselves on the page, fashioned by a manufacturing technique whose functionalism was manifest in the standard nature of its production . . . as well as the standard nature of its product."[94]

The land patent backed—and itself became—currency in this booming economy built on speculation. In lieu of specie came a flood of questionable money whose value did not appear objective, as with gold or silver, but was instead subject to the vagaries of faith and chance. More than any of the dozens of authors writing in this genre, Baldwin focuses most clearly on the workings of finance. "A new theory, not found in the works of political economy, was broached. It was found out that the prejudice in favor of the metals . . . was an absurd superstition; and that, in reality, any thing else, which the parties interested in giving it currency chose, might serve as a representative of value and medium for exchange of property," Baldwin writes. "Accordingly it was decided that Rags, a very familiar character, and very popular, and easy of access, should take [the] place [of gold and silver]. Rags belonged to the school of American progress. . . . It was based on the . . . idea of keeping the imagination of the people excited. . . . The principle of success and the basis of operation though inexplicable in the hurry of the time, is plain enough now: it was faith. Let the public believe that a smutted rag is money, it is money."[95] Paper money littered the United States in the 1830s, especially on the frontier, where it proliferated alongside land speculation, a fact indexed by the explosion in the number of state-chartered banks that issued their own currency, a number that nearly doubled during the 1830s.[96]

When Baldwin memorably notes in one of his sketches, "The State banks were issuing their bills by the sheet, like a patent steam printing-press its issues," it is telling that printed money is figured as the printed word.[97] And when Baldwin designates and explains the "Rag Empire" in the excerpt above, it must be remembered that by the 1830s the word *rags* already referred not just to cheap currency but also to cheap newsprint, since both the money and the newspapers were made of the same material—rags—which was itself composed of what was growing all around Baldwin in Alabama and Mississippi: cotton. So Baldwin's metaphor yoking "bills by the sheet" and periodical issues isn't so much figurative as literal, a real allegory.[98] Similarly, the market speculation materialized in those paper bills finds its linguistic correlate in the wordplay, the exaggeration, that are Southwestern humor's hallmarks, what Constance Rourke, discussing its tall talk and tall tales, properly calls "inflation": "'Absquatulate,' 'slantendiclur,' 'cahoot,' 'catawampus,' 'spyficated,' 'flabbergasted,' 'tarnacious,' 'rampagious,' 'concussence,' 'supernatiousness,' 'rumsquattle.'" Both words and narratives in this genre balloon such that they stretch the boundaries of credibility, "verging aggressively toward the appearance of truth and sheering away again," as she puts it.[99]

As with the speculative bubble of commodity prices in which they grew, the stories' ebullience lay in their unrestrained artifice. Their most memorable characters are unabashed liars, whose fibs are charged with a charismatic grace—con artists of the first rank. Baldwin lionizes both the speculator, who trades in seductive fictions of profit, and the lawyer, who twists legality through the flourish of rhetoric. These are men whose verbal skills are surcharged with a performative force, through whom the art of language can be seen as a vector of power. Baldwin's sketch of the champion liar Ovid Bolus presents a character who embodies the overlap between narrative fictions and fictitious capital. "He adopted a fact occasionally to start with, but, like a Sheffield razor and the crude ore, the workmanship, polish and value were all his own: a Thibet shawl could as well be credited to the insensate goat that grew the wool, as the author of a fact Bolus honored with his artistical skill, could claim to be the inventor of the story," Baldwin writes, and then shortly continues: "How well he asserted the Spiritual over the Material! How he delighted to turn an abstract idea into concrete cash—to make a few blots of ink, representing a little thought, turn out a labor-saving machine, and bring into his pocket money which many days of hard exhausting labor would not procure!"[100] Men like Bolus were slick schemers who thumbed their noses at republican virtues of productive labor, and this genre enacts a transvaluation of values on the tenets of republicanism. Here, those who labor in the earth aren't the chosen people of God, as Thomas Jefferson insisted. Farmers and manual laborers are hardworking suckers. They are dupes to be swindled.

Through characters such as Bolus, this fiction heroizes the immaterial labor of financial speculation, which republicanism denounced.

Beneath Baldwin's sketches and characters lay a truth: the freedom of these white professional men was felt most keenly by exercising the power of words. Language unfettered by convention is made the sign of personal liberty. "What a man does well he must do with freedom. He can no more speak in trammels than he can walk in chains; and he must learn to think freely before he can speak freely," Baldwin writes in a sketch on frontier attorneys, from a land where slaves marched in coffles.[101] This "untrammeled" language springs from the material relations of market and law, which make and remake the world of this plantation frontier, a world of land floats and squatters, a world of insurance scams on slaves buried and resurrected, a world where legal order and human life was dandled on the knee of get-rich-quick schemes.[102] These men's intellect and their will would—and did—bend the world their way, at any expense. Baldwin's sketches are tall tales of self-fashioning, men talking themselves into positions of control, authority, and influence. And again and again, the chicanery of these figures depends materially on the degradation and exploitation of enslaved blacks, defrauded Natives, and imbruted lower-class whites. Kept underfoot, those ousted groups are the very ground on which these men's riches and reputations are built. On the page, those diminished lives are made the backdrop for the scintillate edge of these men's mastery, their intellectual and material superiority. In fiction, the lie told for the sake of its effect on others becomes the sign of these men's authority, and of their authorship. Through the individual creativity of the well-told lie, the material relations aggregated in language are abstracted in the singular work of a personal style, even as language deceptively manipulates social relations for personal gain. ("Like every other eminent artist, [Bolus] brought all his faculties to bear on his art.... A lie never ran away with him, as it is apt to do with young performers; he could always manage and guide it.")[103] Style becomes the calling card of an imagination with the ability to create and to compel, a trace of sovereignty. As seen through Ovid Bolus, the imagination necessary for this frontier world of finance and credit redounds to the "imaginative" work of literature, a mirror play of surplus values.[104] Every bubble of speculation is fabricated from the irreducible materiality of labor. That labor was never going to be performed by these godlike liars, cast as authors of their own fates.

Poised between the facelessness of the folk and the anonymity of administration, these writers were deeply invested in their own individualism, and they consistently remark their own distinct positions and differentiate their presences within the sketches themselves. Without claims either to any sort of barbaric honor (i.e., killing Natives) or to awe-striking money and power (i.e., owning fields full of slaves), their relatively fragile status as white men—their social privilege—rested heavily on their professionalism, and so too on their personalities. Personality was, to a great degree, their most valuable "property." Intangible, subjectively valued, such property partook of the heightened abstractions of the finance economy that defined the Southern frontier of the 1830s. In this moment, to crib from the intellectual historian J. G. A. Pocock regarding similar processes in a different milieu, "Property—the material foundation of both personality and government—has ceased to be real and has become not merely mobile but imaginary."[105] Through the alchemy of paperwork, a unique plot of turf could take the form of a fungible land patent. Through the alchemy of paper money, slaves stooped in a cotton field could take the form of a wildcat bank's dubious currency. And through the alchemy of another paper system, literature, anonymous frontier lawyers and nameless country doctors could become national authors, as their *transcriptions* of salty folk idioms took the form of the *inscriptions* of a stylized personal voice. In so doing, they created not landed, but literary property.[106]

THIS ABILITY TO inscribe their personality onto the page as a form of imaginary property and to render their identity in print as a kind of currency in a way that was marked as peculiarly *American* was the innovation that would demarcate these writers for later critics, within the eventual canon of national literature that would be retrospectively assembled in the twentieth century.[107] They would appear (both to contemporary and later critics) as native *authors* who crafted a native *style*. As opposed to the intense internal focus of the Romantics and the Transcendentalists, for whom style would be the efflorescence of the artistic psyche and the fruit of introspection, the Southern frontier humorists articulated a style marked for its exteriority, built not so much around mastery of oneself as around mastery of one's world. As form, this style would outlive its particular content, accessible to future authors like Twain, who would claim it and refine it.[108] It would survive by feeding on the contrasts between high and low to produce the effect of the literary, expressing an oscillation historically grounded in the production of racial and class difference on the Southern frontier of the 1830s.[109]

And beneath it all lay slavery. So much of the language and oral culture of the enslaved must have been laundered through the figure of the poor white in these stories. In this literary genre, in the Southern frontier society that gives it birth and in the American market where it circulates, the capitalization of the black body founds the real. Slaves and the cotton they produced were "the law and the prophets to the men of the South," as the Scottish traveler James Stirling wrote.[110] "Slave property is the foundation of all property in the South," according to *DeBow's Review*. "When security in this is shaken, all other property partakes of its instability."[111] "If psychic compensation was the 'wages of whiteness,' blackness was the gold standard against which those wages were drawn," as Michael O'Malley writes. Slaves "anchored the sense of white superiority while they enabled the expansion of credit and an astonishing variety of regular and irregular forms of money. Even far from slavery, in the North, the idea of racial inferiority provided a psychic balance to a speculative economy."[112] As genteel professional white men taking part in a cosmopolitan literary print culture, these authors define themselves against the class of people whom their fiction explicitly represents and through whom the larger genre assembles its form and content: poor whites. Their status as provincial and sheltered illiterates yields the authority—in its doubled sense, as authors and as superiors—of these professionals. But the identity of the "poor white" only gains its salience as a category through contrast with blackness and the slave, against blacks as "anticitizens."[113] This also erupts on the page in the characterizing candor of racist epithets, whose frisson of impropriety only redoubles the authenticity of the style. In a character's words from one of these frontier stories, so much is said regarding capitalist transformation, class difference, folk nostalgia, and the slave's value and abjection: "Where's the fun, the frolicking, the fighting? Gone! Gone! The rifle won't make a man a living now—he must turn nigger and work."[114]

4. Literature: 1930s

Only through slavery, then, could poor whites be constituted as a discrete group with a particular culture to be recorded. Only through the associated logic of segregation could that cultural formation be differentiated from the black cultures with which it was completely and inextricably intertwined. This was the emergent project undertaken by the frontier authors of the 1830s. That project would be taken up again by cultural producers a century later, including the literary critics of the 1930s who were aligned with cultural nationalism. Around 1930, in contrast to the moonlight-and-magnolias mythology pegged to the plantation South, whose symbolism remained regional and generically "Southern" (even when it achieved unprecedented popularity, as in *Gone with the Wind*), the provincial character of Southern poor white culture began to dissolve. Around 1930, Southern poor white culture came to seem basically American. The white poor of the South were becoming the *nation's* poor in that decade, and these rural poor, the nation's folk.

Following the example set by the Southwestern authors of the 1830s, primed by a century-long tradition, the Lomaxes and their ilk plunged into the region to resume the erstwhile quest of locating folkways in Southern frontier spaces, usually as archivists asserting their affiliation with the state. At the same time, during the 1930s, literary critics were constructing an ancillary archive of American literature. For these critics, as for public officials, the South could suddenly represent the nation. Indeed, the idea of "the South" was necessary to imagine and to narrate the contradictions that defined the U.S. situation in their contemporary moment: overproduction, shrinking exports, falling prices, declining incomes. Following the crash of 1929 and in the midst of the Great Depression, the South came to symbolize the hardships endured by unemployed masses across the country, as its farmers were being plunged into an even deeper indigence while undergoing what Dorothea Lange and Paul Taylor called "an American exodus" in their book title of 1939. A series of disasters in the region, especially the Flood of 1927, had rendered the colonial situation of the Southern states acutely visible. (Recall, for example, Maury Maverick's excoriation of New York's "Privy Lords of Trade and Plantations, who ... govern the South by remote control.") The discourse of colonialism framed the South in the 1930s.

Public officials and agents, such as the Lomaxes or the FSA photographers, as well as public intellectuals and cultural producers, such as Bernard DeVoto or James Agee, all struggled in varied and oblique ways to comprehend and represent the collective subject produced by the process of Southern enclosure—the laborers of the rural South, both white and black. At the same time, these Southern poor were asserting their voice politically through organizing and geographically through mass migrations northward and westward in search of better conditions.[115] More and more blacks were moving into those regions' cities, and many of those who remained were organizing into interracial groups such as the Southern Tenant Farmers Union, founded in 1934. Amplified by unions and dispersed through migration, this radical populist voice was being "enclosed," as it were, in the state's archives and on the page where it was transmuted into an "American" voice. Through a multifaceted project of archiving, public officials transformed this collective subject into a national "folk" who were projected retrospectively into the past. The past functioned as a container, a cell to which dispossessed Southern laborers were assigned. And in the process, with their unifying praxis opposed by public officials, this collective subject was also, not coincidentally, being segregated. An insistent whitening of the "American folk" transpired during the 1930s. At just the moment that black migrants from the nation's southern periphery were moving into its northern and western centers in historic numbers and as protesting black and white farmers unionized and initiated the Long Civil Rights Movement, cultural producers bore down all the harder on the folk concept and on the color line that partitioned it.[116] Washed into the open, the contradictions of slave racial capitalism that couldn't be resolved in the economic sphere—not least, the sphinx's riddle of the poor white's status—found expression in the domain of culture.

It wasn't that white scholars ignored black contributions to American folk culture. The Lomaxes recorded many blacks in their quest to archive American folk music, seeking performers in supposedly isolated places, especially penitentiaries, not least Lead Belly, whom they promoted into legend. And Howard Odum, a prominent sociologist at Chapel Hill, also collected black folk songs, which he described as "weary and lonesome blues so strange and varied as to reveal a sort of superhuman evidence of the folk soul."[117] For these white scholars, black folk culture was both exemplary and exotic, familiarly American and yet weirdly not. But giving the lie to whatever inclusion this seemed to signal, Odum also wrote: "Little need be said concerning social and political equality. There is no absolute race equality in any sense of the word. The races have different abilities and potentialities."[118] For the Lomaxes, little seemed to distinguish the technology of a phonograph from the technology of a Lead Belly: both were valued for their *record* and *playback* features.[119] And in *Our Singing Country* (1941), remember that the Lomaxes divided their "best" folk singers into two lists—one unmarked and one "Negro." Blacks might be regarded as living repositories of a folk heritage that was American in principle, but that knowledge did not humanize them. They existed behind the Veil. Within the tradition rooted in the slave frontier that was becoming national literature, the shared "folk" language of blacks and whites met different ends. Blacks were construed as strangers within this "American language," however much they had contributed to its vitality, while country whites were regarded as a point of connection with its origin.[120] And while the speech of country whites initiated a continuum with "literature" and its domain of universality, the speech of blacks was constricted to the oral realm of story and song, to animal tales and blues compositions set apart by the question of "African" survivals.

The South's poor whites posed, though, both as a toxin and as a remedy—a *pharmakon*—for scholars and cultural producers. With them, the specters of identity and equality weren't so readily dispelled. Take the assignment for

Fortune magazine that sent James Agee and Walker Evans to Hale County, Alabama, in 1936. The guiding presumption behind that job was that Southern sharecroppers—explicitly *white* Southern sharecroppers—had become, effectively, foreign subjects in their native land, so disfigured by poverty due to the ruthless predation of capitalist agriculture that they were now unrecognizable to their fellow countrymen.[121] (As a rule, this is what makes the Southern, gothic—this mangling and estrangement by domestic colonialism, as with the poor whites in Erskine Caldwell's popular novels *Tobacco Road* and *God's Little Acre* from the early 1930s.) But one doesn't remember Agee and Evans's *Let Us Now Praise Famous Men*, the 1941 book yielded by that *Fortune* assignment, for its gothic overtones. It is remembered instead for its tortuous principles, alternately vexed and vaunted, and for its poetic and pyrotechnic wordsmithery, what one recent critic calls its "torrents and flying buttresses of metaphor and self-analysis."[122] Those aspects owe to how fully Agee and Evans express the contradiction of conundrum and cure that poor whites posed.

Over the course of *Let Us Now Praise Famous Men*, this takes shape as a double bind in which Agee finds himself caught. The project originated as a philippic against the capitalist plunder of these poor farmers' lives, a state of affairs that Agee and Evans regard as criminal. (One of the book's epigraphs is pulled from *The Communist Manifesto*.) That motive fuels the project's documentary impulse, with Agee and Evans taking great care to inventory and to represent these tenant farmers' lives, first as a failed article for *Fortune*, and then as a titanic book project. They undertake an exposé. Somewhere in the writing, though, Agee finds himself snared, philosophically, in whether his subjects are types (Southern tenant farmers) or individuals (a George Gudger, an Ellen Woods). And it is his furious scrambling within that trap, the heat of the friction—damning journalism, damning realism and naturalism, damning the technology of the book, damning representation itself—that makes the writing so luminous.

Agee and Evans manage to expose the systematic depredation of these white Southerners and at the same time to sacralize, rather than to stigmatize, them as poverty's injured. By the close of the book, they have carried their work of redemption so far that their subjects have become saints; indeed, it's hard to imagine them as ordinary humans susceptible to venal lust. Agee and Evans flood them with so much angelic light that they banish all shadows. For Agee, a morning breakfast becomes a Mass, Squinchy Gudger suckling at his mother's breast becomes a Pieta, and in one of the book's multiple endings, he can declare, "Everything that is, is holy."[123] And Evans's photographs are almost explicit in generating this religious iconography: the bedroom fire-

Walker Evans, photograph of Floyd Burroughs' fireplace (1936) (Library of Congress, Washington, D.C.).

place and mantle rendered as a ramshackle altar; young Lucille Burroughs against a wooden wall enhaloed by her straw hat like Piero della Francesca's *Madonna della Misericordia*; a still life of worn-out boots that pays homage to Van Gogh's *A Pair of Shoes*, attempting to restore to the commodity the aura of ritual use. One puts down *Let Us Now Praise Famous Men* puzzled by who needs saving from whom. Is the poverty of these white people a curse or a blessing?

So well conveyed by Agee and Evans, this confusion oriented the larger public debate about the South. Shaped by the discourse of colonialism, that debate can be split into two guiding schools of thought. The first was the regionalism articulated by a coterie of social scientists affiliated with the University of North Carolina at Chapel Hill, scholars such as Rupert Vance, George Tindall, Arthur Raper, and foremost among them, Howard Odum, which exerted tremendous influence on FDR's *Report* (the South as "the nation's No. 1 economic problem"). These men published a series of careful sociological and historical studies during the 1930s, which outlined the South's dire economic plight, in a shared belief that the region's ills could only be redressed through the largesse of the federal government and that the region should be developed along the lines of the rest of the United States. Scholars such as these "replaced the South of Confederate glory, the South of traditional culture, with a South whose very definition was 'that part of the United States whose people are most deprived.'"[124] For the Chapel Hill Regionalists, colonialism had generated a Southern separateness that was precisely the obstacle that had to be overcome. Their rallying cry was the same as Maverick's article: "Let's Join the United States." Poor whites became an alibi for the Keynesian state.

The second school of thought was articulated in the work of the Nashville Agrarians, in literary essays such as those included in the 1930 anthology *I'll Take My Stand*.[125] For these men, the South's colonial situation had, in fact, largely insulated it from the anomie of Northern industrial capitalism, sheltering an organic community and an aesthetic way of life whose days were now numbered. Rather than regionalism with an emphasis placed on the integration of the South within the national whole, this work was instead a celebration of sectionalism, of the South's difference. This was not part of a moonlight-and-magnolias mythos, however: these men had condemned "the high caste Brahmins of the Old South" and "the treacly lamentations of the old school" in their prior incarnation as Vanderbilt's Fugitive poets.[126] For these writers, the South represented a salvific alternative to a national culture corrupted by the rapacity of Northern industrial capitalism. "Suddenly we realized to the full what we had long been dimly feeling," wrote poet Donald Davidson, "that the Lost Cause might not be wholly lost after all. In its very backwardness the South had clung to some secret which embodied, it seemed, the elements out of which its own reconstruction—and possibly even the reconstruction of America—might be achieved."[127] The Agrarians privileged the space of the local and the time of the generational, rather than that of the nation and of historical progress. The small plantation stood as the emblem of this rooted, cyclical world—the idyll of Agrarian cosmology. As it became clear to them that the 1929 crash would not be the death knell for Northern industrial capitalism and that Northerners would not heed the exemplary lessons from Southern society and culture spelled out in *I'll Take My Stand*, many of these Agrarians turned to literature in the late 1930s as a proxy for that lost world. They imputed to the poem, in particular, a bounded and synchronic quality—inoculating it against history and against those destructive changes wrought by capitalism—that they had previously identified with the aesthetic way of life fostered by the plantation.[128]

The Regionalists triumphed in the realm of social policy, as the South's trajectory in subsequent decades veered toward the Sun Belt investments of the 1970s, while the Agrarian New Critics achieved the victory of cultural hegemony during that same time frame, institutionalizing their theories and methods in departments of English literature across the nation. For each, during the 1930s, "the South" became the figurative lens through which one could apprehend "America."[129] In divergent ways, each viewed the plight of the region as a linchpin for the redemption of the nation. And it was the common (white) Southerner who was the fixed object of their regard. Both the Regionalists and the Agrarians could boil down their position to *Save them!*, but for the former, salvation meant intercession, while for the latter, it meant asylum. Both critiques shared a segregationist logic.[130] Farmers who led mythical lives of simplicity and independence, the White Folk became and remained the screen memory that obscured both a black folk and slavery's presence in American cultural history.[131]

Oriented around this White Folk, the Southern nostalgia that had suffused the essays in *I'll Take My Stand* would also provide a foundation for their next incarnation, in the literary sensibility of the New Critics.[132] Scholars have flagged the Southernness of the New Critics, and many take damning note of their birthplace as a group. Biography pins them. The link is suggestive, but as argument, it's flimsy and too circumstantial to be satisfying. What remains to be established is how the New Criticism itself—its aesthetic philosophy and formalist theories—derives coherence from "the South." *I'll Take My Stand* revived and amplified the jargon of authenticity coined by the earlier Southern frontier authors, dialing up their earnest nostalgia while muting their gritty humor.[133] Even if "the South of the past, for all its ways of life, did not produce much 'great' art," as Donald Davidson wrote in that anthology, "The South has been rich in the folk-arts, and is still rich in them—in ballads, country songs and dances, in hymns and spirituals, in folk tales, in the folk crafts of weaving, quilting, furniture-making." (Davidson also mentions his cultural nationalist contemporaries, such as Van Wyck Brooks, "those impassioned scholars who are busily resurrecting Chivers, Kennedy, Byrd, Longstreet, Sut Lovengood, and such minor persons, in their rediscovery of American literature.")[134] For Cleanth Brooks, a central figure in the New Criticism, the South stood in contrast to the anomie of modern society, which he bemoaned. Even if, as Brooks thought, "the Southern community is beginning to dissolve, there is still enough left of it to constitute a real resource for ... writers."[135] In 1936, the poet and critic Allen Tate published

"Notes on Liberty and Property," which lamented the liquid and anonymous character of property under finance capitalism. Tate desired the independence, self-control, and paternalist responsibility that he associated with the agrarian South.[136] He pointed to a great unmooring that plagued contemporary art and literature. "The 'message' of modern art at present is that social man is living, without religion, morality, or art (without the high form that concentrates all three in an organic whole) in a mere system of money references," he wrote.[137] Being "deeply founded in the way of life itself," true art was as opposed to museums as to mass culture.[138] True art ought to express the organic unity of a rooted communal life, where the economic and the aesthetic are intermixed rather than divorced.

The plantation had long embodied a unity between these spheres for the South's paternalist enslavers.[139] The poem conceived by the New Critics bore the watermark of that ideology. Indeed, the New Critical poem should be seen as the valorization of the folk concept set in place a century before by the South's frontier authors—a concept, it will be recalled, that was the counterpart to the slave plantation's expansion, as it fractured social and economic status among whites. Then and there, the folk had become vessels of an authenticity that was always at hazard. For the Agrarian New Critics, the folk themselves having been shucked off, what remained was the folk aesthetic with its aura of genuineness and anteriority—the poem as a small unadulterated world supposedly untouched by capitalism. One need not strain to see that the world metaphorized in such a poem was peculiarly Southern, a world strictly ordered in terms of status, race, and gender, built for elite white men such as themselves. Portrayed as "natural, 'classical,' and timeless," in the words of black studies scholar Clyde Woods, that Southern social order was represented in architectural motifs (pediments, columns, porticoes) and place names (Memphis, Alexandria, Cairo, Luxora) that linked the South to a glorious past of Western civilization that was definitively rooted in slavery.[140] The poem enshrined by the New Critics referred to this order. Its aesthetic coherence predicated a world made by slaves.

From Vernon Parrington's *Main Currents in American Thought* (1927) to F. O. Matthiessen's *American Renaissance* (1941), literary criticism's dominant tendency in the 1930s became the ideological critique of an international capitalist marketplace, which threatened to destroy the promise and the premise of American democracy.[141] (Crucially, this imagined democracy did not include women, blacks, the poor, immigrants, or the indigenous.) For many of these critics, the 1830s represented a Golden Age of the Common Man. By narrating a cultural history aligned with their vision of national democracy, they hoped to synthesize a usable past, as Van Wyck Brooks instructed, to redeem the present. For literary critics "who hoped for the restoration of the democratic past, the Great Crash of 1929 was indeed a miracle. The Great Depression proved to the common man that capitalism was not a path toward reality. Capitalism could provide no essentials, no timeless truths, no social stability. All capitalism offered was meaningless flux," the eminent American Studies scholar David W. Noble writes. "But now in the 1930s, the nation would escape the chaos of the international marketplace. It would return to the stability of the national landscape. Once again there would be an organic unity of the good, the true, and the beautiful. The 1930s would be characterized by a second American renaissance."[142] The presumptive collapse of global capitalism in 1929 presented the possibility that their own era, the 1930s, might be the second coming of the Common Man. By recovering a usable past, they could light a path back to the democratic idyll they had located in the 1830s.

But for the aesthetically devout Agrarian New Critics, such utilitarianism travestied art. The new literary criticism celebrated art's autonomy.[143] The poem was a microcosm that operated on its own terms that were derived from long-established traditions that transcended the flux both of capitalism and of national history. As that principle filtered into literary criticism, the Agrarian New Critics were responsible—far more than nationalist critics such as Van Wyck Brooks, Bernard DeVoto, or Constance Rourke—for the field's institutional framework. It was this new literary criticism that defined and organized university English Departments after the 1930s.[144] The New Critics rejected the methods of cultural nationalism, which they deemed utterly provincial. The New Critics would not compose paeans to the exceptional nature of American democracy. Meanwhile, as a unifying concept for the study of literature, nationalism began losing its purchase. So, while nearly all universities offered some few courses in "American literature" by the mid-1920s, as a field of study it increasingly became the province of the new American Studies programs, shortly to be pursued under the rubric of the "myth and symbol school."[145]

The New Critics substituted a hallowed formalism in place of the nationalists' historicism. Despite being a methodology that renounced the historical, the New Critics' aesthetic theories *did* possess a specific provenance. Their formalism had originated in the Southern Agrarians' folkish aestheticism, and that in turn had derived from the frontier ideologies of the early nineteenth century, part of the 1830s class structure that had produced the South's poor whites as the nation's White Folk—an authentic people set apart from and athwart modern life. So when the New Critics placed the autonomy of literary language at the foundation of literary criticism as an academic discipline, they enshrined at the same time that specific Southern class structure from which those notions of formalism and aesthetic autonomy had been gleaned—aping the cultural nationalism that they rejected and displaced.[146] The poem they conceptualized bore a vestige of this folk tradition. Put simply, the New Critics' formalism also expressed the history of slave racial capitalism. The literariness of American literature was just as rooted in the slave South as its Americanness was.[147]

IN 1938, WHEN Cleanth Brooks and Robert Penn Warren published their groundbreaking textbook, which became a monument of the school's philosophy, it was titled—simply and tellingly—*Understanding Poetry*. Brooks and Warren arranged the contents of their textbook to demonstrate the escalating complexity, irony, and abstraction that could be unified and ordered through poetic form, a sort of teleology. "But very early Cleanth had made a fundamental suggestion," Warren later recalled. "After an introductory section of general discussion, we would get down to individual poems and start with narrative, including folk ballads.... [O]ur whole effort was to show how the non-bookish poetry could lead straight to the bookish." And so their textbook begins with a section on "Narrative Poems," mostly ballads. Ballads represented the most basic poems in this bible of the New Criticism because they were representative of the very basis of poetry. "Folk poetry ... springs from a nonliterary world," in Warren's words, and so it indicates poetry's organic timelessness.[148] Ballads offered a primary example of such a tradition. By beginning *Understanding Poetry* with ballads, Brooks and Warren were both maintaining and breaking with established practice in literary scholarship. Ballads had long been one of the institutional foundations of literary study in America.[149] "It is highly important to see that both the impulse and methods of poetry are rooted very deep in human experience," Brooks and Warren write in their introduction, "and that formal poetry itself represents, not a distinction from, but a specialization of, thoroughly universal habits of human thinking and feeling."[150] Folk poetry and its nonliterary world also referred back to what Allen Tate called the "social basis of aesthetic independence" that these white men had experienced in the plantation South, which had been overwhelmed by the marketplace and its meaningless language. Since a New South could no longer provide them with that basis, these critics hoped to recreate that cultural environment in the English departments where they now resided.[151] For the New Critics, authority was located not in the individual artist, which was a destructive romantic notion, but rather in the work of art itself, which preserved a timeless and universal tradition. Already enjoying the paradigm shift that would seal the decades-long hegemony of the New Criticism, Tate wrote to Davidson in 1942, "You evidently believe that agrarianism was a failure; I think it was and *is* a very great success; but then I never expected it to have any political influence. It is a reaffirmation of the human tradition, and to reaffirm that is an end in itself."[152]

In his first book, *The Relation of the Alabama-Georgia Dialect to the Provincial Dialects of Great Britain* (1935), Cleanth Brooks undertook a similar philological task of linking a feudal Anglo-Saxon culture to a disappearing "feudal" Southern culture.[153] Having studied the eighteenth-century Ballad Revival while at Oxford, Brooks toed a hard line yoking the dialect of that Southern frontier region to an English past, and in doing so, adamantly denying the contributions made by blacks to Southern speech.[154] While any group could develop *folklore*, only some few developed *literature*. While all folk had *a* culture, only some few produced Culture proper. Tradition did not equal civilization.

These notions shaped the New Criticism. Although Brooks and Warren included contemporary ballads such as "Frankie and Johnny," a kernel of antimodernism remained at the center of *Understanding Poetry* and of the New Criticism itself.[155] They ultimately located ballads in the realm of prehistory.[156] With the New Critics, this air of pastness swelled into the stratosphere of the universal. Rooted in tradition, the poem offered a complete version of experience, a paradise not fragmented by contemporary capitalism. For the New Critics, "the artist who has a sense of tradition lets the tradition speak through him. The tradition existed before the artist was born and will exist after he dies," as David W. Noble explains their philosophy. "An artist in 1550, 1650, 1750, 1850, or 1950 is working within the same tradition. An artist in 1750 is telling the same story as was told in 1550 or will be told in 1950." Crucially, this tradition wasn't constrained by national boundaries. New Critics in the United States and England "were rejecting the way in which the term 'tradition' had been limited to a national context," Noble writes. "Literary critics, they agreed, should not try to write about a national tradition in English literature or in American literature. When literary critics wrote about tradition, they should use the term to designate the universal tradition in literature that was critical of the antigenerational and utopian characteristics of the modern world."[157] By beginning their textbook with ballads, the majority of them anonymous, Brooks and Warren exemplified this conception of literary tradition. Because these poems were the avatars of a universal timeless tradition, Brooks and Warren could juxtapose "Lord Randal," a seventeenth-century Child ballad, with "Michael," written in 1800 by William Wordsworth, or "Jesse James," about the late nineteenth-century ex-Confederate outlaw, with an early nineteenth-century poem by Sir Walter Scott set in the Scottish Highlands. Because they believed the great tradition of literature stood outside history, the New Critics could also brand their peers, the cultural nationalists, as heretics within their priesthood of art. With their emphasis on social realism, the cultural nationalists were charged with diluting this great tradition, which must not be sullied by questions about art's political commitments. The New Critics' emphasis on literary form—independent, replete, serene—denied standing to such questions.

Here, formalism encodes historicism. This theory of form expresses a theory of history. And further, the poem so conceived registers a material and actually existing "timelessness" of a sort: that of the cycles that order slave racial capitalism, which superintends the Atlantic world and its "traditions." The historical time of slave racial capitalism is better regarded not as linear progress but as cyclical recurrence, as Ian Baucom has argued, the reiteration of financial bubbles, the repetition of forms.[158] With the New Criticism, jumping beyond the scale of the national, a particular and parochial Anglo-American conception of literature assumed the rank of the universal.[159] More specifically, an aesthetic sensibility cultivated by a coterie of Southern white men who worshipped at the altar of a plantation tradition wrung from the bodies of Natives and slaves was fixed by these men as the Truth of Literature. Their local tradition, which was the fruit of slave racial capitalism, defined the work—and the work—of Art. The apotheosis of this New Criticism, with its pretense to aesthetic universality, coincided with what Henry Luce christened in 1941 as the American Century, with its pretense to global hegemony. The New Criticism became an exponent of Cold War culture and its imperialist designs.[160] Just as the moniker "American Century" uses the language of time to mask the geography of globalization, so too does the New Critics' language of universal and timeless tradition mask the specific place where that aesthetic tradition is established—the nineteenth-century U.S. South.

THIS LINK BETWEEN imperialism and national literature wasn't new. Over the course of at least a century, roughly from the 1830s through and beyond the 1930s, modernization of "the South" had been mutually constituted with a literary discourse of modernism. Both the classification of that literature and the methods of its analysis represent, structurally, a modality of the slave plantation's survival. In what *sounds* American and what *sounds* modern, and in how the American and the modern have been interleaved and made available to literary discourse, the taproot of American literature has drawn its nourishment from the groundwater of slave racial capitalism.

The work and reputation of William Faulkner stand as one example. Emblematic of modernism, Faulkner's idiosyncratic style—oscillating between a high-flown bookish diction and the idiomatic speech of his poor white characters, alongside an almost cubist rendering of the frame narrative—owes a debt to the earlier frontier authors of the "old Southwest." And it was thanks in large part to the labors of the New Critics, searching for a writer of genius in the midst of Cold War culture, that Faulkner did not lapse into the obscurity where he seemed to be headed, but became instead *the* literary artist of the American Century, made a Nobel Laureate in 1949. The content, the style, "Faulkner" himself: all their prestige finds a common source in the history traced by this chapter. Faulkner helped to enshrine the interpretive role of literary elites and in turn, jointly, they projected the vision of a great artist with a complex moral imagination that centered around the nation's slave past.[161]

Even more telling may be the image of a twenty-two-year-old Gabriel García Márquez returning to Aracataca, Colombia, the place of his birth, around 1950 and recognizing in *that* South one he knew from U.S. literature. "The atmosphere, the decadence, the heat in the village were roughly the same as what I had felt in Faulkner. It was a banana-plantation region inhabited by a lot of Americans from the fruit companies which gave it the same sort of atmosphere I had found in the writers of the Deep South," Márquez told an interviewer much later.[162] Faulkner's Yoknapatawpha would become Márquez's Macondo. That moment of recognition by Márquez testifies both to the historical production of "the South" within the United States—a fantasized domestic other that maintained the nation-state imaginatively and materially—*and* to the changing geography of "the South" in the early twentieth century, as it assumed new functions within the global purview of American capitalism. The geographical figure of "the South" was a form and a protocol; it could be replicated elsewhere, endlessly.[163] This is why Márquez could insist on claiming Faulkner, whose fiction so well expresses the jagged "Southern" space-time of American modernism, as not only his forefather but also as a forebear of Caribbean and Latin American literature, a point he hammered home again and again.[164]

In Faulkner's fiction, style encodes the peculiar American relations of colonialism, as style struggles to represent colonialism's absences—or, better put, the absent presence of racial slavery that structures contemporary life in the United States—through a narrative space-time composed of fragments and spirals. The "concept of style" needs to be recoordinated "with some new account of the experience of space, both together now marking the emergence of the modern as such," as Fredric Jameson contends.[165] And as those colonial relations of racial capitalism were transplanted and reproduced in other locales by U.S. imperialism, Faulkner could serve as a paradigm for the likes of Márquez. Márquez too sought to represent American plantations in the American South, which were and were not the same. Style emerges and functions on the Southern frontier in just the way that Jameson suggests, whether in Alabama, Mississippi, or Colombia, whether in 1840, 1936, or 1967. At each point, an "American" style has expressed the schisms that attend the reproduction of the plantation's racial capitalism. Furthermore, modern American style—whether that is keyed in the register of cultural nationalism, as with Mark Twain and his predecessors, or of modernism per se, as with William Faulkner—is peculiarly Southern in provenance *because* of an American imperialism yoked to the expansion of that mode of production.

The work of Southern enclosure has been expressed as the work of American literature. "American literature" names one cultural manifestation of the uneven development endemic to slave racial capitalism. Over the course of the long nineteenth century, uneven development had created a domestic entity known as "the South." Time was refracted when it entered that spatial concept, slowing down and bending like light in water. Fascinated, the mid-nineteenth-century frontier authors toyed with that curiosity of time in their narratives about the region's and the *nation's* folk, their stories sparked by the friction of iconoclastic voices rubbing against the ruling strictures of print culture. Those frontier authors were rediscovered almost a century later amid attempts to bring "the South" within the industrial capitalist fold of the nation-state, particularly during FDR's administration. In this milieu, nationalist literary critics could recognize in those earlier writings a usable past for their invention of a democratic tradition that defined American letters. At the same time, such federal attempts to claim the South fomented a resistance by the Agrarians, who sought to preserve and celebrate the cultural effects of that unevenness. Transforming the aura of timelessness attached to "the South" and its white folk into the language of a formalist literary criticism, their resistance achieved a sweeping cultural victory. Their provincial ideas about tradition, about the poem and the canon, became a threshold to universality, a doorway that was slammed shut for women and minority writers. Meanwhile, already underway by the end of the nineteenth century, with the U.S. push toward a global Monroe Doctrine that gained momentum through the policies and imperialist wars of Woodrow Wilson's administration, racial capitalism's uneven development also produced a *nondomestic* entity of "the South."[166] A globalizing U.S. imperialism generated a South that encompassed Central and South America, and exceeded them.[167]

THESE ENCLOSURES, this style, this folk, all are distortions of a more utopian prospect—whites and blacks toppling the barricades of the color line. Lifting the Veil, some caught a glimpse of another world. That indefatigable collector of black folklore, a novelist devoted to the normal beauty of the lives led by rural blacks in the South, Zora Neale Hurston knew as much. Her life's work occupies a strange relation to this chapter's history, clearly of a piece with it but also a kind of countercurrent. In 1935, for example, she accompanied Alan Lomax on a trip through the South to record folk music for the Library of Congress.[168] And in fact, her oeuvre offers a photo-negative of the American literary formation I've outlined, a more visionary prospect of how the folk can inform the style and voice of American modernism.

In 1950, after a long career she published a summa that served notice on the white culture industry, and on white national culture generally. Pinpointing the widespread "indifference, not to say skepticism, to the internal life of educated minorities," in "What White Publishers Won't Print," Hurston evokes "THE AMERICAN MUSEUM OF UNNATURAL HISTORY," an "intangible built on folk belief," which houses whites' "uncomplicated stereotypes" of nonwhites. "They are lay figures mounted in the museum where all may take them in at a glance. They are made of bent wires without insides at all," she writes. "The American Negro exhibit is a group of two. Both of these mechanical toys are built so that their feet eternally shuffle, and their eyes pop and roll. Shuffling feet and those popping, rolling eyes denote the Negro, and no characterization is genuine without this monotony. One is seated on a stump picking away on his banjo and singing and laughing. The other is a most amoral character before a share-cropper's shack mumbling, about injustice. Doing this makes him out to be a Negro 'intellectual.'" One recognizes the former as an old and treasured relic of slavery, but the latter is of newer vintage, likely created during late-nineteenth-century Populist ferment and reaching maturity in the 1930s with the agricultural organizing done by groups such as the Southern Tenant Farmers Union. That second figure concatenated and dumbed down the elements of Left social realism and documentary to yield a hackneyed type well known by the time of Hurston's piece. Within this museum, there was no space for nonwhites as ordinary people. Blacks could ever only depict the problem of race, whether figured as biological or as sociological. "But for the national welfare, it is urgent to realize that minorities do think, and think about something other than the race problem. That they are very human and internally, according to natural endowment, are just like everybody else," Hurston insists.[169]

This is what made Hurston a radical folklorist. Her work depicts the folk as a composite of everyday people, and folklore as a mundane historical praxis of being human in the world—not as the font of a nationalist culture or of Western civilization. In the predominant model of the American folk, blacks were included only provisionally, as an amalgamation—at once valuable and perverse, premodern and excluded (in fact, "premodern" *because* excluded)—that bore fidelity to the nation's old ways and antique knowledges but also to some imagined African essence. There is always the threat of some "reversion to type," as Hurston notes. "No matter how high we may seem to climb, put us under strain and we revert to type, that is, to the bush. Under a superficial layer of western culture, the jungle drums throb in our veins." She writes, "The realistic story around a Negro insurance official, dentist, general practitioner, undertaker and the like would be most revealing," ordinary humans, neither exceptional nor quaint. "For various reasons, the average, struggling, non-morbid Negro is the best-kept secret in America. His revelation to the public is the thing needed to do away with that feeling of difference which inspires fear, and which ever expresses itself in dislike."[170]

But this revelation would crack the dark mirror into which both a rich white man and a poor white man could gaze and say *I am white*. The poor white could tell himself that he and the rich man were the same, and he would rather live this lie—at whatever cost of violence, whether squandering his own life or taking another's—than face the reality of his impoverishment at the rich man's hands. His is a reality largely shared with those darker peoples behind the Veil, which he cannot admit. Curiosity mingling with contempt, the man of wealth and privilege smirks at the poor white and thinks, *You are not my equal, but...*, and in that moment, the concept of the American folk is born. The contradictions and the failures of whiteness said nearly everything about the American predicament, since even those who fell within the pale of racial supremacy were not protected by its covenant. Even *their* lives were disposable—and often disposed of with their consent. No contradiction more clearly revealed the truth that the United States was a society structured in dominance.[171] "White people in this country will have quite enough to do in learning how to accept and love themselves and each other," James Baldwin wrote in 1962, "and when they have achieved this—which will not be tomorrow and may very well be never—the Negro problem will no longer exist, for it will no longer be needed."[172] The "Negro problem," the "problem of the color line," the problem of American racial difference has been and is still a stratagem of whiteness. And the canon of "American literature" has been its operative.

In 1935, at the end of *Black Reconstruction*, through an excoriation of official history, W. E. B. Du Bois defined whiteness as a system of knowledge and as an ongoing practice of epistemic violence. And that system and practice underpinned the deadly assaults on lives that are devalued both at home and on the other side of the globe. "Imperialism, the exploitation of colored labor throughout the world, thrives upon the approval of the United States, and the United States gives that approval because of the South," he writes.[173] That violence is real, bloody, murderous. It is also destructive in less spectacular ways. Setting watch over a national identity and a timeless tradition, literary criticism guards the entry to Literature—as that reflection of what humans share in common—against those encumbered by too much difference. This Literature has been set as the bar in the high court of liberalism, where personhood has been certified and belonging adjudicated. Here, the particularities of blackness, or queerness, or gender become the only pediment from which an author can permissibly speak. Such authors are consigned—like the fugitive Frederick Douglass before the white abolitionists—to narrate injuries that comprise a spoiled identity. One's identity is politicized, irreversibly, and politics is precluded from the great hall of Art. One is split in two. ("Why did God make me an outcast and a stranger in mine own house? The shades of the prison-house closed round about us all: walls strait and stubborn to the whitest, but relentlessly narrow, tall, and unscalable to sons of night who must plod darkly on in resignation, or beat unavailing palms against the stone, or steadily, half hopelessly, watch the streak of blue above.")[174] To write about being black, or queer, or trans, or woman, or indigenous, or foreign, or poor is to write *only* about those things, and *only* for some few. It is never just to write what is, or might be, newly human.[175] Only ever this twoness. Each exclusion draws a line of partition between us, and within us. The Veil falls, and another world is foreclosed.

Conclusion
In the Trap

Streets like the one she lived on were no accident.
—Ann Petry, *The Street* (1946)

Had readers of *Life* magazine in 1938 picked up October's final issue, they might have noticed two images that bore an uncanny resemblance to each other. Flipping past the solemn stare of the Great Emancipator on the cover ("Abe Lincoln on Broadway"), and a beer ad where Uncle Sam stares at the western horizon ("Which road, America?"), readers saw on the fourth page in *Life's* weekly roundup of pictures a little girl hunched beneath the umbrella she holds, among the pigeons at Trafalgar Square, which crowd her feet and try to roost above her head, and in the layout beside her, someone in a suit who shields their face from the camera with a hat, whom the caption identifies as Greta Garbo. Beneath them both was the photograph of a smartly dressed white woman in profile, staring at a run-down house. Her look is one of concerned dismay. Behind her, almost invisible in the photo's composition, and even more so in the larger spread, a young black girl stares back, both at the woman and at the photographer. Something like wearied disgust colors her expression. The caption reads: "Mary Pickford walked into a back alley in Washington, D.C. The camera registers her look of amazement and the wondering expression of a Negro tenement girl. 'I don't know how human beings can exist in places like these,' said America's onetime sweetheart."

A couple of dozen pages later, included among a handful of color reproductions in a feature on the history of American art, readers encountered a painting by Eastman Johnson, whose title *Life* gives as *Old Kentucky Home*. The painting depicts the backyard of another run-down house, this one utterly ramshackle with its onetime porch now a mess of exposed and busted rafters, its few remaining shingles covered with moss, its windows broken. The yard itself is strewn with debris and peopled with black slaves, with the painting working overtime to muddy the difference between the two. Groups in little vignettes populate the yard: lovers wooing, children playing, a son dancing for his mother, and a young boy admiring an elderly banjo player. And then there's another pair down at the bottom right, who are the fulcrum

SPEAKING OF PICTURES...

The hope of every newscameraman, as he starts out on his daily assignment, is for some lucky break which will give him an exceptional picture. Sometimes he gets his picture before he reaches his assignment, like the London photographer who passed the little girl below. More often the picture is part of the assignment but requires luck and ingenuity. These photographs were part of last week's routine stories, but in each case one photographer outdid himself. The mark of success is that he caught his subject off guard, in the grip of some emotion.

Greta Garbo hid from the camera in New York's expensive Marguery Restaurant. But the mirror betrayed her face and on it the suggestion of sly exultancy at her trick. The angry expression belongs to Robert Reud, a publicity man whom Garbo knew before she was a famous movie star and with whom she never fails to lunch when she visits in New

A little girl was feeding the pigeons in Trafalgar Square in the rain. At first there were only a few and they cooed politely. Then more came and the little girl could not feed them fast enough. They crowded greedily around her and some of them landed on her umbrella, so that she had to hold it tight with both hands. The world was filled with big angry pigeons and the little girl was just about to cry when this photograph was taken.

Mary Pickford walked into a back alley in Washington, D. C. The camera registers her look of amazement and the wondering expression of a Negro tenement girl. "I don't know how human beings can exist in places like these," said America's onetime sweetheart.

Speaking of Pictures, from *Life* magazine (31 October 1938).

for the whole scene, a white mistress who seems to be admitted by her female slave into this world. The white woman in her white dress lit by a diffuse white light is stepping through the gate, across the threshold, staring at the scene. She looks for all the world like Mary Pickford stepping from a time warp. Beneath the Eastman image was reprinted a work by George Caleb Bingham called *The Verdict of the People*, which captures the fray of an election

186 Chapter Four

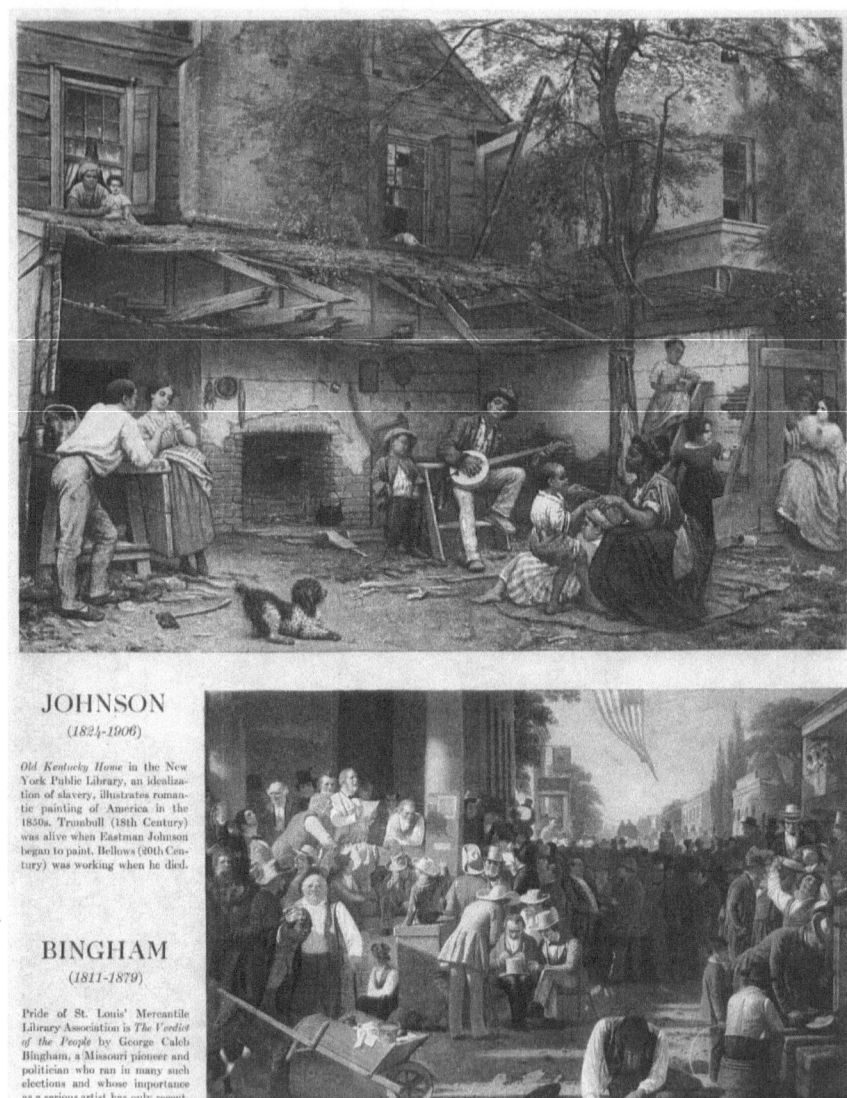

American Art Comes of Age, from Life magazine (31 October 1938).

in a frontier town; one wonders whether readers caught the irony, the contemporary emblems of slavery and democracy cheek-by-jowl.

The similarity between the photograph and the painting is deeper than passing resemblance. When the Eastman was exhibited in 1859, the painting's original title was *Negro Life at the South*, a runaway star at that year's National Academy show, and almost immediately, the painting's titular "South" was misidentified as rural, a plantation scene straight out of a Stephen Foster tune. That's understandable, since its backyard scene is filled with stereotypes plucked from the minstrel stage—an "idealization of slavery," in *Life*'s caption. Understandable, but incorrect, as it turns out. The scene is urban, not rural. "The picture represents several groups of negroes enjoying the air, according to negro fashion, in the rear of one of those dilapidated houses common to Washington City," as a contemporary critic reported. Johnson's "South" was actually the District of Columbia, where he lived and worked. The scene is the lot behind a tavern just east of Johnson's home. The white mistress and Mary Pickford: both "walked into a back alley in Washington, D.C.," to peer at black residents; same place, different time.[1]

If nothing else, the photograph and painting's shared location in the U.S. capital underscores the national character and *longue durée* of slavery's institutions. For the white women in each of these images, slavery's architecture appears where it had not been expected, not in the country but in the city, not in a faraway South but here nearby, and this also comes as a revelation to the white viewer. But then, by the time of this painting's debut, to characterize slavery as rural more or less marked one as urbane. Slavery's "rural" character was at least as ideological as it was descriptive—the byproduct of a culture industry in Northern cities that had subsumed minstrelsy by the late 1850s.[2] It worked hand-in-glove with the project that rendered a distance in space as a distance in time, as described in the introduction, such that the institution's supposed isolation also registered its supposed anteriority to the industrial era. Slavery belonged to another world, in the grammar of the painting, one that was peripheral and going to ruin. More important, those characteristics attached to black people themselves, a population constructed as being at cross-purposes with the "modern" world. There was already a feedback loop in operation: the rural was produced within and abjected by the urban, geography rendered an exponent of racialization. Dereliction and separateness became some of the most salient attributes of blackness. An alibi for comedy and cruelty on the minstrel stage, those attributes supplied the ideological underpinning for an infrastructure of exclusion and abandonment for the growing numbers of black people within cities after the turn of the twentieth century. Of course, those attributes were themselves artifacts of the color line's long history.

Mary Pickford's words may say more than she intends. (And even if no speech bubble rises from the lips of Johnson's white mistress, a shared sentiment structures that scene.) To declare, "I don't know how human beings can exist in places like these" is, most obviously and generously, to express genteel shock at the circumstances of the impoverished. It is the bleating of the liberal reformer, for whom poverty and injustice must always be rediscovered—that obliviousness so characteristic of whiteness. Her words also hang a question mark over the humanity of the residents, as if by "choosing" to stay in such places, they were made to deserve their environment. Pickford seems to imply that despite segregation and lack of means, these residents might ought to consider just moving. As a caption to this triangle of looking—Pickford at the tenement house, the girl at Pickford and the photographer, we at the photograph of the scene—her comment stokes a racializing fantasy. A black geography is born.[3] This space reproduces blackness, and this fictive blackness reproduces the white desire for such a space. Spatial difference and racial difference become locked together, constituting one another. Pickford's "I" is tethered to "places like these" where "human beings" "exist." "Places like these" are a mirror where she can see herself reflected and her own gender, racial, and class identity integrated—and by proxy, so too can the viewer, already so well trained to identify with this particular figure, who was the cinematic ideal of white ladyhood. But as with all fantasy, this space is a screen that hides the real. This white "I" doesn't "know" because it can't; to know would smash it to pieces. Isn't as much said in Pickford's complete dissociation from the little girl right next to her? This girl is fundamentally unseen, invisible, hidden behind a Veil.

THE GIRL HERSELF represents a new generation, at least within the logic of this *Life* photo, as one of the many black children now born and raised within cities. This picture and its subjects witness the consolidation of that geographical formation known as the "ghetto."[4] And in these twinned images, plantation mirrors ghetto, and ghetto mirrors plantation. Even if Washington, D.C., had long had a sizable black population, as evidenced by Johnson's painting, until the Great Migration cities farther north and west did not. Boll weevils and floods, falling cotton prices, the coming of the tractor, lynchings and Jim Crow laws, and elsewhere, wartime labor shortages and the glimmer of a chance at another life, pushed and pulled blacks away from the South. More and more black Southerners fled the terrors and privations of the plantation regime, following the rumors and promises of new freedom, more autonomy, better work.[5]

Upon arrival in those Northern and Western cities, though, blacks found themselves shunted into specific districts. In rural America, a number of towns adopted sundown policies that forbade blacks from staying after dark, or at all, and such policies were enforced by police and mob violence.[6] Many towns and cities originally used racial zoning laws to exclude and segregate them. When those public measures were deemed unconstitutional in 1917, they were replaced by the private agreements known as restrictive covenants.[7]

Through covenants, homeowners could explicitly forbid property from being sold to nonwhites. Its range as a weapon was extended once taken up by the real estate industry and by community builders, who controlled and developed large tracts of land.[8] Invisible barriers now locked blacks out of most neighborhoods. When her family challenged those covenants in court, Lorraine Hansberry recalled how "literally howling mobs surrounded our house," which was "in a hellishly hostile 'white neighborhood,'" and she wrote, "I also remember my desperate and courageous mother, patrolling our household all night with a loaded German Luger, doggedly guarding her four children, while my father fought the respectable part of the battle in the Washington court."[9] Strong-armed by these covenants, blacks were being shut up in slums, tenements, and segregated public housing. In neighborhoods such as Harlem and Chicago's South Side, a housing shortage was made even more acute by wartime freezes on new construction. To meet demand, one-family residences were subdivided into multiple units. These conversions accelerated the depreciation of property values, while at the same time lining the pockets of landlords.[10] The "Bosses of the Buildings take these old houses and convert them into 'kitchenettes,' and then rent them to us at rates so high that they make fabulous fortunes before the houses are too old for habitation," Richard Wright explained in *12 Million Black Voices*. In Wright's example, a seven-room apartment might be broken into seven, one-room apartments, each at a rate of six dollars a week, and so a space that had been rented to whites for fifty dollars per month could now be rented for forty-two dollars *per week*. As buildings decayed, landlords ceased maintenance and stopped paying taxes, since the taxes exceeded the worth of the property. The city then condemned the properties and evicted residents.[11] The nation's first public housing projects during the New Deal allowed some to escape such firetraps, but at the cost of an even more intense segregation, since those projects sequestered blacks even more thoroughly in high-rise ghettos. Federal housing agencies maintained a "neighborhood composition" rule—white projects in white neighborhoods, black projects in black ones—that quashed chances at integration.[12]

Formally color-blind zoning laws replaced the explicitly racial zoning statutes that had been struck down in 1917, but in concert with restrictive covenants, those new ordinances were meant to achieve similar ends. Neighborhoods of single-family homes that were unaffordable to the lower classes were zoned as residential by policymakers. That designation prevented the building of anything other than single-family units, which preserved the whiteness of those neighborhoods. Meanwhile, neighborhoods where blacks resided were often zoned as industrial, which offered far fewer protections to residents or to the properties where they lived. That designation permitted, in black precincts, the construction of rooming houses, as well as the operation of bars, clubs, brothels, and liquor stores. It also allowed industrial development, with its pollution and toxic waste. (These conditions later provided the rationale for "redlining" districts, which denied mortgages to black residents, and thus also denied them homeownership and heritable wealth.)[13] The visible result of invisible planning and policy decisions, blight crippled these neighborhoods, and that blight became equated with blackness itself, in custom and in law. "The blighting of property values and the congesting of the population, whenever the colored or certain foreign races invade a residential section, are so well known as to be within judicial cognizance," one district judge explained. (When the case in question advanced to the Supreme Court in 1926, the justices affirmed the legality of color-blind zoning laws.)[14] The equation of blight and blackness wasn't new, but it was achieving new dominance in its scope, as the nation's black population urbanized. That equation supplied a hardy alibi for residential segregation, a joint project between the public and private sectors, which also stoked white capital accumulation. For the segregators, segregation was immensely profitable.

Black elites already established in the North responded to the influx by doubling down on notions of racial respectability. From the first sociological studies of W. E. B. Du Bois to one of the first fictional migration narratives, Paul Laurence Dunbar's *The Sport of the Gods*, both published at the turn of the century, black elites sounded an alarm about the perils that city life posed to the morality of new country folk.[15] That alarm often reached the pitch of a moral panic about the Future of the Race. Women such as Jane Edna Hunter assumed roles as matriarchs toward young female migrants and, through institutions such as her Working Girls' Home Association, set out to discipline the wayward—in practice, to inculcate in them middle-class moral norms. For both white and black officials, these young women's bodies became the proper objects of surveillance—*not* the economic markets that constrained their lives, as Hazel Carby has argued.[16] Despite the incipient racism and classism of black elites' notions, underneath them lay a concern for the sort of deleterious—and obdurate—ideas that black urban spaces would cultivate in the white mind. And that concern was wholly valid. In the symbolic economy of American blackness, the ghetto would displace the plantation as the originary site of racialization.

Among liberal white reformers, a sea change had begun, which located "race" less in biology than in culture. History's "stuckness" supplanted evolution's determinism. In this new anthropological perspective, a legacy of slavery and a present environment of poverty and slums degraded the race and rendered blacks pathological, inferior, and criminal. These reformers set about working to improve social conditions, equipped with a belief in "progress" and its eventual salvation. But they warned that eventual equality would only come through black discipline, self-reliance, and struggle. In the meantime, there would be white surveillance. With race so defined, liberals could defend black humanity and civil rights, even as they clung to a belief in black inferiority, which, as historian Khalil Gibran Muhammad puts it, might "warrant special attention, but not necessarily special help."[17] As objects for the disciplinary work of reform organizations, black neighborhoods were also subject to discrepant policing. While turning a blind eye toward white wrongdoing in these "vice districts," officers charged blacks for the smallest infractions. The badges of crime and need were pinned on the ghetto and its residents.

YET PEOPLE DID LIVE, and fight back, in the urban neighborhoods of the North and West.[18] New folk cultures emerged: Harlem's Renaissance, St. Louis's blues, the urban blues of Chicago. "Just as in the South, in spite of the Lords of the Land, we managed to keep alive deep down in us a hope of what life could be, so now, with death ever hard at our heels, we pour forth in song and dance," wrote Richard Wright. "Our big brass horns, our huge noisy drums and whirring violins make a flood of melodies whose poignancy is heightened by our love of the sensual, and by our feverish hunger for life."[19] Depicting the migrants leaving the South as anonymous participants in a popular groundswell, Jacob Lawrence's *Migration Series* emblematizes this collective struggle and esprit de corps. In the visual vocabulary of those sixty panels, completed in 1941, Lawrence casts the actions of a disordered mass as the organic movement of a people. Using a graphic style and a basic palette lifted from folk painting, he employs the pictorial language of his subjects to tell their saga—simple colors and shapes in arresting compositions, each captioned to craft a narrative. It is the storybook of a people in motion, a visual history of the folk. "We live on, and our music makes the feet of the whole world dance, even the feet of the poor white workers who live beyond the line that marks the boundary of our lives. Where we cannot go, our tunes, songs, slang, and jokes go," Wright explained. "The common people of the nation grow to love our songs so much that a few of us make our living by creating a haven of song for those who are weary of the barren world of steel and stone reared by the Bosses of the Buildings."[20] This excluded and impoverished space begat new forms of culture. The efflorescence of black cultural production didn't redound to the Americanness of its producers, though, nor did it cement their standing within the nation or serve as final proof of their elemental belonging. Black folk culture could only become American culture once whites appropriated it.

And many whites were drawn to this "haven of song." For them, the ghetto was another frontier, a threshold to a zone apart, where different rules applied and new possibilities beckoned. It was a foreign country, here at home. Especially once white modernists imbued the ghetto with bohemian cachet in the 1910s, affluent whites would travel to Chicago's South Side for jazz or to Harlem's Cotton Club for a show.[21] For whites, the folk culture of urban blacks was exotic, and ripe for plunder. Harlem was in vogue. Many took up slumming. Expeditions were arranged. Whites came "flooding the little cabarets and bars where formerly only colored people laughed and sang, and where now the strangers were being given the best ringside tables to sit and stare at the Negro customers—like amusing animals in a zoo," Langston Hughes wrote.[22] The old speakeasies and black-and-tan joints were upstaged by "new slumming clubs built for tourists," historian Kevin Mumford writes, such as the Cotton Club, Connie's Inn, and Bronzeville's Plantation Café—clubs that "shared at least one common characteristic. African-Americans were employed to perform but were not admitted to the club itself."[23] To venture into the ghetto for new sights, sounds, sensations, and pleasures, and then to return to your home on the other side of town was one of the prerogatives of whiteness—as Mary Pickford and Eastman Johnson's mistress both surely knew. These tourists helped to produce the racial space of the ghetto.[24] Whiteness meant coming and going with impunity, and living elsewhere. Blackness meant being stuck in this place.

What white tourists enjoyed in such venues was, at best, the performance of the performance of black culture. The Cotton Club and the Plantation Café amounted to *Black America* 2.0—another exhibition of "real living scenes in the life of the real Southern negro." "The stage was set up to represent the Land of Cotton with a plantation cabin, rows of cotton bushes, and trees that shot up when the show started," Duke Ellington's son recalled of the Cotton Club's interior. "The bandstand was a replica of a southern mansion, with large white columns and a backdrop painted with weeping willows and slave quarters . . . the whole set was like sleepy-time-down-South during slavery," Cab Calloway noted. "Even the name, Cotton Club, was supposed to convey the Southern feeling. I suppose the idea was to make whites who came to the club feel like they were being catered to and entertained by black slaves."[25] The cabins and cotton and consigned workers of Ambrose Park, described in chapter 2, had moved indoors and uptown. One guidebook of 1931 exclaimed,

"Harlem is a great place, a real place, an honest place, and a place that no visitor should even think of missing."[26] "Real" and "honest"—shows like *Black America* had paved the way for these latter-day gawkers. Commodified and consumed, blackness was the vehicle of white freedom and fulfillment. And, as ever, white desire was mixed with equal parts disgust and danger.

Tourist fascinations, fawning and demeaning, came arm in arm with other, more lethal sorts of attention. Consider Harry Anslinger. A former prohibition agent, who had advocated a massive and overwhelming government response to stop bootleggers, Anslinger was appointed to a small agency in the warrens of the Treasury Department in 1930, the Federal Bureau of Narcotics. Both heroin and cocaine had been outlawed a decade and a half before, control of which was the new bureau's writ, and seeking to increase his agency's power, Anslinger campaigned to criminalize marijuana. His campaign was explicitly racialized. It was also based on bad data and ludicrous hyperbole. "Parents beware!" he warned in a radio address. "Your children ... are being introduced to a new danger in the form of a drugged cigarette, marijuana. Young [people] are slaves to this narcotic, continuing addiction until they deteriorate mentally, become insane, [and] turn to violent crime and murder." He identified black and Mexican Americans as the users and pushers who threatened to corrupt the nation's white youth. And he identified the urban world of jazz as the scene where weed and other drugs had their surest toehold. Jazz "sounded like the jungles in the dead of night," he said, and its players' lives "reeked of filth."[27] Anslinger trained his sights on a single performer who he had heard was addicted to heroin and over whom he had set watch, hounding her with his agents: Billie Holiday.[28] He made her a public example. Double-crossed and set up, she was sentenced to a year in prison, a conviction that stripped her of her cabaret performer's license. Unable to sing, Holiday began to come undone. Anslinger never let up. His agents were stationed at her deathbed. She was handcuffed to the frame while wracked by withdrawal. A methadone prescription was cut off. "They're going to kill me," she told a friend. Anslinger targeted Holiday as a means to launch the century's War on Drugs. Alongside the popular fascination among whites for urban black culture there arose another kind of obsession with blackness, among government officials, bureaucrats, and police. Blackness was deemed pathological and criminal, and required surveillance. It catalyzed the growth of the administrative state.[29]

THE GLAMOROUS STAGE WAS, of course, considerably rarer than the grievous street in the working lives of most ghetto residents (if it was glamor to be a star compelled to use the back entrance). In 1935, in *The Crisis* Ella Baker and Marvel Cooke published an exposé under the title "The Bronx Slave Market." "Any corner in the congested sections of New York City's Bronx is fertile soil for mushroom 'slave marts,'" they wrote. "Rain or shine, cold or hot, you will find them there—Negro women, old and young—sometimes bedraggled, sometimes neatly dressed—but with the invariable paper bundle, waiting expectantly for Bronx housewives to buy their strength and energy for an hour, two hours, or even for a day at the munificent rate of fifteen, twenty, twenty-five, or, if luck be with them, thirty cents an hour." The Depression had enabled a new class of less affluent white women to drive to these Bronx street corners and rent a black servant. "The lower middle-class housewife, who, having dreamed of the luxury of a maid, found opportunity staring her in the face in the form of Negro women pressed to the wall by poverty, starvation and discrimination." Like the mistresses of a century before, they used this "slave market" to purchase their white womanhood. In the North, as in the South, black women were consigned to the drudgery of caring for and keeping up other women's households. (And sometimes they were solicited to care for and to pleasure the bodies of those women's husbands and sons, who "under the subterfuge of work, offer worldly-wise girls higher bids for their time.")[30] Ann Petry described similar perils of predation and privation through the travails of Lutie Johnson, a single mother in Harlem, in her novel *The Street* in 1946. "Washing dishes and clothes and floors and windows," women like Lutie "work because for years now the white folks haven't liked to give black men jobs that paid enough for them to support their families. And finally it gets to be too late for some of them." Petry writes, "Streets like the one she lived on were no accident. They were the North's lynch mobs ... the method the big cities used to keep Negroes in their place."[31] In 1950, Marvel Cooke would revisit and update this exposé in a five-part series; its first words were "I was a slave."[32]

The work available to these black women's husbands and sons was nearly as precarious, as well as dangerous. In William Attaway's *Blood on the Forge*, published in 1941, three sharecropping brothers from Kentucky who face starvation and retribution are enticed northward by a labor agent in 1919. They find themselves working in a steel mill near Pittsburgh, and over the novel's course, each of the brothers is more and less destroyed: the guitar player's hand is crushed; another is blinded in an accident that kills fourteen workers; and, pawn in a union dispute, the eldest is murdered by an immigrant coworker. Not a land of fulfillment, the North was just another hell of dispossession. Locked out of unions, blacks were likely to be employed in industry only when there was a shortage of white laborers, as during wars or strikes. The promised tide of well-paid jobs, which had carried many of these men and their families out of the South, tended to break against the rocky coast of segregation and unemployment.

"Under capitalism," as Michael Denning has noted, "the only thing worse than being exploited is not being exploited." In ghettos, over the coming century, growing numbers would be thrown back onto what he calls "wageless life."[33] However exploited in other ways—exorbitant rents for substandard housing, higher costs of living, predatory lending—residents of the ghetto were often *not* exploited in that one critical way: as laborers. They were unemployed or underemployed in staggering and disproportionate numbers. As early as 1901, in "The Black North: A Social Study," Du Bois pointed out that in comparison with foreign immigrants, "the work of the negroes was the least remunerative, they receiving a third less per week than the other nationalities," and "whereas the Irishmen found economic opportunity wide and growing daily wider, the negro found public opinion determined to 'keep him in his place.'" He traces this exclusion back, most recently, to the Draft Riots of 1863, which weren't just eruptions of rage but "were used as a means of excluding negroes all over the city from lines of work in which they had been long employed." The exclusions were then made permanent.[34] Two decades after his study, in 1921, white mob violence would lay waste to the "Black Wall Street" of Tulsa, a neighborhood made rich by oil discoveries. "I could see planes circling in mid-air. They grew in number and hummed, darted and dipped low. I could hear something like hail falling upon the top of my office building. Down East Archer, I saw the old Mid-Way hotel on fire, burning from its top, and then another and another and another building began to burn from their top," the lawyer Buck Colbert Franklin wrote. Private planes rained bombs of burning turpentine on the black Greenwood district. Residents were machine-gunned down in the streets. Whites looted their homes and businesses before incinerating them. Three hundred people were killed, most of them black. Thirty-five blocks and 1,200 homes were razed. The alibi was an accusation of rape, but the motive was to crush an insubordinate base of black power.[35] Tulsa was one of many urban massacres waged by whites in the opening decades of the twentieth century.[36] That lethal hatred was just the flip side to slumming's racial fetishism.

While the ghetto was home to "native" song and dance that fascinated so many whites, it was also, and more problematically, packed with the bodies of the black natives themselves. The piratical and exterminating animus behind such urban massacres reveals the ghetto's relation to the frontier in other, deeper ways. These are "the lands of no one," in geographer Katherine McKittrick's terms. When Mary Pickford says, "I don't know how human beings can exist in places like these," she picks up a refrain that stretches back toward 1492, when spaces such as the Americas and Africa were conceived as uninhabitable. And yet, their "discovery" posed the contradiction of longtime inhabitants. "So what was geographically at stake when the European center extended itself outward, toward a space that was at once 'nowhere' and inhabited by 'no one,' yet unexpectedly 'there' and 'inhabited,'" McKittrick asks? Racial geographies, which comprise "an overarching system wherein particular spaces of otherness ... were designated as incongruous with humanness."[37] Those who live in the uninhabitable are, by definition, damned, and the "lands of no one" can only ever be filled with the dead and dying—a colonial logic that subtended the plantation, and subsequently the ghetto.[38]

THE 1940S MARKED a racial revolution in the United States, a metamorphosis in the racial formation of blackness that grew out of "a new Black Belt Nation," in Denning's words, "an archipelago of cities across the continent: this *de facto* apartheid became the dominant social fact of American social life in the second half of the twentieth century."[39] Another frontier for white accumulation, the ghetto also produced a culture of terror and a space of death.[40] "It comes as a great shock around the age of 5, 6, or 7 to discover that the flag to which you have pledged allegiance, along with everybody else, has not pledged allegiance to you," James Baldwin said. "It comes as a great shock to see Gary Cooper killing off the Indians and, although you are rooting for Gary Cooper, that the Indians are you."[41] Making that observation, Baldwin echoes the hostility that gave form to Owen Wister's *Virginian*. By that time, 1965, the discourse of colonialism had caught fire among black activists and intellectuals as a way to name their historical relation to the United States, propelled by anticolonial uprisings across the globe.[42] "The dark ghettoes are social, political, educational, and—above all—economic colonies," sociologist Kenneth Clark wrote in 1965. "Their inhabitants are subject peoples, victims of greed, cruelty, insensitivity, guilt, and fear of their masters" (and yet among them, there "exists a surprising human resilience").[43] Two years later, often citing Clark's *Dark Ghetto*, Stokely Carmichael and Charles Hamilton would underline the claim in *Black Power*, writing that "black people in this country form a colony" and "they stand as colonial subjects in relation to the white society."[44] By their lights, this "colony" supplies an unusual surplus: "The lower class has been transformed from production to permanent unemployment. Its value is no longer labor, but dependency," Carmichael and

Hamilton wrote. "Nowhere are people so expendable in the forward march of corporate power as in the ghetto."[45] The truth of black expendability was being literalized through the ongoing process of urban renewal—"Negro removal," as Baldwin put it—that demolished slums to build new infrastructure, hospitals, universities, office buildings, middle-class homes.[46] Rarely was new housing built to replace what had been destroyed. The effect was to intensify segregation and poverty.

Within the ghetto, the atomizing pulse of "market forces" ruptured those family and chosen-family ties that had been the safety net keeping people from free-falling off the perilous perch of Southern sharecropping, with its ever-indebtedness. Structurally ensured, deprivation frayed the mesh of mutual assistance that spanned the void of the government's absence. Migration made longtime affiliations vulnerable, even as new connections were being found in the urban milieu of neighbors and strangers. In anonymous and indifferent cities, these relationships faced the wrecking ball of unemployment, eviction, segregation, and "renewal." And many were wrecked. Once a "city within a city," after the mid-twentieth century, the ghetto became something more like a warehouse. A warehouse is the space where capital sits in suspended animation, in a kind of "live storage" awaiting valorization, and within American racial capitalism, the ghetto approximated a holding tank for the symbolic surplus value of blackness.[47] There, blackness encased its inhabitants—an encasement made concrete and perceptible in the ghetto's degraded built environment, which defied escape. Landscape was known by phenotype, and phenotype known by landscape, as McKittrick puts it.[48] The ghetto's reservoir of cheap labor often went untapped, and then with the coming collapse of Fordism, grew wholly stagnant.[49] And from that vantage of live-or-die necessity, many turned to trade in illegal economies, to *those* black markets.

If a warehouse, then a magazine: this urban armory stocked with "social dynamite" was, according to pundits and policymakers, sure to detonate unless steps were taken. New federal programs in the early 1960s were the first to address the snarl of problems that had emerged in Northern and Western cities. Dubbed the "New Frontier," these policies aimed to upgrade schools, to offer vocational training, and to provide better access to public benefits and health care.[50] They were conceived and implemented as the means to remediate youth delinquency, so that these youth wouldn't transmit a supposed "culture of pathology" to future generations. They meant to rehabilitate not redistribute, to treat symptoms not causes, to reform individuals not structures. They shared the frame of white liberal racism that had been in place since the turn of the century that rested on the notion that history, rather than biology, had diminished and deformed black people. And so, with the butter came the guns. Discipline accompanied disbursement. These social programs were joined with more federal supervision and increased surveillance of these communities.[51] In many states, the benefits meted out under Aid to Dependent Children also authorized agents of the state to make unannounced home visits—raids, in effect—to decide whether recipients maintained a "suitable home" or whether there was a "man in the house," as agents presumed fraud, searched for disqualifications, and patrolled the morality of black mothers.[52]

Police officers soon became the ancillaries of social workers, as crime control was stitched into social services and a War on Poverty morphed into a War on Crime.[53] When the state apprehends someone as black, it construes them first as a nullity, and then as a threat. That imagined threat had arguably called forth and justified the institution of modern police.[54] And it resounded in those policemen who, in the Watts rebellion of 1965, described the situation through recourse to a foreign enemy, as "very much like fighting the Viet Cong."[55] Or in the No Knock, Stop and Frisk laws "which permit a policeman to enter one's home without knocking and to stop anyone on the streets, at will, at any hour, and search him," as Baldwin wrote in his "Report from Occupied Territory" in 1966. "This means that the citizens of Harlem who, as we have seen, can come to grief at any hour in the streets, and who are not safe at their windows, are forbidden the very air."[56]

WHITES STILL FIGURED blackness as a kind of deformity (now imagined to be passed down through spoiled custom rather than through tainted blood), which also posed as a pathogen in the body politic. It importuned treatment, sometimes therapeutic, but most often aggressive. In another register, and at its root, it was alien—what had never, and would never, belong. The slave and her offspring were permanent strangers.[57] By the mid-twentieth century, that ideology no longer pointed toward black recolonization, but instead toward the ghetto as an "occupied territory," in Baldwin's terms, toward the joint campaign of social work and police. By 1965, black youth had been deemed "public enemy no. 1" by the national press.[58] Like "an occupying soldier in a bitterly hostile country," the policeman "represent[s] the force of the white world, and that world's real intentions are, simply, for that world's criminal profit and ease, to keep the black man corralled up here, in his place."[59] Blackness designated the historical mark of a hereditable dispossession. It designated those who existed as the objects rather than the subjects of exchange, whose personhood had only ever articulated culpability for crime and for debts, both moral and pecuniary.[60] The fact of blackness occulted the facts of history.[61]

And through blackness, whites have also dispossessed *themselves* of history. They have created and continually reinvent a baffle against their own historical consciousness and reckoning. "Because they are ignorant of even the recent history of the possessive investment in whiteness—generated by slavery and segregation but augmented by social democratic reform—Americans produce largely cultural explanations for structural social problems," American Studies scholar George Lipsitz writes. These are erroneously construed "as racial problems." In turn, this "fuels a discourse that demonizes people of color for being victimized by these changes, while hiding the privileges of whiteness by attributing them to family values, fatherhood, and foresight—rather than to favoritism."[62] To so conceive blackness as culture—that is, as a corrupt and corrupting practice by both group and individual—is thus also to obscure the history of whiteness.[63] The structural devolves onto the personal. An operative of liberalism, this ideology precludes any cognitive mapping of the collective and historical. History is made to disappear. Ensorcelled, liberalism's subjects are made to forget.[64] Meanwhile, race-as-culture enables slave racial capitalism's ongoing modes of expropriation and domination, which we might— alongside generations of black radicals—simply deem colonialism.

"Its value is no longer labor, but dependency," wrote Carmichael and Hamilton—but what "value" is this exactly? What the "Negro removal" of urban renewal produced, in part, was the whiteness of the suburbs, where European whites could at last shed their ethnic particularities, and propagate a sterile postwar culture of federally subsidized independence in the agar of consumerism and segregation.[65] Urban renewal also hastened the collapse of Fordism, Lipsitz writes, "transforming the U.S. urban economy away from factory production and toward producer services."[66] In other words, renewal structurally reproduced and intensified the "concentrated poverty" of decay and unemployment that it purported to cure. It compounded the dividends of whiteness and multiplied the inestimable expenses of blackness. Each was materialized and symbolized in the spaces of the suburb and the ghetto. Race is not just a *con*ception but a *per*ception, historian Matthew Frye Jacobson points out.[67] And the ghetto functions as a technology of the real. Its built environment trains the white eye, produces the white observer, like a literalized iteration of those phantasmagorias explained in chapter 2. That pedagogy is illustrated in the faces of Johnson's mistress and of Mary Pickford. What the ghetto teaches is a lesson in the false givenness of race. It is an epistemology of whiteness.[68]

IT WAS IN a Cambridge debate of the proposal "The American Dream Is at the Expense of the American Negro" that James Baldwin made his sharp quip about Gary Cooper. Minutes later, he read the U.S. ledger sheet. "Now, we are speaking about expense. I suppose there are several ways to address oneself to some attempt to find what that word means here. From a very literal point of view, the harbors and the ports and the railroads of the country—the economy, *especially* of the Southern states—could not conceivably be what it has become if they had not had and do not still have—indeed and for so long, for so many generations—cheap labor." Taking a subtle knife to liberalism's cherished credos of personhood and historical progress, he charged, "I am stating very seriously and this is not an overstatement: *I* picked the cotton, *I* carried it to market, *I* built the railroads under someone else's whip for nothing, *for nothing*"—he who had been born and raised in twentieth-century Harlem.[69] To watch Baldwin deliver those lines is to watch him cast a kind of spell. Speaking in 1965, possessed by 1865, his words briefly upend history's movement, making its times co-present. In that moment, that echo, his *I* both is and is not his own. From the ghetto, Baldwin speaks for and as the slave. He is a witness to history, and time stands still.

In Los Angeles in the summer of 1965, an incident of police violence against a black mother and her two sons cascaded into the largest urban rebellion in U.S. history, lasting six days, waged by thirty-five thousand people.[70] It would serve as the linchpin for a new carceral regime. Under heightened surveillance of these zones, these camps, broken laws called forth a new "need" for another architecture, of prison upon prison upon prison.[71] The figment of crime supplied government officials with the alibi for an infrastructure of cages, one that still subtends the world we inhabit.[72] By the time of the Watts uprising in 1965, another people had been left derelict on another shore of "freedom"—or was it the same people on the same shore? A century had elapsed since another black uprising struggled to root out chattel slavery. Still, as Baldwin wrote to his nephew, a hundred years of freedom would be celebrated a hundred years too soon.[73] Now—*and all of it is now it is always now*—better than a hundred and fifty years have passed since the Civil War ended and the Reconstruction Amendments were ratified.[74] Some kind of freedom was won, and some kind of captivity remained.[75] The slave's history accumulates.[76] Abolition awaits.

Acknowledgments

Books such as this are usually written under the conditions of tenure, usually guaranteeing a job. This one has been written instead under the conditions of tenuousness that have become the default for laborers in higher education, as they have for laborers everywhere. It has been written on a string of yearly contracts, without certainty of continued employment. It is a product of precariousness and insecurity. These structural conditions have to be acknowledged first and foremost. These conditions help to underwrite the comfort and safety of the tenured—yours, perhaps. If so, your good luck comes with your greater responsibility. If you are in academia, you are implicated in the present catastrophe. Demonstrate solidarity with adjuncts, warn and prepare your students, educate your colleagues and administrators, and make a change. Like the United States, academia is no meritocracy, and everyone deserves financial security.

Coming from where I do and raised as I was, in the coalfields of Virginia, I feel truly lucky to have learned from and shared ideas with such exceptional minds. Often, academia feels like a bureaucracy populated by rote functionaries, and I feel fortunate that this project—and my own intellectual formation—has been nurtured within spaces so committed to interdisciplinary creative thought. All along the way, I have been guided by brilliant and inspiring friends and mentors.

In addition to critiquing early versions of these chapters, Hazel Carby provided discipline, insight, and encouragement at crucial moments during this project. She pointed ways forward at some difficult junctures, which helped bring this book to fruition. Saidiya Hartman has offered generous guidance and invaluable advice and supplied me with a model of what Hannah Arendt called "thinking without a banister." As a teacher, as a writer, and as a mentor, Alex Nemerov demonstrated for me the courage of original thinking, through his imaginative readings of art and cultural history, and by being so willing to disregard orthodox methods.

During my two sojourns at Yale, a number of friends and teachers deserve thanks: Alice Moore, Carlos Miranda, Kathleen Belew, Sara Hudson, Francesca Ammon, Van Truong, Charlie Veric, Ruthie Yow, La Marr Bruce, Brandi Hughes, Kenise Lyons, Mike Amezcua, Tisha Hooks, Andrew Friedman, Ariana Paulson, David Stein, April Merleaux, Karilyn Crockett, Nicole Ivy, Shana Redmond, Sarah Haley, Daniel Gilbert, Amanda Ciafone, Vicki Shepard; Dana Byrd, Ash Anderson, Jenni Sorkin, Suzy Newbury; David Huyssen, Robin Morris, Julia Guarneri, Jason Ward, Stephen Prince; Jacob Yeagley, Christopher Kieran; Laura Wexler and the Photographic Memory Workshop, Michael Denning, Joanne Meyerowitz, and Alicia Schmidt Camacho. Lastly, my inexpressible gratitude goes to Matt Jacobson, who has been unstinting in his support and without whom this book would not have been possible.

Much of the foundational thinking in this project was laid during my time at the University of Minnesota, where I had extraordinary teachers in Karen Till, Tim Brennan, Qadri

Ismael, Paula Rabinowitz, Kevin Murphy, Rod Ferguson, and especially David Noble. Harrod Suarez shared his good humor and intellectual curiosity, and Kim Park Nelson shared her home, her wit, and her extraordinary meals. And though it's odd, after fifteen plus years, to tie them back to Minnesota, I am grateful for the lasting rewards of friendships with Sonjia Hyon and Julietta Singh.

Early drafts of these chapters were researched and written while living in South Bend, Indiana. Richard Pierce in Africana Studies at Notre Dame welcomed me and gave me a chance to teach. Kate Marshall and Ian Newman were the best possible friends and neighbors anyone could have, sharing in gardening and cooking projects. Jason Ruiz offered love and material support, and lots of adventures both near and far from home (not to mention an office and a kitchen, where I could work and play). And I was exceptionally lucky to have one of my oldest and dearest friends living there while I was, Crystal Whitlow, for much-needed emotional ballast (and margaritas), and for knowing me so well.

A fellowship year at Princeton was transformative both in my life and in the life of this project. Thank you to Wallace Best and everyone in African American Studies. Thanks to Daphne Brooks, for her welcoming enthusiasm, and for her work to arrange a colloquium with the four brilliant scholars who agreed to dig deeply into my work and who offered insightful critiques. I am grateful to Tera Hunter, both for her historical insights and for her company; Imani Perry, who urged me to pay more attention to public law and to the architectures of transaction; Walter Johnson, who first suggested my project may not be about what I had thought it was about, and who warned me away from the authoritarianism of cultural studies jargon; and Stephen Best, who has been a paragon for interdisciplinary cultural criticism and a generous advocate. Thanks also to Brian Herrera, Eddie Glaude, Joshua Guild, and Martha Sandweiss. Without the warm friendship of Felix Reitmann, Till Breyer, Leila Adu, Arin Fisher, and especially of Dixa Ramirez, Brittney Edmonds, and Edna Bonhomme, Princeton (and Berlin) wouldn't have been the same.

At the University of Illinois at Urbana–Champaign, I was sustained and inspired by my fellowship at the Program for Research in the Humanities. Thank you to Dianne Harris for her ongoing support, and also to Nancy Castro, David Roediger, Siobhan Somerville, Fiona Ngo, and Jennifer Monson, each of whom inspired me with examples of creative intellect at work. The friendships of Onni Gust, François Proulx, and Ben Bascom gave the Illinois cornfields some queer sparkle. In Chicago, Maud Ellmann and John Wilkinson offered me a beautiful place to live and work for two summers. Annemarie Strassel opened her home to me, and I was saved again and again by the good company of Naomi Paik, Rachel Watson, and Justine Murison (and, albeit from far away, Molly Minturn). A special note of love and gratitude goes to Brian Solem (and his husband Cornell Bar), who spent many evenings with me at Lula Café, plus many nights on the town, and whose friendship made all the difference.

Occasions to share parts of this project at the University of Chicago and at Vanderbilt University leave me in debt to Michael C. Dawson, Amy Dru Stanley, Richard Blackett, Teresa Goddu, and to the many workshop participants at those schools. I'm also grateful for the research funds and for the librarians at Emory University, Duke University, the University of North Carolina at Chapel Hill, the University of Kentucky, the Beinecke Library, the Amon Carter Museum (especially Sam Duncan), and the Smithsonian's National Museum of American History (especially Fath Davis Ruffins and Pete Daniel).

Joan Scott provided encouragement and insight from her editorial post at *History of the Present*. I'm grateful also to my astute and patient editor Mark Simpson-Vos, and to Jessica Newman, and Dominique Moore, at the University of North Carolina Press, as well as the anonymous readers who pointed the way toward a better version of this manuscript. Kerry James Marshall graciously gave me permission to use his astonishing painting *Great America* for the book's cover. Grace Hale and Eric Lott have given me decades-long mentorship.

If anyone deserves their own paragraph in these acknowledgments, it's Dara Orenstein. From the first three-hour lunch we shared in my first week at Yale, she has been a continuous source of brilliance, inspiration, encouragement, and camaraderie. So much of this book is the fruit of our conversations.

The final stretch of this project was completed in Brooklyn, among friends who share a passion for art, self-inquiry, and social justice—Kate Donovan, Vige Millington, Jessie Kindig, Talya Chalef, Harper Keehn, Laura Silverman, and Chrissandra Andrae—who have each made this city feel more like home. Thanks also to Johnny Loritsch, Grayson Crane, and all the folks from Seattle, who have made it such a great second city.

I feel extraordinarily lucky to have lifelong friends to keep me grounded and remind me of who I am, on the regular. Daniel Reid, Deva Woodly Davis, Sarah Landres: thank you for choosing to be my Kin. Bird Cox, my brother, there just aren't enough words in this life for all you've taught me about magic and creativity.

Thanks to my parents, Doug and Sharon, whose love and generosity have enabled me to pursue a life very different from the one I was born into.

And to Will McKeithen, who teaches me every day about care and courage, about new ways to be and to become in the world, and just how sweet (and savory) love can be. Thank you for sharing your life with me.

Notes

Introduction

1. I borrow the phrase from Roediger, *Seizing Freedom*, who builds on Du Bois's concept of the General Strike in *Black Reconstruction*. See also Zimmerman's recent work in "Guinea Sam and Magic Marx."
2. Foner, *Reconstruction*, 77.
3. "Charleston, March 27, 1865," *New-York Daily Tribune*, Tuesday, 4 April 1865, at *History Matters*, http://historymatters.gmu.edu/d/6381.
4. Foner, *Reconstruction*, 77.
5. Foster, "Limitations of Federal Health Care," 356.
6. One official "found that newly freed slaves preferred a life on a leased plantation even with a bad master to the 'great distress and frightful mortality' of the camps." Foster, "Limitations of Federal Health Care," 356. Foster repeatedly notes the discrepancy between white and black mortality rates (with black rates being far higher), whether in the army, hospitals, or camps, so this was not a case of universally substandard care.
7. Downs, *Sick from Freedom*, 27.
8. Marten, *Civil War America*, 213. On black dependency, see also Foner, *Reconstruction*, 57.
9. Foner, *Reconstruction*, 68–69.
10. Pierson, *A Letter to Hon. Charles Sumner*, 6.
11. "The Radical regime in the average state ... lasted less than three and a half years. The amount of good or evil the Radicals could accomplish was limited by this fact if by no other." Woodward, *Origins of the New South*, 22.
12. Stanley, *From Bondage to Contract*, 36, 40.
13. Pierson, *Letter*, 7.
14. Pierson, 7.
15. Testimony of Henry Adams, a discharged black Union soldier from Shreveport, La., in *Report and Testimony of the Select Committee*, part 2, 178–81.
16. Foner, *Reconstruction*, 437.
17. Du Bois, *Black Reconstruction*, 671–75.
18. Du Bois, 506, 698. Most racially specific codes were overturned by the end of 1866, but many of them simply entered state law as versions of the original statues that did not make specific mention of race. See Foner, *Reconstruction*, 209. Between the end of the war and the late 1880s, the black prison population in the South increased at least sixfold, while the number of imprisoned whites remained steady. Ayers, *Vengeance and Justice*, 180.
19. See Ayers, 185–223; Oshinsky, *"Worse Than Slavery,"* 1–109; Lichtenstein, *Twice the Work*; Blackmon, *Slavery by Another Name*; Haley, *No Mercy Here*.
20. Woodward, *Origins of the New South*, 213–15. "It was similar 'to those used for circus animals,' wrote a prison official, except it 'did not have the privacy which would be given to a respectable lion, tiger, or bear.'" Oshinsky, *"Worse Than Slavery,"* 59.

21. Du Bois, *Black Reconstruction*, 700.

22. Cable, *Silent South*, 152. Lichtenstein notes, "felony prisoners were even denied citizenship upon their return" to the community. See *Twice the Work*, 21.

23. See Jaynes, *Branches without Roots*, chapter 3; Thompson, *Reconstruction of Southern Debtors*; Clark, *Pills, Petticoats, and Plows*, chapter 18; Sandage, *Born Losers*, 215–18. In *Development Arrested*, Clyde Woods outlines in searing detail the postwar consolidation of planter hegemony and its innovative epistemologies.

24. *Civil Rights Cases*, 109 U.S. 3 (1883). On lack of enforcement of the act, see Franklin, "The Enforcement of the Civil Rights Act."

25. Citizenship remained structured by its constitutive exclusions. Those exclusions and the concomitant struggles for inclusion would continue to affect Native, Asian, and Latinx peoples in the United States in the decades after the Civil War. See, for example, Hoxie, *This Indian Country*; Jung, *Coolies and Cane*; Molina, *How Race Is Made*; Ngai, *Impossible Subjects*; and Phan, *Bonds of Citizenship*.

26. Deyle, *Carry Me Back*, 60.

27. "Almost without exception, antebellum historians treat slavery as a labor system without acknowledging that it was also a system of capital accumulation," Johnson wrote in *Soul by Soul*, 230n20. This insight has launched a fleet of books in the new histories of capitalism, which treat slavery as just such a system.

28. Hartman, *Lose Your Mother*, 31.

29. See, for example, Loughran, *Republic in Print*, 303–62. See also the second section of chapter 4 in this book.

30. Du Bois, *Black Reconstruction*, 5.

31. I understand slave racial capitalism to name the endless compounding of wealth within a white supremacist regime of exploitation, expropriation, and domination that is oriented around the commodification and degradation of blackness. The term is Walter Johnson's, who defines it in the context of slavery's expansion in the Mississippi Valley in the first half of the nineteenth century, as the tangle of "the science of political economy, the practicalities of the cotton market, and the exigencies of racial domination." See *River of Dark Dreams*, 14. It is also oriented around the exclusion and elimination of Native peoples, and the expropriation of their lands, which was to provide the preconditions for the plantation system. Its racializing protocol isn't restricted to whites, blacks, and Natives. Ever flexible, slave racial capitalism has also subjected Asian and Latinx peoples, as scholars such as Jung, *Coolies and Cane*; Perkinson, *Texas Tough*; and Lowe, *Intimacies of Four Continents* have shown. However, blackness has been and remains a defining pole in the American project, without which other modes of racialization don't achieve coherence.

32. "The Ballot or the Bullet" (1964). Audio and transcript at http://americanradioworks.publicradio.org/features/blackspeech/mx.html.

33. Morrison, *Playing in the Dark*, 50.

34. Blackmon, *Slavery by Another Name*. See also the documentary *13th* (2016), directed by Ava DuVernay, which makes this link explicit.

35. The ruling in the Virginia case *Ruffin v. Commonwealth* infamously deemed the convict the "slave of the state." See Dayan, *Law Is a White Dog*, 60–61.

36. Greeson, *Our South*, 19–41.

37. Stowe, *Uncle Tom's Cabin*, 373–74.

38. Douglass, *My Bondage*, 64.

39. The most fully expressed argument on the incompatibility of plantation slavery and industrial capitalism is in Genovese, *Political Economy of Slavery*. However, Du Bois makes a point of calling slavery an "industrial system" in *Black Reconstruction*, 8. The term *factory* itself enters English usage to name the barracoons off the coast of West Africa. Hartman notes, "The very word 'factory' documents the indissoluble link between England's industrial revolution and the birth of human commodities." See *Lose Your Mother*, 111. As Mary Louise Pratt asks, "For what were the slave trade and the plantation system if not massive experiments in social engineering and discipline, serial production, the systematization of human life, the standardizing of persons?" See *Imperial Eyes*, 36. An excellent historical analysis that lays bare the overlap in political economy between a "modern" North and a "backward" South in the moment of the Civil War can be found in Moore, *Social Origins*, 111–56. See also Richard Slotkin's insights on the overlap of plantation and factory in *Fatal Environment*, 141–50. David Kazanjian offers a close and convincing reading of Marx himself on this point, as he lays out the concepts of "graft" and "articulation" to argue that racial slavery and capitalism were coeval and hitched together, rather than set at odds, in *The Colonizing Trick*, 1–27.

40. In *Business and Slavery*, Foner locates the plantation's metropolitan coffers in New York and studiously transcribes the motivations of the city's proslavery ideologues. Following slavery's money, Foner reveals the North's complicity in the plantation complex, and so skewers the received verities about the Union as some abolitionist stronghold.

41. See Silber, *Romance of Reunion*, 76–77.

42. For more on the use of periodization as a means to establish legitimacy, see Davis, *Periodization and Sovereignty*, which argues that a decision to divide time into specious periods of "feudal" and "modern" underlies the claim to sovereignty and is tantamount to Carl Schmitt's notion of decision.

43. Baptist, *The Half Has Never Been Told*, and Beckert, *Empire of Cotton*, are perhaps the best known among a spate of recent works emphasizing the modernity of the plantation system and the way slavery undergirded the entire national economic system before the Civil War. Critics, including Trevor Burnard, have pointed out that scholars inside and outside the discipline of history have been advancing this argument for some time. See Burnard, "'The Righteous Will Shine.'"

44. See, for example, Menand, *The Metaphysical Club*, ix.

45. For an account of how thoroughly the interests of slaveholders shaped the nation's origins and its originating documents, see Waldstreicher, *Slavery's Constitution*.

46. McClintock, *Imperial Leather*, 374–75.

47. Toscano, "The Open Secret."

48. "'Blackness' both anchored value and, because of this, floated as one of its signifiers; it gave the lie to counterfeits, the suspicion of which always clung to paper money, and became itself a kind of currency. The subsequent circulation of signs of 'blackness' in the U.S. culture industries echoes its economic coloration even as it continues to generate surplus out of its extractions and exchanges." Lott, *Black Mirror*, 23.

49. Wagner, *Disturbing the Peace*, 1.

50. Robinson, *Black Marxism*, 4.

51. Wang, *Carceral Capitalism*, 122.

52. See the concept of the "changing same" in Gilroy, *Black Atlantic*, a concept originally articulated by Leroi Jones (Amiri Baraka).

53. "The captive body ... brings into focus a gathering of social realities as well as a metaphor for *value* so thoroughly interwoven in their literal and figurative emphases that distinctions between them are virtually useless. Even though the captive flesh/body has been 'liberated,' and no one need pretend that even the quotation marks do not *matter*," writes Hortense Spillers, brilliantly yoking value as material and symbolic, "dominant symbolic activity, the ruling episteme that releases the dynamics of naming and valuation, remains grounded in the originating metaphors of captivity and mutilation *so that it is as if neither time nor history, nor historiography and its topics, show movement*, as the human subject is 'murdered' over and over again by the passions of a bloodless and anonymous archaism, showing itself in endless disguise." Spillers, "Mama's Baby," 68 (emphasis added on "so that ...").

54. They tend to neglect the slave as a value-form that simultaneously expresses and masks social relations under a system of capitalist exchange. In other words, they neglect to treat seriously the slave as a commodity. Instead, Afro-Pessimists assume as a given that reified object, the black slave, and then argue for that givenness, producing ontological alibis for a historical process of reification. For prominent examples of Afro-Pessimism, see Wilderson, "Gramsci's Black Marx" and *Red, White and Black*; Sexton, "Afro-Pessimism," *Amalgamation Schemes*, and "People-of-Color-Blindness"; and Warren, *Ontological Terror*.

55. McKittrick, "On Plantations," 955. See also Hartman, *Wayward Lives*.

56. Lowe, *Intimacies of Four Continents*, 7.

57. Stanley, *From Bondage to Contract*, 2.

58. I refer here to emancipation as a public act (not the individual act of, say, Frederick Douglass) and as distinct from manumission. This was one argument Karl Marx made in "On the Jewish Question," where he counters the "political emancipation" for religious minorities advocated by Bruno Bauer—the state's conferral of rights and privileges—with a more thoroughgoing "human emancipation," in which individuals would be free and equal not merely as abstract citizens but as individuals carrying all their particularities and differences. "Emancipation" has required the form of the nation-state in the political philosophy of the West and has meant *national* emancipation.

59. Regarding domination and usurpation, I have in mind the arguments made by Markell in "The Insufficiency of Non-Domination."

60. Lowe, *Immigrant Acts*, 2.

61. For more on these theories of culture and of the role of criticism, see, for example, Jameson, *Marxism and Form*, *The Political Unconscious*, "Culture and Finance Capital," and "The Brick and the Balloon." See also Lowe, *Immigrant Acts* and *Intimacies of Four Continents*, especially chapter 1 in each of those books. At the time of this book's writing and publication, thanks largely to the Movement for Black Lives, there is an expanding public awareness of long-standing structures of exploitation and domination *and* of culture's role as a vehicle of power—a sense that culture isn't neutral and that it bears the past into the present.

62. "The forms and structures that define contemporary society are not immediately available for empirical analysis. What we can grasp are what Marx calls the 'appearances' of the capitalist mode of production, which are themselves not false or illusory but real symptoms of the constitutive elements and forces of society.... In other words, we do not have

access to society or the capitalist mode of production itself as an object of study, but rather only to *representations* of it." Weeks and Hardt, *Jameson Reader*, 4.

63. In Terry Eagleton's concise summation:

> The phrase "cultural materialism" had been coined in the 1980s by Britain's premier socialist critic, Raymond Williams, to describe a form of analysis which examined culture less as a set of isolated artistic monuments than as a material formation, complete with its own modes of production, power-effects, social relation, identifiable audiences, historically conditioned thought-forms. It was a way of bringing an unashamedly materialist analysis to bear on that realm of social existence—"culture"— which was thought by conventional criticism to be the very antithesis of the material; and its ambition was less to relate "culture" to "society," in William's own earlier style, than to examine culture as always-already social and material in its roots. (*Literary Theory*, 198–99)

64. See the "circuit of culture" that frames Stuart Hall's introduction to *Representation: Cultural Representations and Signifying Practices* (1997), which he adopts from Du Gay et al., *Doing Cultural Studies: The Story of the Sony Walkman* (1997). See also Walter Benjamin: "The economic conditions under which a society exists not only determine that society in its material existence and ideological superstructure; they also come to expression. In the case of one who sleeps, an overfull stomach does not find its ideological superstructure in the contents of the dream—and it is exactly the same with the economic conditions of life for the collective. It interprets these conditions; it explains them. In the dream, they find their *expression*; in the awakening, their *interpretation*." *The Arcades Project*, 854–55.

65. Cedric Robinson was the first to coin the term "racial capitalism" in *Black Marxism* (1983), and his scrupulous history of the linkages between "racialism" and capitalism, as well as his conception of blackness and "the negro" as categories, have been influential for this work.

66. Best, *Fugitive's Properties*, 16.

67. Marx writes in the *Grundrisse*: "The exchange of exchange values is the productive, real basis of all *equality* and *freedom*. As pure ideas they are merely the idealized expressions of this basis; as developed in juridical, political, social relations, they are merely this basis to a higher power." Quoted in Kazanjian, *Colonizing Trick*, 18.

68. Postone, *Time, Labor, and Social Domination*, 155. Smallwood, *Saltwater Slavery*, 33–64. Johnson, *Soul by Soul*. Wilderson, "Gramsci's Black Marx." Robinson, *Black Marxism*. On value as a concept more generally, see Postone, and also Marx, *Capital*, 54–87, 97–144. By theorizing the slave as a form of value, I both extend and depart from Marx himself, who regarded the slave as "part and parcel of the means of production," a species of fixed capital machine-bodies that existed only to be used up in the mode of production. On the plantation, "the most effective economy is that which takes out of the human chattel in the shortest space of time the utmost amount of exertion it is capable of putting forth," he writes, and "the duration of [the slave's] life becomes a matter of less moment than its productiveness while it lasts." A life to be "recklessly sacrificed," the slave's body produces only surplus value. The figure of the slave is a doubled figure of surplus in Marx: the black body marked only for profligate waste, a body consumed in the genesis of—and its consumption the very sign of—white wealth, white excess. But as a kind of commodity, as well as a kind of machine, the slave was herself *produced* and *circulated* as a material form and a social form

(in Postone's terms)—a marketed value—and no less a figure of surplus, to be expended or enjoyed at white discretion. See *Capital*, 351, 365–72, 380–81.

69. That point had been hammered for decades in radical black scholarship, and has only recently—thanks largely to the attention of white historians—become de rigueur. See, for example, Du Bois, *Black Reconstruction*; C. L. R. James, *Black Jacobins*; Oliver Cromwell Cox, *Capitalism as a System*; Eric Williams, *Capitalism and Slavery*; Cedric Robinson, *Black Marxism*; and Walter Rodney, *How Europe Underdeveloped Africa*. More recent books in this vein include Baptist, *Half Has Never Been Told*; Beckert, *Empire of Cotton*; Johnson, *River of Dark Dreams*; and *Bankers and Empire* by the black historian Peter James Hudson.

70. See, for example, Johnson, *Soul by Soul*, a brilliant and pathbreaking analysis of the slave commodity that approaches its close with the statement, "That history ended in 1865." Baptist's *The Half Has Never Been Told* ends with an afterword titled, "The Corpse," similarly emphasizing 1865 as a moment of slavery's death. Beckert's *Empire of Cotton* suggests greater continuity before and after 1865 insofar as he notes the expansion of American cotton production through sharecropping, though he disregards cultural production.

71. In his essay on the reemergence of the history of capitalism, Louis Hyman positions its development as a kind of recovery from the hangover of *too much* culture and cultural theory. See Hyman, "Why Write the History of Capitalism?," *Symposium Magazine*, 8 July 2013, http://www.symposium-magazine.com/why-write-the-history-of-capitalism-louis-hyman. There are important exceptions to this trend of disregarding culture and cultural theory, such as La Berge, *Scandals and Abstractions*; McClanahan, *Dead Pledges*; Bernes, *Work of Art*; and with regard to the nineteenth century, Taylor, *Empire of Neglect*.

72. The framing of this book's approach has taken as a guidepost the words of anthropologist David Scott, who writes, "We need a way of describing the regime of slave plantation power in which what is brought into view is less what it restricts and what resists this restriction, less what it represses and what escapes or overcomes this repression, and more the modern conditions it created that positively shaped the way in which language, religion, kinship, and so on were reconstituted." *Conscripts of Modernity*, 115.

73. For insightful work on the temporalities of capitalism, see Sewell, "The Temporalities of Capitalism"; McClanahan, "Investing in the Future"; and Baucom, *Specters of the Atlantic*.

74. Hall, *Cultural Studies*, 23.

75. Blackmon, *Slavery by Another Name*, 248.

76. Johnson, "The Pedestal and the Veil," 306. In Marx's words, which Johnson quotes, "The veiled slavery of the wage-workers in Europe needed, for its pedestal, slavery pure and simple in the new world." See Marx, *Capital*, 711, quoted in Johnson, "The Pedestal and the Veil," 302.

77. Marx, *Capital*, 195.

78. The "chattel principle" is Johnson's concept, in *Soul by Soul*, 19–44. On blackness and exchange, see note 56 of this chapter.

79. James, *Black Jacobins*, 88, 288.

80. La Berge, *Scandals*, 25. La Berge describes her own book as avoiding "a determinist approach, whereby whatever constitutes the economy stands as a theoretical buttress outside literary texts themselves" (23).

81. Grahn Farley, "The Master Norm," 1227.

82. Spillers, "Mama's Baby," 68.

Chapter One

1. Testimony of Ann Ulrich Evans, *Born in Slavery*, Missouri Narratives, vol. 10, http://memory.loc.gov/ammem/snhtml/snhome.html.

2. Testimony of Laura Smalley, in Ira Berlin et al., *Remembering Slavery*, 324.

3. Testimony of Henry Blake, *Born in Slavery*, Arkansas Narratives, vol. 2.

4. Quotations from, respectively, Laura Smalley in Ira Berlin et al., *Remembering Slavery*, 326, Henry Blake, *Born in Slavery*, Arkansas Narratives, vol. 2., and Ann Ulrich Evans, *Born in Slavery*, Missouri Narratives, vol. 10, http://memory.loc.gov/ammem/snhtml/snhome.html.

5. Jake Dunwoodie case, file 50-9-3, box 10788, Record Group 60, Records of the Department of Justice, National Archives, College Park, Md.

6. Berlant, *Cruel Optimism*, 95–117.

7. Wyat, "A Freedman's Speech."

8. I lift the phrase and concept of "white life" from Dylan Rodriguez, *Forced Passages: Imprisoned Radical Intellectuals and the U.S. Prison Regime* (2006), 14.

9. The title referenced is the subtitle to Baptist, *The Half Has Never Been Told: Slavery and the Making of American Capitalism*. Similar questions are asked in both Binder, "The Slavery of Emancipation," and Best and Hartman, "Fugitive Justice," 3–4.

10. Many scholars have made this point generally, but also specifically within the context of late nineteenth-century America. See especially Stanley, *From Bondage to Contract*, and Thomas, *American Literary Realism*. See also Phan, *Bonds of Citizenship*.

11. Baucom, *Specters*, 95.

12. "Liberated capital needed someplace to go." McClanahan, "Investing in the Future," 88.

13. The general strike thesis was advanced by Du Bois in *Black Reconstruction*. It is also the anchor for Roediger, *Seizing Freedom*. Selling the debt of black workers, as white merchants did to white planters seeking labor, was entirely legal, which is to say that black bodies remained objects of a speculative economy. See Daniel, *Shadow of Slavery*, 24.

14. Testimony of James E. O'Hara, Republican congressman from North Carolina, *Report and Testimony*, part 1, 51.

15. O'Malley, *Face Value*, 73–75.

16. Wilderson, "Position of the Unthought," 184.

17. Thompson, *Reconstruction of Southern Debtors*, 6.

18. For a nuanced history of risk and its entanglement with conceptions of freedom and personhood in the United States, see Levy, *Freaks of Fortune*.

19. Foner, *Reconstruction*, 22.

20. Roy, *Socializing Capital*, 132. See also O'Malley, *Face Value*, 105–6.

21. Foner, *Reconstruction*, 22.

22. The changes to federal banking regulations during the Civil War also forbade many types of mortgage lending and required a tremendous amount of capital to obtain a charter. Ransom and Sutch, *One Kind of Freedom*, 109–10.

23. Ayers, *Promise of the New South*, 79.

24. Bensel, *Yankee Leviathan*, 417.

25. For a history and explanation of the bill of lading and the *through* bill of lading, as well as the more widespread changes in cotton financing and transportation, see Nelson, *Iron Confederacies*, 47–70.

26. Reid, *After the War*, 206.

27. Quoted in Ransom and Sutch, *One Kind of Freedom*, 109.

28. On merchants as territorial monopolists, see Ransom and Sutch, 126–48.

29. Quoted in Fite, *Cotton Fields No More*, 5.

30. While I borrow this formulation of the interval from Hartman, *Scenes*, a relevant conception of the "not yet" of historicism is also theorized by Chakrabarty, *Provincializing Europe*, 65, as an "expression ... referring to a process of deferral internal to the very being (that is, logic) of capital."

31. Quoted in Fite, *Cotton Fields No More*, 24. See also 240n21.

32. See Stanley, *From Bondage to Contract*, 1–59.

33. Brinckerhoff in Hartman, *Scenes*, 142.

34. Saidiya Hartman's observation about the slave's condition remains in force for the freed "citizen": "In the arena of affect, the body was no less vulnerable to the demands and the excesses of power. The bestowal that granted the slave a circumscribed and fragmented identity as person in turn shrouded the violence of such a beneficent and humane gesture. Bluntly stated, the violence of subjection concealed and extended itself through the outstretched hand of legislated concern." Hartman, *Scenes*, 94.

35. See Foner, *Business and Slavery*; Martin, "Slavery's Invisible Engine," 817–56; and Du Bois's *Black Reconstruction*, esp. 580–636.

36. *Record in Allgeyer*, 12.

37. Dunwoodie, too, worked near Helena, Arkansas, and filed his report with the Justice Department at Little Rock.

38. *Statement of Pleadings in Allgeyer*, 12. Allgeyer was prosecuted under Act 66, which was passed in 1894 and forbade individuals from contracting an "open marine policy ... [for] insurance on property then in this state, in any marine insurance company which has not complied in all respects with the laws of this state" and subjected violators "to a fine of one thousand dollars for each offense." Cited in *Allgeyer v. Louisiana*, 165 U.S. 578 (1897). The particular law that was contravened, however, was Act 149, which was passed in 1890, and which read in part, "That it shall be the duty of all corporations, domiciled out of the State, doing business in the State, excepting mercantile corporations, to file in the office of the Secretary of State declaration of the place or locality of its domicile, together with the name of its agent or officer in the State representing said corporation upon whom service of process can be made." See Wolff, *Revised Laws of Louisiana*, 153.

39. Beckert, "Emancipation and Empire," 1427.

40. Cooper and Terrill, *American South*, 470, 501. Ayers, *Promise of the New South*, 9.

41. Smith and Cothren, *Cotton*, 436. Beckert notes: "So successful was the reconstruction of cotton growing in the United States that it came to be seen by imperial bureaucrats and capitalists everywhere as a model. . . . The newfound ability of capitalists and states to transform the global cotton-growing countryside with the tools of industrial capitalism allowed for ever more cotton to arrive at ever cheaper prices in the ports of Liverpool, Bremen, Le Havre, Osaka, and Boston. So successful was the recombination of labor, land, capital, and state power that cotton prices in Liverpool not only returned to pre-Civil War levels, but fell further. In 1870, a pound of cotton in the United States had cost 24 cents; in 1894, that price had fallen to just 7 cents—below its cost before the Civil War (when it was about 11 cents)." *Empire of Cotton*, 292, 311.

42. See Beckert, *Empire of Cotton*, and Moore, *Social Origins of Dictatorship and Democracy*, 116.

43. Beckert, *Monied Metropolis*, 22.

44. Beckert, 87.

45. "In 1904 [the South] took the lead over New England in cotton consumed by her mills, and by 1914 was consuming more than all the rest of the country. By 1904 the challenger was surpassing the champion in the production of cotton yarn and five years later was outproducing the rest of the country." Woodward, *Origins of the New South*, 308. Beckert notes, "By 1910, the cotton manufacturing industry of the U.S. South was the world's third largest, after that of Great Britain and the northern states of the Union." *Empire*, 393. On raising tariffs, Moore notes: "The Morrill Tariff of 1861 was the beginning of a sharp upward climb in tariffs. It raised average tariff rates from 20 percent of value to 47 percent, more than double the rates prevailing in 1860. Designed at first to raise revenues for the wartime Union treasury, it established protectionism deeply in American economic policies. The acts of 1883, 1890, 1894, and 1897 granted even more protection." *Social Origins*, 150n75. See also Arrighi, *Long Twentieth Century*, 302.

46. "The political economy of continental industrialization now won out over the political economy of Atlantic trade." Beckert, "Emancipation and Empire," 1435.

47. "By 1900, New York was the national headquarters for the new, modern business structure—the corporation. Nine of the eleven major trusts that emerged after 1882 were headquartered in New York. Gotham's 298 mercantile and manufacturing enterprises valued at more than $1 million totaled more capital than Chicago, Philadelphia, Boston, San Francisco, Baltimore, and St. Louis combined. The total deposits in New York banks equaled those in the rest of the United States. . . . By every important measure—from population density to industrial output to bank deposits to wholesale trade—New York ranked first in the country." Gilfoyle, "Making an American Upper Class," 279.

48. See Aiken, *Cotton Plantation South*, 59–62.

49. "By 1921, twenty-four firms with annual sales of 100,000 bales or more handled 60 percent of the American cotton crop." Woodman, *King Cotton*, 288–89.

50. Wright, *12 Million Black Voices*, 56.

51. Killick, "Transformation of Cotton Marketing," 169.

52. "While the New York Cotton Exchange traded contracts for the future delivery of 5 million bales in 1871–72 (slightly more than the actual harvest), it traded contracts on 32 million bales ten years later—an amount seven and a half times the actual cotton harvest. The global cotton trade now took place not in securing actual cotton, but in speculation on future price movements of the commodity." Beckert, *Empire of Cotton*, 320–21.

53. This is a paraphrase of Fabian, *Card Sharps*, 154.

54. Woodman explains: "In short, hedging involved offsetting each transaction in cotton with an opposite transaction in futures contracts; that is, cotton purchased would be balanced by the sale of a futures contract and cotton sold, by the purchase of a contract. Should prices change, the gain in one transaction would be balanced or cancelled out by a loss in the other, thus obviating the risk inherent in a fluctuating market." *King Cotton*, 293.

55. Woodman, 276.

56. For a good analysis of commodities speculation and its cultural impact, see Fabian, *Card Sharps*, 153–202.

57. Quoted in Woodman, *King Cotton*, 355.

58. Henry S. Reed, quoted in Woodman, 357.

59. "Over 36 percent of the loans came from New York, or more than three times as much as was borrowed in New Orleans, the largest Southern money market in the cotton trade." Woodman, 355–56.

60. Arrighi, *Long Twentieth Century*, 6–7.

61. Each shift occurs in a moment dominated by finance capital, and it is important to note that per this chapter's earlier discussion, the national debt forms a crucial mechanism in the theory that Arrighi elaborates. The Civil War sparked this shift toward domestic capital accumulation in the United States. Cotton dominated the trade relationship between the United States and Britain. "On the export side, cotton constituted the largest share of exports from the United States to Great Britain. . . . Cotton made up the bulk of all overseas exports from 1815 through 1860, giving the United States substantial credits to purchase overseas goods and services. Cotton produced in the United States became more and more important to the British economy, and the bulk of British cotton came from the United States . . . reaching an astounding 88.5 percent in 1860, or 92 percent according to one source." Blatt and Roediger, *Meaning of Slavery*, 22. See also Beckert, *Empire of Cotton*, 243. According to Richard Bensel, "At the same time the Treasury was assuming a larger and more substantial role in the economy, the Civil War was hastening the development of capital markets and a strong financier class. In the first instance, financial insecurity engendered by the crisis detached American investment from European, particularly British, financing. . . . The withdrawal of European investment strongly encouraged domestic capital accumulation and the emergence of a distinctly American class of financiers." *Yankee Leviathan*, 248–49. As argued earlier, the Bankruptcy Act of 1867 effectively transfers the value of slave bodies, following formal abolition, into Northern finance capital that's then funneled back into the plantation in the form of credit.

62. According to Arrighi's chronology, the nineteenth century's great depression of 1873 to 1896 marks the signal crisis in the British regime of accumulation. I'm proposing that we backdate the onset of that crisis to coincide with the changes effected by the Civil War.

63. Baldwin, *Cross of Redemption*, 129.

64. On police power's definition (or lack thereof), see *Lawton v. Steele*, 152 U.S. 133 (1894); see also Ernst Freund, quoted in Wagner, *Disturbing the Peace*, 11.

65. Novak, *People's Welfare*, 106.

66. Pleading of Branch K. Miller, *Statement of Pleadings in Allgeyer*, 26–27.

67. *Statement of Pleadings in Allgeyer*, 19.

68. See Baptist, *Half Has Never*, 329–30.

69. Here is the wording of the court's opinion: "The 'liberty' mentioned in that amendment means, not only the right of the citizen to be free from the mere physical restraint of his person, as by incarceration, but the term is deemed to embrace the right of the citizen to be free in the enjoyment of all his faculties; to be free to use them in all lawful ways; to live and work where he will; to earn his livelihood by any lawful calling; to pursue any livelihood or avocation; and for that purpose to enter into all contracts which may be proper, necessary, and essential to his carrying out to a successful conclusion the purposes above mentioned." *Allgeyer v. Louisiana*, 165 U.S. 578 (1897).

70. See Best, *Fugitive's Properties*, 321n63.

71. Calder, *Financing the American Dream*, 94.

72. Calder, 96. He notes: "The most popular single text was Benjamin Franklin's 'The Way to Wealth.' By 1928, this collection of Poor Richard's economic aphorisms had been printed in over one thousand editions" (84).

73. Fabian, *Card Sharps*, 130.

74. Quoted in Fleming, *Freedmen's Savings Bank*, 149.

75. Quoted in Fleming, 145–48.

76. Gilbert, "Comptroller of the Currency," 127.

77. Roy, *Socializing Capital*, 130.

78. Roy, 133.

79. "The new organization of Northern wealth was not comparable to the petty bourgeoisie which seized power after the overthrow of European feudalism. It was a new rule of associated and federated monarchs of industry and finance wielding a vaster and more despotic power than European kings and nobles ever held. It was destined to subdue not simply Southern agrarianism but even individual wealth and brains in the North which were creating a new petty bourgeoisie of small merchants and skilled artisans." Du Bois, *Black Reconstruction*, 345–46.

80. "The war and Reconstruction had definitively shifted the location of citizenship from the individual states to the national level, a centralization of government power made visible by the circulation of the first national currency and the emancipation of the slaves." Hale, *Making Whiteness*, 6.

81. Best, *Fugitive's Properties*, 158.

82. Marx, *Capital*, 754.

83. "Government stock is a promise to repay at a future date; from the inception and development of the National Debt, it is known that this date will in reality never be reached, but the tokens of repayment are exchangeable at a market price in the present," as J. G. A. Pocock explains in *Virtue, Commerce, and History* (112). See also Bensel, *Yankee Leviathan*, 241.

84. Bensel, 283–84. See also Beckert on the Browns and Barings, in *Empire of Cotton*, 240.

85. On railroads and bonded debt, see Nelson, *Iron Confederacies*, 147–48, but also much of chapter 7.

86. Nelson, 156.

87. Beckert, *Empire of Cotton*, 353.

88. The cotton trade "was essential to specie importation through foreign exchange operations." Bensel, *Yankee Leviathan*, 301.

89. Bensel, 317. Foner, *Reconstruction*, 22.

90. Bensel, *Yankee Leviathan*, 403. Bensel explains the process this way:

> [Cotton] was a "global commodity" with well-established grades, commercial links, and transportation routes. All of these were particularly strong and well-developed between the American South and Great Britain (Liverpool in particular). Credit rode these connections with British capital moving the crop across the Atlantic. The banking houses that specialized in these transactions also moved railroad bonds (primarily) across the Atlantic. When sold in Britain, the British paid in (gold-denominated) pounds which recrossed the Atlantic and liquidated cotton debts. But this still left a

substantial imbalance in American-British trade which was made up by British exports to the United States. These exports came through the tariff system which skimmed gold off imports (in the form of, of course, a tax). That gold, in turn, serviced federal debt (both principal and interest). The railroads turned dollars into the gold the federal government released into the economy and sent it back across the Atlantic as dividends on railroad bonds. (Personal correspondence, 3 October 2016)

91. Roger L. Ransom notes in *Conflict and Compromise*: "After the war, the federal government committed itself to the retirement of the large war debt. This policy was pursued with particular vigor between 1866 and 1878, when the outstanding interest-bearing debt of the federal government fell from $2.3 billion to $1.8 billion; by 1893, the total had fallen to only $587 million" (287). In "Explaining America's Surge," Douglas A. Irwin notes that this moment when the debt was largely retired was also the moment of a U.S. "transition from exporting raw materials and primary products to exporting processed materials and manufactured goods," which took place "in the period from 1895 to 1910" (1). Foner writes in *Reconstruction*, "Accelerating the emergence of an American industrial bourgeoisie, the war tied the fortunes of this class to the Republican party and the national state" (21).

92. This widely circulating claim was most famously made by Williams in *Capitalism and Slavery*, noting, for example, that in eighteenth-century Liverpool "the red-brick Customs House was blazoned with Negro heads" (63).

93. Cotton remained the leading U.S. export into the twentieth century. By 1880, the amounts exported exceeded prewar levels, and hovered between 20 and 30 percent of all exports through the onset of World War I. See Beckert, *Empire of Cotton*, 292, and calculations from *Statistical Abstract of the United States* in Irwin, "Explaining America's Surge," 28.

94. On the national debt as a lever of primitive accumulation, see Walker, "Primitive Accumulation."

95. *Ruffin v Commonwealth*, 62 Va. 790 (1871).

96. Read, *Micro-Politics of Capital*, 26.

97. King, *Southern States*, 53.

98. Read, *Micro-Politics of Capital*, 26.

99. Regarding the "intensive" and "extensive," see Read, *Micro-Politics of Capital*, on the subjective affects generated by capitalism.

100. Hartman, *Scenes*, 125.

101. Thomas, *American Literary Realism*, 42.

102. See Du Bois, *Black Reconstruction*, chapter 4, "The General Strike," and for a more recent discussion of historians' neglect of Du Bois's thesis, see Roediger, *Seizing Freedom*.

103. Fortune, *Black and White*, 14.

104. This quantitative impulse reached an apogee in Ransom and Sutch, *One Kind of Freedom* (1977), which split the difference, arguing that the economic situation of sharecroppers was better than that of slaves but that merchants were little territorial monopolists who charged exorbitant interest rates, curtailing any possibility of either economic or geographic mobility by sharecroppers. For other works on "planter persistence," see Daniel, *Shadow of Slavery* (1972); Wayne, *The Reshaping of Plantation Society* (1983); Bartley, *Creation of Modern Georgia* (1983); Wiener, *Social Origins of the New South* (1978); Billings, *Planters and the Making of a New South* (1979); Campbell, *Southern Community in Crisis*

(1980); Powell, *New Masters* (1980); Formwalt, "Antebellum Planter Persistence" (October 1981); Townes, "Effect of Emancipation in Large Landholdings" (August 1979). See also the review essay by Foner, "Reconstruction Revisited" (1982).

105. An excellent overview of this historiography can be found in Coclanis and Marler, "The Economics of Reconstruction."

106. Daniel, *Shadow of Slavery*, 174.

107. Binder, "Slavery of Emancipation," 2063–101. And, of course, the Thirteenth Amendment itself explicitly preserves slavery as punishment for a crime.

108. Blackmon, *Slavery by Another Name*, 248.

109. In a recent essay on the new history of capitalism, Jeffrey Sklansky points out its preoccupation with commodities and finance and its neglect of labor. And, as he notes in "Labor, Money, and the Financial Turn," "If the face of capital in the new history is that of finance, the face of labor is that of slavery, and the two are as closely entwined as manufacturing and wage labor were in earlier scholarship" (40). On the relationship between slavery and capitalism, see, especially, Johnson, "The Pedestal and the Veil," 299–308.

110. See, for example, Blackmon, *Slavery by Another Name*, which is framed metonymically as *a* story of *a* man (one Green Cottenham) and which portrays "neoslavery," as Blackmon terms it, as a story of murderous brutality, albeit one profitable to local businessmen and corporate titans, whose habitat is the convict labor camps of the South.

111. For another version of the critique I make here, see McKittrick, "Plantation Futures," 1–15. She describes how the geography of the plantation has produced and continues to produce blackness as nonhuman, generating "particular spaces of otherness—for purposes here, black geographies ... designated as incongruous with humanness" (6).

112. Spillers, "Mama's Baby," 68. Baucom, *Specters of the Atlantic*, 333. See also Sewell, "The Temporalities of Capitalism," 517–37.

113. James Baldwin's comments were made in a debate with William F. Buckley at Cambridge University in 1965. See Eckman, *Furious Passage*, 15. Jackson, *Soledad Brother*, 233. Kincaid, "In History," 1.

114. La Berge, "Scandals and Abstractions," 52.

115. See, for example, Levy, *Freaks of Fortune*, on the nineteenth-century origins of the link between managing risk and securing freedom.

116. Alexander, "The Limits of Freedom," 406n38.

117. "It can now be argued that what we call 'debt' in the Americas is the political economy that results in the formation of 'race,' given that we understand race to be a social hierarchy with no biological grounding." Mirzoeff, "The Debt-Prison System." This also applies to the red herring of white sharecroppers in the South who were caught up in this credit economy. To the extent that these workers appeared degraded by debt and impoverishment, they appeared less than white, and a scandal. Those workers, however, were still also paid the wages of whiteness, to cite Roediger, after Du Bois, in *Wages of Whiteness*. Furthermore, as Ransom and Sutch have shown in *One Kind of Freedom*, more whites than blacks owned land in the South, including poor whites: "For each and every wealth class, black owners of real estate held a smaller fraction of their wealth in land than did their white counterparts" (85–86). See the tables and calculations on those pages as well.

118. Testimony of Henry Adams, in *Report and Testimony*, 180–81.

119. See Hahn, "Hunting, Fishing, and Foraging," 37–64.

120. "The South's colonial relationship to the North in the postwar economy was, for example, so pronounced that northeastern and midwestern commercial interests were able to purchase some 85 percent of the more than 2.5 million acres of public land sold in lots of 5,000 or larger in Louisiana and Mississippi between 1880 and 1888. Purchases by outside interests were smaller in other southern states but still amounted to a quarter or more of sales." Bensel, *Yankee Leviathan*, 418n5.

121. Gilbert, "Comptroller of the Currency," 126.

122. Fleming, *Freedmen's Savings Bank*, 71–72.

123. "Government securities were replaced with speculative stocks and mortgages on worthless property. Political influence was used to obtain loans, and trustees borrowed liberally from the bank for private purposes. Jay Cooke and Co. virtually controlled the bank between 1870 and 1873. The company borrowed half a million dollars at five percent while the depositors received six. Henry Cooke, Jay Cooke's brother and President of the First National Bank of Washington, part of the Cooke empire, was a member of the financial committee of the Freedman's Savings Bank. He used the Freedman's Bank to aid his own institution by transferring poor securities connected with bad transactions from the First National to the Freedman's Bank, so that the latter was made to hold the questionable paper of the First National. As the first Territorial Governor of the District of Columbia, he permitted the District to borrow vast sums, collateralized by worthless securities, for grand projects." Gilbert, "Comptroller of the Currency," 127.

124. Quoted in Fleming, *Freedmen's Savings Bank*, 145–48.

125. Quoted in Fleming, 109. Douglass was appointed the figurehead of the bank just before its collapse. Of that position he wrote: "The fact is, and all investigation shows it, that I was married to a corpse. The false building, with its marble counters and black walnut finishings, was there, as were the affable and agile clerks and the discreet and colored cashier; but the Life, which was the money, was gone." Quoted on p. 93.

126. "It took nine years, from 1874 to 1883, for the commissioners and then the comptroller of the currency to realize upon the assets of the defunct company and pay the depositors a substantial amount of their savings.... In all, the commissioners and the comptroller of the currency declared five dividends, which paid off 62 percent of the Bank's indebtedness.... Although the commissioners had spoken as if they were deluged with deposit books, only 29,996 depositors of an eligible 61,131 sent in their passbooks for the first dividend, and the statistics showed that these were the wealthier depositors.... The first dividend set the pattern for succeeding ones; each year the number of claimants declined, so that after the final dividend was paid in 1883, less than 18,000 depositors had received the full 62 percent." Osthaus, *Freedmen, Philanthropy, and Fraud*, 211–13. Osthaus's final chapter, "The Bank's Legacy," includes copious details of the insults and catastrophes heaped on the bank's depositors by pirates, legislators, and bureaucrats following the bank's scurrilous devastation.

127. Appel, "Finance Is Just Another Word," 159–73.

128. "And the sensible freedmen made no demands of their own; they did not even have real lives of their own to be remembered. Their 'freedom' in the midst of the war became only a rarely mentioned disjuncture, a reality only as it was refused, a strange misfortune lost in the mists of reconciliation." Blight, *Race and Reunion*, 224, regarding the white literature of reconciliation. On the functions of indebtedness, see Hartman, *Scenes*, 125–63.

129. "By this means the merchant knows how large to make his bill. He lets the colored man come and buy a few things, run up an account, charging four or five prices for everything. For instance, he will charge twenty to twenty-five cents a pound for sugar, for which you or any white man would pay eight or nine cents; or twenty-five cents a pound for bacon, for which you would have to pay six or seven cents. . . . If the colored man refuses to pay the bill, which, as I have said, is always made large enough to cover the value of the entire crop, after paying the rent, the merchant comes into court and sues him. The white man brings his itemized account into court; the colored man has no account, and of course he is beaten in the suit, and the cost is thrown onto him. They stand against him if he cannot pay it. And colored men soon learn that it is better to pay any account, however unjust, than to refuse, for he stands no possible chance of getting justice before the law." Testimony of John Milton Brown, black schoolteacher turned sheriff in Friar's Point, Mississippi, in *Report and Testimony*, part 2, 362.

Chapter Two

1. "William Harnett: Trompe l'Oeil."
2. The notion of the era's culture of skepticism is discussed in Leja, *Looking Askance*. The Victor ad from 1908 is reproduced on p. 126.
3. Leja, 142.
4. Quoted in Leja, 140.
5. Leja, 144.
6. Troutman, "William Michael Harnett's *Attention, Company!*," 10.
7. Greenberg, "Towards a Newer Laocoon," 35. Greenberg discerned in trompe l'oeil a fidelity to medium specificity, even if nascently, which would govern high modernism as an article of faith. For Greenberg, medium specificity assumed the language of sensation and depended on sensual clarity—just as music appeals directly to the ear, so painting should appeal immediately to the eye—and that puzzle locates for him the concerns of modernism. While this account is an old one and has come in for drubbing, the four writers who have written most perceptively about the logic of trompe l'oeil still locate it within a discourse of modernism, either as its apotheosis via the economy (Walter Benn Michaels) or as part of machine culture (Mark Seltzer) or in relation to the machined commodity (David Lubin) or in a hermeneutics of suspicion (Michael Leja). On the logic of still-life painting and trompe l'oeil generally, see Seltzer, *Bodies and Machines*, 121–45.
8. Much has been written about Harnett. For the fullest treatment, see Frankenstein, *After the Hunt*. See also Michaels, *Gold Standard*, 161–67; Lubin, "Masculinity, Nostalgia, and the Trompe l'Oeil Still Life Paintings of William Harnett," chapter 6 in *Picturing a Nation*, 273–319; and Leja, "Touching Pictures by William Harnett," chapter 4 in *Looking Askance*, 125–52. This chapter departs from the usual itinerary for arguments in American art history, a discipline that often has great difficulty imagining ways to organize its inquiries that do not take the artist's life, however broadly understood, as the historical limit and cultural boundary of any question's relevance. Recent work at the intersection of African American studies and art history has begun to challenge this framework. See, for example, Cheng, *Second Skin*; Copeland, *Bound to Appear*; English, *How to See a Work of Art*; and Fleetwood, *Troubling Vision*.

9. "The effect produced is of 'truth,'" writes Roland Barthes, of the direct gaze in Richard Avedon's portraits. "The gaze, rendered here in an emphatic manner by the photographer (in the past, this could be done by the painter), acts as the very organ of truth." Barthes, "Right in the Eyes," in *Responsibility of Forms*, 240.

10. There are perhaps three other figure paintings by Harnett. None utilize the wall and none attempt the frontality and flatness of the trompe l'oeil style. I have discovered only one other trompe l'oeil painter, Victor Dubreuil, who included unphotographed figures in his works.

11. "A vibrating tension is set up as the objects struggle to maintain their volume against the tendency of the real picture plane to re-assert its material flatness and *crush them to silhouettes*." Greenberg, "Towards a Newer Laocoon," 35 (emphasis mine).

12. In this regard, it is part of a lineage, since blackness had long been an aesthetic figure at white command and disposal: the master commanding performances in the slave yard, the buyer appraising the "fancy girl" on the auction block, the white actor performing on the minstrel stage. And in the high modernism of the early twentieth century, blackness would again assume its role as an aesthetic figure in that economy of "love and theft" known as primitivism. For more on these cultural dynamics, see Lott, *Love and Theft*, 20, which also deals with the "oscillation between currency and counterfeit" that attends blackness a quarter century before. For more on the connection between primitivism and modernism, see Lemke, *Primitivist Modernism*; Hutchinson, *Indian Craze*; Ngai, "Black Venus"; and Miller, "Black Dandy."

13. A factual and contemporary South was replaced by a fictional and nostalgic South, which Northerners eagerly consumed. It was not so much that they forgot about the South as that they preferred the new legend over the actual reality. See Silber, *Romance of Reunion*, and Cox, *Dreaming of Dixie*. Prince, *Stories of the South*, deals well with the proliferation of black images meant for Northern consumers.

14. Marx, *Capital*, 49.

15. As one effect of this occlusion in public attention and public memory, the South would be the subject of repeated discoveries by journalists and cultural producers for at least the next century, a peripheral outpost that occasionally popped into focus as a forgotten part of the nation, whether during Reconstruction, the Great Depression, or the War on Poverty. For more, see the introduction and chapter 4.

16. Derrida, *Specters of Marx*.

17. Jameson, "Modernism and Imperialism," 51.

18. Fanon, *Black Skin*, 14.

19. As quoted in Blight, *Race and Reunion*, 73, 75.

20. Toll, *Blacking Up*, 120. O'Malley argues with insight about the unexpected connections between black soldiers and greenback currency. "During the Civil War, Americans conflated the greenbacks—paper declared to be money by legislative enactment—with African American soldiers, enlisted by legislative fiat.... The debate over race and equality in Reconstruction used the same language, and the same logic, as the debate over money." *Face Value*, 83, 106.

21. The strains of this legacy still shape liberalist historiography, of which Blight's *Race and Reunion* might stand as a premier example. In Blight's account, two neat options are presented to explain the war's legacy: a good emancipationism and a bad reconciliationism. This, perhaps necessarily, entails hagiographic reductions of Abraham Lincoln and Frederick Douglass. Just as the former's strident racism is erased, so too, Blight's account down-

plays the latter's critical black radicalism—where membership in the state is viewed not as an end in itself, but as a means toward the work of freedom and abolition.

22. This definition of the nation comes from Anderson, *Imagined Communities*, 7.

23. Cohen's *Reconstruction of American Liberalism* examines the clash and reconciliation of liberalism's two wings in the writings of Gilded Age intellectuals, which, she argues, laid the groundwork for the modern American liberalism we have inherited. For a brilliant discussion of the ongoing confusion of personhood, property, and slavery in U.S. law and culture, see Best, *Fugitive's Properties*.

24. My introduction to this triptych and my reading of it owe to Nudelman, *John Brown's Body*, 155–61.

25. *Ruffin v. Commonwealth* (1871) adjudged a Virginia felon to be a "slave of the state." That case has received much contemporary attention in scholarship on the Thirteenth Amendment's infamous loophole, and in the cultural currents that this triptych embodies, we can begin to see the designation of "slave of the state" not only in its negative aspect but also as revealing power's more positive and productive facets.

26. Douglass, *Narrative*, 43.

27. "His gesture of allegiance, saluting as he applies to the government for money, mirrors the servile gesture of the 'contraband' who doffs his hat to recruiting officer. Far from entitling the black soldier to autonomy, physical suffering leaves him dependent on the federal government." Nudelman, *John Brown's Body*, 156. Perhaps of note here, too, is the role of the "provost marshal," who was part magistrate and part police officer, associated not with recruiting but with discipline and custody.

28. One cannot help but note the formal identity between early, Dunning-era histories of Reconstruction and their liberal counterparts today: both structure black freedom as "failure" and "tragedy," with the values assigned to each side merely transposed.

29. See Morgan, *Laboring Women*, 69–106; Spillers, "Mama's Baby"; Sublette, *The American Slave Coast*; Hartman, "The Belly of the World."

30. Regarding Haiti's founding documents after the Haitian Revolution, but entirely applicable here, Sibylle Fischer writes, "The political unconscious of radical antislavery was not the nation-state." *Modernity Disavowed*, 271.

31. Letter included in *Free at Last*, 454–56.

32. See Walker, *Appeal*, and Garnet, "An Address to the Slaves." Harnessing the philosophy of yeomanry, not unlike Walker, Garnet says, "Think how many tears you have poured out upon the soil which you have cultivated with unrequited toil and enriched with your blood; and then go to your lordly enslavers and tell them plainly, that you *are determined to be free*" (202).

33. "A Typical Negro," 429–30.

34. Oliver Wendell Holmes Sr. draws an extended comparison between skin and the photographic image in "The Stereoscope and the Stereograph," 738–49.

35. For a thoroughgoing critique of the spectacle of black suffering and its role in liberal ideologies, see the introduction in Hartman, *Scenes of Subjection*, 3–14.

36. Johnson, *Soul by Soul*, 146.

37. Goodyear, "Photography."

38. Goodyear, "Photography." See also Wood, *Blind Memory*, 267–71.

39. Quoted in Goodyear, "Photography."

40. Douglass, *My Bondage*, 220–21.

41. Gates, *Figures in Black*, 108.

42. My inspiration for this point comes from Saidiya Hartman's suggestion that the pen in the gash effaces the wound, but that it's also tethered to that effacing, such that Douglass's form and style might be symptomatic rather than determining of subjectivity. Lecture for "Narratives of Slavery," Columbia University, 26 October 2006.

43. Douglass, *Narrative*, vii, 4–5, 16.

44. Fried, *Realism, Writing, Disfiguration*, 18.

45. Writing in a historical moment marked by the compulsive public display of the mortally wounded black body, shown repeatedly in viral videos of murders inflicted by a police force sanctioned by the state and by the white public, one realizes again the thoroughgoing and structural entrenchment of this dynamic of a black subjectivity adjudicated by a white liberalist suspicion. Douglass, *My Bondage*, 219.

46. Anne Norton writes perceptively of this aspect of liberalism:

> The liberal individual, bearing rights, . . . became an abstraction. Individuality, once an attribute of certain bodies, became an abstraction assignable to any body, and to no body. Corporations, lacking the embodiment—much less the bodily integrity—that individuality once designated, acquired that status in law. Men, who had once held rights in their bodies, who had made their bodies the title and the means to citizenship, now supplemented those (natural rights) with the creation of literary selves. The idea of individuality overcame the represented bodies of men, replacing that which it purported to represent. Individuality acts as supplement. Disembodiment removed liberalism one step further from the inscription of rank at birth that had marked feudalism. Disembodiment moved liberalism one step closer to the rule of reason. African Americans once held as slaves could be held to be equals. Women, once held to be constitutionally inferior, could be ascribed constitutional rights. Individuality, and the rights of man with it, could be extended to any body. The promise of disembodiment became the promise of liberalism. (Norton, "Engendering Another American Identity," 131–32)

47. These questions are indebted to Brilliant, *Portraiture*, 1–44.

48. "Installing a set of objects upon a ledge, at a distance, as the endpoint of the viewer's gaze, these still-life paintings make the viewer's position that of a secure subject, a full-blown individual, comfortably and even complacently eyeing a group of things separate from himself. Almost as surely as these paintings show objects they imply subjects." Nemerov, *The Body of Raphaelle Peale*, 4.

49. Lubin, *Picturing*, 308.

50. Barthes, "Right in the Eyes," 240.

51. On the counterfeit as a practice of freedom, see Young, "How Not to Be a Slave," in *The Grey Album*, 21–64. On the slipperiness of money's value represented in and as art, see Weschler, *Boggs*.

52. *New-York Tribune*, 2 June 1895, 10.

53. "Wild Negro Chants and Dances," *New York Times*, 25 May 1895, 9.

54. *New-York Tribune*, 4 June 1895, 5.

55. For an account of San Juan and the interplay of segregation and U.S. imperial might, which focuses on their brother division, the Tenth Cavalry, see Amy Kaplan, "Black and Blue at San Juan Hill," in *Cultures of United States Imperialism*, 219–36.

56. The most detailed account of *Black America* and the closely related show *The South before the War* has been written by Webb, "Authentic Possibilities," 63–82.

57. On these dynamics, see Hartman, *Scenes of Subjection*, 29–30.

58. "The Stage," *Washington Post*, 20 October 1895, 19.

59. Miller, *Segregated Sound*, 85–120, includes an incisive analysis of the rhetoric of authenticity that was used to promote *Black America*, which Miller ties both to long-standing ploys of the minstrel tradition and to an emergent academic discourse around folklore.

60. *New York Clipper*, 19 July 1879, quoted in Toll, *Blacking Up*, 205.

61. Toll, 206.

62. *Hartford Courant*, 18 October 1879, 1.

63. Kittler, *Gramophone, Film, Typewriter*, 37.

64. "Black America," *Boston Daily Globe*, 14 July 1895, 27.

65. "Wild Negro Chants and Dances," *New York Times*, 25 May 1895, 9.

66. Although it combined most of these new elements, *Black America* was one of many "plant shows" in this decade, which included *The South before the War, Slavery Days, Way Down South, The Old South*, and *Darkest America*. Abbott and Seroff attribute the introduction of scenic realism in these shows to *The South before the War*, which premiered in 1892. And indeed, Billy and Cordelia McClain, an African American couple who worked for and helped manage *South before the War*, provided the creative backbone for *Black America*. I would suggest that it wasn't until the later show that the novel elements of scenic realism and spectacle present in *South before the War* reached fruition. See Abbott and Seroff, *Out of Sight*, 360–69.

67. "Black America," *Boston Daily Globe*, 14 July 1895, 27.

68. *Boston Daily Globe*, 18 July 1895, 4.

69. *New-York Tribune*, 4 June 1895, 11.

70. "Music and Drama," *Boston Daily Globe*, 7 July 1895, 18. "Black America," *Boston Daily Globe*, 14 July 1895, 27.

71. "Nate Salsbury's 'Black America' as Written by Harry Tarleton of Taos for Rebecca Salsbury James," Nate Salsbury Papers, Billy Rose Theatre Collection, New York Public Library, box 1, folder 24. Webb, "Authentic Possibilities," 80.

72. "Music and Drama," *Boston Daily Globe*, 7 July 1895, 18.

73. "Music and Drama," *Boston Daily Globe*, 7 July 1895, 18.

74. Publicity statement, The South before the War Company Papers in the Irving S. Gilmore Music Library of Yale University. MSS 87, box 1, folder 1.

75. My claim about the finale is somewhat speculative. McClain and his wife, Cordelia, worked on *South before the War* until 1894, which was when this third act was commissioned by that show's producers. McClain drafted a script titled *Before and after the War* that year, an incredibly similar title for a piece that marked out an incredibly similar plot to *Black America*'s third act. McClain's script ended with "The Emancipation Proclamation of the Slave" and what he called "the great tableaux of Abraham Lincoln." It seems quite likely, to me at least, that the finales for both shows were written by him. See Webb, "Authentic Possibilities," 77–79. For the attribution of *Black America*'s creative genius to McClain, see Fletcher, *100 Years*, 29, 97. Abbott and Seroff write, "Much of the success of the *South before the War* is attributable to Billy McClain, the creative genius of its first two big seasons." *Out of Sight*, 362. Citing Tom Fletcher's book, which suggests that McClain "understood *Black Amer-*

ica as a production designed to create jobs," Miller claims: "Evidence suggests that at least some—I suspect a significant number—of the show's bit players were local residents, no more 'southern' than the legion of migrants who had recently made New York home. *Black America* succeeded, from Fletcher's perspective, precisely because it featured local celebrity performers who were already favorites with New York audiences." *Segregated Sound*, 119.

76. Quoted in Abbott and Seroff, *Out of Sight*, 364. This was echoed, in a way, by the producer Nate Salsbury, who told a *Washington Post* reporter that *Black America* intended "to show the people of the North the better side of the colored man and woman of the South." And one of the show's early scholars wrote in 1947 that the show was "a first effort to make some presentation of the Negro as a person." Quoted by David Fiske, "The Plantation in Brooklyn: Nate Salsbury's *Black America* Show," http://newyorkhistoryblog.org/2014/01/07/the-plantation-in-brooklyn-nate-salsburys-black-america-show. One wonders, too, whether the McClains might have been aware of and inspired by *The Mirror of Slavery*, the antislavery panorama created by the black abolitionist and fugitive slave Henry Box Brown in 1850, which was another historical meditation on the contradictions between blackness and American nationalism. See Brooks, *Bodies in Dissent*, chapter 2, 66–130.

77. Marx, "On the Jewish Question," 9.

78. Thomas Sergeant Perry, "William Dean Howells," *Century* 23 (March 1882): 683–84, quoted in Wonham, *Playing the Races*, 6.

79. The advent of this evolutionary narrative in black minstrelsy is attributed to William Foote's Afro-American Specialty Company, an all-black troupe from 1891. According to Abbott and Seroff, "Its theme of 'Negro evolution' was considered too progressive for mainstream America. The Afro-American Specialty Company was designed for export, and for that, it lasted less than a year" (146). See Abbott and Seroff, *Out of Sight*, 145–51.

80. "Wild Negro Chants and Dances," *New York Times*, 25 May 1895, 9. Disregarding even the implicit separate-but-equal logic in "a country *for them*" and the imputed subservience of their "appeals," such moments were themselves troubled. It was this same reviewer who extolled, two short paragraphs later, "the happy, careless life" enjoyed by "the negroes of slavery days."

81. In 1892, Harris wrote: "[N]either fictive nor illustrative art has any business with types. It must address itself to life, to the essence of life, which is character, which is individuality. Missing these it misses its true function." Quoted in Wonham, *Playing the Races*, 9.

82. Wonham, 9.

83. Quoted in Wonham, 10.

84. "The Cotton Exchange at 'Black America,'" *New-York Tribune*, 12 June 1895, 11.

85. *New-York Tribune*, 2 June 1895, 10.

86. "Scenes at 'Black America,'" *New-York Tribune*, 9 June 1895, 12.

87. "Black America," *Boston Daily Globe*, 14 July 1895, 27.

88. Henry Grady, "Against Centralization," speech at the University of Virginia, 25 June 1889; quoted in Best, "The Subject of Property," 80.

89. Before 1865, the enslaved could not alienate their labor power in the market; rather, they were themselves capital, and its subjects of accumulation, part and parcel of the very means of production. Marx excepts in his discussion of labor power "slaves, bondsmen, etc." who "themselves form part and parcel of the means of production." Marx, *Capital*, 668.

90. David A. De Armond of Missouri, quoted in Logan, *Betrayal of the Negro*, 90.
91. Harris, *Uncle Remus*, xvii (emphasis mine).
92. *New-York Tribune*, 4 June 1895, 5.
93. *Boston Daily Globe*, 7 July 1895, 18.
94. *New-York Tribune*, 4 June 1895, 11.
95. *Boston Daily Globe*, 18 July 1895, 4.
96. "The Stage," *Washington Post*, 20 October 1895, 19.
97. Rydell, *All the World's*, 88.
98. Benjamin, *Arcades Project*, 805.
99. "Black America," *Boston Daily Globe*, 14 July 1895, 27.
100. Miller, "The Panorama," 34–69.
101. I write "again" because the category of "the South" has long incorporated imperialist aims. See, for example, Greeson, *Our South*, and Johnson, *River of Dark Dreams*.
102. Miller, "The Panorama," 46–47.
103. "Scenes at 'Black America,'" *New-York Tribune*, 9 June 1895, 12.
104. Warner, "Mass Public," 385. Michael Warner and Lauren Berlant, both eminent scholars of liberal culture, have addressed brilliantly formulated essays to these questions of citizenship, publicity, disembodiment, and the commodity form. Berlant reads the various incarnations of *Imitation of Life* (novel, movie, remake), and Warner ponders the forms and meanings of iconicity in American culture. Both Berlant and Warner write from a position aligned with white emancipation, although their critical ostentation leaves that position undisclosed. (In this, I cannot help but notice a structural similarity with liberalism itself.) Both proceed from a presumption that their subjects—black or white, minoritized or not—*pursue* publicity. For them, the iconicity of the public figure implicitly promises the reconciliation of embodiment and abstraction, which have been set at odds by the structure of the public sphere. As Berlant puts it, "since the commodity is the modern embodiment of the legitimate 'artificial person,' Americans in the text equate personal emancipation through it with shedding the collectively shared body of pain to gain a solitary protected self" (122–23). But theirs can only be characterized as a normative position, one they problematize but nevertheless insistently occupy as critics. Questions linger that neither of them addresses (because, within their framework, neither of them can answer): Why presume that those whose bodies and personas are most susceptible to being commodified would ever regard publicity's "artificial personhood" as potentially liberatory? Why would the "minoritized" necessarily seek more publicity than they already endure? Both authors "inadvertently" reinforce the position of whiteness as the invisible norm that all desire to occupy. See Warner, "Mass Public," and Berlant, "National Brands, National Body: *Imitation of Life*," chapter 3 of *The Female Complaint*, 107–44.
105. "The law attempted to resolve the contradiction between the slave as property and the slave as person/laborer or, at the very least, to minimize this tension by attending to the slave as both a form of property and a person," writes Saidiya Hartman. "This effort was instrumental in maintaining the dominance of the slave-owning class, particularly in a period of national crisis concerning the institution. The increasing recognition of the slave person in the period 1830–1860 was an effort to combat the abolitionist polemic about the degradations of chattel status and the slave's lack of rights." Hartman, *Scenes*, 93.
106. Crary, *Suspensions of Perception*, 74–75.

107. "Mode of production," as Jason Read has argued, comprises more than the means of manufacture and the biological reproduction of labor's existence. "*There is a production of subjectivity necessary to the constitution of the capitalist mode of production*," he writes. "For a new mode of production such as capital to be instituted it is not sufficient for it to simply form a new economy, or write new laws, it must institute itself in the quotidian dimensions of existence—it must become habit." Read, *Micro-Politics of Capital*, 36 (emphasis in original).

108. Debord, *Society of the Spectacle*, 24. On the concept of spectacle, see also Clark, *Painting of Modern Life*, 3–22, and Wark, *Beach Beneath the Street*.

109. Debord, *Society of the Spectacle*, 150. Clark writes, "The concept of the spectacle is thus an attempt—a partial and unfinished one—to bring into theoretical order a diverse set of symptoms which are normally treated, by bourgeois sociology or conventional Leftism, as anecdotal trappings affixed somewhat lightly to the old economic order: 'consumerism,' for instance, or 'the society of leisure'; the rise of mass media; the expansion of advertising, the hypertrophy of official diversions (Olympic games, party conventions, *biennales*)." *Painting of Modern Life*, 9.

110. As David Harvey has noted: "If capital only made things that lasted a 100 years it would have died a long time ago. So increasingly it starts to focus its attention on the production of something that is ephemeral, doesn't last very long, is instantly disposable so it even produces products that are instantly disposable and of course spectacle is an instantaneous production. Production is not instantaneous but the consumption is instantaneous. So increasingly urbanisation has become a vehicle for the cultivation of spectacle." Harvey, "There Is No Way."

111. Jameson, "Culture and Finance Capital," 251.

112. Jameson, 258, 264.

113. On black stereotypes in advertising, see Hale, *Making Whiteness*, 121–97. On the popularity of "coon songs" and Tin Pan Alley, see Lemons, "Black Stereotypes," and Dormon, "Shaping the Popular Image." On black representation in early cinema, see Robinson, *Forgeries of Memory*. On plantation thematics in jazz clubs, see Ogren, *The Jazz Revolution*. Cab Calloway recalled, "The whole set was like a sleepy time down South during slavery, [and] the idea was to make whites who came feel like they were being catered to and entertained by black slaves." Quoted in Dinerstein, *Origins of Cool*, 43.

114. Because it is oriented partly around fetishes tied to the emergence of commodity racism, nationalism also profited from this commerce in blackness. The new nationalism of reconciliation required blackness as commodity spectacle, much as the "old" nationalism had required the unbounded market in chattel slaves. Regarding nationalism as a scopic politics of commodity spectacle, see McClintock, *Imperial Leather*, esp. chapters 5 and 10.

115. Blackface minstrelsy and the market in Tomitudes—the popular items of material culture that depicted Harriet Beecher Stowe's famous characters—preexist and predict these developments. For more on the affective economy of Tomitudes, see Bernstein, *Racial Innocence*.

116. So Du Bois writes, in the first sentences of *Souls*, revealing blackness as a world of meaning that is all encompassing: "Herein lie buried many things which if read with patience may show the strange meaning of being black here at the dawning of the Twentieth Century. . . . I have sought here to sketch, in vague, uncertain outline, the spiritual world in which ten thousand Americans live and strive." *Souls*, vii. Marx also uses the figure of the

veil when describing the fetishism of commodities within capitalism: "The life-process of society, which is based on the process of material production, does not strip off its mystical veil until it is treated as production by freely associated men, and is consciously regulated by them in accordance with a settled plan." *Capital*, 80.

117. Debord, *Society of the Spectacle*, 17.

118. Hale, *Making Whiteness*, 168.

119. Crary, "Spectacle, Attention, Counter-Memory," 99.

120. "Capital was kick-started by the rape of the African continent . . . 'the socio-political order of the New World' was kick-started by approaching a particular body (a black body) with direct relations of force, not by approaching a white body with variable capital. Thus, one could say that slavery—the 'accumulation' of black bodies regardless of their utility as labourers through an idiom of despotic power—is closer to capital's primal desire than is waged oppression—the 'exploitation' of unraced bodies that labour through an idiom of rational/symbolic (the wage) power: A relation of terror as opposed to a relation of hegemony." Wilderson, "Gramsci's Black Marx," 230.

121. Farley, "The Apogee," 1229.

122. Twain, *Pudd'nhead Wilson*, 9.

123. Langston Hughes, introduction to *Pudd'nhead Wilson*, by Mark Twain, xi.

124. Twain, *Pudd'nhead Wilson*, 141.

125. Twain, 143.

126. Twain, 27.

127. Twain, 5.

128. Twain, 142.

129. For another treatment of the connections between *Pudd'nhead Wilson* and *Plessy*, see chapter 2, "Mark Twain and Homer Plessy," in Sundquist, *To Wake the Nations*, 225–70.

130. Best, *Fugitive's Properties*, 345n85.

131. *Plessy v. Ferguson*, 163 U.S. 537 (1896).

132. For another treatment of these issues, see Kahn, "Controlling Identity," 755–81.

133. Sundquist, *To Wake the Nations*, 269.

134. "Scenes at 'Black America,'" *New-York Tribune*, 9 June 1895, 12.

135. Collins, "Portraits of Slave Children," 187–88.

136. "White and Colored Slaves," *Harper's Weekly*, 30 January 1864, 71. See Collins, "Portraits of Slave Children," 187–210, and chapter 2 of Mitchell, *Raising Freedom's Child*, 51–90.

137. The girls' images may have incited viewers' imaginations in other ways. "The girls' portraits invited viewers—particularly male viewers—to imagine them as the light-skinned 'fancy girls' for sale in the New Orleans slave market, young women highly valued for their service as concubines to the white men of the South. These photographs presented a female body that existed somewhere between the real and the imagined, in this respect much like pornographic photography of the nineteenth century." Mitchell, *Raising Freedom's Child*, 64.

138. "White and Colored Slaves," *Harper's Weekly*, 30 January 1864, 71.

139. Wiegman, *American Anatomies*, 21.

140. Spillers, *Black, White, and In Color*, 318. Sundquist, *To Wake the Nations*, 268.

141. King references here the thought of Martin Buber. Quoted in Binder, "Slavery of Emancipation," 2098n154.

142. Collins, "Portraits of Slave Children," 189.

143. McElroy's *Philadelphia City Directory, for 1859*, 294.

144. Quoted in Davis and Haller, *Peoples of Philadelphia*, 168.

145. There is nothing to prove or disprove Isaac White's presence on the Philadelphia leg of the tour.

146. Kathleen Collins suggests in her article that Isaac was present only in New York and did not travel to Philadelphia. There is, however, no evidence of this, although there are no extant photographs taken of him in that city. The letter in *Harper's* only takes care to mention the three white children who were expelled from the Philadelphia hotel.

147. This handwritten caption on the photograph can be found in the Photographs and Prints Division, Schomburg Center for Research in Black Culture, The New York Public Library.

148. Holmes, "The Stereoscope," 747–78. Allan Sekula writes: "Would it be absurd for me to suggest that Holmes is describing something analogous to the capitalist exchange process, whereby exchange values are detached from, and exist independently of, the use values of commodities? The dominant metaphor in Holmes's discussion is that of bourgeois political economy; just as use value is eclipsed by exchange value, so the photographic sign comes to eclipse its referent. For Holmes, quite explicitly, the photograph is akin to money." "Traffic in Photographs," 22.

149. Of note here are Jameson's words on the deterritorialization endemic to finance capital and its cultures. Deterritorialization "implies a new ontological and free-floating state, one in which the content . . . has definitively been suppressed in favor of the form, in which the inherent nature of the product becomes insignificant, a mere marketing pretext, while the goal of production no longer lies in any specific market, any specific set of consumers or social and individual needs, but rather in its transformation into that element which by definition has no context or territory, and indeed no use value as such, namely, money." "Culture and Finance Capital," 260. See also Cheng, *Second Skin*, which offers arguments related to this chapter's, but in a psychoanalytic register. Cheng reads the naked skin of black performer Josephine Baker as a means of articulating the aesthetics of blackness with an emergent modernist style.

150. Hale, *Making Whiteness*, 199–240.

151. Frankenstein, *Illusions of Reality*.

Chapter Three

1. Wister, *The Virginian*, 125.

2. Morrison, *Playing in the Dark*, 5.

3. Hine and Faragher, *Frontiers*, 125. See Painter, *Exodusters*. See also *Report and Testimony*.

4. Bold, *Frontier Club*, 135.

5. In the gloss by Carl Schmitt, this process is the "terrestrial fundament" of "all further law," "the reproductive root in the normative order of history." Schmitt, *Nomos*, 42–49.

6. Noting how settlers "carry" law wherever they voyage, the jurist William Blackstone later wrote, "if an uninhabited country be discovered and planted by English subjects, all the English laws then in being, which are the birthright of every subject, are immediately there in force." Quoted in Pateman, *Contract and Domination*, 55–56.

7. On Meigs's plan, see O'Malley, *Face Value*, 44–46. On the actual history of turning this land into a commodity, see Johnson, *River of Dark Dreams*, 34–45.

8. Stiles, *Jesse James*, 236.

9. Agnew, *Worlds Apart*, 82–83, 188–90.

10. See, for example, Alexander Nemerov's analysis of Western genre paintings in "Doing the 'Old America,'" 285–343.

11. Jameson, "Magical Narratives," 135–63.

12. For another argument along these lines, see Kuenz, "The Cowboy Businessman." Kuenz writes: "Among middle-class white men in particular, the changes in the social and economic organization of the United States brought on by post–Civil War growth posed special challenges as traditional notions of masculine identity grounded in an ethic of individualism and self-production confronted an economy where that ethic no longer had a sure place. While the culture at large continued to sing the praises of the self-made man, he who was a product of his own free labor, the emerging corporate world was steadily making his success both less likely and irrelevant" (106).

13. Hopkins, *The Magazine Novels of Pauline Hopkins* (1990), 358.

14. Patterson, "'Kin' o' Rough Justice Fer a Parson,'" 449.

15. Carby, introduction to Hopkins, *Magazine Novels*, xliii.

16. "The cataclysmic events of the Civil War have obscured in our present century the fact that, for at least half of the decades prior to the war, all states lying beyond the Appalachians were thought to share a unified Western consciousness. Even stranger to Americans living today would be the commonly accepted assumption that the roots of this new Western culture were Southern. This conviction that Western interests would ultimately merge with those of the South helps explain New England's staunch opposition to the Louisiana Purchase of 1803, to the War of 1812, and to the Mexican War of 1846." Watson, *Yeoman Versus Cavalier*, 12.

17. Bold, *Frontier Club*, 226.

18. Kilbride, "Fanny Kemble and Frances Butler Leigh," 109. "Major Butler had a considerable personal interest in the enslaved population. This fact influenced his actions at the convention, where his position on slavery was forthright, and his arguments for its preservation numerous and contentious. No slave state delegate had more to do with fitting those held in bondage into the United States Constitution than did he." Bell, *Major Butler's Legacy*, xx. See also Sublette, *American Slave Coast*, 293.

19. Payne, *Owen Wister*, 10.

20. Wister, *That I May Tell You*, 3.

21. Wister, *Virginian*, viii.

22. "For the first time, a cowboy was a gentleman and hero, but nobody realized then that the book was the master design on which thousands of Westerns would be modeled. Its hero was the first cowboy to capture the public's imagination.... Before this, cowboys had been depicted as murderous thugs.... The Virginian himself is the progenitor of the cowboy as a folk figure." Wister, *Owen Wister Out West*, 2.

23. Slotkin, *The Fatal Environment*, 100, 105 (emphasis added).

24. Slotkin, *Gunfighter Nation*, 17–18.

25. Slotkin, 170. Payne, *Owen Wister*, 80. Black flesh, too, was a bonanza commodity in the 1850s, when there was a bubble in slave prices. See Johnson, *River of Dark Dreams*.

26. Among its many problems, Turner's thesis ignores the projection of the concept of the frontier beyond the continental United States, which would achieve a crystalline historical realization five years later in 1898. For an example of such projection, see Norris, "The Frontier Gone at Last," 69–81.

27. Slotkin, *Gunfighter Nation*, 61.

28. Sklansky, *The Soul's Economy*, 171–204.

29. Marginalism intended to reassert capitalists' dominion over profits and wages by arguing that their outlays in fixed capital provided the very conditions for labor's productivity. "The marginal 'product' of capital . . . was the difference between the total output of a given labor force before and after investment in and installation of new plant and equipment," writes James Livingston. "The increase in the marginal product of labor—and so in the wages of labor—was now theoretically dependent on the maintenance of productive investment, which was itself a function of past income accruing to capital. . . . Capital could hereafter appear as a factor of *production*." Livingston, *Pragmatism*, 56. This account of marginalism and its historical context comes from chapter 2 of his book, esp. 49–56.

30. Donohue, *Freedom from Want*, 65–66. Donohue also sketches the rise of marginalism in Europe and the conditions for its success in the United States in the 1890s.

31. Sklansky, *Soul's Economy*, 207.

32. Kuenz, "The Cowboy Businessman," 117.

33. For a different take on the early Western genre's preoccupation with forms of control, in this case the artist (and Wister's friend) Frederic Remington's pictures of the West as a fantasy of social control of a restive urban underclass, see Nemerov, "Doing the 'Old America.'"

34. Alfred D. Chandler Jr. notes, "as the first salaried manager in the country, the plantation overseer was an important person in American economic history. . . . The overseer was expected to know the strengths and weaknesses of his foremen, or 'drivers,' and even many of the field hands themselves." *The Visible Hand*, 65.

35. "In the mid-1790s, Philadelphia, capital of a nation recently born of revolution, was teeming with exiles driven from their homes by a cycle of revolution sweeping the Atlantic world. Some came from France, victims of one or another political purge. But many more had come from the Caribbean, particularly Saint-Domingue, fleeing slave revolution . . . white masters and merchants, previously rich and now reduced to dependence." Dubois, *Avengers*, 8.

36. See Kilbride, *An American Aristocracy*.

37. Butler Place may well have been built by a French expatriate fleeing from the Haitian Revolution. Wister's biographer notes, "A Frenchman had built the main house of this estate in 1790, before the Butler family acquired it in 1810." Payne, *Owen Wister*, 10–11.

38. See, for example, Richards, *The California Gold Rush*.

39. The conceit of Wister's joke also bears a striking resemblance to a Southwestern frontier story (a genre discussed in chapter 4) by John Gorman Barr, "A Lively Village; or Brisk Speculation in a New Commodity," in which a "speculator in cats" (likely a verbal play on wildcat banks) convinces a town to use cats as their primary currency. Reprinted in Cohen and Dillingham, *Humor of the Old Southwest*, 400–414.

40. On the relationship between chattel and cattle in the context of slave law, see Dayan, *Law Is a White Dog*, 125–27.

41. Sublette, *American Slave Coast*, 9.

42. Kemble, *Journal of a Residence*, 331–32 (emphasis mine on "the Virginians").

43. Like a dystopic vision of the Southern plantation after 1865, Wister wrote for the stage production of *The Virginian* in 1904 the song "Ten Thousand Cattle Straying (Dead Broke)": "*Ten thousand cattle straying, / They quit my range and travell'd away, / And it's 'sons-of-guns' is what I say, / I am dead broke, dead broke this day. / Dead broke.*" These lyrics sound like nothing so much as an enslaver bemoaning abolition's reversal of his fortunes. In *West of Everything*, Jane Tompkins also suggests that cattle occupy something like the position of the slave in the Western; see chapter 5, "Cattle," 111–23.

44. Wister has thus set about rewriting that other canonical American tall tale about frogs, Mark Twain's "The Celebrated Jumping Frog of Calaveras County" (1865). Twain's yarn, too, concerns a speculator, albeit in the simpler form of a compulsive gambler, named Jim Smiley. A man who will bet on anything—"if there was a dog-fight, he'd bet on it; if there was a cat-fight, he'd bet on it; if there was a chicken-fight, he'd bet on it; why, if there was two birds setting on a fence, he would bet you which one would fly first"—Jim Smiley emerges the fool at the end of Twain's story. Twain's gambler gets his comeuppance, in true republican fashion. But with his story of the Virginian and the frogs, Wister performs a transvaluation of values on Twain's tale. For Wister, the speculator is the hero. Twain, *The Celebrated Jumping Frog*, 11–12.

45. For a social and economic history of the "trust movement" and its relation to risk, see chapter 8 of Levy, *Freaks of Fortune*, 264–307.

46. Livingston, *Pragmatism*, 44. In the context of this argument, it is worth pointing out that this fear and repugnance toward unproductive labor was a stalwart in arguments made by Northern advocates of free labor against Southern planter "aristocrats," both before and after the Civil War. In the antislavery discourse of free labor, the South was recurrently framed as an atavistic relic of the Old World, which was ordered through caste, status, and hierarchy, as opposed to free labor's supposed ideals of meritocracy, egalitarianism, and democracy. Just to take one, of innumerable, examples: the abolitionist Wendell Phillips declared in his speech "Under the Flag" in April 1861, "The North *thinks*—can appreciate argument—is the nineteenth century—hardly any struggle left in it but that between the working class and the money-kings. The South *dreams*—it is the thirteenth and fourteenth century—baron and serf—noble and slave." Frederick Douglass and Harriet Beecher Stowe also rely on this sort of feudal rhetoric. Phillips, *Speeches*, 399.

47. Livingston, *Pragmatism*, 54.

48. The Virginian's "plain" provenance and corporate trajectory also then exemplifies Livingston's claim that procapitalists "hailed the new division of labor between owners and managers as the dawn of scientific procedure in business enterprise and the source of social mobility for the sons of the working class. In their view, the corporations would become the recruiting ground for talent from families without social connection or inherited wealth." Livingston, *Pragmatism*, 177. It is entirely possible that Wister means his character's provenance from "old Virginia" to legitimate the planter's authority for a new era, while also intending his yeoman stock to use an older era's "productive" manual labor to legitimate a newer corporate era's "unproductive" mental labor. In other words, with the names of the novel and the character, Wister imports the South into the West to draw an analogy between the planter and the corporate capitalist.

49. Wolf, "The Labor of Seeing," 298.

50. Lippmann, *Drift and Mastery*, 55–56.
51. See, for example, the classic history by Wiebe, *The Search for Order*.
52. Sklansky, *Soul's Economy*, 201.
53. Though in a different register, the importance of language over action in *The Virginian* is a central argument of Mitchell, *Westerns*, 94–119.
54. See Susman, "Personality," 271–85.
55. Freud, *The Joke*, 98.
56. Freud, 173, 145.
57. Freud, 98 (emphasis in original).
58. Freud, 132. Freud's description recurs to a metaphor that likens the "economy of the psyche" to economies of scale wherein expansion of a business reduces its costs of manufacture, "lessens" its "running costs." For Freud, the mind itself is incorporated—not just literally included by the body, but also figuratively functioning as a systematized and integrated "business concern." Our mental corporation produces the commodity of pleasure, and it operates with the capital of psychic energy. What the mind wants is to optimize its output of pleasure while dialing back its "expenditure" of this energy. As Freud conceives it, psychic energy is continually being expended through inhibitions to desire, through various forms of "psychical damming-up" (114). The joke might be understood as a device that saves on this labor—a kind of scientific management for the mind, the discovery of a more efficient technique. "The process in the joke's first person [i.e., the teller] produces pleasure by lifting inhibition, reducing local expenditure," he writes (151). The innovations of joke-work mean that "the same activity can now be managed at a lower cost." Freud, *The Joke*.
59. From the diary of Sidney George Fisher, quoted in Tompkins, *West of Everything*, 146, original in Bell, *Major Butler's Legacy*, 400–401.
60. Payne, *Owen Wister*, 214.
61. Canetti, *The Conscience of Words*, 27.
62. Equiano, *Interesting Narrative*, 55. Cugoano, *Thoughts*, 9.
63. Canetti's fantasy reveals the integral connection between this figure of absolute power and a figure of absolute degradation. One of the profound insights provided by the contemporary theories of sovereignty elaborated by Giorgio Agamben has been this revelation—that the figure of sovereignty is jointly articulated with the figure of a life that exists only to die at its hands. One of its profound shortcomings is Agamben's refusal to consider, as originary to sovereign power, the scenes of racial terror in the colonies, on the plantations. See Agamben, *Homo Sacer*, and for his analysis of racism (as European anti-Semitism) in its conjunction with sovereign power, see the third book in his tetralogy, *Remnants of Auschwitz*, 82–86, 155–56. A critique of Agamben's exclusion of race can be found in Sexton, "People-of-Color-Blindness," 31–56.
64. Nemerov, *Frederic Remington*, 38.
65. Freud, *The Joke*, 128.
66. On the fantasy of black extinction, see Fredrickson, *The Black Image*, 154–64, 246–55. For a critique of such colonization schemes, see Walker, *Appeal*, 70–74. On Walker and Jefferson, see Kazanjian, *The Colonizing Trick*, 89–138. On Stowe, see Brown, *Domestic Individualism*, 13–38.
67. Fredrickson, *Black Image*, 252.
68. Benjamin, *Arcades Project*, 111, 497.

69. Arendt, *Origins*, 189–90, 217.

70. McCarthy, *Blood Meridian*, 260–61.

71. Foucault, *Society*, 254. This theme is developed across Sylvia Wynter's oeuvre, but see, for example, "1492: A New World View," 5–57.

72. McKittrick, "Plantation Futures," 6–7.

73. Potts, "Quality Inequality," 231.

74. Kaplan, *Anarchy of Empire*, 120.

75. Statistic on lynchings from Painter, *Standing at Armageddon*, 166. Du Bois, *Souls*, 55.

76. Du Bois, "Another Open Letter," 233.

77. Regarding how the discourse that criminalized blackness itself as a state of being was assembled during these years, see Muhammad, *Condemnation of Blackness*. How this reservoir functions in the contemporary moment is examined in Wang, *Carceral Capitalism*, 151–92.

78. See, for example, Spear, "Origins of the Urban Ghetto," 153–66. This assertion also comports with what the geographer Katherine McKittrick terms the "lands of no one," in which she includes the plantation and the ghetto, as part of colonialism's "overarching system wherein particular spaces of otherness—for purposes here, black geographies—were designated as incongruous with humanness." She writes, "So in our present moment, some live in the unlivable, and to live in the unlivable condemns the geographies of marginalized to death over and over again." McKittrick, "Plantation Futures," 6–7.

79. Wells, *The Light of Truth*, 493.

80. Du Bois, *Darkwater*, 94–95.

81. An extensive account of the auction can be found in Bell, *Major Butler's Legacy*, 311–40.

82. Gikandi, *Slavery*, 158.

83. Canetti, *Conscience of Words*, 27.

84. Payne, *Owen Wister*, 73. It was almost exactly one year before the Supreme Court would hand down its decision in the *Santa Clara* railroad case (10 May 1886) that would grant corporations legal personhood—surely an auspicious time to be working in a law office such as Francis Rawle's.

85. "Among middle-class white men in particular, the changes in the social and economic organization of the United States brought on by post–Civil War growth posed special challenges as traditional notions of masculine identity grounded in an ethic of individualism and self-production confronted an economy where that ethic no longer had a sure place. While the culture at large continued to sing the praises of the self-made man, he who was a product of his own free labor, the emerging corporate world was steadily making his success both less likely and irrelevant." Kuenz, "The Cowboy Businessman," 106.

86. Walter Johnson traces the lineaments of this order:

> When the Scottish traveler James Stirling suggested in 1857 that cotton and Negroes were "the law and the prophets to the men of the South," he was suggesting that the foundational commodities on which the Southern social order was based were both the limiting condition and the leading indicators of the course of Southern history—the law and the prophets. This never-ending, ever-changing conversation was a way for white men to measure the progress of their political economy. Their sense of economic time—of proper and improper development, of beckoning possibility and cautionary

warning—was indexed through the comparison of the prices of cotton and slaves. (*River of Dark Dreams*, 374)

87. On the structure of antagonisms among the settler, the Native, and the slave, see Wilderson, *Red, White, and Black*.

88. On the relation between delaying and promising, I have in mind Brook Thomas's discussion of contract, here in relation to the philosophy of David Hume: "[P]romises are especially important in establishing commitments to those beyond our immediate circle of friends and family. Indeed, distance seems to be a dynamic part of the dynamic of promising, since a promise is almost always evoked when delivery on an obligation involves a delay. Promises, therefore, are ideally suited for the transfer of goods that are absent in either time or space." On a somewhat larger scale, what this brings into focus is how the space of territory and the space of markets overlap. Thomas, *American Literary Realism*, 30.

Chapter Four

1. Scharnhorst, *Owen Wister*, 159.
2. Lomax, *Cowboy Songs*, vii–viii.
3. Lomax, xvii, xxiv, xxvi. Lomax was not the first American folklorist to appeal to organic metaphor. Collecting spirituals in the South during his Civil War deployment, Thomas Wentworth Higginson wrote in the *Atlantic Monthly* in June 1867, "I could now gather on their own soil these strange plants, which I had before seen as in museums alone. . . . Writing down in the darkness, as I best could—perhaps with my hand in the safe covert of my pocket—the words of the song, I have afterwards carried it to my tent, like some captured bird or insect, and then, after examination, put it by." http://www.theatlantic.com/past/docs/issues/1867jun/spirit.htm.
4. Lomax, *Cowboy Songs*, xxi.
5. Karl Hagstrom Miller notes a slippage in some early folklorist work that equated the mountain South of Appalachia with the region as a whole. "It was a subtle but important categorical slip. The implicit equation between the mountains and the South marked the entire region as a place apart from the rest of the nation. It suggested that the South maintained a homogenous musical culture defined by its antiquity, its primitive ideals, and its ignorance of northern styles." Miller, *Segregated Sound*, 105. Of course, the Appalachian Mountains were also stitched into the fabric of national commerce and national culture; that region's isolation was also as much figment as reality.
6. Lomax, *Our Singing Country*, xxiii–xxiv.
7. See Wright, *12 Million Black Voices*, 79–86. "News comes that there are better places to go, but we know that the next place will be as bad as the last one. Yet we go. Our drifting is the expression of our hope to improve our lives" (86). "Of all the elements of [rural] transformation [to capital-intensive farming], mechanization proves the most elusive to chart. In a sense, it was like a wave that had gained momentum since the turn of the century and was about to break over the rural South," writes historian Pete Daniel. "Mechanization in the Cotton Belt actually started in the western growing areas and spread east. . . . [M]any commercial farmers took the first step toward mechanization in the 1930s, and they often used government money to purchase tractors. With an assured parity price, they could invest with some certainty of paying off debts. According to one study, each tractor displaced several

families, and the 111,399 tractors introduced into cotton-growing states in the 1930s displaced from 100,000 to 500,000 families or from a half-million to two million people. Of the 148,096 fewer farm operators over the 1930s, mechanization displaced from one-fifth to two-fifths." Daniel, *Breaking the Land*, 175.

8. Maguire and Brown, *On Shares*, 90–91.

9. FDR's other signal New Deal reforms weren't generous to Southern farmers and their families, as historian Jacquelyn Dowd Hall has pointed out. "When unemployment insurance was enacted in 1935, for example, it did not extend to agricultural and domestic workers, whom reformers did not see as independent, full-time breadwinners, and on whom the South's low-wage economy depended. As a result, 55 percent of all African American workers and 87 percent of all wage-earning African American women were excluded from one of the chief benefits of the New Deal." Hall, "Long Civil Rights," 1241.

10. "The enclosure movement in the Delta was not, as some have argued, based on the transition from feudalism into capitalism; rather, it marked the movement from capital-scarce, labor-intensive plantation production to capital-intensive, labor-surplus neo-plantation production. In the process, millions fled the South in horror, and thousands of African American communities were destroyed seemingly overnight." Woods, *Development Arrested*, 127. "Just as Theodore Roosevelt posed as a trustbuster while acquiescing to business demands for rationalization, Franklin D. Roosevelt secured strong support from bottom-rung farmers while the USDA implemented policies advocated by top-rung commercial farmers." Daniel, "Crossroads of Change," 447.

11. Daniel, *Shadow of Slavery*, 163.

12. The "effect of the [Southern] migration on US national culture was tremendous," Michael Denning argues in *The Cultural Front*, leading to "a 'southernization' of American culture," though he locates its impact later, in the decades after World War II. Denning, *Cultural Front*, 35.

13. "Just as agency programs were weighted toward the tenant-laden South and the migrant-laden West, the photographic collection *as a whole* was weighted toward the same regions. Thus, while 11 percent of the United States population lived in the West (1940 census), the region was represented in 21.9 percent of the total RA [Resettlement Administration]/FSA photos, and while the South held 31.5 percent of the country's population, it was represented in 42.4 percent of the photos. On the other side of the coin, North Central states composed 30.3 percent of the population but only 22.8 percent of the photos; Northeastern states 27.2 percent of the population, only 12.9 percent of the photos." Natanson, *Black Image*, 69.

14. Stange, *Symbols*, 130.

15. For example, the peonage statute would not cover situations in which workers were hired with the promise of pay, which then never came. Here, the employer was seen technically to be "indebted" to the worker. Repeated over and over in the Department of Justice form letters to the supplicating farmers were the sentences, "Peonage is a condition of compulsory service based upon the indebtedness of the peon to the master. The basal fact is indebtedness." See the Peonage Complaint File in the General Records of the Department of Justice, Record Group 60, National Archives, College Park, Md. Box 10787, which is filled with direct appeals to the president.

16. Maverick, "Let's Join."

17. See Noble, *Death of a Nation*, 151–214.

18. The classic scholarship on this process, which was taking place across Western nations in this era, can be found in Eric Hobsbawm, "Inventing Traditions" and "Mass-Producing Traditions: 1870–1914" (which also makes reference to the United States), in Hobsbawm and Ranger, *Invention of Tradition*.

19. See Brodhead, *School of Hawthorne*, 201–11.

20. Brooks, *America's Coming-of-Age*, 109, 39.

21. These authors are listed in Brodhead, *School of Hawthorne*, 56. John Lomax's mentor at Harvard, Barrett Wendell, had published his *Literary History of America* in 1900, which "defended American literature with faint praise" and "did not question the assumption that whatever was of value in it was a product of New England and therefore predominantly British in spirit." In 1925, another scholar "remarked that the title of Wendell's book should have been 'A Literary History of Harvard University, with Incidental Glimpses of the Minor Writers of America.'" Graff, *Professing*, 212. This elitism was also, of course, racist: "Barrett Wendell at the turn of the century still regretted the freeing of the slaves, an event he blamed for having permanently 'lowered the personal dignity of public life, by substituting for the traditional rule of the conservative gentry the obvious dominance of the less educated classes.'" Graff, 83.

22. Graff, 125. The remark was made by Charles Hall Grandgent in 1912 regarding new artistic movements such as postimpressionism, cubism, and futurism.

23. See, for example, Bridgman, *Colloquial Style*, and Lemke, *Vernacular Matters*. The quest had its forebears: "elegance iz most generally found in a plain, neet, chaste phraseology," Noah Webster wrote in 1790, in example of his phonetic spelling theory. Quoted in Bridgman, *Colloquial Style*, 43. "The language of the street is always strong. . . . Cut these words and they would bleed; they are vascular and alive; they walk and run," Emerson wrote in his journals in 1849. (His praise was not without its racial presumptions about the folk, since Emerson designates this speech as, unsurprisingly, "vigorous Saxon.") Quoted in Matthiessen, *American*, 35. "Slang, profoundly consider'd, is the lawless germinal element, below all words and sentences, and behind all poetry," Walt Whitman wrote in 1885, a poet who had become for these insurgents something of a patron saint. Whitman, "Slang in America," in *Portable Walt Whitman*, 557.

24. Noble, *Death of a Nation*, 80.

25. Matthiessen, *American*, 628. Relevant to the arguments made later in this chapter, according to Graff, Matthiessen "managed to transform the organic social conservatism of Eliot and the Agrarians into a celebration of the democratic spirit. Matthiessen's book comprehensively fused cultural criticism and academic literary history with the New Criticism's method of explication and its themes of complexity, paradox, and tragic vision." Graff, *Professing*, 219.

26. This strand is associated with the critical work of Perry Miller in *The New England Mind: The Seventeenth Century* (1939) and later in *Errand into the Wilderness* (1956, though the essays comprising it were published in journals beginning in the 1930s). Miller redeemed the Puritans after they had been tarnished by Parrington. This competing strand "would shortly come to define the widely expounded 'romance' interpretation of American literature: the central role of the Puritans; the continuity from Puritan to Transcendentalist to modernist; the cultivation of symbolic perception and of intensity of experience divorced from society; the primacy of Manichaean dualism and unresolved moral and epistemological conflict in the American imagination." Graff, *Professing*, 218. The strand I am tracing in this chapter is associated instead with a realist disposition in literary criticism. A necessary caveat: this romance/realism dichotomy that structured midcentury Ameri-

can literary criticism is a false binary, which naturalizes the nation-state and its constitutive exclusions, as scholars in the 1980s and 1990s would consistently and trenchantly argue. Cindy Weinstein and Christopher Looby point out: "For a long time, what made American literature distinctive, even exceptional, was held to be its aesthetic particularity: its characteristic 'organic form,' its embrace of romance rather than realism, its colloquial style, or some other discovered or invented aesthetic quality. Then it came about that this critical use of aesthetic categories to identify and analyze American literature was considered spurious and morally suspect—held to constitute a dangerous and morally blameworthy evasion of history and political reality." Weinstein and Looby, *American Literature's Aesthetic Dimensions*, 1.

27. The crucial difference between the fiction associated with the Northwest (such as James Fenimore Cooper's Leatherstocking Tales) and that of the Southwest was the orientation toward the frontier culture. For the former, the frontier represented a zone of anticulture (which with Free Soil politics and the germ of a more recognizable Western genre would later become a zone of self-culture). Its hero was a loner pitted against "savages" (both Natives and poor whites) in a wilderness. It was also what Richard Slotkin calls a "one-man precapitalist utopia." See *Fatal Environment*, 105. For the latter, often satirical in tone, the "egalitarian" culture of slavery's frontier could be valorized. Southwestern literature portrayed social relations and communities, and indeed depended on the representation of society and its contradictions for its defining humor. Obviously, this was crucial for the conception of a folk culture. See Saxton, *Rise and Fall*, 183–203. Henry Nash Smith writes: "It is true that . . . the Southwest produced its own striking symbols, embodied in the newspaper sketches and oral tales which were called, collectively, Southwestern humor. These symbols were also destined to survive the Civil War and to have important consequences for American literature. They formed the tradition out of which developed Mark Twain." *Virgin Land*, 152. William Faulkner said, "In my opinion, Mark Twain was the first truly American writer, and all of us since are his heirs, we are descended from him." *Faulkner at Nagano*, 88. And Ernest Hemingway famously wrote, "All modern American literature comes from one book by Mark Twain called Huckleberry Finn." *Green Hills*, 17.

28. Brooks, "On Creating," 337–41. Judy, *(Dis)forming*, 58.

29. Edmund Wilson would make this point decades later in his classic *Patriotic Gore*, when he noted the revival of the work of George Washington Harris, perhaps the most famous of the Southern frontier humorists, and his character Sut Lovingood. "These stories were collected, in 1867, in a volume called *Sut Lovingood: Yarns Spun by a Nat'ral Born Durn'd Fool*, which was reviewed by Mark Twain in a San Francisco paper and to which he perhaps owed something; but Harris's work, after his death in 1869, seems to have been soon forgotten, and it was only in the thirties of the present century that—in the course of the recent excavations in the field of American literature—such writers as Bernard DeVoto, Constance Rourke, and F. O. Matthiessen began to take an interest in Sut Lovingood." Wilson, *Patriotic Gore*, 508.

30. *The Beginnings of Critical Realism in America: Main Currents in American Thought*, vol. 3 (1927), 86. Quoted in Noble, *Death of a Nation*, 87.

31. Twain writes:

And now here I was, in a country where a right to say how the country should be governed was restricted to six persons in each thousand of its population. For the nine hundred and ninety-four to express dissatisfaction with the regnant system and propose to change it, would have made the whole six shudder as one man, it would have been so disloyal, so dishonorable, such putrid black treason. So to speak, I was become a stockholder in a corporation where nine hundred and ninety-four of the members furnished all the money and did all the work, and the other six elected themselves a permanent board of directors and took all the dividends. It seemed to me that what the nine hundred and ninety-four needed was a new deal. (*Connecticut Yankee*, 101–2)

32. DeVoto, *Mark Twain's America*, 99, 243. Van Wyck Brooks had published a book titled *The Ordeal of Mark Twain* in 1920, but for Brooks, Twain succeeded *despite* his frontier situation. "A desert of human sand!—the barrenest spot in all Christendom, surely, for the seed of genius to fall in" (*Ordeal of Mark Twain*, 30)—a sentiment that stems from one famously expressed by H. L. Mencken in "Sahara of the Bozart" in 1917 that the South was "almost as sterile, artistically, intellectually, culturally, as the Sahara Desert" (*Mencken Chrestomathy*, 184). For DeVoto, he succeeded *because* of his frontier situation. The intellectual historian Kerwin Klein notes that DeVoto's *Mark Twain's America* "was one of the first critical texts to construct the Twain that most of us have grown up with, one of America's great authors." *Frontiers*, 217.

33. Rourke, *American Humor*, 61–64.

34. Matthiessen, *American*, 637. See also Leo Marx, who writes: "In Hawthorne and James criticism arose from a comparison of America to tradition, to the past. In Whitman and Twain, on the other hand, the criticism was based on egalitarian standards. It came from a comparison of an actual America with an idealized democratic vision of the nation's destiny. From the beginning the vernacular was more than a literary, technique—it was a view of experience." *Pilot*, 17.

35. See, for example, chapter 1 of Johnson, *River of Dark Dreams*, and chapter 4 of Baptist, *Half Has Never*. The term "factories in the field" comes from a different historical context; see McWilliams, *Factories*.

36. Rogin, *Fathers*, 251–52. On the work of surveyors, see Johnson, *River of Dark Dreams*, 35–37. On the connections between the New York business world and the plantation South, see Foner, *Business & Slavery*.

37. Sellers, *Market Revolution*, 408.

38. Baptist, *Half Has Never*, 322.

39. Blacks in the North were not safe from this market, as the Fugitive Slave Laws made clear, and as did their repeated testimony of fear and anxiety about being (re)captured, even as free blacks, as in the case of Solomon Northup.

40. Loughran, *Republic*, 314.

The Embargo Act of 1807, the Non-Intercourse Act of 1808, and various customs duties all defined a legal line between the "internal" economy of the United States and the global economy of the late nineteenth century, dividing the Valley from the global economy by inscribing across the mouth of the Mississippi a line between the inside and the outside. They were ways of making the U.S. national sovereignty represented by the Louisiana Purchase material, in the form of economic practice.... [T]he 1808 law closing the Atlantic slave trade to the United States ... forwarded an emergent idea of the "nation" as the container of its own economy, over and against the insatiable logic of an economy that could commodify anything—even a tiny child. (Johnson, *River*, 27)

See also the arguments made by Sublette in *American Slave Coast*, chapter 2, "Protectionism, or the Importance of 1808."

41. Loughran, *Republic*, 309–10.

42. Sellers, *Market Revolution*, 403–4.

43. Quoted in Sellers, 404. As W. E. B. Du Bois notes: "After all, abolition represented capital. The whole movement was based on mawkish sentimentality, and not on the demands of the workers, at least of the white workers." *Black Reconstruction*, 25. On the power dynamics of the contract, see Stanley, "Legends of Contract Freedom," in *From Bondage*.

44. "Abolitionism, although resisted by much of the bourgeoisie, muted class conflict over wage slavery to become the vanguard of capitalist liberalism.... Suffusing free-labor enterprise with antislavery altruism, it would eventually endow the bourgeois state with hegemonic sanctity." Sellers, *Market Revolution*, 405.

45. Baptist, *Half Has Never*, 311.

46. Porter, *Big Bear*, vii.

47. Thorpe, *Hive*, 6. The literary critic Lloyd Pratt cites Thorpe's comment in *Archives of American Time*, which focuses on three genres essential to the construction of a national literature, one of which is Southwestern humor. "In important ways, these genres have been central stabilizing influences and touchstones of this field in moments of transition and consolidation. If they are not the keystone in the arch of American literature, then they are among its most important voussoirs" (21). Thorpe is quoted on p. 133.

48. Thus, DeVoto, remarking on Augustus Baldwin Longstreet, the first of these Southwestern humorists: "Longstreet declared his intention of recording what he had seen ... to produce laughter by exhibiting what they had seen and heard in the world of reality." See *Mark Twain's America*, 243. On the four best of these writers: "[T]hey are this literature achieving realism. It is as the fulfillment of their beginnings, as a realist writing in the comic tradition, that Mark Twain achieves his permanence in American literature." *Mark Twain's America*, 257. And more generally: "In the work of these [writers] the humor of the frontier became a literature." *Mark Twain's America*, 257; see also p. 44. Constance Rourke states: "Within these tales character and custom in small sections of the Southwest were portrayed with such close and ready detail as to provide something of a record of the time and place." *American Humor*, 64. F. O. Matthiessen on George Washington Harris: "Because he possessed a keen eye and ear, [he] could use it as a means to portray the frontier life with both realism and fantastic extravagance—the union of incongruities most natural to American humor.... Harris possesses on the comic level something of what Melville does on the tragic, the rare kind of dramatic imagination that can get movement directly into words." *American Renaissance*, 642, 644.

49. Quoted in Bridgman, *Colloquial*, 54–55.

50. Rourke, *American Humor*, 67.

51. This is what Leo Marx would later revere in the canonical *Adventures of Huckleberry Finn*. "The largest boast of *Huckleberry Finn* is reserved for the language itself—its capacity to take on the dignity of art, to replace the elevated style of Longfellow or Cooper.... Vernacular narration is the key to Mark Twain's style just as it is the key to Whitman's. Twain uses a naive character and his naive language to convey a highly complicated state of mind. But the point of view and the idiom finally are inseparable: together they form a style. And it is this style that lends immediacy to the affirmation without which the book would be

morally empty." *Pilot*, 15–16. Marx also explicitly links Twain to this Southwestern literature, even quoting from Thorpe's story, "The Big Bear of Arkansas" (1841).

52. Pratt, *Archives of American Time*, 136, 127.

53. Cohen and Dillingham, *Humor*, xx.

54. Sellers, *Market Revolution*, 267.

55. See David Roediger on the desire of Whigs to be associated with "rural white common people" around 1840, including their adoption of "symbols like Davy Crockett's coonskin cap." *Wages*, 98. "Competition in manipulating vernacular characterization was one aspect, perhaps a crucial one, in the transformation of previously upper-class institutions—not only political partiers but the press and theater, schools and denominational churches, even the anti-slavery movement—into mass media of ideological expression and controversy. Whigs and Democrats vied for preeminence, but the Democrats won most of the rounds." Saxton, *Rise and Fall*, 84.

56. Pratt, *Archives*, 126–27.

57. Cohen and Dillingham, *Humor*, xxiv. Also quoted in Pratt, *Archives*, 140.

58. Johnson, *River of Dark Dreams*, 5.

59. Sellers, *Market Revolution*, 408.

60. "And most of the slaveholding minority were small farmers, half owning five slaves or fewer and three-fourths fewer than ten," Sellers notes. "At the peculiar institution's apogee in 1860, only 19 percent of the southern people belonged to families owning any human property, while 42 percent were free nonslaveholders, and 37 percent were enslaved." Sellers, *Market Revolution*, 279.

61. Johnson, *River of Dark Dreams*, 4–5.

62. Rogin, *Fathers*, 253–54.

63. Rogin, 264.

64. "State factional politics, western-elite support for Indian removal, and the high status of Jackson's territorial appointees all suggest that Jackson's support came from frontier leaders like himself, hungry for national power and able to organize the mass of frontier voters." Rogin, 265–66.

65. Jackson's "internal-improvements and Bank vetoes, his nullification proclamation, and his removal of government deposits from the U.S. Bank all asserted unprecedented executive prerogatives and a new theory of political representation. The legislature represented elite interests; the executive embodied the popular will. This doctrine infused life into the nascently bureaucratic federal executive, the informal group of presidential advisers, and the specialized party apparatus. Jackson was the first modern President." Rogin, 267.

66. Rogin, 294.

67. Sellers, *Market Revolution*, 280. Du Bois also notes this surge of poor white outmigration from Southern states, where they had been replaced by enslaved labor, and he makes clear their antipathy toward black workers, which shaped the politics of settler colonial expansion into the West. In his chapter "The White Worker," he writes:

> The resultant revolt of the poor whites, just as the revolt of the slaves, came through migration. And their migration, instead of being restricted, was freely encouraged. As a result, the poor whites left the South in large numbers. In 1860, 399,700 Virginians were living out of their native state. From Tennessee, 344,765 emigrated; from North Carolina, 272,606, and from South Carolina, 256,868. The majority of these had come to

the Middle West and it is quite possible that the Southern states sent as many settlers to the West as the Northeastern states, and while the Northeast demanded free soil, the Southerners demanded not only free soil but the exclusion of Negroes from work and the franchise. They had a very vivid fear of the Negro as a competitor in labor, whether slave or free. It was thus the presence of the poor white Southerner in the West that complicated the whole Free Soil movement in its relation to the labor movement. (*Black Reconstruction*, 28)

68. Sellers, *Market Revolution*, 408. Southern lands would not be subjected to literal enclosure—the fencing of the open range—until the late nineteenth century. Not coincidentally, this followed the conferral of formal freedom to the enslaved. Turning the commons of the open range, used by both poor whites and poor blacks, into private property compelled the entry of independent farmers into the rigged economy of sharecropping. See Hahn, "Hunting, Fishing," 37–64. For a more nuanced account of the politics and racialism that governed this process, see also Brown, "Free Men," 117–37.

69. Southern emigrants who favored abolition were not, therefore, antiracist. The fight for Free Soil in the West was not just a fight to exclude slavery but also, especially, to ban blacks. See Du Bois, *Black Reconstruction*, 28n69.

70. Much of what Karl Marx writes regarding the French peasantry in *The Eighteenth Brumaire* (1852) could as well apply to the South's poor whites in this Jacksonian moment:

The allotment farmers are an immense mass, whose individual members live in identical conditions, without, however, entering into manifold relationships with one another. Their method of production isolates them from one another, instead of drawing them into mutual intercourse. This isolation is promoted by the poor means of communication in France, together with the poverty of the farmers themselves.... In so far as millions of families live under economic conditions that separate their mode of life, their interests and their culture from those of the other classes, and that place them in an attitude hostile toward the latter, they constitute a class; in so far as there exists only a local connection among these farmers, a connection which the individuality and exclusiveness of their interests prevent from generating among them any unity of interest, national connections, and political organization, they do not constitute a class. Consequently, they are unable to assert their class interests in their own name, be it by a parliament or by convention. They can not represent one another, they must themselves be represented. (71)

And, like Bonaparte, Andrew Jackson "does not represent the revolutionary, it represents the conservative farmer; it does not represent the farmer, who presses beyond his own economic conditions, his little allotment of land, it represents him rather who would confirm these conditions; it does not represent the rural population, that, thanks to its own inherent energy, wishes, jointly with the cities, to overthrow the old order, it represents, on the contrary, the rural population that, hide-bound in the old order, seeks to see itself, together with its allotments, saved and favored by the ghost of the Empire; it represents not the intelligence, but the superstition of the farmer; not his judgment, but his bias; not his future, but his past" (72).

71. Du Bois, *Black Reconstruction*, 26. A thoroughly researched historical account of these Southern poor whites, including the machinations by which planters accrued land for the

consolidating and expanding cotton empire, can be found in Keri Leigh Merritt, *Masterless Men: Poor Whites and Slavery in the Antebellum South* (2017).

72. Johnson, *River of Dark Dreams*, 56, 71.

73. Forret, *Race Relations*, 77. Forret notes that this trade was strictly prohibited by law, with one South Carolina law of 1817 subjecting whites who contravened the statute to an exorbitant fine "not exceeding one thousand dollars, and imprisonment not exceeding a term of twelve months, nor less than one month." *Race Relations*, 96. He also writes, "Slaves and poor whites in the antebellum South engaged in a range of sexual contacts, from apparently loving unions of varying duration to violent sexual assaults and the myriad forms of coerced sex that seamlessly connected these extremes." *Race Relations*, 184. David Roediger also writes: "In certain places and at certain times between 1607 and 1800, the 'lower sorts' of whites appear to have been pleasantly lacking in racial consciousness.... In any case, racial lines were often drawn quite waveringly at the bottom of society." *Wages*, 24. Jacqueline Jones also details this illicit trade in chapter 6 of *American Work*, 191–218. See also McCurry, *Masters*, 116–21. McCurry cites a statement made by the Savannah River Anti-Slave Traffick Association in 1846 that claimed the poor white trafficker to be "more potent than the abolitionist" because he "seduces [the slave's] affections from his master, renders him unable to endure and insubordinate to discipline, prepares his mind for insurrection, burning and murder, and both ensures a speedy decay and stimulates a violent dissolution of our domestic institutions." *Masters*, 120. See also Merritt, *Masterless Men*, 123–30, especially on the sexual relations between poor white women and enslaved men.

74. Johnson, *River of Dark Dreams*, 47, 57. Forret also notes the contradictory location of poor whites within the slave plantation regime, often employed as overseers or patrollers by the planter class but who also possessed the means to subvert the system. As he documents, the historical archive contains fleeting glimpses of poor whites who assisted slaves in their escapes from bondage and who banded with slaves in insurrectionary plots. See *Race Relations*, chapter 3, "Poor Whites in Slave Control and Slave Resistance," 115–56.

75. "'Freedom' was constituted through a narrative dialectic that rested simultaneously on a spatialization of the 'unfree' as exteriority and a temporal subsuming of that unfreedom as internal difference or contradiction. The 'overcoming' of internal contradiction resolves in 'freedom' within the modern Western political sphere through displacement and elision of the coeval conditions of settler dispossession, slavery, and indentureship in the Americas. In this sense, modern liberal humanism is a formalism." Lowe, *Intimacies*, 39.

76. Bridgman, *Colloquial Style*, 51.

77. Benjamin, *Work of Art*, 23. As the volume's editor, Michael W. Jennings, notes: "A work of art may be said to have an aura if it claims a unique status based less on quality, use value, or worth per se than on its figurative distance from the beholder.... This is in effect a description of the inevitable fetishization of the work of art, less through the process of its creation than through the process of its transmission.... The auratic work exerts claims to power that parallel and reinforce the larger claims to political power of the class for whom such objects are most meaningful: the ruling class." *Work of Art*, 15.

78. Warner, *Letters*, 17.

79. "Of course, the ideological function of a tradition is to create unity out of disunity and to resolve the social contradiction or differences, between texts." Carby, *Cultures*, 147. Raymond Williams notes that the coalescing of "literature" as a concept entails "first, a shift

from 'learning' to 'taste' or 'sensibility' as a criterion defining literary quality; second, an increasing specialization of literature to 'creative' or 'imaginative' works; third, a development of the concept of 'tradition' within national terms, resulting in the more effective definition of 'a national literature.'" *Marxism*, 48.

80. The context for Adorno's critique was the philosophy of Martin Heidegger, who thoroughly romanticizes rural folk life. Adorno, *Jargon*, xii–xiii.

81. Adorno, 38–39.

82. Jameson, *Political Unconscious*, 87.

83. Adorno, *Jargon*, 47–48. In *Minima Moralia*, Adorno spells out the domination inherent to such literary play with dialects, as well as the retaliatory root of dialect's difference.

> To play off workers' dialects against the written language is reactionary.... The language of the subjected ... domination alone has stamped, so robbing them further of the justice promised by the unmutilated, autonomous word to all those free enough to pronounce it without rancor. Proletarian language is dictated by hunger. The poor chew words to fill their bellies. From the objective spirit of language they expect the sustenance refused them by society; those whose mouths are full of words have nothing else between their teeth. So they take revenge on language. Being forbidden to love it, they maim the body of language, and so repeat in impotent strength the disfigurement inflicted on them. (*Minima Moralia*, 102)

84. Writing about "black English" in what can be understood as a kind of cognate to these differences in speech on the Southwestern frontier, Barbara Fields notes: "The speech patterns of Afro-Americans do not reflect a stronger survival of African linguistic patterns among Afro-Americans, as compared to Anglo-Caribbeans. Instead, they testify to the greater prevalence, strength, and rigidity in the United States, as compared to the United Kingdom, of segregated schooling, residence, and sociability, especially among the working class." *Racecraft*, 168–69. In other words, dialect isn't the vestige of some prior cultural practice; rather, dialect manifests the lived experience of those threats and dangers that are being endured by its speakers.

85. Quoted in Cohen and Dillingham, *Humor*, 376 (emphasis in original).

86. Jameson, *Marxism and Form*, 334. See also D. A. Miller, *Jane Austen, or the Secret of Style* (2005).

87. Adorno, *Jargon*, 13.

88. "The process of the specialization of 'literature' to 'creative' or 'imaginative' works is very much more complicated. It is in part a major affirmative response, in the name of an essentially general human 'creativity,' to the socially repressive and intellectually mechanical forms of a new social order: that of capitalism and especially industrial capitalism. The practical specialization of work to the wage-labour production of commodities; of 'being' to 'work' in these terms; of language to the passing of 'rational' or 'informative' 'messages'; of social relations to functions within a systematic economic and political order: all these pressures and limits were challenged in the name of a full and liberating 'imagination' and 'creativity.'" Williams, *Marxism*, 49–50.

89. Johnson, *River of Dark Dreams*, 34–36.

90. "The land office was politically significant in the newly emerging states of the West as the customs service was in the port cities of the East. As one Senate committee reported in

1840, 'few places ... afford[ed] such ready and certain means ... of extending favors and accommodation to a large and influential portion of the community, as those attached to the land system.' In part, the importance of the land office resulted from its size and from the public funds spent annually to maintain it. In 1833 there were fifty-three land districts throughout the West; in 1837, there were sixty-two. Each district had its own staff, and in addition there was a staff of 8 surveyors general and 126 deputy surveyors. By 1840 the cost of this administrative machinery was nearly $350,000 per year." Nelson, *Roots*, 27.

91. Rohrbough, *Land Office*, 266.

92. Rohrbough, 262.

93. See Kafka, *Demon of Writing*, 116. Kafka also includes this Marx citation: "Bureaucracy is the imaginary state alongside the real state. It is the spiritualism of the state. Hence everything acquires a double meaning: a real meaning and a bureaucratic one; in like fashion, there is both real knowledge and bureaucratic knowledge (and the same applies to the will)." *Demon of Writing*, 119.

94. Zakim, "Paperwork," 38.

95. Baldwin, *Flush Times*, 81–83.

96. "Some 379 banks issued paper money in 1832, the year Andrew Jackson issued his famous veto [of the Second Bank of the United States]. That number jumped to 439 the next year, 489 the year after, and 569 in 1836—and leaped still further to 661 in 1837 and 691 in 1838 ... reaching a peak of 711 in 1840." Mihm, *Nation of Counterfeiters*, 180.

97. Baldwin, *Flush Times*, 83.

98. For an explanation of this dynamic in early nineteenth-century Britain, see Poovey, "'The Paper Age,'" in *Genres*, 153–69.

99. Rourke, *American Humor*, 58–60.

100. Baldwin, *Flush Times*, 4–5.

101. Baldwin, 230.

102. In his sketch of naive old-society Virginians adjusting to the libertine frontier, Baldwin writes, "*He* knew nothing of the elaborate machinery of ingenious chicane—such as feigning bankruptcy—fraudulent conveyances—making over to his wife—running property—and had never heard of such tricks as sending out coffins to the graveyard, with negroes inside, carried off by sudden spells of imaginary disease, to be 'resurrected,' in due time, grinning, on the banks of the Brazos." *Flush Times*, 93. Baldwin refers to the scams of John Murrell, which are the subject of Rothman, *Flush Times*, and which are also a subject in Johnson, *River of Dark Dreams*, chapter 2.

103. Baldwin, *Flush Times*, 14–15.

104. Baldwin makes the authorial connection between lying and fiction explicit: "Dickens and Bulwer can do as much lying, for money too, as they choose, and no one blame them, any more than they would blame a lawyer regularly *fee'd* to do it; but let any man, gifted with the same genius, try his hand at it, not deliberately and in writing, but merely orally, and ugly names are given him, and he is proscribed!" *Flush Times*, 17–18.

105. Pocock, *Virtue*, 112.

106. "The paradigm of property for Blackstone, as for other eighteenth-century jurists, was land, and it was on the model of the landed estate that the concept of literary property was formulated," according to Mark Rose, *Authors*, 7. Rose also links the emergence of copyright as literary property to the prevalence of paper money; see *Authors*, 129.

107. It must be noted that against the grain of the trends I'm setting out, many of these writers published their pieces under pseudonyms, a fact that reflects a more long-standing "principle of negativity," as Michael Warner calls it, associated with the publications of private persons. That is, to enter the public discourse of print, under this earlier dispensation of republicanism, was to become abstract and universal, to shed temporarily the concrete particularity of the private interested person. In doing so, one assumed the *virtue* of the citizen in this republic of letters. One published oneself—submitted to publication—for the sake of the public good, not for the sake of personal considerations. And alongside this self-negating model of virtue existed the standard of politeness, that other regulating model of personhood within the public discourse of print. Politeness, as Warner argues, was not a civic category, like virtue, but a market category. By mediating one's social value and reflecting one's aspirations for esteem and distinction, politeness was a mode of genteel self-fashioning. *Letters*, 132–38. So against this cultural backdrop, not least in its unapologetic bawdiness, Southern frontier humor thoroughly contravened these norms of virtue and politeness through its incipient, but insistent, style; it was a way of writing whose imprimatur was conspicuousness rather than constraint and the amplification of the exceptional voice rather than its muting (even as the frame narrative maintained a semblance of decorum). These authors "wanted to do something in the writing line, did not expect to be paid for it, liked to publish under a pseudonym, and sometimes regretted at a later date having indulged in such a dubious pastime," worrying that their tales "would injure their professional status," according to Cohen and Dillingham. *Humor*, xix. These authors established a precedent. That they aren't famous to us doesn't negate the importance of their example. It only suggests that they were part of an emergent paradigm, crosscut by other historical currents.

108. Summarizing V. L. Parrington's viewpoint and bearing on this geographical delineation, David W. Noble notes: "Emerson, Thoreau, and Whitman were artists from the Northeast who were inspired by the democratic promise of the Mississippi Valley. But Twain was the first major writer from the valley of democracy." *Death of a Nation*, 87.

109. According to Fredric Jameson's analysis, the situation finds an analogy in the contemporary Nikolai Gogol, also writing in the 1830s and 1840s, and his formal importance for Russian literature:

> For Gogol's starting point is not a "vision of life," not a meaning, but rather a style, a particular type of sentence: he wishes to transpose to the level of the art-story the gestures and storytelling techniques characteristic of the traditional Russian skaz, or oral yarn (something on the order of the American tall tale or the stories of Mark Twain, as the Formalists were fond of pointing out). It is therefore a misconception to imagine that in Gogol form is adequate to content: on the contrary, it is because Gogol wishes to work in a particular kind of form, and to speak in the tone of voice of the skaz, that he casts about for raw materials appropriate to it, for anecdotes, names, piquant details, sudden shifts in manner. It now becomes clear why neither the grotesque nor the pathetic can be seen as the dominant mode of the story: for the skaz lives by their opposition, by their abrupt alternation with each other. (Jameson, "Metacommentary," 11)

110. Quoted in Johnson, *River of Dark Dreams*, 374.
111. Quoted in O'Malley, *Face Value*, 76.
112. O'Malley, 45, 80.

113. Roediger, *Wages*, 57.

114. Thomas Bangs Thorpe, "The Disgraced Scalp-Lock," in Cohen and Dillingham, *Humor*, 354.

115. "What united New Dealers between 1932 and 1965 was not a social-democratic vision but a common assault on the privileges of northern capital," Richard Bensel writes. *Yankee Leviathan*, 433. He notes that it was only in the New Deal that the "cross-sectional inversion of class alignments of the two major parties" (421) came to an end—that is, Democrats represented the white working classes while Republicans represented the black working classes. "This problem persisted until the New Deal restructuring of the political economy partially nationalized the class structure of national party competition by bringing blacks and labor into the Democratic party" (433).

116. On the periodization of the Civil Rights movement, see Dowd Hall, "Long Civil Rights." See also Gilmore, *Defying Dixie*.

117. Wagner, *Disturbing*, 30. Decades earlier, nineteenth-century enthusiasts had extolled the importance of the black spiritual, a form that had enjoyed mass appeal. Filene, *Romancing*, 29–31.

118. Howard Odum, *Social and Mental Traits of the Negro* (1910), 286. Quoted in Filene, *Romancing*, 31.

119. One of the Lomaxes' major innovations was to directly record folk singers performing their songs. This "meant that for the first time there was a way to stick a pipeline right down into the heart of the folks where they were and let them come on like they felt," as Alan Lomax recalled (Filene, *Romancing*, 56). "Purity was now attributed not just to specific folk songs (e.g., Child ballads) but to the folk figures who sang them." *Romancing*, 58. They promoted Lead Belly as both "the living embodiment of America's folk song tradition, a time capsule that had preserved the pure voice of the people" and as a "savage, untamed animal" forced to perform in his convict clothes "for exhibition purposes." *Romancing*, 58–59.

120. Relevant here is Raymond Williams's explanation of philology and philosophies of language wherein studies of "the speech of conquered and dominated peoples [and] the 'dialects' of outlying or socially inferior groups [were] theoretically matched against the observer's 'standard,' were regarded as at most 'behaviour,' rather than independent, creative, self-directing life. North American empirical linguistics reversed one part of this tendency, restoring the primacy of speech in the literal absence of 'standard' or 'classical' texts. Yet the objectivist character of the underlying general theory came to limit even this, by converting speech itself to a 'text'—the characteristically persistent word in orthodox structural linguistics. Language came to be seen as a fixed, objective, and in these senses 'given' system, which had theoretical and practical priority over what were described as 'utterances' (later as 'performance'). Thus the living speech of human beings in their specific social relationships in the world was theoretically reduced to instances and examples of a system which lay beyond them." Williams, *Marxism and Literature*, 27.

121. Early in *Let Us Now Praise Famous Men*, before he has met the Ricketts, Woods, and Gudgers, Agee writes of one landowner, "nearly all his tenants were negroes and no use to me." Agee and Evans, *Let Us Now*, 24.

122. Sullivan, "Southern Exposures."

123. See, respectively, Agee and Evans, *Let Us Now*, 80, 390, and 406.

124. Leuchtenberg, *White House*, 108.

125. A thorough and nuanced cultural history of the Fugitives-cum-Agrarians-cum-New Critics can be found in Maxwell, *Indicted South*, which traces the politics behind these transforming groups alongside their critical reception.

126. Quoted in Hale, *Making Whiteness*, 257.

127. Quoted in Rubin, introduction to Southerners, *I'll Take My Stand*, ix. In *The Attack on Leviathan* (1938), Donald Davidson voiced a trenchant critique of the Regionalists.

128. See Noble, *Death of a Nation*, chapter 4; Jancovich, *Cultural Politics*; Bové, *Mastering Discourse*, chapter. 3; O'Kane, "Before the New Criticism"; Pickering, "The Roots of New Criticism." Many critics have grappled with the relationship between the ideas of the Agrarians and the New Critics. Most often, these two groups are differentiated and then put into relation, either of agreement or of disagreement. Within the context of this chapter, however, and of the book itself, that dichotomy begins to come undone when contemplated within the *longue durée* of slave racial capitalism in America. The racialized class structure endemic to that system renders that dichotomy moot by introducing the figure of the slave, and hence of the poor white. This offers purchase both for historicizing the formalism of the New Critics *and* for engaging a formalist quality within this capitalist history, which allows for a clearer explication of their aestheticism, not only in its continuity with agrarianism but also for what it shares with the contemporary literary criticism of the New York Intellectuals, who are often pitted as defining antagonists for the New Critics.

129. In this moment of colonial discourse, the geography of "America" as an economic zone begins again, for some, imaginatively to exceed the geography of "America" as a nation-state. Apprehending the South as an underdeveloped region that might include the spaces of accumulation in Latin America could force a recognition of the spatial disjuncture between the United States and "America." See, for example, chapter 1 of Grandin, *Empire's Workshop*.

130. Hale, *Making Whiteness*, 257.

131. The "concept of a 'screen memory' [is] one which owes its value as a memory not to its own content but to the relation existing between that content and some other, that has been suppressed." Freud, *Freud Reader*, 126.

132. See notes 136 and 157 for references.

133. In essays from *I'll Take My Stand* such as John Crowe Ransom's "Reconstructed but Unregenerate," Donald Davidson's "A Mirror for Artists," Andrew Lytle's "The Hind Tit," and John Donald Wade's "The Life and Death of Cousin Lucius," one is consistently struck by the Agrarians' recourse to the frontier discourse assembled by those Southern authors a hundred years earlier. The notion that those poor whites excluded from the largesse of slave racial capitalism were in possession of some elemental and anachronistic existence, genuine and endangered, had been fully subsumed by 1930 into the historical consciousness of these "Twelve Southerners."

134. Davidson, "A Mirror for Artists," in Southerners, *I'll Take My Stand*, 54–55.

135. Jancovich, *Cultural Politics*, 20.

136. Tate wrote that "finance-capitalism has become so top-heavy with a crazy jig-saw network of exchange-value that the individual citizen is wholly at the mercy of the shifting pieces of the puzzle at remote points where he cannot possibly assert his own needs and rights. This was not originally the American system. We began with the belief that society should be supported by agriculture, the most stable basis of society because it is relatively

less dependent upon the market than any other kind of production." "Notes on Liberty and Property," 601. Of this desire, one might be unsurprised to learn that Tate's own rural Kentucky boyhood had been decidedly more itinerant. In Tate's wry recollection, "we might as well have been living, and I been born, in a tavern at a crossroads." His father's business required the family to move as often as three times a year, and by the time he was twelve, his parents had divorced and his father's ventures had failed. http://www.english.illinois.edu/maps/poets/s_z/tate/life.htm.

137. Quoted in Schwartz, *Creating Faulkner's Reputation*, 75.

138. Southerners, *I'll Take My Stand*, xxvi. "The truly artistic life is surely that in which the aesthetic experience is not curtained off but is mixed up with all sorts of instruments and occupations pertaining to the round of daily life. It ranges all the way from pots and pans, chairs and rugs, clothing and houses, up to dramas publicly performed and government buildings." Donald Davidson, "A Mirror for Artists," in *I'll Take My Stand*, 39–40.

139. The classic example is George Fitzhugh, *Cannibals All* (1857).

140. Woods, *Development Arrested*, 51.

141. Counterexamples of leftist critics from this decade include V. F. Calverton, Granville Hicks, Russell Blankenship, and Bernard Smith.

142. Noble, *Death*, 88. "With the death of capitalism, Jacksonian democracy had become, as Arthur Schlesinger Jr. had written [in *The Age of Jackson* (1945)], a usable past for Franklin Roosevelt's New Deal." Noble, *Death*, 80. The "1930s were a decade that promised to restore the democracy of the 1830s by defeating the capitalism imported from Europe in the 1870s." Noble, *Death*, 237.

143. "What is meant by the . . . conception of some historically provisional 'autonomy of the sign' is then that staking out and roping off of an area of henceforth 'literary' language (or of the language of painting or music) so that its perception as an object is felt to be distinct from the speech—and sounds and colors—of everyday life, at the same time that its hitherto conventional referential content is suspended and at length problematized." Jameson, "The Existence of Italy," 202.

144. "Between 1935 and 1945 this 'New Criticism' became more persuasive for younger teachers of literature than the commonly accepted approach to the study of American literature in the mid-1930s—the historical." Noble, *Death*, 131.

145. See Graff, *Professing*, 212. As late as 1936, the critic Howard Mumford Jones complained, "in this country education in English literature is education in British literature." See Shumway, *Creating American*, 202. Although F. O. Matthiessen pointed the way with *American Renaissance*, Henry Nash Smith's *Virgin Land* (1950) is usually considered the first example of the symbol-myth school and his article "Can 'American Studies' Develop a Method" (1957) as the first statement of the school's program.

146. Noble points out that despite surface parallels between the pastoralism of Parrington, Matthiessen, and the symbol-myth school and that of the Southern Agrarians, they actually referred to very different world orders, different conceptions of space, time, and history, aligned respectively with the national and the local. The Agrarians rejected the dictates of historical progress, specifically as they were embodied in the Northern industrialist push for a "New South," because these dictates led to the capitalist fragmentation of local communal integrity. For them, time "was experienced as generational. There was no sequence of past, present, and future." Noble, *Death*, 135. "For the Southern Agrarians . . .

the sacred was to be found simultaneously in the universal and the local, but not in the nation." Noble, *Death*, 142.

147. There are no shortage of books on the New Criticism and its politics. If the traditional view had been that the New Critics rejected politics to focus solely on the text, abjuring the "extrinsic" for the "intrinsic" in their terms, that view was upset by Graff, *Professing*, which articulated the politics animating their supposed apoliticism, how they hoped to reveal that the "moral and social significance [of] literature ... became a function of the formal texture of the work itself rather than something external or superadded" (148). "Whatever one may think of their predominantly conservative politics, the fact remains that first-generation New Critics were neither aesthetes nor pure explicators but culture critics with a considerable 'axe to grind' against the technocratic tendencies of modern mass civilization" (149). See especially chapters 3 and 9 in Guillory, *Cultural Capital*: "to redefine the social space of literary culture as *necessarily* institutional. The school becomes the site at which the practice of reading can be cultivated in such a way as to preserve the cultural capital of literature (signified ... as a kind of *sacredness*), just because its social space can be conceived as a space of deliberate and strategic withdrawal, as the withdrawal of literary culture from 'the world'" (165). Furthermore, "In discovering that literature was intrinsically difficult, these new students also discovered at the same moment why it needed to be studied *in the university*" (172). Graff's work had been preceded by Fekete, *Critical Twilight*, which excoriated John Crowe Ransom's formalism. In a rather hermetically sealed account, Jancovich, *Cultural Politcs*, argues for a continuity in the cultural politics of the Agrarians and the New Critics, though he dwells little on the *formal* continuity between them and doesn't situate his account in a deeper history of the region or the nation. This cultural overlap was picked up again somewhat more recently in a cursory overview by Pickering, "The Roots of New Criticism." Perhaps the most astute account of the New Critics' ideas and how they are situated with the Agrarians as well as other American intellectual traditions can be found in Noble, *Death of a Nation*. However, while many of these critics explicate the intellectual continuities between the Agrarians and the New Critics, and worry over them, none that I've encountered have asserted the relationship between their Southern aesthetic tradition and history of racial slavery. This chapter aims to draw that link.

148. Robert Penn Warren, "Brooks and Warren," 2.

149. As one of the discipline's principal objects of analysis, ballads had helped to constitute the "department of English" in the United States. "The emergence of philology in the latter half of the nineteenth century constituted the place of the ballad in the curriculum of English literature," writes ballad scholar Steve Newman. *Ballad Collection*, 190. The first professorship in English at Harvard was conferred on Francis James Child, a philologist and scholar of Shakespeare, whose lifework was his compilation *The English and Scottish Popular Ballads*. When Child identified 305 true ballads, no more and no less, which he printed along with all their 1,300 variants in a ten-part series between 1882 and 1898, he created the very definition of a canon. "For him"—and for the New Critics, one might add—"the ballad is popular not in the sense of belonging to the lower classes but rather shared by high and low as part of a feudal world, prior to 'the art of printing,' the Reformation, and 'the intrusion of cold reflection into a world of sense and fancy,'" Newman writes, quoting Child (*Ballad Collection*, 193). The Child canon was meant to preserve what is "permanent

and universal in the heart of man," which had been secreted in true ballads before they were corrupted by the marketplace of print culture (Newman, *Ballad Collection*, 193). "True" ballads preceded the arrival of the printing press in Britain in 1475, meaning the ballad belonged to a prelapsarian world. Filene, *Romancing*, 13–14.

150. Brooks and Warren, *Understanding Poetry*, 9.

151. Noble, *Death*, 143.

152. Hagenstein et al., *American Georgics*, 254.

153. Many folklorists began seeking living remnants of Francis Child's canonical ballads among the rural whites of the Appalachian Mountains. Filene, *Romancing*, 15–18. Child himself had no patience for the notion of a ballad tradition in the United States. Others, such as John Lomax, with whom this chapter began, argued that not only did the "Anglo-Saxon ballad spirit" survive but also that "[t]his spirit is manifested both in the preservation of the English ballad *and* in the creation of local songs." Lomax, *Cowboy Songs*, xvii (emphasis mine). Lomax's project on cowboy songs was shepherded into print by George Lyman Kittredge, another philologist, who had been Child's student and was his successor at Harvard. Szwed, *Alan Lomax*, 9. What unified the field in this moment was the shared belief that, in Kittredge's words, "The text is the thing." Folklorists in the field and philologists in their studies had a shared focus on language and its relation to a canon of knowledge, and a shared disposition as scientists. It was not until the 1930s when Lomax, his son Alan, and their 350-pound Dictaphone recorder would wend their way through the American South archiving songs played by the folk themselves that there emerged a concern with the context of these texts and with the personal histories of these balladeers. Until then, in universities, this was the province of literature. The ballad was usually construed as the expression of a collective: *das Volk dichtet*, in Jakob Grimm's words, "the folk makes the poem." Filene, *Romancing*, 16, 49–50.

154. Newman, *Ballad Collection*, 260n95.

155. "[I]n the anthology they edited along with R. W. B. Lewis, *American Literature: The Makers and the Making* (1973) . . . Warren included and enthusiastically commented upon not only traditional ballads, Native American chants, 'Frankie and Johnny' and 'Jesse James' but also Wobbly songs, the works of Woody Guthrie, and especially the blues from Jelly Roll Morton to Bessie Smith to Robert Johnson, even mentioning a remake by the Rolling Stones." Newman, *Ballad Collection*, 215.

156. Raymond Williams writes of the late nineteenth century, "*Folksong* came to be influentially specialized to the pre-industrial, pre-urban, pre-literate world, though *popular* songs, including new industrial work songs, were still being actively produced. Folk, in this period, had the effect of backdating all elements of popular culture, and was often offered as a contrast with modern popular forms, either of a radical and working-class or of a commercial kind." *Keywords*, 93.

157. Noble, *Death*, 142–43. Thus, Donald Davidson in *I'll Take My Stand*: "What I should particularly like to note is that the specious theory that an 'independent' country ought to originate an independent art, worthy of its national greatness, did not originate in the South" (55–56).

158. See Baucom, *Specters*, and Sewell, "Temporalities."

159. Beginning in the late 1930s with the efforts of the New Critics, *literature* comports with what the Caribbean theorist Michel Rolph-Trouillot terms a "North Atlantic universal," one

of those "words that project the North Atlantic experience on a universal scale that they themselves helped to create." These concepts "are particulars that have gained a degree of universality," Trouillot writes, "but because they are rooted in a particular history, they evoke multiple layers of sensibilities, persuasions, cultural assumptions, and ideological choices tied to that localized history. They come to us loaded with aesthetic and stylistic sensibilities; religious and philosophical persuasions; [and] cultural assumptions." "North Atlantic," 847.

160. See, for example, Saunders, *Cultural Cold War*, esp. chapter 15, "Ransom's Boys." See also Walhout, "The New Criticism," 861–71.

161. See Schwartz, *Creating Faulkner's Reputation*, esp. chapter 3. Of special note in the context of this chapter is Faulkner's *Absalom, Absalom!* (1936), a novel explicitly concerned with the Mississippi frontier of the 1830s and with its protagonist Thomas Sutpen's ruthless ambition. *Absalom, Absalom!* is a novel preoccupied with the relationship between form and history, and how meaning is transmitted and degraded over time.

162. Márquez, "Art of Fiction." Thanks to Dara Orenstein for pointing me to this interview.

163. See Greeson, *Our South*. As the white Southern activist and organizer Myles Horton noted, "Appalachia and the South . . . have a lot in common with Third World countries or Third World segments within other countries." *Long Haul*, 213. See also Frank, "Development of Underdevelopment," 17–31.

164. On the relationship between modernism and imperialism, Jameson writes, "Such spatial disjunction has as its immediate consequence the inability to grasp the way the system functions as a whole. [National literature cannot] include this radical otherness of colonial life, colonial suffering, and exploitation, let alone the structural connections between that and this, between absent space and daily life in the metropolis" See "Modernism and Imperialism," 51. Marquez: "I believe that the greatest debt that we Latin American novelists have is to Faulkner. . . . Faulkner is present in all Latin American fiction." Quoted in Zamora, *Writing the Apocalypse*, 201n14. Bell-Villada, *Garcia Marquez*, 82.

165. Jameson, "Modernism and Imperialism," 54.

166. "Because the Monroe Doctrine prohibited Europeans from interfering in Latin America, the United States became (by its own fiat) the sole 'civilized nation'—in Roosevelt's terms—allowed to invade countries in the Americas," as Nell Irvin Painter writes. "Between 1900 and 1917 the United States exercised this right repeatedly, not only in the Dominican Republic and Panama but also in Cuba, Nicaragua, Haiti, and Mexico." This was followed and supplemented by the "dollar diplomacy" of the Taft administration, a "soft" imperialism that leveraged U.S. financial power toward the corporate control of foreign markets. During his time in office, Woodrow Wilson would invade more Latin American countries than any prior president. Painter, *Standing*, 174.

167. On the relationship between geographical imaginings of the South and of America, and their relation to literary production, see also Greeson, *Our South*, and Raul Coronado, *A World Not to Come: A History of Latino Writing and Print Culture* (2013).

168. Carby, *Cultures*, 176. Carby argues that Hurston's notions of the black folk were also complicated. Hurston clung to a static conception of culture that privileged the "authentic" blackness of the rural folk. "Hurston's representation of the folk is not only a discursive displacement of the historical and cultural transformation of migration, but also a creation of a folk who are outside of history." *Cultures*, 172. Carby ends with a question as pertinent

to this chapter's history of "American literature" as to "African American literature": "how does cultural authenticity come to be situated so exclusively in the rural folk?" *Cultures,* 182.

169. Hurston, "What White Publishers Won't Print," 117–19.

170. Hurston, 117–21.

171. Hall, "Race, Articulation."

172. Baldwin, "Letter from a Region."

173. Du Bois, *Black Reconstruction,* 707.

174. Du Bois, *Souls,* 3.

175. I allude to what Sylvia Wynter calls the "New Human Project," which her philosophical oeuvre has sought to advance. See, especially in the context of this chapter, Wynter, "Unsettling the Coloniality," 257–337, and "Rethinking 'Aesthetics,'" 237–79.

Conclusion

1. These details and this comparison can be found in Davis, "Eastman Johnson's *Negro Life,*" 67–92.

2. See chapter 3 in Lott, *Love and Theft,* esp. 76.

3. I use "black geography" in the sense described by McKittrick, "Plantation Futures," 1–15.

4. On the history of this geographical formation, see Spear, "Origins," 153–66, and Duneier, *Ghetto.* See also Sugrue, *Origins.*

5. See, for example, Wilkerson, *Warmth.*

6. Rothstein, *Color of Law,* 42.

7. Racial zoning laws were declared unconstitutional by the Supreme Court in *Buchanan v. Warley* (1917), as part of the court's consistent interpretation of the Fourteenth Amendment as a shrine to "freedom of contract" during the Lochner Era. See Rothstein, *Color of Law,* chapter 1. For more on racially restrictive covenants, see Gotham, *Race, Real Estate.* Gotham succinctly defines those contracts: "As legally enforceable contractual agreements between property owners and neighborhood associations, restrictive covenants prohibited the sale, occupancy, or lease of property and land to certain racial groups, especially blacks" (38). See also Connolly, *A World More Concrete.*

8. Gotham, *Race, Real Estate,* 39–40.

9. *New York Times,* 24 April 1964. For more on Chicago's specific history along these lines, see Satter, *Family Properties.* For more on Hansberry, see Perry, *Looking for Lorraine.*

10. Duneier, *Ghetto,* 31.

11. Wright, *12 Million,* 104, 116.

12. Rothstein, *Color of Law,* 19–24, 31–32. The "federal government's housing rules pushed ... cities into a more rigid segregation than otherwise would have existed" (24).

13. Rothstein, 48–50.

14. Rothstein, 53. As Ibram X. Kendi notes, "As early as 1793, a White minister protested that 'a Negro hut' had depreciated property values in Salem. . . . The vicious housing cycle had already begun. Racist policies harmed Black neighborhoods, generating racist ideas that caused people not to want to live next to Blacks, which depressed the value of Black homes, which caused people not to want to live in Black neighborhoods even more, owing to low property values." *Stamped,* 170.

15. Within an incisive critique of structural racism in Northern cities, Du Bois wrote in "The Black North: A Social Study" (1901) that "the conditions under which these new immigrants are now received are of such a nature that very frequently the good are made bad and the bad made professional criminals. One has but to read Dunbar's 'Sport of the Gods' to get an idea of the temptations that surround the young immigrant." It was in *The Philadelphia Negro* (1899) that Du Bois expounded his notions of a "talented tenth" and a "submerged tenth."

16. Carby, "Policing," 738–55. There were a few public voices that avoided the trap of cultural pathology, such as the black reformer Fannie B. Williams, who blamed the effects of racism and segregation that kept blacks in "the worst portions of the city" and confined them to precarious and menial labor. See Muhammad, *Condemnation*, 109. See also Hartman, *Wayward Lives*.

17. Muhammad, *Condemnation*, 113.

18. See McKittrick, "On Plantations," 947–63.

19. Wright, *12 Million*, 126–28.

20. Wright, 130.

21. In exploring this history, Kevin Mumford defines modern slumming as "social superiors temporarily exploiting people and institutions on the margins, usually for pleasure, leisure, or sexual adventure." *Interzones*, 143. The historian Chad Heap writes, "Since its initial coinage in the mid-1880s, the word *slumming* has always implied some sense of venturing not only beneath one's own social standing but also beyond the parameters of one's local neighborhood." *Slumming*, 103.

22. Hughes, "When the Negro Was in Vogue," in *Collected Works*, 176.

23. Mumford, *Interzones*, 151. Mumford points out that whites could also enjoy their slumming adventures on the written page, in novels such as Carl Van Vechten's *Nigger Heaven*. Like travelogues and guidebooks, these novels often included a glossary of black words and phrases. *Interzones*, 145–46.

24. On the multiple racial, sexual, and class fantasies that were being played out by these white tourists, see Heap, *Slumming*, chapters 3 and 5.

25. Quoted in Lock, *Blutopia*, 88.

26. Mumford, *Interzones*, 155.

27. Hari, *Chasing*, 17–18.

28. For more on Holiday, see Griffin, *If You Can't*.

29. See Harcourt, *Counterrevolution*, and Hinton, *War on Poverty*.

30. Baker and Cooke, "Bronx Slave Market," 330.

31. Petry, *The Street*, 388–89, 323.

32. The series was published in five installments in *The New York Compass* (January 1950). On the racialization of care labor and service work, see Glenn, "From Servitude." See also Nadasen, *Household Workers*. On black women's lives in these new urban spaces, see also Hartman, *Wayward Lives*.

33. Denning, "Wageless Life." Denning's aphorism is cribbed from the British economist Joan Robinson.

34. Du Bois, "The Black North."

35. Keyes, "Long-Lost Manuscript." The historian Destin Jenkins notes that the race war in Tulsa also stripped blacks of their assets, which contributed to the racial wealth gap. Jenkins, "The Racial Wealth Gap."

36. For more on the numerous massacres in these years, which took place in East St. Louis, Illinois, Atlanta, Chicago, Philadelphia, New York, and elsewhere, see Ida B. Wells, *The East St. Louis Massacre: The Outrage of the Century* (1917) in *Light of Truth* and Du Bois, *Darkwater*, 94–95. Drake and Cayton note that fifty-eight bombs were hurled at black homes in the years surrounding the Chicago "riot" of July 1919, "which took at least thirty-eight lives, resulted in over five hundred injuries, destroyed $250,000 worth of property, and left over a thousand persons homeless." *Black Metropolis*, 64–65.

37. McKittrick, "Plantation Futures," 6.

38. Hence, as she notes, there emerged the form of the "plantation," whose purpose it was "to plant" the wastes and deserts of America. The hard labor of clearing and cultivating these impossible spaces fell to blacks and natives, who were dishumanized and condemned. Their unaccounted lives were to be expended so that "human civilization" there could flourish.

39. Denning, *Cultural*, 33, 36.

40. Taussig, "Culture of Terror."

41. Baldwin, *Collected Essays*, 714–15.

42. For one genealogy of anti-imperialism in the civil rights movement, see the conclusion to Rana, *Two Faces*, 326–48. See also Singh, *Black Is a Country*.

43. Clark, *Dark Ghetto*, 11. Much of chapter 3 details the colonial dynamics of the ghetto, although Clark refrains from explicitly labeling it as such.

44. Carmichael and Hamilton, *Black Power*, 5. A useful overview of this contemporary debate can be found in Katz, *Undeserving Poor*, 68–84. Harold Cruse drew this comparison even earlier, in 1962, in "Revolutionary Nationalism," where he described the relation of blacks to the United States as one of "domestic colonialism." In *From #BlackLivesMatter*, the revolutionary socialist Keeanga-Yamahtta Taylor rejoins this debate, arguing against the use of this colonialist framework on orthodox terms. As she notes, these midcentury black activists and intellectuals get at a core truth by deploying that discourse in that decolonizing moment. Taylor doesn't suggest what concept might better name such thoroughgoing dispossession and underdevelopment that aggrandizes another's profit and power. See *From #BlackLivesMatter*, 195–97.

45. Carmichael and Hamilton, *Black Power*, 148–49.

46. Rothstein, *Color of Law*, 127. In a 1963 interview with Kenneth Clark, Baldwin said, "most cities are engaged in . . . something called urban renewal, which means moving Negroes out: it means Negro removal, that is what it means. The federal government is an accomplice to this fact." Baldwin, *Conversations*, 42.

47. I am grateful to Dara Orenstein for this conceptualization of the warehouse. For more on its history, see her book *Out of Stock*. On the symbolic surplus value of blackness, see Lott, *Black Mirror*.

48. I borrow this formulation from Ansfield, "Still Submerged," 127.

49. "Although characterized by the expansion of the middle class, the decades after World War II witnessed slow economic growth, frequent recessions, and the displacement of untrained and unskilled labor through automation. These developments hit African Americans harder than they hit the rest of the U.S. population. . . . The AFL-CIO estimated [in 1963] that at just 12 percent of the total U.S. population, black workers represented some

36 percent of long-term, or 'relatively permanent,' unemployed Americans." Hinton, *From the War*, 28

50. Hinton, 30.

51. Hinton, 45–49.

52. Rules declared ineligible those children "whose mother associates with a man in a relationship similar to that of husband and wife" or a wife whose "unwillingness to live with her husband" was the reason for her living singly (regardless of domestic abuse), so long as the father was "willing to live with and support his family." For records of such domestic surveillance, see, for example, the federal report "Illegitimacy and Its Impact on the Aid to Dependent Children Program" (1960), in Mink and Solinger, *Welfare*, 174–91. The "man-in-the-house" rule was struck down by the Supreme Court in 1968 in *King v. Smith*. The most astute analysis of this discursive knot of blackness and gender remains Spillers, "Mama's Baby."

53. "Policymakers believed that cultural pathology explained the high rates of reported crime in African American neighborhoods, and as a result of these racist assumptions, positioned crime control as the primary social service provided to segregated communities suffering from high rates of poverty and unemployment. By shifting power within domestic urban programs from social workers to law enforcement authorities, federal policymakers introduced far more punitive forms of social control in neighborhoods that had experienced unrest or that seemed vulnerable to rebellion." Hinton, *From the War*, 100.

54. See Wagner, *Disturbing the Peace*, 58–115.

55. Hinton, *From the War*, 69.

56. Baldwin, "Report," in *Collected Essays*, 735.

57. See Hartman, *Lose Your Mother*, 3–18.

58. Hinton, *From the War*, 72.

59. Baldwin, "Fifth Ave., Uptown," in *Collected Essays*, 176.

60. See Smallwood, *Saltwater Slavery*; Wagner, *Disturbing the Peace*; Hartman, *Scenes of Subjection* and *Lose Your Mother*; Dayan, *The Law Is a White Dog*.

61. Robinson, *Black Marxism*, 4.

62. Lipsitz, "Possessive Investment," 379.

63. On the history of whiteness, see Painter, *History of White People*, and, in an American context, Jacobson, *Whiteness*.

64. Lipsitz, "Possessive," 381.

65. Lipsitz, 373.

66. Lipsitz, 375.

67. Jacobson, *Whiteness*, 9.

68. The "ghetto is essentially a sociospatial device that enables a dominant status group in an urban setting simultaneously to ostracize and exploit a subordinate group endowed with negative symbolic capital, that is, an incarnate property perceived to make its contact degrading by virtue of what Max Weber calls 'negative social estimation of honour.' Put differently, it is a relation of ethnoracial control and closure built out of four elements: (i) stigma; (ii) constraint; (iii) territorial confinement; and (iv) institutional encasement. The resulting formation is a distinct *space*, containing an ethnically homogeneous population.... The ghetto, in short, operates as an *ethnoracial prison*: it encages a dishonoured

category and severely curtails the life chances of its members in support of the 'monopolization of ideal and material goods or opportunities' by the dominant status group dwelling on its outskirts." Wacquant, "From Slavery," 50–51.

69. "James Baldwin Debates William F. Buckley (1965)."

70. Hinton, *From the War*, 64.

71. In addition to Hinton, see Murakawa, *First Civil Right*.

72. For an authoritative history of crime as a malleable and racializing concept, see Muhammad, *Condemnation*, as well as Muhammad, "Where Did All," 72–90.

73. Baldwin, *Collected Essays*, 295. As his student Barbara Jeanne Fields notes, C. Vann Woodward claimed the civil rights movement "completed a nineteenth-century agenda, rather than tackling a twentieth-century one." Fields further critiques the liberal wing of that movement, writing that while "'Freedom now!' was a slogan to inspire the sacrifice of livelihood and even of life. 'Integration now!' could scarcely inspire the expenditure of breath required to shout it." Fields, *Racecraft*, 161–62.

74. Morrison, *Beloved*, 248.

75. I want to recall here this excerpt also included in the introduction: "The captive body, then, brings into focus a gathering of social realities as well as a metaphor for *value* so thoroughly interwoven in their literal and figurative emphases that distinctions between them are virtually useless. Even though the captive flesh/body has been 'liberated,' and no one need pretend that even the question marks do not *matter*, dominant symbolic activity, the ruling episteme that releases the dynamics of naming and valuation, remains grounded in the originating metaphors of captivity and mutilation so that it is as if neither time nor history, nor historiography and its topics, show movement, as the human subject is 'murdered' over and over again by the passions of a bloodless and anonymous archaism, showing itself in endless disguise." Spillers, "Mama's Baby," 68.

76. This is the fundamental tenet of historical—and hence, cultural—materialism, by my lights: not history's progress, but its accretion. This is one lesson of the Spillers excerpt in the previous note. "Time does not pass but accumulates. Why? Because what has begun does not end but endures. . . . Because history comes to us not only as [Benjaminian] flash or revelation but piling up." Baucom, *Specters*, 333.

Bibliography

Archives Consulted

General Records of the Department of Justice, Record Group 60. National Archives, College Park, Md.
Nate Salsbury Papers. Billy Rose Theatre Collection, New York Public Library.
Nathan Salsbury Papers. American Literature Collection, Beinecke Rare Book and Manuscript Library, Yale University.
Record Group 101, Records of the Comptroller of the Currency, Letters Rec'd by the Commissioner of the Freedman's Savings and Trust Company and by the Comptroller, 1870–1914. National Archives, College Park, Md.
The South before the War Company Papers. Irving S. Gilmore Music Library of Yale University.
Thomas D. Clark's Mercantile Records of the South, 1816–1940. University of Kentucky.

Published Sources

13th (2016) dir. Ava DuVernay.
Abbott, Lynn, and Doug Seroff. *Out of Sight: The Rise of African-American Popular Music, 1889–1895*. Jackson: University Press of Mississippi, 2002.
Adorno, Theodor. *The Jargon of Authenticity*. New York: Routledge, 2003.
———. *Minima Moralia: Reflections from Damaged Life*. Translated by E. F. N. Jephcott. New York: Verso, 2005.
Agamben, Giorgio. *Homo Sacer: Sovereign Power and Bare Life*. Translated by Daniel Heller-Roazen. Stanford: Stanford University Press, 1998.
———. *Remnants of Auschwitz: The Witness and the Archive*. Translated by Daniel Heller-Roazen. Brooklyn: Zone, 1999.
Agee, James, and Walker Evans. *Let Us Now Praise Famous Men*. Boston: Houghton Mifflin, 2001. First published in 1941.
Agnew, Jean-Christophe. *Worlds Apart: The Market and the Theater in Anglo-American Thought*. New York: Cambridge University Press, 1986.
Aiken, Charles S. *The Cotton Plantation South since the Civil War*. Baltimore: Johns Hopkins University Press, 1998.
Alexander, Gregory S. "The Limits of Freedom of Contract in the Age of Laissez-Faire Constitutionalism." In *The Fall and Rise of Freedom of Contract*, edited By Francis H. Buckley. Durham, N.C.: Duke University Press, 1999.
Anderson, Benedict. *Imagined Communities: Reflections on the Origin and Spread of Nationalism*. New York: Verso, 1983.
Ansfield, Bench. "Still Submerged: The Uninhabitability of Urban Redevelopment." In *Sylvia Wynter: On Being Human as Praxis*, edited by Katherine McKittrick, 124–41. Durham, N.C.: Duke University Press, 2014.

Appel, Hannah Chadeayne. "Finance Is Just Another Word for Other People's Debts: An Interview with David Graeber." *Radical History Review* 118 (2014): 159–73.

Arendt, Hannah. *The Origins of Totalitarianism*. New York: Harcourt, Brace, 1951.

Arrighi, Giovanni. *The Long Twentieth Century: Money, Power, and the Origin of Our Times*. New York: Verso 2010.

Ayers, Edward L. *Promise of the New South: Life after Reconstruction*. New York: Oxford University Press, 1992.

———. *Vengeance and Justice: Crime and Punishment in the 19th-Century American South*. New York: Oxford University Press, 1984.

Baker, Ella, and Marvel Cooke. "The Bronx Slave Market." *The Crisis*, November 1935, 330–31.

Baldwin, James. *Collected Essays*. New York: Library of America, 1998.

———. *Conversations with James Baldwin*. Edited by Fred L. Stanley and Louis H. Pratt. Jackson: University Press of Mississippi, 1989.

———. *The Cross of Redemption: Uncollected Writings*. New York: Vintage, 2011.

———. "James Baldwin Debates William F. Buckley (1965)." *The Riverbends Channel*, 27 October 2012, video, 58:57. https://youtu.be/oFeoS41xe7w.

———. "Letter from a Region in My Mind." *New Yorker*, 17 November 1962. https://www.newyorker.com/magazine/1962/11/17/letter-from-a-region-in-my-mind.

Baldwin, Joseph Glover. *The Flush Times of Alabama and Mississippi*. New York: Appleton, 1853.

Baptist, Edward. *The Half Has Never Been Told: Slavery and the Making of American Capitalism*. New York: Basic, 2014.

Barthes, Roland. *The Responsibility of Forms: Critical Essays on Music, Art, and Representation*. Translated by Richard Howard. New York: Hill & Wang, 1985.

Bartley, Numan V. *The Creation of Modern Georgia*. Athens: University of Georgia Press, 1983.

Baucom, Ian. *Specters of the Atlantic: Finance Capital, Slavery, and the Philosophy of History*. Durham, N.C.: Duke University Press, 2005.

Beckert, Sven. "Emancipation and Empire: Reconstructing the Worldwide Web of Cotton Production in the Age of the American Civil War." *American Historical Review* 109, no. 5 (December 2004): 1405–38.

———. *Empire of Cotton: A Global History*. New York: Knopf, 2014.

———. *The Monied Metropolis: New York City and the Consolidation of the American Bourgeoisie, 1850–1896*. Cambridge: Cambridge University Press, 2001.

Bell, Malcolm, Jr. *Major Butler's Legacy: Five Generations of a Slaveholding Family*. Athens: University of Georgia Press, 2004.

Bell-Villada, Gene H. *Garcia Marquez: The Man and His Work*. Chapel Hill: University of North Carolina Press, 2010.

Benjamin, Walter. *The Arcades Project*. Translated by Howard Eiland and Kevin McLaughlin. Cambridge: Belknap, 1999.

———. *The Work of Art in the Age of Its Technological Reproducibility and Other Writings on Media*. Translated by Edmund Jephcott and Harry Zohn. Cambridge, Mass.: Harvard University Press, 2008.

Bensel, Richard. *Yankee Leviathan: The Origins of Central State Authority in America, 1859–1877*. Cambridge: Cambridge University Press, 1990.

Berlant, Lauren. *Cruel Optimism*. Durham, N.C.: Duke University Press, 2011.
———. *The Female Complaint: The Unfinished Business of Sentimentality in American Culture*. Durham, N.C.: Duke University Press, 2008.
Berlin, Ira, et al., eds. *Free at Last: A Documentary History of Slavery, Freedom, and the Civil War.* New York: New Press, 1992.
———. *Remembering Slavery: African Americans Talk about Their Personal Experiences of Slavery and Freedom*. New York: New Press, 1998.
Bernes, Jasper. *The Work of Art in the Age of Deindustrialization*. Stanford: Stanford University Press, 2017.
Bernstein, Robin. *Racial Innocence: Performing American Childhood from Slavery to Civil Rights*. New York: NYU Press, 2011.
Best, Stephen. *The Fugitive's Properties: Law and the Poetics of Possession*. Chicago: University of Chicago Press, 2010.
———. "The Subject of Property: Race, Prosthesis, and Possession in American Culture, 1865–1927." PhD diss., University of Pennsylvania, 1997.
Best, Stephen, and Saidiya Hartman. "Fugitive Justice." *Representations* 92 (Fall 2005): 1–13.
Billings, Dwight. *Planters and the Making of a New South: Class, Politics, and Development in North Carolina, 1865–1900*. Chapel Hill: University of North Carolina Press, 1979.
Binder, Guyora. "The Slavery of Emancipation." *Cardozo Law Review* 17 (1996): 2063–101.
Blackmon, Douglas. *Slavery by Another Name: The Re-Enslavement of Black Americans from the Civil War to World War II*. New York: Doubleday, 2008.
Blatt, Martin H., and David Roediger, eds. *The Meaning of Slavery in the North*. New York: Garland, 1998.
Blight, David. *Race and Reunion: The Civil War in American Memory*. Cambridge: Belknap, 2001.
Bold, Christine. *Frontier Club: Popular Westerns and Cultural Power*. New York: Oxford University Press, 2013.
Born in Slavery: Slave Narratives from the Federal Writers' Project, 1936–1938. http://memory.loc.gov/ammem/snhtml/snhome.html.
Bové, Paul A. *Mastering Discourse: The Politics of Intellectual Culture*. Durham, N.C.: Duke University Press, 1992.
Bridgman, Richard. *The Colloquial Style in America*. New York: Oxford University Press, 1966.
Brilliant, Richard. *Portraiture*. Cambridge, Mass.: Harvard University Press, 1991.
Brodhead, Richard. *The School of Hawthorne*. New York: Oxford University Press, 1986.
Brooks, Cleanth, Jr., and Robert Penn Warren. *Understanding Poetry: An Anthology for College Students*. New York: Henry Holt, 1938.
Brooks, Daphne. *Bodies in Dissent: Spectacular Performances of Race and Freedom, 1850–1910*. Durham, N.C.: Duke University Press, 2006.
Brooks, Van Wyck. *America's Coming-of-Age*. New York: B. W. Huebsch, 1915.
———. "On Creating a Usable Past." *Dial* 64 (11 April 1918): 337–41.
———. *The Ordeal of Mark Twain*. New York: Dutton, 1920.
Brown, Gillian. *Domestic Individualism: Imagining Self in Nineteenth-Century America*. Berkeley: University of California Press, 1990.

Brown, R. Ben. "Free Men and Free Pigs: Closing the Southern Range and the American Property Tradition." *Radical History Review* 108 (Fall 2010): 117–37.

Burnard, Trevor. "'The Righteous Will Shine Like the Sun': Writing an Evocative History of Antebellum American Slavery." *Slavery and Abolition: A Journal of Slave and Post-Slave Studies* 36, no. 1 (2015): 180–85.

Cable, George Washington. *The Silent South, Together with The Freedman's Case in Equity and the Convict Lease System*. New York: Scribner, 1885.

Calder, Lendol. *Financing the American Dream: A Cultural History of Consumer Credit*. Princeton, N.J.: Princeton University Press, 1999.

Campbell, Randolph B. *A Southern Community in Crisis: Harrison County, Texas, 1850–1880*. Austin: Texas State Historical Society, 1980.

Canetti, Elias. *The Conscience of Words*. New York: Seabury, 1979.

Carby, Hazel. *Cultures in Babylon: Black Britain and African America*. New York: Verso, 1999.

———. "Policing the Black Woman's Body in an Urban Context." *Critical Inquiry* 18, no. 4 (Summer 1992): 738–55.

Carmichael, Stokely, and Charles V. Hamilton. *Black Power: The Politics of Liberation in America*. New York: Vintage, 1992. First published in 1967.

Chakrabarty, Dipesh. *Provincializing Europe: Postcolonial Thought and Historical Difference*. Princeton, N.J.: Princeton University Press, 2000.

Chandler, Alfred D., Jr. *The Visible Hand: The Managerial Revolution in American Business*. Cambridge, Mass.: Harvard University Press, 1977.

Cheng, Anne Anlin. *Second Skin: Josephine Baker and the Modern Surface*. New York: Oxford University Press, 2013.

Clark, Kenneth. *Dark Ghetto: Dilemmas of Social Power*. New York: Harper & Row, 1965.

Clark, T. J. *The Painting of Modern Life: Paris in the Art of Manet and His Followers*. Princeton, N.J.: Princeton University Press, 1984.

Clark, Thomas D. *Pills, Petticoats, and Plows: The Southern Country Store*. New York: Bobbs-Merrill, 1944.

Coclanis, Peter A., and Scott Marler. "The Economics of Reconstruction." In *A Companion to the Civil War and Reconstruction*, edited by Lacy K. Ford. Blackwell, 2005. Blackwell Reference Online.

Cohen, Hennig, and William B. Dillingham, eds. *Humor of the Old Southwest*. Athens: University of Georgia Press, 1994. First published in 1964.

Cohen, Nancy. *The Reconstruction of American Liberalism, 1865–1914*. Chapel Hill: University of North Carolina Press, 2002.

Collins, Kathleen. "Portraits of Slave Children." *History of Photography* 9, no. 3 (July–September 1985): 187–210.

Connolly, Nathan D. B. *A World More Concrete: Race and the Remaking of Jim Crow South Florida*. Chicago: University of Chicago Press, 2014.

Cooper, William J., Jr., and Thomas E. Terrill. *The American South: A History*. Lanham, Md.: Rowman & Littlefield, 2008.

Copeland, Huey. *Bound to Appear: Art, Slavery, and the Site of Blackness in Multicultural America*. Chicago: University of Chicago Press, 2013.

Cox, Karen L. *Dreaming of Dixie: How the South Was Created in American Popular Culture*. Chapel Hill: University of North Carolina Press, 2011.

Cox, Oliver Cromwell. *Capitalism as a System*. New York: Monthly Review, 1964.
Crary, Jonathan. "Spectacle, Attention, Counter-Memory." *October* 50 (Autumn 1989): 96–107.
———. *Suspensions of Perception: Attention, Spectacle, and Modern Culture*. Cambridge: MIT Press, 1999.
Cruse, Harold. "Revolutionary Nationalism and the Afro-American." *Studies on the Left* 2, no. 3 (1962).
Cugaono, Ottobah. *Thoughts and Sentiments on the Evil and Wicked Traffic of the Slavery and Commerce of the Human Species*. New York: Cambridge, 2013. First published in 1787.
Daniel, Pete. *Breaking the Land: The Transformation of Cotton, Tobacco, and Rice Cultures since 1880*. Urbana: University of Illinois Press, 1985.
———. "Crossroads of Change: Cotton, Tobacco, and Rice Cultures in the Twentieth-Century South." *Journal of Southern History* 50, no. 3 (1984): 429–56.
———. *The Shadow of Slavery: Peonage in the South, 1901–1969*. Urbana: University of Illinois Press, 1972.
Davis, Allen F., and Mark H. Haller. *The Peoples of Philadelphia: A History of Ethnic Groups and Lower-Class Life, 1790–1940*. Philadelphia: Temple University Press, 1973.
Davis, John. "Eastman Johnson's *Negro Life at the South* and Urban Slavery in Washington, D.C." *Art Bulletin* (March 1988): 67–92.
Davis, Kathleen. *Periodization and Sovereignty: How Ideas of Feudalism and Secularization Govern the Politics of Time*. Philadelphia: University of Pennsylvania Press, 2008.
Dayan, Colin. *The Law Is a White Dog: How Legal Rituals Make and Unmake Persons*. Princeton, N.J.: Princeton University Press, 2011.
Debord, Guy. *The Society of the Spectacle*. Translated by Donald Nicholson-Smith. New York: Zone, 1994. First published in 1967.
Denning, Michael. *The Cultural Front: The Laboring of American Culture in the Twentieth Century*. New York: Verso, 1996.
———. "Wageless Life." *New Left Review* 66 (November–December. 2010): 79–97.
Derrida, Jacques. *Specters of Marx: The State of the Debt, the Work of Mourning, and the New International*. Translated by Peggy Kamuf. New York: Routledge, 1994.
DeVoto, Bernard. *Mark Twain's America*. Boston: Little, Brown, 1932.
Deyle, Steven. *Carry Me Back: The Domestic Slave Trade in American Life*. New York: Oxford University Press, 2005.
Dinerstein, Joel. *The Origins of Cool in Postwar America*. Chicago: University of Chicago Press, 2017.
Donohue, Kathleen. *Freedom from Want: American Liberalism and the Idea of the Consumer*. Baltimore: Johns Hopkins University Press, 2003.
Dormon, James H. "Shaping the Popular Image of Post-Reconstruction American Blacks: The 'Coon Song' Phenomenon of the Gilded Age." *American Quarterly* 40, no. 4 (1988): 450–71.
Douglass, Frederick. *My Bondage and My Freedom*. New York, 1855.
———. *Narrative of the Life of Frederick Douglass, an American Slave*. New York: Dover. First published in 1845.
Downs, Jim. *Sick from Freedom: African-American Illness and Suffering during the Civil War and Reconstruction*. New York: Oxford University Press, 2012.

Drake, St. Clair, and Horace R. Cayton. *Black Metropolis: A Study of Negro Life in a Northern City*. Chicago: University of Chicago Press, 2015. First published in 1945.

Dubois, Laurent. *Avengers of the New World: The Story of the Haitian Revolution*. Cambridge, Mass.: Harvard University Press, 2005.

Du Bois, W. E. B. "Another Open Letter to Woodrow Wilson." *The Crisis* (September 1913): 233.

———. "The Black North: A Social Study." *New York Times*, 17 November 1901. http://movies2.nytimes.com/books/00/11/05/specials/dubois-north.html.

———. *Black Reconstruction in America: An Essay toward a History of the Part Which Black Folk Played in the Attempt to Reconstruct Democracy in America, 1860–1880*. New York: Free Press, 1999. First published in 1935.

———. *Darkwater: Voices from within the Veil*. New York: Harcourt, Brace, 1920.

———. *The Souls of Black Folk*. Chicago: A. C. McClurg, 1903.

Du Gay, Paul, et al., eds. *Doing Cultural Studies: The Story of the Sony Walkman*. Thousand Oaks: Sage, 1997.

Duneier, Mitchell. *Ghetto: The Invention of a Place, the History of an Idea*. New York: FSG, 2016.

Eagleton, Terry. *Literary Theory*. Minneapolis: University of Minnesota, 2008. First published in 1983.

Eckman, Fern Marja. *The Furious Passage of James Baldwin*. Lanham: Rowman & Littlefield, 2014. First published in 1966.

English, Darby. *How to See a Work of Art in Total Darkness*. Cambridge, Mass.: MIT Press, 2010.

Equiano, Olaudah. *The Interesting Narrative and Other Writings*. New York: Penguin, 2003. First published in 1789.

Fabian, Ann. *Card Sharps, Dream Books, and Bucket Shops: Gambling in 19th-Century America*. Ithaca, N.Y.: Cornell University Press, 1990.

Fanon, Frantz. *Black Skin, White Masks*. Translated by Charles Lam Markmann. New York: Grove Press, 1967.

Farley, Anthony Paul. "The Apogee of the Commodity." *DePaul Law Review* 53 (2003–4): 1229–46.

Faulkner, William. *Absalom, Absalom!* New York: Random House, 1936.

———. *Faulkner at Nagano*. Tokyo: Kenkyusha, 1959.

Fekete, John. *The Critical Twilight: Explorations in the Ideology of Anglo-American Literary Theory from Eliot to McLuhan*. London: Routledge & Kegan Paul, 1977.

Fields, Karen E., and Barbara J. Fields. *Racecraft: The Soul of Inequality in American Life*. New York: Verso, 2012.

Filene, Benjamin. *Romancing the Folk: Public Memory and American Roots Music*. Chapel Hill: University of North Carolina Press, 2000.

Fischer, Sibylle. *Modernity Disavowed: Haiti and the Cultures of Slavery in the Age of Revolution*. Durham, N.C.: Duke University Press, 2004.

Fiske, David. "The Plantation in Brooklyn: Nate Salsbury's *Black America* Show," last modified 7 January 2014. http://newyorkhistoryblog.org/2014/01/07/the-plantation-in-brooklyn-nate-salsburys-black-america-show.

Fite, Gilbert C. *Cotton Fields No More: Southern Agriculture, 1865–1980*. Lexington: University Press of Kentucky, 1984.

Fleetwood, Nicole. *Troubling Vision: Performance, Visuality, and Blackness*. Chicago: University of Chicago Press, 2011.

Fleming, Walter L. *Freedmen's Savings Bank: A Chapter in the Economic History of the Negro Race*. Westport, Conn.: Negro Universities Press, 1970. First published in 1906.

Fletcher, Tom. *100 Years of the Negro in Show Business*. New York: Da Capo Press, 1984.

Foner, Eric. *Reconstruction: America's Unfinished Revolution, 1863–1877*. New York: Harper & Row, 1988.

———. "Reconstruction Revisited." *Reviews in American History* 10, no. 4 (1982): 82–100.

Foner, Philip S. *Business and Slavery: The New York Merchants and the Irrepressible Conflict*. Chapel Hill: University of North Carolina Press, 1941.

Formwalt, Lee W. "Antebellum Planter Persistence: Southwest Georgia—A Case Study." *Plantation Society in the Americas* 1 (October 1981): 410–29.

Forret, Jeff. *Race Relations at the Margins: Slaves and Poor Whites in the Antebellum South*. Baton Rouge: Louisiana State University Press, 2006.

Fortune, T. Thomas. *Black and White: Land, Labor, and Politics in the South*. New York: Washington Square Press, 2007. First published in 1884.

Foster, Gaines M. "The Limitations of Federal Health Care for Freedmen, 1862–1868." *Journal of Southern History* 48 (1982): 349–72.

Foucault, Michel. *"Society Must Be Defended": Lectures at the Collège de France, 1975–1976*. Translated by David Macey. New York: Picador, 2003.

Frank, Andre Gunder. "The Development of Underdevelopment." *Monthly Review* 18, no. 4 (1966): 17–31.

Frankenstein, Alfred. *After the Hunt: William Harnett and Other American Still Life Painters, 1870–1900*. Berkeley: University of California Press, 1969.

———. *Illusions of Reality*. Fort Worth: Amon Carter Museum, 1977.

Franklin, John Hope. "The Enforcement of the Civil Rights Act of 1875." *Prologue* 6 (1974): 225–35.

Fredrickson, George M. *The Black Image in the White Mind: The Debate on Afro-American Character and Destiny*. New York: Harper & Row, 1971.

Freud, Sigmund. *The Freud Reader*. Edited by Peter Gay. New York: Norton, 1995.

———. *The Joke and Its Relation to the Unconscious*. Translated by Joyce Crick. New York: Penguin, 2002. First published in 1905.

Fried, Michael. *Realism, Writing, Disfiguration: On Thomas Eakins and Stephen Crane*. Chicago: University of Chicago Press, 1987.

Garnet, Henry Highland. "An Address to the Slaves of the United States of America" [1843]. In *Lift Every Voice: African American Oratory, 1787–1900*, edited by Philip S. Foner and Robert James Branham, 198–205. Tuscaloosa: University of Alabama Press, 1998.

Gates, Henry Louis, Jr. *Figures in Black: Words, Signs, and the Racial Self*. New York: Oxford University Press, 1987.

Genovese, Eugene D. *The Political Economy of Slavery*. New York: Pantheon, 1965.

Gikandi, Simon. *Slavery and the Culture of Taste*. Princeton, N.J.: Princeton University Press, 2011.

Gilbert, Abby L. "The Comptroller of the Currency and the Freedman's Savings Bank." *Journal of Negro History* 57, no. 2 (April 1972): 125–43.

Gilfoyle, Timothy. "Making an American Upper Class." *Reviews in American History* 30, no. 2 (June 2002): 279–87.

Gilmore, Glenda. *Defying Dixie: The Radical Roots of Civil Rights*. New York: Norton, 2008.

Gilroy, Paul. *The Black Atlantic: Modernity and Double Consciousness*. New York: Verso, 1993.

Glenn, Evelyn Nakano. "From Servitude to Service Work: Historical Continuities in the Racial Division of Paid Reproductive Labor." *Signs* 18, no. 1 (1992): 1–43.

Goodyear, Frank H., III. "Photography Changes the Way We Record and Respond to Social Issues." *click!*, Smithsonian Institution, accessed 20 December 2011, http://click.si.edu/Story.aspx?story=297 (site discontinued).

Gotham, Kevin Fox. *Race, Real Estate, and Uneven Development: The Kansas City Experience, 1900–2010*. 2nd ed. Albany: SUNY Press, 2014.

Graff, Gerald. *Professing Literature: An Institutional History*. Chicago: University of Chicago Press, 1987.

Grahn-Farley, Maria. "The Master Norm." *DePaul Law Review* 53, no. 3 (2004): 1215–28.

Grandin, Greg. *Empire's Workshop: Latin America, the United States, and the Rise of the New Imperialism*. New York: Metropolitan, 2006.

Greenberg, Clement. "Towards a Newer Laocoon." In *Perceptions and Judgments, 1939–1944*, vol. 1 of *Collected Essays and Criticism*. Chicago: University of Chicago Press, 1988.

Greeson, Jennifer Rae. *Our South: Geographical Fantasy and the Rise of National Literature*. Cambridge, Mass.: Harvard University Press, 2010.

Griffin, Farah Jasmine. *If You Can't Be Free, Be a Mystery: In Search of Billie Holiday*. New York: Free Press, 2001.

Guillory, John. *Cultural Capital: The Problem of Literary Canon Formation*. Chicago: University of Chicago Press, 1993.

Hagenstein, Edwin C., et al. *American Georgics: Writings on Farming, Culture, and the Land*. New Haven, Conn.: Yale University Press, 2011.

Hahn, Steven. "Hunting, Fishing, and Foraging: Common Rights and Class Relations in the Postbellum South." *Radical History Review* 26 (1982): 37–64.

Hale, Grace Elizabeth. *Making Whiteness: The Culture of Segregation in the South, 1890–1940*. New York: Vintage, 1995.

Haley, Sarah. *No Mercy Here: Gender, Punishment, and the Making of Jim Crow Modernity*. Chapel Hill: University of North Carolina Press, 2016.

Hall, Jacquelyn Dowd. "The Long Civil Rights Movement." *Journal of American History* (March 2005): 1233–63.

Hall, Stuart. *Cultural Studies 1983*. Durham, N.C.: Duke University Press, 2016.

———. Introduction to *Representation: Cultural Representations and Signifying Practices*. London: Sage, 1997.

———. "Race, Articulation, and Societies Structured in Dominance." In *Sociological Theories: Race and Colonialism*, 305–44. Paris: UNESCO, 1980.

Harcourt, Bernard. *The Counterrevolution: How Our Government Went to War against Its Own Citizens*. New York: Basic, 2018.
Hari, Johann. *Chasing the Scream: The First and Last Days of the War on Drugs*. New York: Bloomsbury, 2015.
Harris, Joel Chandler. *Uncle Remus, His Songs and His Sayings*. New York: Appleton, 1895. First published in 1880.
Hartman, Saidiya. "The Belly of the World: A Note on Black Women's Labors." *Souls* 18, no. 1 (2016): 166–73.
———. *Lose Your Mother: A Journey along the Atlantic Slave Route*. New York: FSG, 2006.
———. *Scenes of Subjection: Terror, Slavery, and Self-Making in Nineteenth-Century America*. New York: Oxford University Press, 1997.
———. *Wayward Lives, Beautiful Experiments: Intimate Histories of Social Upheaval*. New York: Norton, 2019.
Harvey, David. "There Is No Way You Can Change the World without Changing Your Ideas!" *LeftEast*, last modified 13 December 2016. http://www.criticatac.ro/lefteast/david-harvey-interview-2016.
Heap, Chad. *Slumming: Sexual and Racial Encounters in American Nightlife*. Chicago: University of Chicago Press, 2008.
Hemingway, Ernest. *Green Hills of Africa*. New York: Simon & Schuster, 2015. First published in 1935.
Hine, Robert V., and John Mack Faragher. *Frontiers: A Short History of the American West*. New Haven, Conn.: Yale University Press, 2007.
Hinton, Elizabeth. *From the War on Poverty to the War on Crime: The Making of Mass Incarceration in America*. Cambridge, Mass.: Harvard University Press, 2016.
Hobsbawm, Eric, and Terrence Ranger, eds. *The Invention of Tradition*. Cambridge: Cambridge University Press, 1983.
Holmes, Oliver Wendell, Sr. "The Stereoscope and the Stereograph." *The Atlantic*, June 1859, 738–49.
Hopkins, Pauline. *The Magazine Novels of Pauline Hopkins*. New York: Oxford University Press, 1990.
Horton, Myles. *The Long Haul*. New York: Doubleday, 1990.
Hoxie, Frederick. *This Indian Country: American Indian Activists and the Place They Made*. New York: Penguin, 2012.
Hudson, Peter James. *Bankers and Empire: How Wall Street Colonized the Caribbean*. Chicago: University of Chicago Press, 2017.
Hughes, Langston. *Collected Works*. Vol. 13. Columbia: University of Missouri Press, 2002.
Hurston, Zora Neale. "What White Publishers Won't Print." In *Within the Circle: An Anthology of African American Literary Criticism from the Harlem Renaissance to the Present*, edited By Angelyn Mitchell, 117–21. Durham, N.C.: Duke University Press, 1994.
Hutchinson, Elizabeth. *The Indian Craze: Primitivism, Modernism, and Transculturation in American Art, 1890–915*. Durham, N.C.: Duke University Press, 2009.
Hyman, Louis. "Why Write the History of Capitalism?" *Symposium Magazine*, 8 July 2013. http://www.symposium-magazine.com/why-write-the-history-o f-capitalism-louis-hyman.

Irwin, Douglas A. "Explaining America's Surge in Manufactured Exports, 1880–1913." 23 July 2001. https://www.dartmouth.edu/~dirwin/docs/Surge3wp.pdf.
Jackson, George. *Soledad Brother: The Prison Letters of George Jackson.* Chicago: Lawrence Hill, 1994. First published in 1970.
Jacobson, Matthew Frye. *Whiteness of a Different Color: European Immigrants and the Alchemy of Race.* Cambridge, Mass.: Harvard University Press, 1998.
James, C. L. R. *Black Jacobins: Toussaint L'Ouverture and the San Domingo Revolution.* New York: Vintage, 1963. First published in 1938.
Jameson, Fredric. "The Brick and the Balloon: Architecture, Idealism and Land Speculation." *New Left Review* (March/April 1998): 25–46.
———. "Culture and Finance Capital." *Critical Inquiry* (Autumn 1997): 246–65.
———. "The Existence of Italy." In *Signatures of the Visible*, 155–230. New York: Routledge, 1992.
———."Magical Narratives: Romance as Genre." *New Literary History* 7, no. 1 (Autumn 1975): 135–63.
———. *Marxism and Form: Twentieth-Century Dialectical Theories of Literature.* Princeton, N.J.: Princeton University Press, 1971.
———. "Metacommentary." *PMLA* 86, no. 1 (1971): 9–18.
———. "Modernism and Imperialism." In *Nationalism, Colonialism, and Literature*, 43–68. Minneapolis: University of Minnesota Press, 1990.
———. *The Political Unconscious: Narrative as a Socially Symbolic Act.* Ithaca, N.Y.: Cornell University Press, 1981.
Jancovich, Mark. *The Cultural Politics of the New Criticism.* New York: Cambridge University Press, 1993.
Jaynes, Gerald. *Branches without Roots: Genesis of the Black Working Class in the American South.* New York: Oxford University Press, 1986.
Jenkins, Destin. "The Racial Wealth Gap and the Problem of Historical Narration." *Process: A Blog for American History*, last modified 27 June 2017. http://www.processhistory.org/jenkins-racial-wealth-gap.
Johnson, Walter. "The Pedestal and the Veil: Rethinking the Capitalism/Slavery Question." *Journal of the Early Republic* 24 (Summer 2004): 299–308.
———. *River of Dark Dreams: Slavery and Empire in the Cotton Kingdom.* Cambridge, Mass.: Harvard University Press, 2013.
———. *Soul by Soul: Life inside the Antebellum Slave Market.* Cambridge, Mass.: Harvard University Press, 1999.
Jones, Jacqueline. *American Work: Four Centuries of Black and White Labor.* New York: Norton, 1998.
Judy, Ronald A. T. *(Dis)forming the American Canon: African-Arabic Slave Narratives and the Vernacular.* Minneapolis: University of Minnesota Press, 1993.
Jung, Moon-Ho. *Coolies and Cane: Race, Labor, and Sugar in the Age of Emancipation.* Baltimore: Johns Hopkins University Press, 2006.
Kafka, Ben. *The Demon of Writing: Powers and Failures of Paperwork.* Brooklyn: Zone, 2012.
Kahn, Jonathan D. "Controlling Identity: Plessy, Privacy, and Racial Defamation." *DePaul Law Review* 54 (2005): 755–81.

Kaplan, Amy. *The Anarchy of Empire in the Making of U.S. Culture.* Cambridge, Mass.: Harvard University Press, 2002.
Kaplan, Amy, and Donald E. Pease, eds. *Cultures of United States Imperialism.* Durham, N.C.: Duke University Press, 1993.
Katz, Michael B. *The Undeserving Poor: America's Enduring Confrontation with Poverty.* New York: Oxford University Press, 2013. First published in 1989.
Kazanjian, David. *The Colonizing Trick: National Culture and Imperial Citizenship in Early America.* Minneapolis: University of Minnesota Press, 2003.
Kemble, Fanny. *Journal of a Residence on a Georgian Plantation, in 1838–39.* New York: Harper, 1863.
Kendi, Ibram X. *Stamped from the Beginning: The Definitive History of Racist Ideas in America.* New York: Nation Books, 2016.
Keyes, Allison. "A Long-Lost Manuscript Contains a Searing Eyewitness Account of the Tulsa Race Massacre of 1921." *Smithsonian.com,* last modified 27 May 2016. https://www.smithsonianmag.com/smithsonian-institution/long-lost-manuscript-contains-searing-eyewitness-account-tulsa-race-massacre-1921-180959251.
Kilbride, Daniel. *An American Aristocracy: Southern Planters in Antebellum Philadelphia.* Columbia: University of South Carolina Press, 2006.
———. "Fanny Kemble and Frances Butler Leigh." In *Georgia Women: Their Lives and Times,* edited by Ann Short Chirhart and Betty Wood, 1:106–29. Athens: University of Georgia Press, 2009.
Killick, J. R. "The Transformation of Cotton Marketing in the Late Nineteenth Century: Alexander Sprunt and Son of Wilmington, N.C., 1884–1956." *Business History Review* 55, no. 2 (Summer 1981): 143–69.
Kincaid, Jamaica. "In History." *Callaloo* 20, no.1 (Winter 1997): 1–7.
King, Edward. *The Southern States of North America.* Vol. 1. London, 1875.
Kittler, Friedrich. *Gramophone, Film, Typewriter.* Stanford: Stanford University Press, 1999.
Klein, Kerwin. *Frontiers of Historical Imagination: Narrating the European Conquest of Native America, 1890–1990.* Berkeley: University of California Press, 1997.
Kuenz, Jane. "The Cowboy Businessman and 'The Course of Empire': Owen Wister's *The Virginian.*" *Cultural Critique* 48 (Spring 2001): 98–128.
La Berge, Leigh Clare. "Scandals and Abstractions: 1980s Finance and the Revaluation of American Culture." PhD diss., New York University, 2008.
———. *Scandals and Abstractions: Financial Fiction of the Long 1980s.* New York: Oxford University Press, 2014.
Leja, Michael. *Looking Askance: Skepticism in American Art from Eakins to Duchamp.* Berkeley: University of California Press, 2004.
Lemke, Sieglinde. *Primitivist Modernism: Black Culture and the Origins of Transatlantic Modernism.* New York: Oxford University Press, 1998.
———. *The Vernacular Matters of American Literature.* New York: Palgrave, 2009.
Lemons, J. Stanley. "Black Stereotypes as Reflected in Popular Culture, 1880–1920." *American Quarterly* 29, no. 1 (1977): 102–16.
Leuchtenberg, William. *The White House Looks South: Franklin D. Roosevelt, Harry S. Truman, Lyndon B. Johnson.* Baton Rouge: Louisiana State University Press, 2005.

Levy, Jonathan Ira. *Freaks of Fortune: The Emerging World of Capitalism and Risk in America*. Cambridge, Mass.: Harvard University Press, 2012.

Lichtenstein, Alex. *Twice the Work of Free Labor: The Political Economy of Convict Labor in the New South*. New York: Verso, 1996.

Lippmann, Walter. *Drift and Mastery: An Attempt to Diagnose the Current Unrest*. New York: Mitchell Kennerley, 1914.

Lipsitz, George. "The Possessive Investment in Whiteness: Racialized Social Democracy and the 'White' Problem in American Studies." *American Quarterly* 47, no. 3 (1995): 369–87.

Livingston, James. *Pragmatism and the Political Economy of Revolution, 1850–1940*. Chapel Hill: University of North Carolina Press, 1994.

Lock, Graham. *Blutopia: Visions of the Future and Revisions of the Past in the Work of Sun Ra, Duke Ellington, and Anthony Braxton*. Durham, N.C.: Duke University Press, 1999.

Logan, Rayford Whittingham. *The Betrayal of the Negro, from Rutherford B. Hayes to Woodrow Wilson*. New York: Da Capo Press, 1997. First published in 1954.

Lomax, John A. *Cowboy Songs and Other Frontier Ballads*. New York: Sturgis & Walton, 1910.

———. *Our Singing Country: Folk Songs and Ballads*. Mineola: Dover, 2000. First published in 1941.

Lott, Eric. *Black Mirror: The Cultural Contradiction of American Racism*. Cambridge: Belknap, 2017.

———. *Love and Theft: Blackface Minstrelsy and the American Working Class*. New York: Oxford University Press, 1993.

Loughran, Trish. *The Republic in Print: Print Culture in the Age of U.S. Nation Building, 1770–1870*. New York: Columbia University Press, 2007.

Lowe, Lisa. *Immigrant Acts: On Asian American Cultural Politics*. Durham, N.C.: Duke University Press, 1996.

———. *Intimacies of Four Continents*. Durham, N.C.: Duke University Press, 2015.

Lubin, David. *Picturing a Nation: Art and Social Change in Nineteenth-Century America*. New Haven, Conn.: Yale University Press, 1994.

Maguire, Jane, and Ed Brown. *On Shares: Ed Brown's Story*. New York: Norton 1976.

Markell, Patchen. "The Insufficiency of Non-Domination." *Political Theory* 36, no. 1 (2008): 9–36.

Márquez, Gabriel García. "The Art of Fiction No. 69." *Paris Review* 82 (Winter 1981). http://www.theparisreview.org/interviews/3196/the-art-of-fiction-no-69-gabriel-garcia-marquez.

Marten, James Alen. *Civil War America: Voices from the Home Front*. New York: Fordham University Press, 2007.

Martin, Bonnie. "Slavery's Invisible Engine: Mortgaging Human Property." *Journal of Southern History* 76, no. 4 (2010): 817–56.

Marx, Karl. *Capital*. Vol. 1. Translated by Samuel Moore and Edward Aveling. New York: International Publishers, 1967.

———. *The Eighteenth Brumaire of Louis Bonaparte*. Translated by Daniel De Leon. New York: International Publishers, 1898.

———. "On the Jewish Question." In *Selected Writings*, edited by Lawrence H. Simon, 1–26. Indianapolis: Hackett, 1994.
Marx, Leo. *The Pilot and the Passenger: Essays on Literature, Technology, and Culture in the United States.* New York: Oxford University Press, 1988.
Matthiessen, F. O. *American Renaissance: Art and Expression in the Age of Emerson and Whitman.* New York: Oxford University Press, 1941.
Maverick, Maury. "Let's Join the United States." *Virginia Quarterly Review*, Winter 1939. http://www.vqronline.org/essay/lets-join-united-states.
Maxwell, Angie. *The Indicted South: Public Criticism, Southern Inferiority, and the Politics of Whiteness.* Chapel Hill: University of North Carolina Press, 2014.
McCarthy, Cormac. *Blood Meridian, or The Evening Redness in the West.* New York: Random Houe, 1985.
McClanahan, Annie. *Dead Pledges: Debt, Crisis, and Twenty-First Century Culture.* Stanford: Stanford University Press, 2016.
———. "Investing in the Future: Late Capitalism's End of History." *Journal of Cultural Economy* 6, no. 1 (2013): 78–93.
McClintock, Anne. *Imperial Leather: Race, Gender, and Sexuality in the Colonial Conquest.* New York: Routledge, 1995.
McCurry, Stephanie. *Masters of Small Worlds: Yeoman Households, Gender Relations, and the Political Culture of the Antebellum South Carolina Low Country.* New York: Oxford University Press, 1997.
McElroy's Philadelphia City Directory, for 1859. Philadelphia: Edward C. & John Biddle, 1859.
McKittrick, Katherine. "On Plantations, Prisons, and a Black Sense of Place." *Social and Cultural Geography* 12, no. 8 (December 2011): 947–63.
———. "Plantation Futures." *Small Axe* 42 (November 2013): 1–15.
McWilliams, Carey. *Factories in the Field: The Story of Migratory Farm Labor in California.* Boston: Little, Brown, 1939.
Menand, Louis. *The Metaphysical Club: A Story of Ideas in America.* New York: FSG, 2001.
Mencken, H. L. *A Mencken Chrestomathy.* New York: Vintage, 1982.
Merritt, Keri Leigh. *Masterless Men: Poor Whites and Slavery in the Antebellum South.* New York: Cambridge University Press, 2017.
Michaels, Walter Benn. *The Gold Standard and the Logic of Naturalism.* Berkeley: University of California Press, 1987.
Mihm, Stephen. *Nation of Counterfeiters: Capitalists, Con Men, and the Making of the United States.* Cambridge, Mass.: Harvard University Press, 2007.
Miller, Angela. "The Panorama, the Cinema, and the Emergence of the Spectacular." *Wide Angle* 18, no. 2 (April 1996): 34–69.
Miller, Karl Hagstrom. *Segregated Sound: Inventing Folk and Pop Music in the Age of Jim Crow.* Durham, N.C.: Duke University Press, 2010.
Miller, Monica L. "The Black Dandy as Bad Modernist." In *Bad Modernisms*, edited by Douglas Mao and Rebecca L. Walkowitz, 179–205. Durham, N.C.: Duke University Press, 2006.
Mink, Gwendolyn, and Rickie Solinger, eds. *Welfare: A Documentary History of Policy and Politics.* New York: NYU Press, 2003.

Mirzoeff, Nicholas. "The Debt-Prison System," posted 11 April 2012. http://www.nicholasmirzoeff.com/O2012/2012/04/11/the-debt-prison-system.
Mitchell, Lee Clark. *Westerns: Making the Man in Fiction and Film*. Chicago: University of Chicago Press, 1996.
Mitchell, Mary Niall. *Raising Freedom's Child: Black Children and Visions of the Future after Slavery*. New York: NYU Press, 2008.
Molina, Natalia. *How Race Is Made in America: Immigration, Citizenship, and the Historical Power of Racial Scripts*. Berkeley: University of California Press, 2014.
Moore, Barrington, Jr. *Social Origins of Dictatorship and Democracy: Lord and Peasant in the Making of the Modern World*. Boston: Beacon, 1966.
Morgan, Jennifer. *Laboring Women: Reproduction and Gender in New World Slavery*. Philadelphia: University of Pennsylvania Press, 2004.
Morrison, Toni. *Beloved*. New York: Vintage, 2004. First published in 1987.
———. *Playing in the Dark: Whiteness and the Literary Imagination*. Cambridge, Mass.: Harvard University Press, 1992.
Moten, Fred. "Knowledge of Freedom." *CR: The New Centennial Review* 4, no. 2 (Fall 2004): 269–310.
Muhammad, Khalil Gibran. *The Condemnation of Blackness: Race, Crime, and the Making of Modern Urban America*. Cambridge, Mass.: Harvard University Press, 2010.
———. "Where Did All the White Criminals Go? Reconfiguring Race and Crime on the Road to Mass Incarceration." *Souls* 13, no. 1 (2011): 72–90.
Mumford, Kevin. *Interzones: Black/White Sex Districts in Chicago and New York in the Early Twentieth Century*. New York: Columbia University Press, 1997.
Murakawa, Naomi. *The First Civil Right: How Liberals Built Prison America*. New York: Oxford University Press, 2014.
Nadasen, Premillaa. *Household Workers Unite: The Untold Story of African American Women Who Built a Movement*. Boston: Beacon Press, 2015.
Natanson, Nicholas. *The Black Image in the New Deal: The Politics of FSA Photography*. Knoxville: University of Tennessee Press, 1992.
Nelson, Scott Reynolds. *Iron Confederacies: Southern Railways, Klan Violence and Reconstruction*. Chapel Hill: University of North Carolina Press, 1999.
Nelson, William E. *The Roots of American Bureaucracy, 1830–1900*. Cambridge, Mass.: Harvard University Press, 1982.
Nemerov, Alexander. *The Body of Raphaelle Peale: Still Life and Selfhood, 1812–1824*. Berkeley: University of California Press, 2001.
———. "Doing the 'Old America': The Image of the American West, 1880–1920." In *The West as America: Reinterpreting Images of the Frontier, 1820–1920*, edited by William Truettner, 285–343. Washington, D.C.: Smithsonian, 1991.
———. *Frederic Remington and the American Civil War: A Ghost Story*. Stockbridge, Mass.: Norman Rockwell Museum, 2006.
Newman, Steve. *Ballad Collection, Lyric, and the Canon: The Call of the Popular from the Restoration to the New Criticism*. Philadelphia: University of Pennsylvania Press, 2007.
Ngai, Mae. *Impossible Subjects: Illegal Aliens and the Making of Modern America*. Princeton, N.J.: Princeton University Press, 2003.

Ngai, Sianne. "Black Venus, *Blonde Venus*." In *Bad Modernisms*, edited by Douglas Mao and Rebecca L. Walkowitz, 145–78. Durham, N.C.: Duke University Press, 2006.
Noble, David W. *Death of a Nation: American Culture and the End of Exceptionalism*. Minneapolis: University of Minnesota Press, 2002.
Norris, Frank. "The Frontier Gone at Last." In *Responsibilities of the Novelist*, 69–81. New York: Doubleday, 1903.
Norton, Anne. "Engendering Another American Identity." In *Rhetorical Republic: Governing Representations in American Politics*, edited by Frederick M. Dolan and Thomas L. Dumm, 125–42. Amherst: University of Massachusetts Press, 1993.
Novak, William J. *The People's Welfare: Law and Regulation in Nineteenth-Century America*. Chapel Hill: University of North Carolina Press, 1996.
Nudelman, Franny. *John Brown's Body: Slavery, Violence, and the Culture of War*. Chapel Hill: University of North Carolina Press, 2002.
Ogren, Kathy J. *The Jazz Revolution: Twenties America and the Meaning of Jazz*. New York: Oxford University Press, 1989.
O'Kane, Karen. "Before the New Criticism: Modernism and the Nashville Group." *Mississippi Quarterly* 51, no. 4 (Fall 1998): 683–97.
O'Malley, Michael. *Face Value: The Entwined Histories of Money and Race in America*. Chicago: University of Chicago Press, 2012.
Orenstein, Dara. *Out of Stock: The Warehouse in the History of Capitalism*. Chicago: University of Chicago Press, 2019.
Oshinsky, David M. *"Worse Than Slavery": Parchman Farm and the Ordeal of Jim Crow Justice*. New York: Free Press, 1996.
Osthaus, Carl R. *Freedmen, Philanthropy, and Fraud: A History of the Freedman's Savings Bank*. Urbana: University of Illinois Press, 1976.
Painter, Nell Irvin. *Exodusters: Black Migration to Kansas after Reconstruction*. New York: Norton, 1976.
———. *The History of White People*. New York: Norton, 2010.
———. *Standing at Armageddon: The United States, 1877–1919*. New York: Norton, 1989.
Pateman, Carole, and Charles W. Mills. *Contract and Domination*. Malden, Mass.: Polity, 2007.
Patterson, Martha H. "'Kin' o' Rough Jestice Fer a Parson': Pauline Hopkins's *Winona* and the Politics of Reconstructing History." *African American Review* 32, no. 3 (Autumn 1998): 445–60.
Payne, Darwin. *Owen Wister: Chronicler of the West, Gentleman of the East*. Dallas: Southern Methodist University Press, 1985.
Perkinson, Robert. *Texas Tough: The Rise of America's Prison Empire*. New York: Metropolitan, 2010.
Perry, Imani. *Looking for Lorraine: The Radiant and Radical Life of Lorraine Hansberry*. Boston: Beacon Press, 2018.
Petry, Ann. *The Street*. Boston: Houghton Mifflin, 1946.
Phan, Hoang Gia. *Bonds of Citizenship: Law and the Labors of Emancipation*. New York: New York University Press, 2013.
Phillips, Wendell. *Speeches, Lectures, and Letters*. Boston: Redpath, 1863.

Pickering, Edward D. "The Roots of New Criticism." *Southern Literary Journal* 41, no. 1 (2008): 93–108.
Pierson, H. W. *A Letter to Hon. Charles Sumner, with Statements of Outrages upon Freedmen in Georgia, and an Account of my Expulsion from Andersonville, Ga., by the Ku-Klux Klan*. Washington, D.C., 1870.
Pocock, J. G. A. *Virtue, Commerce, and History: Essays on Political Thought and History, Chiefly in the Eighteenth Century*. Cambridge: Cambridge University Press, 1985.
Poovey, Mary. *Genres of the Credit Economy: Mediating Value in Eighteenth- and Nineteenth-Century Britain*. Chicago: University of Chicago Press, 2008.
Porter, William T., ed. *The Big Bear of Arkansas and Other Sketches*. Philadelphia: Peterson, 1843.
Postone, Moishe. *Time, Labor, and Social Domination: A Reinterpretation of Marx's Critical Theory*. Cambridge: Cambridge University Press, 1993.
Potts, Jason. "Quality Inequality: *The Virginian* and the Invention of Meritocracy." *Studies in American Fiction* 40, no. 2 (2013): 231–57.
Powell, Lawrence. *New Masters: Northern Planters during the Civil War and Reconstruction*. New Haven, Conn.: Yale University Press, 1980.
Pratt, Lloyd. *Archives of American Time: Literature and Modernity in the Nineteenth Century*. Philadelphia: University of Pennsylvania Press, 2010.
Pratt, Mary Louise. *Imperial Eyes: Travel Writing and Transculturation*. New York: Routledge, 1992.
Prince, Steven. *Stories of the South: Race and the Reconstruction of Southern Identity, 1865–1915*. Chapel Hill: University of North Carolina Press, 2014.
Rana, Aziz. *The Two Faces of American Freedom*. Cambridge, Mass.: Harvard University Press, 2010.
Ransom, Roger L. *Conflict and Compromise: The Political Economy of Slavery, Emancipation, and the American Civil War*. Cambridge: Cambridge University Press, 1989.
Ransom, Roger L., and Richard P. Sutch. *One Kind of Freedom: The Economic Consequences of Emancipation*. 2nd ed. Cambridge: Cambridge University Press, 2001.
Read, Jason. *The Micro-Politics of Capital: Marx and the Prehistory of the Present*. Albany: SUNY Press, 2003.
Reid, Whitelaw. *After the War: A Southern Tour*. New York, 1866.
Report and Testimony of the Select Committee of the United States Senate to Investigate the Causes of the Removal of the Negroes from the Southern States to the Northern States. S. Rpt. 693. Washington, D.C., 1880.
Richards, Leonard L. *The California Gold Rush and the Coming of the Civil War*. New York: Vintage, 2008.
Robinson, Cedric. *Black Marxism: The Making of the Black Radical Tradition*. Chapel Hill: University of North Carolina Press, 2000. First published in 1983.
———. *Forgeries of Memory and Meaning: Blacks and the Regimes of Race in American Theater and Film before World War II*. Chapel Hill: University of North Carolina Press, 2007.
Rodney, Walter. *How Europe Underdeveloped Africa*. New York: Verso, 2018. First published in 1972.
Rodriguez, Dylan. *Forced Passages: Imprisoned Radical Intellectuals and the U.S. Prison Regime*. Minneapolis: University of Minnesota Press, 2006.

Roediger, David. *Seizing Freedom: Slave Emancipation and Liberty for All*. New York: Verso, 2014.
———. *Wages of Whiteness: Race and the Making of the American Working Class*. New York: Verso, 1991.
Rogin, Michael. *Fathers and Children: Andrew Jackson and the Subjugation of the American Indian*. New York: Transaction, 1991.
Rohrbough, Malcolm J. *The Land Office Business: The Settlement and Administration of American Public Lands, 1789–1837*. New York: Oxford University Press, 1968.
Rose, Mark. *Authors and Owners: The Invention of Copyright*. Cambridge, Mass.: Harvard University Press, 1993.
Rothman, Joshua D. *Flush Times and Fever Dreams: A Story of Capitalism and Slavery in the Age of Jackson*. Athens: University of Georgia Press, 2012.
Rothstein, Richard. *The Color of Law: A Forgotten History of How Our Government Segregated America*. New York: Liveright, 2017.
Rourke, Constance. *American Humor: A Study of the National Character*. New York: NYRB, 2004. First published in 1931.
Roy, William G. *Socializing Capital: The Rise of the Large Industrial Corporation in America*. Princeton, N.J.: Princeton University Press, 1997.
Rydell, Robert W. *All the World's a Fair*. Chicago: University of Chicago Press, 1984.
Sandage, Scott A. *Born Losers: A History of Failure in America*. Cambridge, Mass.: Harvard University Press, 2005.
Satter, Beryl. *Family Properties: Race, Real Estate, and the Exploitation of Black Urban America*. New York: Henry Holt, 2010.
Saunders, Frances Stonor. *The Cultural Cold War: The CIA and the World of Arts and Letters*. New York: New Press, 2013.
Saxton, Alexander. *Rise and Fall of the White Republic: Class Politics and Mass Culture in Nineteenth-Century America*. New York: Verso, 1990.
Scharnhorst, Gary. *Owen Wister and the West*. Norman: University of Oklahoma Press, 2015.
Schmitt, Carl. *The Nomos of the Earth*. Candor, N.Y.: Telos, 2006.
Schwartz, Lawrence H. *Creating Faulkner's Reputation: The Politics of Modern Literary Criticism*. Knoxville: University of Tennessee Press, 1988.
Scott, David. *Conscripts of Modernity: The Tragedy of Colonial Enlightenment*. Durham, N.C.: Duke University Press, 2004.
Sekula, Allan. "The Traffic in Photographs." *Art Journal* 41, no. 1 (Spring 1981): 15–25.
Sellers, Charles. *The Market Revolution: Jacksonian America, 1815–1846*. New York: Oxford University Press, 1991.
Seltzer, Mark. *Bodies and Machines*. New York: Routledge, 1992.
Sewell, William H., Jr. "The Temporalities of Capitalism." *Socio-Economic Review* 6 (2008): 517–37.
Sexton, Jared. "Afro-Pessimism: The Unclear Word." *Rhizomes* 29 (2016). https://doi.org/10.20415/rhiz/029.e02.
———. *Amalgamation Schemes: Antiblackness and the Critique of Multiracialism*. Minneapolis: University of Minnesota Press, 2008.
———. "People-of-Color-Blindness: Notes on the Afterlife of Slavery." *Social Text* 103 (2010): 31–56.

Shumway, David R. *Creating American Civilization: A Genealogy of American Literature as an Academic Discipline*. Minneapolis: University of Minnesota Press, 1994.

Silber, Nina. *The Romance of Reunion: Northerners and the South, 1865–1900*. Chapel Hill: University of North Carolina Press, 1993.

Singh, Nikhil Pal. *Black Is a Country: Race and the Unfinished Struggle for Democracy*. Cambridge, Mass.: Harvard University Press, 2004.

Sklansky, Jeffrey. "Labor, Money, and the Financial Turn in the History of Capitalism." *Labor* 11, no. 1 (2014): 23–46.

———. *The Soul's Economy: Market Society and Selfhood in American Economic Thought, 1820–1920*. Chapel Hill: University of North Carolina Press, 2002.

Slotkin, Richard. *The Fatal Environment: The Myth of the Frontier in the Age of Industrialization, 1800–1890*. New York: Atheneum, 1985.

———. *Gunfighter Nation: The Myth of the Frontier in Twentieth-Century America*. New York: Atheneum, 1992.

Smallwood, Stephanie. *Saltwater Slavery: A Middle Passage from Africa to American Diaspora*. Cambridge, Mass.: Harvard University Press, 2007.

Smith, C. Wayne, and J. Tom Cothren, eds. *Cotton: Origin, History, Technology, and Production*. New York: Wiley, 1999.

Smith, Henry Nash. *Virgin Land: The American West as Symbol and Myth*. Cambridge, Mass.: Harvard University Press, 1950.

Southerners, Twelve. *I'll Take My Stand: The South and the Agrarian Tradition*. New York: Harper, 1962. First published in 1930.

Spear, Allan. "The Origins of the Urban Ghetto, 1870–1915." In *Key Issues in the Afro-American Experience*, edited by Nathan Huggins et al., 153–66. New York: Harcourt Brace Jovanovich, 1971.

Spillers, Hortense. *Black, White, and In Color: Essays on American Literature and Culture*. Chicago: University of Chicago Press, 2003.

———. "Mama's Baby, Papa's Maybe: An American Grammar Book." *Diacritics* (Summer 1987): 64–81.

Stange, Maren. *Symbols of Ideal Life: Social Documentary Photography in America*. New York: Cambridge University Press, 1989.

Stanley, Amy Dru. *From Bondage to Contract: Wage Labor, Marriage, and the Market in the Age of Slave Emancipation*. New York: Cambridge University Press, 1998.

Stiles, T. J. *Jesse James: Last Rebel of the Civil War*. New York: Knopf, 2002.

Stowe, Harriet Beecher. *Uncle Tom's Cabin; or, Life Among the Lowly*. New York: Signet, 1998. First published in 1852.

Sublette, Ned, and Constance. *The American Slave Coast: A History of the Slave-Breeding Industry*. Chicago: Lawrence Hill, 2016.

Sugrue, Thomas. *The Origins of the Urban Crisis: Race and Inequality in Postwar Detroit*. Princeton, N.J.: Princeton University Press, 1996.

Sullivan, John Jeremiah. "Southern Exposures." *Bookforum* (June/July/August 2013). https://www.bookforum.com/print/2002/a-long-lost-manuscript-both-complements-and-rivals-a-classic-work-of-depression-era-documentary-reportage-11650.

Sundquist, Eric J. *To Wake the Nations: Race in the Making of American Literature*. Cambridge: Belknap Press, 1993.

Susman, Warren. "Personality and the Making of Twentieth-Century Culture." In *Culture as History: The Transformation of American Society in the Twentieth Century*, 271–85. New York: Pantheon, 1984.
Szwed, John. *Alan Lomax: The Man Who Recorded the World*. New York: Viking, 2010.
Taussig, Michael. "Culture of Terror—Space of Death: Roger Casement's Putumayo Report and the Explanation of Torture." *Comparative Studies in Society and History* 26, no. 3 (July 1984): 467–97.
Taylor, Christopher. *Empire of Neglect: The West Indies in the Wake of British Liberalism*. Durham, N.C.: Duke University Press, 2018.
Taylor, Keeanga-Yamahtta. *From #BlackLivesMatter to Black Liberation*. Chicago: Haymarket, 2016.
Thomas, Brook. *American Literary Realism and the Failed Promise of Contract*. Berkeley: University of California Press, 1997.
Thompson, Elizabeth Lee. *The Reconstruction of Southern Debtors: Bankruptcy after the Civil War*. Athens: University of Georgia Press, 2004.
Thorpe, T. B. *The Hive of "The Bee-Hunter."* New York: Appleton, 1854.
Toll, Robert. *Blacking Up: The Minstrel Show in Nineteenth Century America*. New York: Oxford University Press, 1977.
Tompkins, Jane. *West of Everything: The Inner Life of Westerns*. New York: Oxford University Press, 1992.
Toscano, Alberto. "The Open Secret of Real Abstraction." *Rethinking Marxism* 20, no. 2 (April 2008): 273–87.
Townes, A. Jane. "The Effect of Emancipation in Large Landholdings, Nelson and Goochland Counties, Virginia." *Journal of Southern History* 45 (August 1979): 403–12.
Trouillot, Michel-Rolph. "North Atlantic Universals: Analytical Fictions, 1492–1945." *South Atlantic Quarterly* 101, no. 4 (Fall 2002): 839–58.
Troutman, Maralynn. "William Michael Harnett's *Attention, Company!*" PhD diss., University of Oklahoma, 1977.
Twain, Mark. *The Celebrated Jumping Frog of Calaveras County, and Other Sketches*. London: Routledge, 1867.
———. *A Connecticut Yankee in King Arthur's Court*. New York: Harper, 1889.
———. *Pudd'nhead Wilson*. New York: Bantam, 1981. First published in 1893.
Wacquant, Loïc. "From Slavery to Mass Incarceration: Rethinking the 'Race Question' in the US." *New Left Review* 13 (January–February 2002): 41–60.
Wagner, Bryan. *Disturbing the Peace: Black Culture and the Police Power after Slavery*. Cambridge, Mass.: Harvard University Press, 2010.
Waldstreicher, David. *Slavery's Constitution: From Revolution to Ratification*. New York: Hill & Wang, 2009.
Walhout, Mark. "The New Criticism and the Crisis of American Liberalism: The Poetics of the Cold War." *College English* 49, no. 8 (December 1987): 861–71.
Walker, David. *Appeal to the Coloured Citizens of the World*, edited by Peter P. Hinks. University Park: Pennsylvania State University Press, 2000. First published in 1830.
Walker, Gavin. "Primitive Accumulation and the State-Form: National Debt as an Apparatus of Capture." *Viewpoint Magazine*, last modified 29 October 2014. https:

//viewpointmag.com/2014/10/29/primitive-accumulation-and-the-state-form-national-debt-as-an-apparatus-of-capture.

Wang, Jackie. *Carceral Capitalism*. South Pasadena: Semiotext(e), 2018.

Wark, McKenzie. *The Beach Beneath the Street: The Everyday Life and Glorious Times of the Situationist International*. New York: Verso, 2011.

Warner, Michael. *The Letters of the Republic: Publication and the Public Sphere in Eighteenth-Century America*. Cambridge, Mass.: Harvard University Press, 1990.

———. "Mass Public and the Mass Subject." In *Habermas and the Public Sphere*, edited by Craig J. Calhoun, 377–401. Cambridge: MIT Press, 1992.

Warren, Calvin L. *Ontological Terror: Blackness, Nihilism, and Emancipation*. Durham, N.C.: Duke University Press, 2018.

Warren, Robert Penn. "Brooks and Warren." *Humanities* 6, no. 2 (April 1985): 1–3.

Watson, Ritchie Devon, Jr. *Yeoman versus Cavalier: The Old Southwest's Fictional Road to Rebellion*. Baton Rouge: LSU Press, 1993.

Wayne, Michael. *The Reshaping of Plantation Society: The Natchez District, 1860–1880*. Urbana: University of Illinois Press, 1983.

Webb, Barbara L. "Authentic Possibilities: Plantation Performance of the 1890s." *Theatre Journal* 56 (2004): 63–82.

Weeks, Kathi, and Michael Hardt. *The Jameson Reader*. Oxford: Blackwell, 2000.

Weinstein, Cindy, and Christopher Looby, eds. *American Literature's Aesthetic Dimensions*. New York: Columbia University Press, 2012.

Wells, Ida B. *The Light of Truth: Writings of an Anti-Lynching Crusader*, edited by Mia Bay. New York: Penguin, 2014.

Weschler, Lawrence. *Boggs: A Comedy of Values*. Chicago: University of Chicago Press, 1999.

Whitman, Walt. *The Portable Walt Whitman*. New York: Penguin, 1977.

Wiebe, Robert H. *The Search for Order, 1877–1920*. New York: Hill & Wang, 1967.

Wiegman, Robyn. *American Anatomies: Theorizing Race and Gender*. Durham, N.J.: Duke University Press, 1995.

Wiener, Jonathan. *Social Origins of the New South: Alabama, 1860–1885*. Baton Rouge: Louisiana State University Press, 1978.

Wilderson, Frank B., III. "Gramsci's Black Marx: Whither the Slave in Civil Society?" *Social Identities* 9, no. 2 (2003): 225–40.

———. "The Position of the Unthought: An Interview with Saidiya V. Hartman." *Qui Parle* 13, no. 2 (Spring/Summer 2003): 183–201.

———. *Red, White & Black: Cinema and the Structure of U.S. Antagonisms*. Durham, N.J.: Duke University Press, 2010.

Wilkerson, Isabel. *The Warmth of Other Suns: The Epic Story of America's Great Migration*. New York: Knopf, 2010.

"William Harnett: Trompe l'Oeil." Accessed 28 July 2019. https://www.nga.gov/features/slideshows/william-harnett.html.

Williams, Eric. *Capitalism and Slavery*. Chapel Hill: University of North Carolina Press, 1944.

Williams, Raymond. *Keywords: A Vocabulary of Culture and Society*. New York: Oxford University Press, 1976.

———. *Marxism and Literature*. Oxford: Oxford University Press, 1977.
Wilson, Edmund. *Patriotic Gore: Studies in the Literature of the American Civil War*. New York: Oxford University Press, 1962.
Wister, Fanny Kemble, ed. *Owen Wister Out West: His Journals and Letters*. Chicago: University of Chicago Press, 1958.
———, ed. *That I May Tell You: Journals and Letters of the Owen Wister Family*. Wayne, Pa.: Haverford House, 1979.
Wister, Owen. *The Virginian*. Mineola: Dover, 2006. First published in 1902.
Wolf, Bryan J. "The Labor of Seeing: Pragmatism, Ideology, and Gender in Winslow Homer's *The Morning Bell*." *Prospects: An Annual of American Cultural Studies*, October 1992, 273–318.
Wolff, Solomon, ed. *Revised Laws of Louisiana*. New Orleans, 1897.
Wonham, Henry B. *Playing the Races: Ethnic Caricature and American Literary Realism*. New York: Oxford University Press, 2004.
Wood, Marcus. *Blind Memory: Visual Representations of Slavery in England and America, 1780–1865*. New York: Routledge, 2000.
Woodman, Harold D. *King Cotton and His Retainers: Financing and Marketing the Cotton Crop of the South, 1800–1925*. Columbia: University of South Carolina Press, 1990.
Woods, Clyde. *Development Arrested: The Blues and Plantation Power in the Mississippi Delta*. New York: Verso, 1998.
Woodward, C. Vann. *Origins of the New South: 1877–1913*. Baton Rouge: Louisiana State University Press, 1951.
Wright, Richard. *12 Million Black Voices*. New York: Viking, 1941.
Wyat, Bayley. "A Freedman's Speech" (Philadelphia, 1866). *An American Time Capsule: Three Centuries of Broadsides and Other Ephemera*. http://hdl.loc.gov/loc.rbc/rbpe .15901.40b.
Wynter, Sylvia. "1492: A New World View." In *Race, Discourse, and the Origins of the Americas: A New World View*, edited by Vera Hyatt and Rex Nettleford, 5–57. Washington, D.C.: Smithsonian, 1995.
———. "Rethinking 'Aesthetics': Notes toward a Deciphering Practice." In *Ex-iles: Essays on Caribbean Cinema*, edited by Mbye Cham, 237–79. Trenton, N.J.: Africa World Press, 1992.
———. "Unsettling the Coloniality of Being/Power/Truth/Freedom: Towards the Human, after Man, Its Overrepresentation—An Argument." *CR: The New Centennial Review* 3, no. 3 (2003): 257–337.
X, Malcolm. "The Ballot or the Bullet" (1964). http://americanradioworks.publicradio .org/features/blackspeech/mx.html.
Young, Kevin. *The Grey Album: On the Blackness of Blackness*. Minneapolis: Graywolf, 2012.
Zakim, Michael. "Paperwork." *Raritan* (Spring 2014): 34–56.
Zamora, Lois Parkinson. *Writing the Apocalypse: Historical Vision in Contemporary U.S. and Latin American Fiction*. Cambridge: Cambridge University Press, 1989.
Zimmerman, Andrew. "Guinea Sam Nightingale and Magic Marx in Civil War Missouri: Provincializing Global History and Decolonizing Theory." *History of the Present* 8 (Fall 2018): 140–76.

Index

abolition, 1, 13–16, 19, 63–64, 200; and black objectification, 65–72, 97, 101, 183; contra emancipation, 10, 15; failure of, 4–8, 40–43, 54, 239n43; as financial arrangement, 20–25, 29–30, 38–40, 44–45, 89, 214n61; and market culture, 150, 239nn43–44; and spatial imagination of United States, 149–50
Adorno, Theodor, 159–160, 243n83. *See also* authenticity
Afro-Pessimism, 9, 208n54
Agee, James, 152, 168–71
Agricultural Adjustment Act (AAA), 140
Allgeyer v. Louisiana (1897), 25–32, 58, 212n38, 214n69
American Anti-Slavery Society, 149–50
American Renaissance, 146, 157, 175
American Studies, 175
Anslinger, Harry, 193
Arrighi, Giovanni, 29, 214nn61–62
Attention, Company! (1878), 51–58, 72–73, 90–92, 96, 99–104
authenticity: and realism, 53, 73–74, 84, 87; and blackness, 84, 87, 96, 103–4; and the folk, 153, 157–61, 173, 251n168
Ayers, Edward, 84

Baker, Ella, 194
Baldwin, James, 30, 42, 43, 105, 138, 196–200
ballads: importance to literary study, 139, 173, 176–78, 249n149, 250n153, 250n155
Bankruptcy Act (1867), 20–22, 45, 214n61
banks, 5, 20, 27, 34–35, 213n47; decline of, in the South, 22–23; Freedman's Savings, 32–34, 44–45, 218n123; of the United States, 155, 240n65; and paper money, 27, 29, 35, 155, 163–64, 244n96

Benjamin, Walter, 84, 128, 129, 157, 209n64, 256n76
Best, Stephen, 12, 35, 94
Birth of a Nation, The (1915), 90, 147
Bit of War History, A (1865–66), 58–62, 64, 86
Black America (1895), 73–88, 189
Black Codes, 3
blackness: as aesthetic, 53–56, 73, 192–93, 220n12; commodification of, 54, 56, 89–91, 103–4, 207n48, 220n12; exchange value of, 5, 9, 13–14, 54–56, 72; and geography, 187–92, 196–200, 217n111; as indebtedness, 17, 37–38, 43; as spectacle, 80, 87–91, 103–4; and U.S. nationalism, 4–6, 8–9, 127–28, 167, 226n114
Black Power (1967), 18, 196
Blood Meridian (1985), 129–30
bonanza (speculative bubble), 108, 113–14, 116–17, 120, 121, 128, 229n25
Bronx Slave Market, 194
Brooks, Cleanth, 173, 176, 177
Brooks, Van Wyck, 145, 173, 175, 238n32
Butler, Pierce, 111, 118, 134

Calhoun, John, 31
Canetti, Elias, 127
Carby, Hazel, 111, 190, 251n68
Chapel Hill Regionalists, 171–73
chattel: etymology, 119, 230n40; slavery, 5, 10, 13, 14, 68, 90, 137, 200, 226n114; status, 9, 14, 54, 95
cinema, 51, 86–86, 88, 90
citizenship, 4, 10–11, 19, 56–58, 71, 78, 167, 206n25; and Fourteenth Amendment, 19, 25, 214n69; logic of, 64; and masculinity, 62; and national debt, 19, 34–38, 44

Civil Rights Act (1875), 4
Civil War: and black citizenship, 56–72; and finance capital, 34–38, 45; and periodization of slavery, 7; and *The Virginian*, 111–12, 118–19, 126–28
Clark, John Bates, 114–15, 122. *See also* marginalism
Colfax massacre, 3
colonialism: and ghetto, 196–200, 233n78, 254nn43–44; and liberalism, 10, 25, 29, 42, 242n75; and modernism, 55–56, 179–80, 251n164; and U.S. South, 44, 141–43, 147, 168–73, 218n120, 247n129; settler colonialism, 106–7, 112, 115, 123, 136–37, 162, 240n67. *See also* liberalism
commodity: logic of slavery, 4–6, 54–55, 71–72, 80, 83–85, 208n54, 209n69, 225n104; as spectacle, 8–9, 14, 51, 72, 87, 89–91, 98–104, 226n114; speculation, 113–14, 119–21, 128, 164; as form of value, 12–14, 54. *See also* cotton; slave; blackness; personhood
contraband: slaves as, 2, 59–62, 64–65
contract, 21–33, 83, 89; freedom of, 26, 30–31; labor, 2, 17–20, 43; and liberalism, 10, 19, 23–33, 233n48; and commodification of black personhood, 20–25, 38, 39–40, 101–2
Cooke, Jay, 22, 34, 44, 218n123
Cooke, Marvel, 194
Cooper, James Fenimore, 113, 150, 237n27, 239n51
corporation: growth of, 34–36, 38–39, 89, 112, 213n47; plantation and emergence of, 26–30, 31–32, 45, 215n90, 214n61; rights and freedoms of, 19, 26, 29–32, 58, 212n38, 233n84; and emergence of the Western, 109, 112–15, 121–25, 130, 132, 135–37, 229n12, 231n48, 233n84
cotton: market, 22–23, 36–30, 31, 40, 45, 214n61; production, 18, 27, 36–37, 73–74, 79–84, 119, 140, 149, 154–55, 212n41

Cotton Club, 90, 192
cowboy, 15, 105, 112, 119, 139, 229n22; black, 106; as manager, 108, 113, 129, 132; as overseer, 136
Crary, Jonathan, 51, 88–89, 91. *See also* spectacle
Crash of 1929, 140, 168, 172, 175
credit: abolition as relation of, 38–40, 44–45; and citizenship, 34–37, 43; via sharecropping system, 20–25, 27–30, 31–32, 89. *See also* debt; finance
Crèvecœur, J. Hector St. John de, 7, 108
crop-lien laws, 20–24, 45
cultural materialism, 10–12, 209n63, 256n76

Debord, Guy, 88–89, 91. *See also* spectacle
debt: and captivity, 14, 17–18, 24, 25, 30, 31–38, 44–45, 134, 142, 211n13; national, 19, 22, 34–38, 44, 215n83, 216n91, 214n61; and racialization, 43, 198, 217n117. *See also* credit; finance
deterritorialization, 19, 28–29, 32, 54–55, 228n149
DeVoto, Bernard, 146–47, 168, 175, 237n29, 238n32, 239n48
dialect, 157–60, 177, 243n83, 246n120
Douglass, Frederick, 1, 7, 44, 61, 68–70, 72, 73, 74, 78, 83, 96, 183, 218n125, 220n21; *Narrative of*, 69–70
Du Bois, W. E. B., 4, 5, 35, 134, 155–56, 190, 195, 253n15; *Black Reconstruction*, 3, 13, 17, 40, 183, 207n39, 211n13, 215n79, 239n43, 240n67; concept of "the Veil," 90, 133, 226n116

emancipation: contra abolition, 10; proclamation, 22, 35, 96; as legacy of Civil War, 56–58, 78–9, 223n75; liberal framework of, 19, 62–64, 71, 78, 87–88, 208n58, 225n104
English departments, 173, 175, 176, 249n149

Equiano, Olaudah, 127
Evans, Walker, 169–71

Farm Security Administration (FSA), 141–42, 146, 154, 168, 235n13
feudalism: as ideological, 7–8, 207n42, 231n46, 235n10
finance, 20–25, 26–30, 32, 34–36, 42, 55, 89, 112, 163–66, 214n61, 217n109, 228n149. *See also* credit; debt
Flood of 1927, 140, 141, 168
folk: and national literature, 147–48, 157–61, 173–77, 180, 250n153; and segregation, 138–40, 169–70, 173, 181–83, 191–92; Southern origins of, 15, 139–40, 141–142, 146–48, 168–69, 180, 234n5, 250n153. *See also* ballads
Foner, Eric, 22, 41
Foucault, Michel, 130
Fourteenth Amendment, 4; and corporate rights, 19, 26, 30–31, 58; and financialization of slave's value, 19, 25, 33, 38, 39, 101–3; and freedom of contract, 19, 30–31; and national debt, 34–38. See also *Allgeyer v. Louisiana*; citizenship; contract
Freedman's Bank, 33–34, 44–45, 218n123
Freedmen's Bureau, 2–3
freedpersons' schools, 96–100
Freud, Sigmund, 116, 125, 127, 232n58, 247n131
frontier: and ghetto, 192, 195–97; and literary style, 146–48, 150–53, 157–61, 169, 177, 180, 238n32, 239n48, 245n107, 247n133; as history, 106–7, 128, 132, 135; and slavery, 6, 106–8, 111, 120–21, 135–37, 146, 149, 152–56, 166–67, 169, 237n27, 244n102; and Turner's thesis, 112, 114, 230n26; as zone of speculation, 107–8, 110, 113, 121, 123, 128–32, 135, 162–67

Garnet, Henry Highland, 64, 221n32
Garrison, William Lloyd, 69–70, 150
general strike, 1, 20

genre: of frontier humor, 146–47, 150–53, 156–61, 163–67, 237n27; as historical form, 11, 15, 135; of novel, 109; on painting, 51–53, 72–73, 86; of Western, 105–7, 109–10, 113, 124, 128–29, 135–37, 230n33, 237n27. *See also* trompe l'oeil painting
ghetto, 16, 133–34, 188–200, 233n78, 255n68
Gone With the Wind, 147, 167
Gordon (slave), 64–68, 70–73, 83, 86, 96
Grady, Henry, 83
Greenberg, Clement, 52, 219n7, 220n11

Hansberry, Lorraine, 189
Harnett, William, 51–52, 73, 100–101, 219n8
Harris, George Washington, 147, 158, 237n29, 239n48
Harris, Joel Chandler, 79, 83, 224n81
Hartman, Saidiya, 9, 39, 41
history: of capitalism, 13, 41–42, 91, 210n70, 217n109; emplotment as tragedy, 41, 62, 221n28; frontier as origin, 106–7, 128, 137, 228n5; of Reconstruction, 40–42; and repetition, 9–10, 24, 29, 42, 200, 208n53; and materialism, 11, 200, 209n64, 256n76
Hobbes, Thomas, 107, 109, 128, 130
Holiday, Billie, 193
Hopkins, Pauline, 110–11
Hurston, Zora Neale, 181–82, 251n168

I'll Take My Stand (1930), 172–73
imperialism, 5, 35, 55, 84–86, 106–8, 129–32, 178–81, 183, 251n164, 251n166
insurance, 26, 29, 31, 165

Jackson, Andrew, 131, 153–55, 162, 240nn64–65, 241n70
James, Jesse, 108, 109, 178
Jameson, Fredric, 55, 89, 160, 180, 228n149, 245n109, 251n164
Johnson, Andrew, 2

Johnson, Walter, 5, 14, 66, 154, 156, 161–62, 206n31, 209n69
joke, 115–136 passim; theory of, 116, 125–27, 232n58

Kazanjian, David, 12, 207n39
Kemble, Fanny, 111, 120, 121
Ku Klux Klan, 3, 6, 108

Lawrence, Jacob, 191
Let Us Now Praise Famous Men (1941), 170–71, 246n121
liberalism: and colonialism, 25, 29, 39; critique of, 10, 13–14, 16, 63–64, 78, 199–200, 256n73; definition, 58, 88, 222n46, 242n75; as display of wounds, 70–72, 222n45; historians and, 41, 64, 220n21; and realism, 76–77; and white supremacy, 10, 16, 29, 39, 70–72, 183, 190–91, 197–98, 225n104
Lincoln, Abraham, 33, 74, 78, 184, 220n21. *See also* general strike
Lochner era, 32, 252n7
Lomax, John (and Alan), 139–40, 145, 168, 169, 181, 236n21, 246n119, 250n153. *See also* ballads
Lowe, Lisa, 10–11

Malcolm X, 6
management: cowboy as, 108, 113–16, 121–23, 129, 136; of racialized populations, 132–38; and slavery, 149, 230n34
marginalism, 114–15, 122, 230n29
market revolution, 149–56 passim
Márquez, Gabriel García, 179–80
Marx, Karl: on liberalism, 76, 78, 208n58, 209n67, 241n70; on national debt, 35–38; on value-form, 12–13, 54, 226n116
Matthiessen, F. O., 146, 147, 174, 236n25, 237n29, 239n48, 248n146
McClain, Billy and Cordelia, 76–79, 223n66, 224n76
McKittrick, Katherine, 130, 196–97, 233n78

mechanization, 83, 140
Meigs, Henry, 107, 109
merchants: and coercion, 17, 18, 39, 45, 219n129; and credit, 20–24, 27, 29, 37, 42, 45, 216n104
minstrelsy, 55, 57, 74–76, 78, 105, 142, 187; and plantation, 74–75, 79, 185; and realism, 74, 224n79
modernism, 52, 55, 89, 145, 152, 157, 178–81, 192, 219n7, 220n12, 251n164
modernization, 7, 15, 141–43, 149, 178
Morrison, Toni, 6, 106, 138

Nashville Agrarians, 172–75, 180, 247n133, 248n146, 249n147. *See also* New Critics
National Banking Act (1863), 22, 34
nationalism, 8–9, 45, 56–58, 67–68, 112, 118, 126–28, 134, 226n114; and cultural production, 10–11, 14–16, 145–51, 158–59, 166–69, 174–83
Negro Life at the South (1859), 184–87, 192, 199
New Critics, 148, 173–79, 247n128, 249n147
New Deal, 140–42, 146, 147, 189, 235n9, 246n115, 248n142
New York City: and plantation finance, 22, 35, 45, 54–55, 80, 89, 142, 207n40. *See also Black America*
North: as ideological concept, 7–8, 187, 207n39; and literature, 145, 146, 150, 152, 157; and plantation finance, 5, 17, 22, 32–30, 39, 45, 80, 89, 142, 207n40, 215n79, 214n61; and slave as value-form, 21, 53–56, 66–68, 88–89; and segregation, 2, 97–99, 188–200. *See also* ghetto; South

Odum, Howard, 169, 171

panorama, 85–87, 224n76
paper money, 22, 34–35, 52, 161, 163–67, 207n48, 220n20, 244n96, 244n106

paperwork, 26, 142, 161–63, 166, 244n93
Parrington, Vernon Louis, 146, 174, 236n26
periodization, 207n42, 209n69, 231n46
personality: white, as property, 110, 124–25, 163, 165–66
personhood: black, as commodity spectacle, 54–56, 80, 83–88, 90–91, 95–96, 101–4; of corporations, 26, 29, 58, 233n84; as means of expropriation, 18–19, 21, 23–25, 38–39, 55, 198, 200. *See also* Fourteenth Amendment
Petry, Ann, 184, 194
Philadelphia: and *Attention, Company!*, 52, 97–100; and Owen Wister, 111, 118, 135, 230n35
photography: and racialization, 52, 64–68, 97–103, 184–85, 187–88, 227n137; of Southern folk, 141, 146, 168, 170–71, 235n13
Pickford, Mary, 184–88, 192, 196, 199
plantation: and imperialism, 107, 120, 128, 137, 179–80, 254n38; as modern system, 4–6, 15, 19–25, 36–40, 44–45, 54–56, 142, 149, 178, 196, 206n31, 207n39, 210n71, 233n78, 235n10; as preserve of pastness, 7–8, 172, 174; as spectacle, 73–75, 79–88, 192; and southern enclosure, 140–41, 155–56; urban, 185–90, 192, 196; and *Virginian*, 111–12, 116, 119–20, 126, 128, 132, 136–37
Plessy v. Ferguson, 30, 94–96, 98, 99
police power, 30–31, 58, 133, 198, 222n45
poor whites: as national folk, 15, 139–41, 146–48, 151, 167, 175, 182, 247n133; and relations with slaves, 43, 156–57, 167, 242nn73–74; representations of, 150–53, 156–61, 169–71, 179, 241n70, 247n133; sidelined by plantation's expansion, 154–55, 240–41nn67–68
portraiture, 53–55, 72–73, 78, 84, 86, 100–101
prison, 3–4, 6–7, 27, 40, 200
privacy: in *Pudd'nhead Wilson*, 93–96; right to, 93–94; and whiteness, 88, 95–6, 98

producerism, 114, 121–23
publicity: and blackness, 72, 87, 91, 94–95, 98, 100, 225n104

railroads, 3, 5, 20, 42, 58, 108, 112, 116, 135, 200, 233n84; and bonded debt, 35, 215n90; and cattle, 119; as infrastructure for cotton markets, 23, 26, 27–28, 35, 36; and slaves, 120
realism: and blackness, 21, 53–56, 73–80, 85–87, 91; and caricature, 79; and liberalism, 76–78; and literature, 145, 151, 157–58, 170, 178, 236n26, 239n48; and painting, 51–53, 72–73; scenic, 74–76, 85, 223n66; and spectacle, 89
Reconstruction, 2–6, 18, 36–38, 74, 100, 108, 147, 172, 215n80; abandonment of, 3, 36–38, 96; amendments, 4, 200; histories of, 6, 12–13, 41–42, 62, 183, 221n28
Robinson, Cedric, 9, 209n65
Roosevelt, Franklin Delano, 140, 142, 146, 171, 180, 235n9, 235n10, 248n142. *See also* New Deal
Roosevelt, Theodore, 74, 126, 132, 138–39, 235n10
Rourke, Constance, 146, 147, 151, 164, 175, 237n29

Salsbury, Nate, 73–76, 79–80, 84
Santa Clara v. Southern Pacific Railroad (1885), 58, 233n84
Searchers, The (1956), 105, 107
segregation, 2, 16, 39, 91–92, 98–99, 103, 132–34, 142–43, 243n84; of American folk, 140, 148, 167–69, 173; and *Plessy v. Ferguson*, 30, 94–96; in ghettos, 90, 133–34, 184, 188–200, 253n16, 255n53
settler colonialism, 107, 112, 115, 123, 136–37, 153, 162, 240n67, 242n75
sharecropping, 4, 21–24, 28, 43, 89, 140–42, 170–71, 181, 194, 197, 216n104, 217n117, 241n68. *See also* contract; cotton

slave: body as artifact, 65–70, 82; as chattel, 11–12, 23, 32, 59–62, 68, 98–99, 107–8, 119–21, 134, 167, 225n105; as enemy, 126–28, 136; as a form of value, 5–6, 11–12, 18–22, 30, 35, 37–38, 39, 44–45, 54, 56, 71–72, 84, 89–90, 102–4, 166, 208n54; as general equivalent, 4–5, 20, 22, 39, 167; as machine, 68–69, 82–83; narratives, 68–70; white, 97–99, 101. *See also* blackness

slave racial capitalism, 9, 12–13, 16, 30, 45, 88–91, 99, 104, 116, 136–37, 141, 148, 152, 169, 178–180, 199–200, 206n31, 207n39, 247n128

slavery: continuity of, after 1865, 13, 40–43, 62, 71–72, 89, 148, 178–80, 194, 200; as foundation of United States, 5–9, 12, 16, 18, 20, 64, 148–49, 152, 200; as national system, 18, 38, 40, 54–55, 137, 146, 149, 167, 187, 200, 226n114, 238n40; as "peculiar institution," 5–6

soldiers: and citizenship, 58–67, 71, 76, 86, 221n27; and Civil War, 33, 43, 56, 58, 67, 100–101; and minstrel stereotypes, 57–58; Ninth Cavalry, 74, 86

South: as colony, 54–55, 141–42, 168, 170–72, 218n120, 247n129, 251n163; enclosure of, 15–16, 140–42, 148–49, 155, 240n67, 241n68; financial transformation, 17–45 passim; frontier, 105–8, 146–57, 160–67, 177, 229n16, 237n27; as ideological concept, 6–8, 42, 148–49, 173, 178–81, 187, 220n13, 231n46, 247n129; as imperialist, 85–86, 130, 179–81, 183, 225n101, 247n129; representations of, 74–76, 80–86, 88, 141–42, 147, 150–53, 156, 160–61, 167, 170, 178–81, 185–87, 192, 220n13, 223n66, 235nn12–13; western and, 111–12, 116, 118–20, 229n16, 231n48. *See also* North

spectacle, 8, 51, 56, 72, 80, 85, 87, 95, 101, 226n110, 226n114; definition, 88–91, 226n109

speculation: as commodity bonanzas, 113–14, 116, 119, 121, 136; in cotton, 27–28, 45, 213n52; and frontier, 107–8, 110, 128–30, 135–37, 152, 154, 161–67, 230n39, 231n44; and gambling, 128–30; and imagination, 107, 121–22. *See also* finance

Spillers, Hortense, 9, 16, 99, 208n53, 255n52

Spirit of the Times, 151–52, 158

state: alienation of, 35–38, 44, 78, 244n93; claims on life, 56, 60–62, 65, 71; police powers, 30–31, 58, 133, 198, 221n25, 222n45

still-life painting, 15, 51, 53, 54, 73, 85, 86, 103, 171

Stowe, Harriet Beecher, 7, 67, 74, 128

style, 11, 15, 55, 69; in American literature, 146–52, 157–61, 165–66, 179–81, 239n51

Sut Lovingood (1867), 147, 158, 237n29

Tate, Allen, 173, 176, 247n136
Taylor, Frederick Winslow, 83
Thirteenth Amendment, 4, 6, 19, 41, 221n25
Tourgée, Albion, 94–95
trompe l'oeil painting, 15, 51–55, 73, 85, 86, 96, 103, 219n7
Tulsa massacre (1921), 133, 195, 253n35
Turner, Frederick Jackson, 108, 114, 230n26
Twain, Mark, 54, 79, 152, 237n29, 238n32, 38, 245nn108–9, 231n44; as apotheosis of frontier literature, 146, 157, 166, 180, 237n27, 239n48, 51; and New Deal, 146; *Pudd'nhead Wilson*, 54, 91–93

Uncle Tom's Cabin (1852), 7, 128

value-form (form of value). *See* blackness; slave; slave racial capitalism
"The Veil" (Du Bois), 133, 169, 181, 182, 183, 188, 226n116; and concept of spectacle, 90–91

Warren, Robert Penn, 176–78, 250n155
Warren, Samuel, and Louis Brandeis: "Right to Privacy," 93–95

Washington, D.C., 31, 44, 79, 184–88, 218n123
Watts Rebellion (1965), 198, 200
Wells, Ida B., 9, 134
western. *See* genre
White, Isaac, 101–4
whiteness: and hermeneutics of suspicion, 66–72, 96; and liberalism, 10, 15–16, 30, 39, 70–72, 183, 190–91, 197–98, 222n45, 225n104; and poverty, 140–43, 147–48, 151–57, 160, 165, 167, 170–72, 175, 179, 182, 217n117, 240n67, 241n70, 242n73; as property, 94–96, 99, 106; of slaves, 97–101; and subjectivity, 56, 88, 90–96, 103, 106, 115, 121–25, 136, 182, 187–88, 192–93, 199; and supremacy, 1–200 passim; and theft, 17–21, 32–40, 42–44, 64, 90, 154, 189–90, 192, 196, 219n129, 227n120
Wister, Owen, 109, 111–15, 118, 120–24, 131–32, 134–39, 196, 231n43, 231n44; racism of, 126
world's fairs, 75, 84, 86
Wright, Richard, 17, 28, 138, 140, 189, 191
Wynter, Sylvia, 9, 130, 233n71, 252n175

www.ingramcontent.com/pod-product-compliance
Lightning Source LLC
Chambersburg PA
CBHW030528230426
43665CB00010B/801